A Theology of Paul the Apostle, Part Two

A Theology of Paul the Apostle, Part Two

Cross and Atonement

G. ROGER GREENE

PICKWICK *Publications* · Eugene, Oregon

A THEOLOGY OF PAUL THE APOSTLE, PART TWO
Cross and Atonement

Pickwick Publications
An Imprint of Wipf and Stock Publishers
199 W. 8th Ave., Suite 3
Eugene, OR 97401

www.wipfandstock.com

PAPERBACK ISBN: 978-1-6667-4586-3
HARDCOVER ISBN: 978-1-6667-4587-0
EBOOK ISBN: 978-1-6667-4588-7

Cataloguing-in-Publication data:

Names: Greene, G. Roger, author.

Title: A theology of Paul the apostle, part two : cross and atonement / G. Roger Greene.

Description: Eugene, OR: Pickwick Publications, 2023 | Includes bibliographical references and index.

Identifiers: ISBN 978-1-6667-4586-3 (paperback) | ISBN 978-1-6667-4587-0 (hardcover) | ISBN xxx-978-1-6667-4588-7 (ebook)

Subjects: LCSH: Paul, the Apostle, Saint. | Bible. Epistles of Paul—Theology. | Atonement—Biblical teaching.

Classification: BT265.2 G744 2023 (print) | BT265.2 (ebook)

JUNE 20, 2023 9:47 AM

This work is dedicated to my two sons, Ramsey and Jason,
each of whom has brought a father much joy.

Contents

Theology of Paul the Apostle Outline

Preface

A RUDE graphitto scratched in the plaster on a building wall near the Palatine Hill in Rome portrays a human figure with the head of a donkey outstretched on a Roman cross. The accompanying inscription, crudely scratched in Greek, reads: "Alexamenos worships [his] god." The dating of the graphitto is difficult, but it would apparently fall between the late first century to the late third century. It is usually interpreted as a mocking depiction of Christian worship in the time frame in which it falls.

The graphitto offers not so mute testimony to the immense task faced by the earliest Christians, Paul included, to embrace and proclaim a gospel based upon the historical fact of Roman crucifixion. Jesus's death on a Roman cross could not be denied. Yet, what sense did it make to proclaim Jesus of Nazareth as "Lord of the world," when he had been put to death on a wooden cross as an insurrectionist by the Romans. The graphitto well captures a gentile perspective, while from a Jewish perspective Jesus's death on a cross could even be interpreted as representative of the curse of God (cf. Gal 3:13; Deut 21:23). Paul himself recognized the difficulty of the seeming foolishness of the "word of the cross," although he had come to recognize that gospel word as the power of God (1 Cor 1:18–25).

Paul himself was originally numbered among the doubters. His strength of feeling led him to become an ardent persecutor of the fledgling Christian church (cf. Gal 1:13–14; Acts 9). But then, Paul was called to proclaim the Gospel of God as the fulfilment and flowering of his own Judaism and apocalyptic hopes.

The Christian movement, from the time of its earliest inception as a Jewish sect of believers who trusted in "the Way" (cf. Acts 9:2), has been compelled to properly interpret the meaning of Jesus's death on a Roman cross. In the very earliest kerygma available to us (1 Cor 15:3–5; Phil 2:8; Acts 2), one is confronted with the elliptical Gospel of God—Jesus was killed, Jesus was raised. What did that mean in a first century Greco-Roman world?

In a formative period of Christian theologies, one should respect Paul's own uniqueness. One should seek to hear Paul's own understanding of what he terms "the Gospel of God." One should not expect Paul's thought to be identical to that of the writer of 1 Peter or the author of Hebrews, for example. First Peter 2:21–25 is a significant passage that in some current editions of *Novum Testamentum Graece* is arranged as hymnic or traditional material rather than simple prose. It appears in an imperatival, exhortative context and offers the example of Christ in indicative terms as proper motivation for living the Christian life. However, it focuses upon and lays stress to Christ's suffering and death upon the cross for sins.

> For unto this you were called, because indeed Christ suffered in your behalf [ὑπὲρ ὑμῶν], leaving for you all an example in order that you may be caused to follow in his steps, who did not commit sin nor was deceit found in his mouth, who when he was cursed did not respond with a curse, while suffering he did not threaten, but he gave [himself] over to the one who judges rightly; who himself bore our sins in his body upon the tree, in order that while we are those who die to sins, we shall live in righteousness, by whose wound you were healed. For all of you were like sheep wandering astray, *but* now you have been turned back to the shepherd and guardian of your souls (1 Peter 2:21–25, original translation).

It should be noted that unless otherwise indicated, translation of New Testament passages in the current work is that of the present author. For those who know Greek, the author will frequently introduce Greek terms and call attention to verb tenses employed by Paul. English aids will also be given.

Regardless of who may have written 1 Peter, which sounds rather sermonic, Paul is not "Peter" and his thought is not identical to that of Peter, although they may both echo early Christian kerygma. Paul himself speaks in terms of dying unto Sin (not "sins") and living unto righteousness. Paul does not, however, speak of Christ bearing our sins (plural) in his body upon the cross ("the tree"). He simply does not. Where is the supportive verse or passage? One cannot legitimately criticize Paul because he does not espouse the view of Peter or that of the writer to the Hebrews.

Neither should one read their views back into Paul in dogmatic fashion. Paul, for example, seldom mentions "repentance" (μετάνοια, 2 Cor 7:9; Rom 2:4; 2 Tim 2:25) and "forgiveness" (ἀφίημι, 1 Cor 7:11–13; Rom 1:27; 4:7). Paul never mentions the word "disciple" (μαθητής), but then neither does the remainder of the New Testament outside of the Gospels and Acts. Much theology has been attributed or ascribed to Paul that is simply not to be found *in Paul*. If one seeks to understand the theology *of Paul*, one needs to consider Paul in his own right apart from or in comparison to and contrast with the larger Christian tradition. But then the questions arise and the problems begin. Which letters, indeed, come from Paul himself? What appears to be their central theme or themes? Was there development in his thought?

The salutations of each of Paul's letters commend "grace and peace from God the Father and the Lord Jesus Christ" to those earliest Christians who made up the congregations of his churches, folk whom he metaphorically identified as the "body of Christ" and "saints." Though seldom realized, Paul's salutations are in reality the initial introduction to Pauline theology and actually set the tone for the nature of Paul's theology as that is to be found expressed in his letters.

Paul is often understood as an early Christian theologian and as the theologian of the "cross." Contemporary atonement theory regularly appeals to Pauline texts in support of any given perspective regarding "the atonement." The significance of this doctrine in Christian soteriology calls for examination and search for clarity in Pauline texts that have been claimed as supportive documentation of particular atonement theories.

To comprehend Paul, one must consider multiple matrices, not only the theological one. Just as there is an historical background matrix for Paul's perspectives, so also is there a foreground of Christian history. It is ultimately the foreground to which the present readers and the current author belong. The author chooses a significant issue (atonement) to pursue in the context of historical summary in order to demonstrate how we got to where we are. Thereby, the two volumes of this current work, *Theology of Paul the Apostle*, constitute a whole—Paul's eschatological gospel along with cross and atonement. Volume one proceeds from establishing a theological prolegomena to the development of Paul's *theo*logical understanding of the Gospel of God in the context of developing early Christianity. The second and current volume of the present work examines a specific element of the Gospel ellipse in the light of its soteriological significance. It probes what could be termed a "storm center" in Pauline theology.

Paul's "in Christ" theology is understood in the light of the underlying eschatological realities that inform the new epoch of God's indicative, realities that in fact bring the eschatological community into being. How that community is to live is informed by Paul's cross imperative. How Paul's understanding of the cross has been interpreted is addressed by the issue of atonement and the historical appropriation of Paul in the context of the early historical development of Christianity.

One, of course, may consult the table of contents *and the separate, provided outline* to gain a total overview of the work. The outline provided in each volume is representative of the entire two part work. The dual, complete outline representing both volumes provides a convenient and ready reference as to the total content of the entire work. Throughout this work, the primary concern is Paul's *theo*logy, with anthropology being a secondary applicational concern, even though the two areas of theology and anthropology may not ultimately be separated by human interpreters interested in an integrated gospel.

Several issues set forth in the first part of this work should be repeated here. As indicated in the preface to part one, the first issue is that of anachronism. Terms like "gospel," "salvation," "lord," and "savior" were terms applied to Augustus Caesar and his rule even prior to the Christ event. All of these terms appear in Paul's letters and are applied to Christ or the Gospel of God. On the other hand, Paul never uses the word "Christian" at all, either with reference to himself, his churches, or individual believers in Christ. Luke indicates that the disciples were first called "Christian" (Χριστιανός) in

Antioch (Acts 11:26). The only other occurrences of the word "Christian" in the entire New Testament are to be found in Acts 26:28 and 1 Peter 4:16. The word "Christian" thus occurs only three times in the entire New Testament. Paul never uses the word "disciple" either, although he does use repeatedly the phrase "in Christ."

The reader should also again be advised thereby that for clarity's sake, the words "Christian" and "Christianity"(when applied either to Paul or the earliest church of his day) are used in this work anachronistically. No satisfactory alternatives have yet been proposed, such that it becomes cumbersome and perhaps misleading to use alternatives such as "believers in Christ" *et alli*. The term "Jews" to describe Jews is accurate, even though it may suggest a certain anachronism. There was no single expression of Judaism in Paul's day and Judaism certainly was changed after 70 CE. "Gentiles" should be spelled "gentiles," for it is a non-ethnic designation much like "pagans." To use an alternate term like "non-Jews" or "not-Jewish" would likewise lack a certain clarity. While acknowledging anachronism, this work will thus make use of the words "Christian," "Jews," and "gentiles" to describe relevant people or groups as appropriate.

In dealing with the conceptual Gospel of God, the word "Gospel" will be capitalized in this volume. Paul's personal understanding or proclamation of that Gospel will not be capitalized. It will be cited as "gospel of Paul." No one, Paul included, has a complete understanding of the Gospel of God. By nature of the case, there is a distinguishing difference that should be realized and acknowledged. Our own perspective is always partial or limited.

There have been many and multiple monographs that have addressed the topic of the cross and its atonement value from both a specific Pauline view as well as the more general view of either the New Testament or systematic theology. The church as a whole has wrestled with these issues for 2,000 years. The focus of the present work is a reconsideration of Paul's understanding in the light of what Paul himself wrote and in the light of how Paul has been understood in the context of Christian history. It is the longstanding developmental interpretation of New Testament texts, including Paul, that has brought us to the present time.

To repeat a quote from the preface in part one of the present work. It is hoped that what is written here will be accessible for those who may be at the comparative beginning of an earnest pilgrimage with Paul. And for the specialists in the field, the writer hopes to bring familiar things or things too little noticed to the fore. Repetition is not a bad thing. Reflection, new or old, is always a good thing.

In the end, to hear Paul "speak" is to be confronted afresh by the freedom of the Gospel of God, at least as Paul understood it within his first century matrices and within the context of his apostolic calling. Paul himself was a part of the overall matrix of earliest Christianity. Examination of Paul's letters themselves must remain an ever-present priority, otherwise, any discussion is only derivative. Secondary treatments of Paul must be measured in the light of the letters themselves. Attention will be given to the application of Paul's thought in a postmodern age. Such consideration may involve confirmation, challenge, and correction. It may call for change or reaffirmation. Paul, the "apostle of the cross," needs to be heard, for the ministry and thought of Paul may provide a significant way forward for those seeking to live "in Christ" in a postmodern world.

Acknowledgments

As this work is drawn to completion, the author feels that he has come to a way station in his journey with the apostle Paul—a bit of a *respite* in what has been a far more lengthy journey than the author ever anticipated in the beginning. *Webster's Collegiate Dictionary* defines "respite" in terms of "a temporary delay" and an "interval of rest or relief." The interval of rest or relief is certainly welcome, for now other things may be addressed and attention may become diversified once again. On the other hand, the phrase "a temporary delay" offers a more intractable omen, an ominous foreboding or foreshadowing that the author has not yet reached the end of a much greater journey that is yet to unfold.

The author is very thankful and grateful for all of those who have enabled him to arrive at this particular way station. No one is a self-made person, for one always stands on the shoulders of, or joins hands with, those who have gone this way before. The present work has germinated over many years. Seminary professors of long ago introduced a young theological student to the serious study and appreciation of Paul as found in both English and Greek texts. They offered an opportunity to begin an earnest pilgrimage with Paul that has continued throughout a lengthy teaching career. The pilgrimage has afforded opportunity for introducing the apostle Paul to yet new generations of undergraduate students and laypersons alike. The many scholar students of Paul whose names appear in footnotes and the bibliography of the present work have proven to be able dialogue partners who have guided, informed, challenged, and corrected the present writer in both agreement and disagreement.

Appreciation is expressed to my immediate editor and project manager, Chris Spinks, who was always available to answer every question the author posed to him promptly with efficiency and effectiveness. Appreciation is also expressed to Matt Wimer, Managing Editor at Wipf and Stock, for his flexibility and ready willingness to address any issue that the author had. The author likewise expresses appreciation to the entire production staff at Wipf and Stock, including persons unknown to the author by name, who have worked through the entire production process to ultimately bring a work like this into being as a published work. The author would be remiss if he did not express a word of future thanks to those at Wipf and Stock who will engage in the marketing process after publication.

To my two colleagues at Mississippi College, Michael Johnson and Eddie Mahaffey, the author again expresses a debt of gratitude for their willingness to allow lengthy manuscripts on Pauline theology to intrude upon and guide many, many lunch-time discussions. Their questions and corrections, along with their suggestive insights and contributions have made this current work on Paul's theology to be a much better work than it otherwise would have been. Their abiding friendship and support for this writer extends beyond what anyone could fairly ask.

An extra-special debt of love and appreciation is expressed to my wife, Mary Ann, who has served as a tireless editor of what has been written as well as a willing dialogue partner for what in many instances was about to be written. She has supported the project through all the years of its development with full encouragement and without complaint, even when the dining room table remained covered with books and paper and even when bookshelves filled with books on Paul began to multiply in hallways and bedrooms. She has read through the manuscripts many times over.

This present work on *Theology of Paul* is presented in two volumes, such that it seems altogether fitting to dedicate the work to my two sons, Ramsey and Jason, each of whom this father is justly proud. Jason, the artist, provided original cover art for the two volumes. Ramsey, the engineer, provided thoughtful commentary along the way. This father loves and appreciates you guys!

Abbreviations

AD	*Anno Domini, "In the year of the Lord"*
ABD	*The Anchor Bible Dictionary.* 6 vols. Edited by David Noel Freedman. New York: Doubleday, 1992.
2 Apol.	Justin Martyr, *Second Apology*
2 Bar	2 Baruch
Adv. Marc.	Tertullian, *Against Marcion*
Ant.	Josephus, *Jewish Antiquities*
aor.	aorist tense in Greek
BAGD	*A Greek-English Lexicon of the New Testament and Other Early Christian Literature.* Walter Bauer. 2nd ed. Translated and adapted by William F. Arndt and F. Wilbur Gingrich. Revised and augmented by F. Wilbur Gingrich and Frederick W. Danker. Chicago: The University of Chicago Press, 1979.
BC	Before Christ
BCE	Before the common era
c.	circa
CE	Common era
cf.	compare
Com. Gal.	Luther, *Commentary on Galatians*
Comm. Rom.	Origen, *Commentary on Romans*
Conf.	Augustine, *Confessions*
Cor	Corinthians (1 and 2)
cp.	compare
d.	died, deceased
Dem. ev.	Eusebius, *Demonstration of the Gospel*
Dial.	Justin Martyr, *Dialogue with Trypho*
Did.	The Didache
Eph	Ephesians

Epist.	Abelard, *Epistle ad Rom.*
Euchir.	Augustine, *Enchiridion on Faith, Hope, and Love*
Exod	Exodus
Faust.	Augustine, *Against Faustus the Manichaean*
Gal	Galatians
Gen	Genesis
gen.	genitive case in Greek
Haer.	Irenaeus, *Against Heresies*
Heb	Hebrews
IDB	*The Interpreter's Dictionary of the Bible.* 4 vols. Edited by George A. Buttrick. Nashville: Abingdon, 1976.
Inc.	Athanasius, *On the Incarnation*
Ign. *Smyrn.*	Ignatius, *To the Smyrnaeans*
Ign. *Trall.*	Ignatius, *To the Trallians*
Ign. *Rom.*	Ignatius, *To the Romans*
Instit.	Calvin, *Institutes*
Isa	Isaiah
J. W.	Josephus, *Jewish War*
Jer	Jeremiah
Lev	Leviticus
LXX	Septuagint, Greek translation of the Old Testament
Macc.	Maccabees (1 to 4)
Matt	Matthew
NAB	*New American Bible*
NIV	*New International Version*
NPNF	*Nicene and Post Nicene Fathers*, Series 1. Edited by Philip Schaff. Reprint. Peabody, MA: Hendrickson, 1999.
NPNF2	*Nicene and Post Nicene Fathers*, Series 2. Edited by Philip Schaff. Reprint. Peabody, MA: Hendrickson, 1999.
NRSV	*New Revised Standard Version*
obj.	objective, as in objective genitive
part.	participle in Greek
Pet	Peter (1 and 2)
pf.	perfect verb tense in Greek
Phil	Philippians
pl.	Plural number, as in the pronoun "you"
Ps	Psalms
Rom	Romans

RSV	*Revised Standard Version*
Sam	Samuel (1 and 2)
SBL	Society of Biblical Literature
Serm.	Augustine, *Sermons*
STA	Greene, "Source Tradition of Acts"
sub.	subjective, as in subjective genitive
TDNT	*Theological Dictionary of the New Testament*. 10 vols. Edited by Gerhard Kittel and Gerhard Friedrich.. Translated and edited by Geoffrey W. Bromily. Grand Rapids: William B. Eerdmans, 1964–76.
Thess	Thessalonians (1 and 2)
Tim	Timothy (1 and 2)
Trin.	Augustine, *On the Trinity*
Wis.	Wisdom of Solomon

1

Paul's Gospel and the Cross

ONE of the most certain historical facts about Jesus is the fact that he died on a Roman cross during the time when Pontius Pilate was governor of Judea. Many contemporary scholars date Jesus's death to April 7, 30 CE. His death is a fact even immortalized in the Apostles' Creed. *Over time*, the cross became the central, concrete symbol of Christianity itself and the central reality within Christian theology.

At the beginning of the twentieth century in a work known as *The Fundamentals*, Dyson Hague and Franklin Johnson wrote from a very conservative perspective, as they stressed a view of substitutionary atonement. According to varying doctrinal standards of major church bodies, the atonement was seen as fundamental to the faith. According to Johnson, the Christian world as a whole has believed in a substitutionary atonement "ever since it began to think." Athanasius stated the doctrine as clearly and fully as any other writer. As Johnson asserted, "All the great historic creeds which set forth the atonement at any length set forth a substitutionary atonement."[1] Or as Hague stated, "The Atonement is Christianity in epitome. It is the heart of *Christianity as a system*; it is the distinguishing mark of the Christian religion."[2] Hague saw a substantial unity among the representative standards of leading Protestant churches. Church creeds and confessions set forth the death of Christ as the central fact of Christianity. The Apostles' Creed is a case in point, for it passes over the life and ministry of Christ "in order that the faith of the Church in all ages may at once be focused upon His sufferings and His death."[3] Perhaps surprisingly, in the light of his conservative position,

1. Johnson, "Atonement," 3:64. Johnson exhibits a tendency toward sweeping overstatement.

2. Hague, "At-one-ment by Propitiation," 3:79. One should note the supplied emphasis, which is not original.

3. Hague, "At-one-ment by Propitiation," 3:93. The Apostles Creed states the following: *"I believe in God, the Father almighty, Creator of heaven and earth, and in Jesus Christ, his only Son, our Lord, who was conceived by the Holy Spirit, born of the Virgin Mary, suffered under Pontius Pilate, was crucified, died and was buried; he descended into hell; on the third day he rose again from the dead; he ascended into heaven, and is seated at the right hand of God the Father almighty; from there he will come to judge the living and the dead. I believe in the Holy Spirit, the holy catholic Church, the communion of the*

Hague acknowledged the historical consciousness of the early church "did not seem to be alive to the necessity of the formation of any particular theory of the atonement."[4] There appears to be more truth in Hague's statement than in Johnson's, and perhaps more truth than even Hague realized.

The Matter of Atonement

The word *atonement* itself is open to diverse definition. Its roots are found in Middle English as a synonym for *reconciliation* (i.e., at-one-ment). The English word "atone" is derived from the phrase "at one" and suggests a harmonious relationship with another. In broad usage, "atonement" originally suggested "at-one-ment" or "reconciliation." In more restricted theological usage the term has come to be used to refer to the process or means by which hindrances or obstacles to reconciliation between human beings (or God and human beings) and God may be removed, such that a proper relationship may be restored.[5] The theological doctrine of atonement generally deals with human sin and the remedy for that sin before God. While *conceptually* frequent in the Old Testament, the actual word "atonement" only occurred once in the King James New Testament as a synonym for "reconciliation" in Rom 5:11.[6]

While the New Testament (Paul included) may use various metaphors to affirm the truth of atonement, the metaphors do not explain how Christ cancels out the effects of human sin or the manner in which Christ reconciles human beings to God. It is not surprising that imagery is drawn from the sacrificial practices of Judaism, where atonement was associated with the shedding of blood and subsequent death (Eph 5:2). Paul can also use an obedience metaphor (Phil 2:8). Paul can also use the imagery of "buying," which implies a price paid (1 Cor 6:20; 7:23; Gal 3:13; 4:5). Without using the word "ransom," Paul can speak of the effect of being set free (Gal 5:1) and of redemption (Col 2:14; Eph 1:7) in terms of forgiveness of sins. God himself puts forth that which alleviates the penalty of guilt (Rom 3:25), as he acts in Christ to re-create and rehabilitate humanity. Throughout, Paul appears not so much to emphasize the means, as he does the end result of that which is attained through Christ. And the end

---

saints, the forgiveness of sins, the resurrection of the body, and life everlasting. Amen." The creed moves from miraculous birth to Jesus's death on a cross, without addressing anything in between. The entire ministry of Jesus is omitted. Is that not important for faith and practice that is Christian?

4. Hague, "At-One-Ment by Propitiation," 3:86.

5. Mitton, "Atonement," 309–13.

6. The *RSV* replaced "atonement" with "reconciliation," such that the actual word does not appear in the *RSV* or more modern versions of the New Testament, unless the translation seeks to preserve a theological view. McGrath suggests that "atonement theory" as applied to the "work of Christ," while used extensively in the nineteenth and twentieth centuries, is a rather cumbersome and unhelpful currency in which to discuss "soteriology." See McGrath, *Christian Theology*, 319. The present writer would still affirm that the term "atonement" maintains a significant presence in the contemporary theological landscape in soteriological discussion of conceptual Pauline perspectives pertaining to the Gospel of God.

result is found even in all of Paul's salutations—"Grace and peace from God the Father and the Lord Jesus Christ."

The Matter of "Sin"

Paul's overriding description of humanity apart from Christ is that of humanity enslaved to "sin." Paul conceives "sin" as a stance or attitude, a state or condition which also has social dimensions. Paul can also personify "sin" as "Sin" and view it as an enslaving power. Paul's letters do not view "sin" as the simple, accumulative violations of moral law (or "moral peccadillos," as some have described it), but as a controlling power over humanity. In other words, "Sin" is perceived by Paul as a power and a force which gives rise to our own rebellion, enslavement, and death, while "sins" are but the symptom of the underlying cause of a climate of our own rebellion, alienation, and idolatry wrought by the power of "Sin."[7]

For Paul, sin is "unGodliness" (spelled with a capital "G"), because it represents a willful disregard of God, It includes idolatry or the worship of substitute gods. It is thereby not "godlessness" but "Godlessness." The first century was not a "godless" world. There were "gods" worshipped everywhere. Idolatry, in fact, involves many false gods (Rom 1:21–23). This is made plain in Rom 1:18–32, with its predominant vocabulary of ἀσέβεια ("ungodliness") and ἀδικία ("wickedness"). Romans 1:18–32, in particular, makes use of the words ἀδικία and ἀσέβεια to describe sin as a stance taken against God. This stance results in distorted and broken social relationships, such that "God's wrath" simply lets sin run its course in terms of sexual disorders and social injustices. When the concept of God is distorted in idolatry, the result is human injustice and disorder, i.e., a failure to live as God intended humans to live. Distortion of the divine results in the distortion of humanity. From a Jewish perspective shared by Paul, the problem was idolatry.

As one refuses the identity of "creature," one turns away from God the Creator. So, for Paul the matter of "godlessness or ungodliness" is not simply the rejection of God, but it is also idolatry.[8] Human existence itself is distorted by setting up false gods. Rejection or falsification of the truth leads to the acceptance of a lie for the truth. That this is deliberate choice carries with it ethical implications (Rom 1:18, 25). Sin carries with it destruction of relationships. The "lack of righteousness" (ἀδικία) of human beings is the opposite of God's δικαιοσύνη ("righteousness"). God's justice is his fidelity to relationship, such that human injustice suggests a lack of fidelity, i.e., infidelity (cf. Rom 6:3; 3:5; 9:14). When moved toward idolatry, religion itself becomes "another ideological tool to justify activity that really oppresses and dehumanizes."[9] The truth

7. To reiterate, the present writer uses the capitalized form "Sin" to refer to the personified force and "sin" or "sins" to refer to the symptomatic actions of humankind.

8. Tambasco, *Atonement*, 36.

9. Tambasco, *Atonement*, 39.

is suppressed by ἀδικία ("wickedness") or lack of righteousness. The result is idolatry that reinforces injustice (Rom 1:18).

Paul uses the word ἁμαρτία in Rom 6:12–13, a word which etymologically suggests "missing the target." "Sin," as a human action, becomes a failure to manifest and reflect the "glory of God." To live as a "praise of God's glory" is the purpose of humankind according to Paul (cf. Eph 1:6, 12, 14). When Paul uses the word in the plural ("sins"), he is usually reflecting Old Testament usage (cf. 1 Thess 2:16 [cf. Gen 15:16]); Rom 4:7; 11:27) or a liturgical formula (1 Cor 15:3; Gal 1:4). When Paul uses the term in the singular, overwhelmingly he suggests "Sin" as a personified power or force. This is especially apparent in Rom 5–8, as Sin becomes alive as an entity that enters us and controls us, thereby leading to all manner of rebellion. "Sin" becomes a villain that makes "Everyone" a victim, as it dwells within one (Rom 7:20), exercising internal possession and control (Rom 6:16–17; 7:5). One is powerless against its onslaught.

There is a solidarity in Sin, the origin of which is attributed to Adam, the solution to which by way of contrast is solidarity in Christ (Rom 5:12–21, esp. 15–19). Paul blends a causality in Adam (cf. Rom 5:12–14; 4 Ezra 7:118; 2 Bar 54:15–19) with our own causality. The translation of Rom 5:12d has given rise to misunderstanding. Augustine followed the Vulgate which translated the ἐφ' ᾧ of the underlying Greek as "in whom," such that the entire clause read "in whom all sinned." This gave rise to Augustine's doctrine of "original sin" as a quasi-biological inheritance that neglected to affirm our own responsibility. One is thus born with a "black mark on the soul" that needs to be washed away in baptism, even and especially in new-born infants. Adam's sin is our sin *and* our guilt. Such a perspective, if accurate, would have called for ἐν ᾧ ("in whom"), which is not what is written in the Greek. What is written is ἐφ' ᾧ, better translated "because" or "given the fact that." Shared responsibility for sins and their consequence is set forth.

Adam sinned and let Sin loose in the world. Each human being since Adam has been born into an environment in which Sin reigns. Yet each one has become "the Adam of one's own soul," as one sins deliberately and inevitably (cf. 2 Bar 54:15, 19). Paul makes more explicit in Rom 5:13–14 what he introduced in verse 12. A stated law or command of God (such as Adam had) turns sin into a direct transgression when that law or command is violated. Paul recognizes that sinning existed objectively from the time of Adam, but that it is not subjectively imputed *as transgression* apart from the giving of the Law. With the advent of Mosaic Law, sin is exposed with clarity and thereby sin becomes even more sinful, as it takes on the character of transgression.

As with Sin, Paul can personify Law.[10] While Paul sees the Law as "holy and just and good" (Rom 7:12; cf. Gal 3:19; 7:10), as an accomplice to Sin, it has negative qualities and consequences. The Law, of course, has to be implemented; not to implement it

---

10. Just as Paul personified Sin, so Law may be understood in similar fashion. One may use the word with a capital "L" to suggest a personified reality, or *the* Torah, or as "law" to specify the will of God that is to be implemented by human beings.

is to remain in a state of sinfulness. The deeper problem, however, is that Sin employs the Law as a lackey and petty tyrant and uses it to kill. Sin preceded the Law in the epoch from Adam to Moses as a rebellious stance against God. Once the Law is given, sin becomes transgression, or direct violation of a stated will of God. The power of Sin is able to thwart the "holy and just and good" gift of God, such that it actually intensifies sins.

If one begins first with the Law as law, then sin becomes a transgression or a breaking of law and becomes centered upon legalism. This leads to a detrimental view of God and his justice in terms of one who must reward or punish on the basis of legal standing. It can even become idolatrous. As Tambasco observes, if one begins with sin as transgression, the impression is given that God gave the Law as a contractural punishment for those who would not keep it. Such an impression is diametrically opposite of one that suggests God gave the Law as an aid to help his people to respond to him and accept his gifts already offered.[11] The real focal point in the Old Testament is reformative justice in the light of maintenance of covenant and not retributive justice.

The Justice of God

The acknowledged central theme of Romans is the "righteousness" or "justice" (δικαιοσύνη) of God which defines the Gospel of God (Rom 1:16–17). The δικ- root in Greek may express either "rightness" or "justice," such that "righteousness" should not be understood simply in terms of a passive moral quality.[12] The present writer has suggested the concept of "rectification" as an alternative of understanding, such that the phrase ἡ δικαιοσύνη θεοῦ could be translated "the rectifying activity of God" or "the rectification of God" as a subjective genitive of activity toward his creation, including humankind. It should not be understood as simply a static attribute.

The Wrath of God.

In Paul's usage the phrase "wrath of God" does not point to vindictive emotion within God or capricious activity. It points to an effective quality and not an affective quality. As Tambasco correctly describes, Paul sees God's wrath to be the negative side of God's saving action, the mirror image of God's justice.[13] There is a qualitative theological difference between human anger and divine anger in biblical thought, even though the same words may be used for either. God's anger, however, is described in anthropomorphic terms (how else?), but all of the characteristics of God are above and beyond those of humanity. As the book of James (lit., "Jacob") reminds, "The anger of man does not work the righteousness of God" (James 1:20). Anger in human

11. Tambasco, *Atonement*, 47.

12. Louw and Nida, *Greek-English Lexicon Semantic Domains*, 1:744–45.

13. Tambasco, *Atonement*, 31–33. Cf. Rom 1:17–18.

kind may be sharply distinguished from God's wrath. Divine "wrath" is seen to be the natural outworking of the divine will. Just as the "righteousness" or "justice" of God is "revealed" in the Gospel of God unto salvation (Rom 1:16–17), so also the "wrath" of God is revealed against impiety (ἀσέβεια) and unrighteousness/injustice (ἀδικία) (Rom 1:18).

Romans 1:18–32 offers the longest treatment of God's wrath in Paul's understanding. It occurs in the pre-eminent letter to the Romans—a book which reflects his mature theology. As Rom 1:24, 26, 28 indicate, "wrath" carries its own condemnation as God "gives over" human beings to their own devices and sinfulness, with consequent self-destruction. Human freedom is respected, but sin brings its own punishment and destruction. Yet even divine wrath (as Paul understands it) is seen to be in the service of God's justice. Just as God's righteousness or justice (his "rectifying" nature) is revealed, so is divine wrath (Rom 1:17–18).

God does not act on a human basis even in the Old Testament—he is God and not man (Hos 11:8–9). Even in the early days of his ministry, Paul affirmed that God had not destined human beings for wrath but for salvation "through our Lord Jesus Christ" (1 Thess 5:9). God seeks to extend his mercy upon all (Rom 11:32). As a revealed correlative of God's saving justice in Christ (which Paul sees as eschatological), God's wrath is likewise understood as an eschatological reality.[14] While there is present anticipation of future reality (1 Thess 1:10; Rom 1:18; 2:9; 3:5; 5:9), wrath as Paul conceives it also begins in the present (1 Thess 2:16; Rom 1:24, 26, 28).

The Righteousness/Justice of God.

A cursory view of the Old Testament reveals that God's justice is associated with many varied functions that characterize his saving activity. It is expressly contrasted with his punishing wrath, which is often seen to be "God's allowing sin to reap its own consequences."[15] Time and time again, God reaches out in covenant faithfulness to restore an unfaithful covenant people. While often perceived or interpreted as retributive justice, God's intent is really reformative justice or rectification. God's justice is not divorced from his mercy, but rather both describe his complementary saving activity. While other notes could be stressed, it is important to see that his saving justice is directed not just toward personal salvation but toward human situations marred by the effects of political and social injustices.

Paul did not found Christianity, nor was he the only one in early Christianity wrestling with understanding the Christ event. Whether Pauline or traditional, references like 1 Cor 1:30 and Rom 3:25 are formulations of God's saving justice, i.e., his saving activity manifest in Christ, or, his rectifying activity. God's justice is far more than a divine attribute; it is God's activity. While Paul's conception has its forensic

14. See Greene, part one of the present work.

15. Tambasco, *Atonement*, 21.

aspects, Paul portrays a God who calls not just individuals but the entire cosmic order to account. He does not passively condemn human beings out of a rote legalism, but he seeks to rescue human beings from condemnation and self-destruction. He seeks to enable human beings to become fully human, as they were intended to be in creation.

Paul describes God's justice in terms of saving and rehabilitating justice. He never defines it in terms of God's wrath or as "vindictive punishment for sin."[16] In this, Paul develops Jewish and Christian traditions. There is a parallel between the revelation of the righteousness (rectification) of God and the power of the Gospel of God unto salvation (Rom 1:16–17). Paul's concern in the early chapters of Romans, for example, is to establish a level playing field between Jews and gentiles based upon faithfulness and not covenant privilege. At the same time, Paul seeks to establish the covenant faithfulness of God even in the face of human infidelity (Rom 3:1–5).[17]

The Need of Atonement

Disobedience of the will of God by humanity—i.e., sins and transgressions—creates a context of alienation and estrangement from God, such that barriers of alienation must be removed through some process that restores relationship. In the Old Testament, God as the wronged and greater party established what was deemed necessary; he provided the means by which forgiveness could be obtained. With the development of Torah, proper relationship could be maintained through the sacrificial system, even though its efficacy had its limitations.

The New Testament relates "atonement" to the Gospel of God in Christ in terms inevitably drawn from sacrificial practice, in the light of association with Jesus's death on a Roman cross. The practice of literal sacrifice belonged to the religious matrices of both the Jewish and Greco-Roman worlds. According to *traditional* thought, in Christ, and particularly in his cross-death, humanity finds what it needs to have one's sins forgiven and one's life reconciled to God. The New Testament speaks with one voice concerning the need for atonement and the fact of atonement. Human beings need to be reconciled to God. The Gospel proclaims human beings are reconciled to God through Christ, the result of which is peace with God (Rom 5:1; Eph 2:14–16). Yet no precise explanation is specified as to *how* this is achieved. Pursuit of understanding suggests one need come to a better appreciation of Paul's conceptualization of "sin," "wrath," and "righteousness" or "justice," and perhaps even "at-one-ment" itself.

16. Tambasco, *Atonement*, 20.

17. While not Paul, Jesus's parable of the Loving Father who had two sons ("The Prodigal Son," so called, Luke 15:11–32), is illustrative of broken relationships in need of restoration and healed only by acceptance of a father's grace through a change of mind-set (repentance) on the part of the son. Even though the younger son "repented," the only way a "son" can become a son is to develop a mind-set of "sonship" and be treated like one. Jesus's parable is open-ended and has great rhetorical effect, for in reality, according to the story, we don't know what happened to either "son." The parable certainly illustrates restorative justice rather than retributive wrath.

Paul affirms humanity's need for atonement in the light of sin and estrangement characterized by downright hostility (Col 1:21). Without God because of alienation (Eph 2:12; 4:18), humanity is seen to be hostile to God and even seen to be enemies of God (Rom 8:7; 5:10). This is true for *both* Jew and gentile, for "all have sinned" (Rom 3:23). There has been deliberate disobedience of the will of God, with the consequent degrading of human life. One continues to lack "the glory of God" (Rom 3:23; cf. Eph 1:6, 12, 14). God is by nature neither complacent nor indulgent; he does not treat sin as though it does not matter. God is not indifferent (Gal 6:7), although God stands on the side of life and not death, which is the reason he acts to redeem and reconcile (cf. Rom 6:23; Eph 2:1), not only from symptomatic human actions of sinning, but also from powers of Sin that enslave and kill.[18]

God seeks to save humanity from that which destroys, hence, the sending of his Son in love and mercy. While we were sinners Christ died "for us" (Rom 5:8), such that the atoning work of Christ is particularly associated in some way with his cross-death (1 Cor 11:25; Rom 3:25; 5:10; Eph 2:13). Christ's action of self-giving does not stand in contrast to the self-giving of God the Father (2 Cor 5:19; Rom 2:25; 8:32). Rather, the two stand in concord. Through the self-giving action of God and that of Christ, the opportunity of "salvation" and reconciliation is extended to human beings, who may now be freed and restored (1 Thess 5:10; 2 Cor 5:14–15; Rom 5:1–2, 9–10). However, an opportunity extended does not automatically mean an opportunity embraced or achieved.

The Role of the Law

Paul expresses the view that the Law not only defines evil, but it actually appeals to our own self-interests so as to entice or provoke evil. The Law thus becomes an unwitting accomplice of Sin, that power already dormant within us. The Law actually brings Sin to life, provoking our sinfulness (cf. Rom 7:8–11). The Law removes ignorance by calling sin what it is, and in the process increases our guilt (Rom 7:13). Paul makes another point in Galatians that is not explicit in Romans, namely, the Law is likened to a παιδαγωγός or guardian slave responsible for minor children. By way of analogy, Paul suggests the Law served a commendable, but preparatory role prior to Christ (Gal 3:24–25). Paul recognizes, however, that this was a very temporary function. No law has been given which could ultimately "make alive"; if that were the case,

---

18. The etiological story of Adam is most often seen as a story of judgment, and it is. However, it is also a story of redemption. Adam and Eve are not summarily put to death by God. Rather, God acted to redeem, a point often overlooked. In this instance, transgression and human aggression became the etiological explanation for enmity between humans and snakes, pain in childbirth, female subjection, and general human toil, as well as the origin of death as an explanation for man's now brief life. We see that sin has consequences, but we have generally overlooked the redemptive aspects of God's actions, in favor of emphasizing divine wrath or judgment. In Gen 1:21 God is even portrayed as making garments of skin to clothe Adam and Eve—garments of animal skin to clothe Adam and Eve!

then "righteousness" would be on the basis of law (cf. Gal 3:21–22). The codified Law remains external—it can inform human beings, but it cannot motivate one to obey. And then, even so, it may contribute to idolatry. Personified, "Law" ends up being an unwitting accomplice of "Sin," actually provoking one to sin. The end result is "Death."

In Paul's view, Law reinforces the dominion of Sin that leads to Death. Among other "powers," they are realities of the Present Evil Age from which God's power in Christ is able to rescue us. How does Paul's view of freedom from Sin, Law, and Death by means of Christ's death *and* resurrection compare with popular views of the means of atonement?

The Tyrant of Death

"Death" becomes the final, ruling tyrant over humanity. Metaphorically, Paul speaks in terms of the death of relationships as a result of unrighteousness; he centers upon more than just biological reality. Paul uses metaphorical descriptions of both life and death, understood in qualitative and personal terms (cf. Rom 7:5, 9–10; 8:10). Paul can use anthropological terms in different ways to describe human beings. His three major words of "body, spirit, and flesh" (σῶμα, πνεῦμα, and σάρξ) describe an entire human being from different perspectives rather than "parts" of a human being. All three terms may be understood in the sense of the capability or quality of relationships of the self. "Flesh" (σάρξ) can be used by Paul to refer to life lived in a manner turned away from God, as contrasted with the "spirit" (πνεῦμα) or life lived turned toward God.[19]

Life "in the flesh" becomes that which improperly exalts the self, which is characterized by the distortion of all relationships. One turns from proper relationships with God, self, and others. It is self-destructive and results in the *breakdown* of the individual and the *breakup* of relationships with God, creation, and others. Paul describes "works of the flesh" in Gal 5:19–21 with examples of things that cripple or destroy social and divine relationships. To enter such a realm is to enter the realm of "Death."

Physical death brings with it the end of all of our endeavors and relationships. While on the one hand death is a natural part of creaturely existence since the time of Adam, on the other hand a premature, untimely, or violent death is seen in the Old Testament to be evil. Physical death can at times be attributed to a sinful life or sinful society, such that death comes as a consequence of sin. This, of course, is illustrated by the story of the "Fall" and its aftermath in Gen 2–3. Death thus takes on a predominate role as that which is associated with the consequences of sin.

Apocalyptic imagery of the late Old Testament and intertestamental period can view both metaphorical and biological death as a power to be conquered, hence, "Death" capitalized. Paul develops his teaching against the backdrop of apocalyptic

---

19. See Greene, *Paul's Eschatological Gospel*, part one of the present work.

thought, such that Death/death in all its dimensions is but the finishing end of a long process related to Sin/sin. Sin pays "wages," regularly and periodically, which result in "death" (Rom 6:23). Paul personifies Death and sees it as a total power, having both a present and a future reality, having both a spiritual and physical dimension, having the identity as "the last enemy to be destroyed" (1 Cor 15:26).

Cross Terminology in Paul

Gordon Fee, among other things, assumes that the cross is the focus of Paul's gospel, that the saving event is the *crucifixion* (cf. 1 Cor 1:13, 17, 18, 23; 2:2, 8; cf. 5:7). Christ's death was "for all of you" (ὑπὲρ ὑμῶν; 1 Cor 1:13; 11:24) or "for our sins" (ὑπὲρ τῶν ἁμαρτιῶν; 1 Cor 15:3).[20] He acknowledges that it is not easy to determine exactly how Paul understood Christ's death "for us," but concludes that 1 Cor 15:3 likely reflects the language of Isaiah 53 (*LXX*). The suffering servant bears the sins of many, reflecting the language of atonement drawn from both the Exodus and the sacrificial system. As Fee states, "The death of Christ 'for our sins' means that one died on behalf of others to satisfy the penalty and to overcome the alienation," which for Paul includes forgiveness of past sins and deliverance from the bondage of one's sinfulness.[21]

In the context of 1 Corinthians, the cross becomes the ultimate expression of both God's power and wisdom. God has "'out-smarted' the wise and 'overpowered' the strong."[22] The understanding of God and his ways is at issue in 1 Cor 1:10—4:21, such that, as Fee states, the crucifixion of Christ effected salvation for all of the "called." He revealed the essential character of God, further made known in the servant character of Paul's apostleship (1 Cor 3:5; 4:1–2, 9–13).

The cross appeared as sheer folly in usual thought, although Paul learned that a crucified Messiah was God's counter of overcoming the human idolatries of seeking signs and fascination with human wisdom. If there was to be a gospel at all, Paul and the other early Christians had to account for the death of Christ by crucifixion. Fee exhibits a typical assumption of cross theology for Paul, drawn from Christian theology. Paul himself does not emphasize "forgiveness of sins" in 1 Corinthians or even elsewhere in his uncontested letters (cf. use of ἄφεσις, Col 1:14; Eph 1:7). While crucifixion language is rather heavy in 1 Cor 1–2 *for Paul*, it appears in the context of factionalism and a misunderstanding or misrepresentation of the gospel in Corinth.

For Paul, the way God "out-smarted" the wise and "overpowered" the strong was through the resurrection of Christ, not through his crucifixion. Ultimately, the last enemy called "Death" could not hold him (cf. 1 Cor 15). First Corinthians 5:7 refers to Christ's death in terms of a Passover theme (which is a celebrative, deliverance theme),

---

20. Fee, "Theology of 1 Corinthians," 37–58. In keeping with the ground rules of the SBL seminar, Fee writes as if 1 Corinthians were Paul's only extant letter.

21. Fee, "Theology of 1 Corinthians," 49.

22. Fee, "Theology of 1 Corinthians," 42.

while 1 Cor 11:24 belongs to the Lord's Supper tradition. First Corinthians 15:3 *and* 15:4 are acknowledged as traditionary material by Paul, although he apparently stands in agreement with it. Reference to Isaiah 53 *in Paul* is very thin or even illusory. How easy it is to read Christian theology into Paul based upon texts other than Paul.

Following his exposition of 1 Cor 1:18—2:5, Charles Cousar concludes that a striking picture of God's purposes is given in the story of the crucified Christ. First of all, God stands as the "hidden figure behind the vivid drama of the cross." According to Cousar, the crucifixion is not blamed on a human source and becomes the occasion of God's self-revelation. Second, God is revealed as free and sovereign, as not bound to human categories and expectations. Third, God's self-revelation occurs in the message of the crucified one, thus exposing the idolatrous nature of human wisdom and providing the basis for epistemology. Fourth, the self-revelation through the preaching of the cross proves God to be a saving God. Fifth, God chooses what is weak and powerless to shame the wise and the strong. Sixth, God's power is made available to the entire community, as ultimate authority is exercised through the cross. And finally, the community finds its unity in the message of the cross, which exposes self-deception and cultivates God's "foolish weakness."[23]

It should be noted that nothing that Cousar says makes God to be the perpetrator or even the supporter of Jesus's crucifixion or Jesus's death, whether or not such would be intended by Cousar. In the present writer's perspective, it becomes a question of *intent* versus *result*. Texts that are most often translated and interpreted to suggest divine intent should be more appropriately understood in terms of either divine result or Christian living. There is nothing of a "plan moving toward a conclusion," i.e., God sent Jesus to die in order to make atonement, or, even more specifically, to die by crucifixion. Rather, there is result born of what turned out to be eschatological event in Paul's understanding—i.e., Jesus was put to death on a Roman cross, *but God raised him from the dead.*

Followed by the resurrection, a Roman cross itself becomes a powerful symbol of the overcoming of Roman sins, political Jewish sins, and that of the powers. Death is overcome by new life, which in turn is available to those "in Christ." Paul's structural emphases on the crucifixion in his polemics with the Corinthian Christians are *not* essentially different from the kerygma in Acts in terms of their resultant meaning. This may be pursued in terms of a perceived "theology of the cross" attributed to Paul.

Cousar makes the point that there is "no instance of a 'crucified-resurrected' formula in the Pauline letters."[24] However, one truly cannot "break apart" the death and resurrection. And, Paul was more confessional and doxological than he was "formulaic." Obviously, there could be no resurrection—life out of death—without the death of Christ. On the other hand, however, one can have death without positing resurrection. Yet the death apart from resurrection would not have the same meaning,

23. Cousar, *Theology of the Cross*, 35.
24. Cousar, *Theology of the Cross*, 23.

no matter how much it might be described in terms of sacrificial and cultic imagery. No less a figure than John Calvin realized that point. Any contemporary discussion of the "death of Jesus" or "cross theology" should always be carried out in the light of the assumed concomitant reality of the resurrection. Aspective theology at its best is always born of the light of the whole gospel. And, if Pauline, it should recognize not just a "cross" theology predicated upon the post-Pauline development of atonement theories, but it should focus upon Paul's own emphases.

Cross and Kerygma

According to Green, drawing upon Hengel, Paul uses two stereotypical expressions for the atoning significance of the cross.[25] He speaks of the "giving up" of Jesus for the salvation of humankind either as a divine act or in terms of self-giving (Gal 1:4; 2:19–20; Rom 4:25; 8:32). There is also a "dying formula" *present* in Paul, i.e., "Christ died *for us*"—cf. 1 Thess 5:10; 1 Cor 15:3; 2 Cor 5:14, 15; Rom 5:6, 8. The question may be asked, what emerges when one begins to examine the texts offered in support? The *cross* is nowhere mentioned directly in any of these texts, except by implication in Gal 2:19 where Paul says he has been "crucified with Christ." While Paul mentions the death of Christ in behalf of all (ὑπὲρ πάντων) in 2 Cor 5:14–15, the overall context has to deal with Christian living in terms of new creation and reconciliation. Paul mentions the twin aspects of his full gospel in 2 Cor 5:15, Christ *died* and *was raised* "in our behalf," that we might be reconciled to God and become his ambassadors in a ministry of reconciliation.[26]

Paul's overall argument in 2 Cor 5:14–21 relates Christ's death to these themes. Even the oft-quoted 2 Cor 5:21 should likely be related to these themes, as well, rather than to atonement theory. Paul relates sin and death and life in the flesh (κατὰ σάρκα). Christ lived in the flesh and died at the hands of sinful humankind, but God raised him from the dead. Paul expresses a salvation-resurrection theme in 1 Thess 5:9–10, which occurs in an imperatival context. In Rom 4:25 Paul uses παραδίδωμι to point out that Christ was handed over because of our trespasses (διὰ τὰ παραπτώματα) and raised because of our justification. In Rom 8:32 God did not spare his own son, but gave him over in behalf of us all, "how will he not 'grace' all things to us together with him." The suggestion is that God gave Christ over to Death, i.e., he allowed him to die without doing anything by way of intervention. God had yet a trump card to play in terms of resurrection and exaltation. Many treatments of Rom 8:32 do not take into account the "rest of the story," in which Jesus's death is but an interim point. Divine intervention came at the point of resurrection.

25. Green, "Death of Christ," 202.

26. What Paul affirms in 2 Cor 5:15 highlights the fact that ὑπὲρ ὑμῶν cannot be legitimately translated "in our place" as some interpreters of the Atonement are wont to do. If Christ was raised "in our place," one is confronted with what could be termed "substitutionary resurrection."

Galatians 1:4 makes the point that Jesus gave himself in behalf of our sins (*keryg-ma*) to deliver us from the Present Evil Age. In addition, Gal 2:19–20 is a significant reference. Paul has died *to* the Law *through* the Law, in order that he might live to God: "I have been crucified together with/in Christ," who is identified as the Son of God, "who loved [aor. part.] me and gave [aor. part.] himself in my behalf."[27] First Corinthians 15:3 states that Christ died in behalf of (ὑπέρ) our sins according to the scriptures. This is not only kerygmatic tradition, but it represents interpretation of Old Testament Scripture. Romans 5:6 indicates that at the right season, Christ died in behalf of the godless, while we were still weak, i.e., while we were in the flesh and under the power of Sin, Christ died. Prior to the resurrection, under the ruling powers of the Present Evil Age, Christ died. Romans 5:8 states that God commended his own love to us, because while we were sinners Christ died in our behalf. That verse need not be understood in the sense that it was on the basis of Christ's death that God "commended" his love.

There may be a "dying" strain present in Paul's thought, but just because θανατάω appears doesn't mean it is a "formula." Historically speaking, Christ *died* and he *died on a cross*. Neither could be denied, although Paul himself tends to mention Christ's *death* more than specifically *his death on a cross* (see Appendix A). We should perhaps not confuse the two realities and read "cross" into Paul where he only mentions "death." When Paul mentions the death of Christ, he is acknowledging the historical kerygma. When he mentions "cross," he tends to mention it in an imperatival context of Christian identity and called-for action. According to Hengel, the Pauline phrase "Christ died for us" becomes the most frequent and most important *confessional* statement in Paul and primitive Christianity.[28] Regardless of how Hengel uses the expression, a confessional statement extends far beyond literalization of the words in terms of implied meanings, especially in a "high-context" societal setting. Paul aligns himself with the foundations of shared faith in the primitive Christian tradition and builds upon them.

Paul reflects on the meaning of the crucified Christ at Corinth and Colossae in large part so as to counter competing ideas. At Corinth the word of the cross counters wrong-headed thinking about the nature of present existence, as Paul must speak against the "wisdom of the world" and status-seeking enthusiasts. The scandalous cross of Christ is presented as the "power of God," such that "Christ crucified" and the community oriented around the crucified Christ (1 Cor 1:18–31) uproots social, philosophical, and even soteriological norms of the Corinthians. Paul's text mocks the

---

27. The aorist tense in Greek is the "default" tense. It offers a non-descriptive, single perspective summary of the action. While it may at times refer to a singular occurrence of an action, it is a common false assumption that it automatically refers to a singular, punctiliar action. The aorist tense is "without horizon," it is "a-oristic."

28. Hengel, *Atonement*, 37.

"self-confident pretensions"[29] of the Corinthians with a highly ironic presentation of God's "foolishness" and "weakness" as compared with their self-assumed theological position of "wisdom" and "strength," thus sharply exposing their own misguided religious and intellectual certitudes.

Paul's initial preaching among the Corinthians intended to establish their faith as that solidly based upon the power of God to overcome death and raise the dead (i.e., the death and resurrection of Christ as the Gospel of God). What developed in Corinth called for correction—a kind of retrospective remediation to correct a false understanding of both the indicative and the imperative held by the Corinthians. The nature of Jesus's death and the reality of bodily resurrection had apparently both come under fire, thus calling the indicative of the Gospel into question. The pride expressed in spiritual excesses and assumptive human wisdom was undermining a proper Christian imperative in living out the Christian faith. First Corinthians as a whole has to address both aspects of the Gospel of God, yet it proved to be a very "painful" experience for both the Corinthians and for Paul in his relations with the Corinthian Christians.

What has developed in terms of atonement perception attributed to Paul also calls for correction, in the light of what Paul himself says. Repeated attention to a handful of prooftexts is not representative of Paul's larger contextual eschatological perspectives. Such attention to atonement theories has led to a neglect of Paul's cross-imperative.

To the Colossians, Paul presents a cosmic Christ who reconciled the whole cosmos to God, including all the astral powers. This happens through the flesh and blood, life and death of Christ—"through him God was pleased to reconcile to himself all things . . . by making peace through the blood of his cross" (Col 1:20; cf. 1:14; 2:13–14; 3:13). Death on a cross which logically should suggest certain defeat is paradoxically and powerfully turned into victory through the action of resurrection. Appeasement of astral powers is not the means of access to God, nor is quasi-gnostic spiritualizing the way to discipleship and Christian identity. One lives with ethical behavior in the material world, reconciled to God, in freedom independent of the powers. "Peace" is made through the "blood of the cross" in the light of resurrection life and triumph even over Death.

"Peace" is achieved through divine victory over the powers. Nothing could be more powerful than the divine demonstration of life wrought from death. The "war" is for all intents and purposes over, such that the principalities and powers have been disarmed and made a public spectacle in a divine victory procession (Col 2:12–15). That is Paul's affirmation—"peace through the blood of his cross." What appeared to be defeat *by* the powers becomes rather the defeat *of* the powers in Christ's resurrection.

Elsewhere, Jesus's life as God's obedient Son is center stage. Jesus's obedience is seen most clearly and profoundly in his own willingness to embrace suffering,

29. Cousar, *Theology of the Cross*, 33.

rejection, and excruciating and shameful death by crucifixion. One may reference interpretation given in Phil 2:6–11 once again. Christ's death becomes the highest expression of his life, *establishing for us* a pattern of a life characterized by love and obedience, as Tambasco correctly stresses.[30] As Green states, "Paul shows how Christian thought and life build on the foundational event of the cross of Christ."[31] McGrath calls further attention in other ways—"The death of Christ is significant, not simply as an historical event, but through the preaching of the word (Rom 10:14) and the subsequent evoking of faith."[32] When one considers the issue, it is history in the service of theology; it is theology making sense of history, i.e., what does Jesus's rather ignominious death on the cross mean in terms of the Gospel of God? What does it mean in terms of foundational theological understanding? What does it say about the nature of God? And the response of God to Sin/sin? And then, what does it mean in terms of Christian living?

Ultimately, as will be argued later, Paul's specific focus upon the cross moves more in the realm of the imperative than it does in the realm of the indicative.[33] Even the significant passage in Phil 2:6–11 is introduced with a strong imperative—"Have this mind among yourselves which [was] also in Christ Jesus" (Phil 2:5b), which is most certainly a contributional application of the passage by Paul. The presence of the imperative is Pauline, regardless of whether or not Paul appropriates an early Christian hymn. It is likewise followed by an emphasis upon the imperative.

Cousar admits that the apostolic kerygma recorded in the speeches in Acts contains a definite accusatory element in connection with the crucifixion, which is contrasted with a following statement of God's vindication in the resurrection (cf. Acts 2:23–24; cf. 2:36; 3:13–15; 10:39–40; 13:28–30). It is certainly a kerygmatic emphasis with which Luke agrees. According to Cousar, Paul's letters nowhere indicate a set of charges for Jesus's death, followed by a statement of divine vindication. "The pattern so prominent in Acts has no place in Paul at all."[34]

While the *pattern* may have no place in Paul, it is a weak argument from silence to assume Paul would not hold to such a viewpoint. It is likely he would not have stated it so directly as Luke did some twenty or more years later.[35] Secondly, such a viewpoint does appear to be implicit in Paul, *although* Paul really begins with the

30. Tambasco, *Atonement*, 72.

31. Green, "Death of Christ," 203.

32. McGrath, "Theology of the Cross," 194.

33. See Gorman, *Cruciformity.*

34. Cousar, *Theology of the Cross*, 90. It needs to be remembered that Paul writes much earlier than Luke.

35. David Brondos affirms that Paul offers the same basic story of redemption as the remainder of the New Testament. Cf. Brondos, *Paul on the Cross*. Given the temporal considerations, one might say in reverse that the basic story of redemption in Paul is reflected in the subsequent New Testament writings. Indeed, one should also be reminded that we are not privy to all of Paul's theology, but only that which is expressed through his letters, his "epistolic" theology.

event of death rather than historical forces leading up to it. This is perhaps to affirm Paul really focuses upon resurrection and the risen Christ, for which death must be the necessary prelude. Paul's focus is ultimately not accusation, but rather affirmation. That is ultimately Luke's focus as well, although he has different purposes afoot.

Paul's concern is with the eschatological change of the Ages, which is really absent from Luke's emphasis. As Beker correctly suggests, Jesus's resurrection is not the closure event of the incarnation but the inauguration of the new and final day.[36] The resurrection anchors the promise of God's future. It is the firstfruit. It calls forth the gift of the Spirit, the guarantee of future inheritance. These are the Pauline emphases. Paul has a different focus, but that does not mean he would not espouse or support the kerymatic emphasis found in Acts based upon historical event, even though Luke's later *pattern* may be absent. The earliest Christians struggled with the meaning of Christ's death even as they recounted historical details. With an eye on past eschatological events, Paul looks to the future fulfilment and culmination of that inaugurative eschatology.

The "Blood" of Christ

The term "blood" occurs only twelve times in Paul (out of ninety-seven times in the New Testament). Three occurrences have to do with "flesh and blood" as a metaphor for humankind in one's current state of existence (Gal 1:16; 1 Cor 15:50; Eph 6:12). Romans 3:15 (Isa 59:7) has to do with the taking of human life. The other eight references have to do with the "blood" of Christ.[37]

The references in 1 Corinthians are related to the celebration of the Lord's Supper. First Corinthians 10:16 points to participation in Christ's life at the Supper. First Corinthians 11:25 speaks of the new covenant "in Christ's blood," while 1 Cor 11:27 speaks of the "body and blood of the Lord." Romans 3:25 points to the *place* of expiation or "provision" which God has set forth, through faith, "in his blood." Romans 5:9 makes the point that having been "right wised" in/by his blood, we shall be saved through him (δι' αὐτοῦ) from wrath. The phrase expresses indirect agency, behind whom stands God as the direct agent of the action.

In Eph 1:6–7 Paul stresses that the church is to be a praise unto the grace of God with which he graced us in the Beloved One, in whom we have redemption through his blood, the forgiveness of trespasses, according to the wealth of his grace. The phraseology appears to be euphemistic for the death of Christ. The way of resurrection occurred, and had to occur, through death, i.e., "the blood of Christ." Participation in the "body and blood" associated with the Supper points to communion and a continuing identity with Christ, i.e., a cross imperative based upon an historical indicative.

36. Beker, *Paul the Apostle*, 156.
37. 1 Cor 10:16; 11:25; 11:27; Rom 3:25; 5:9; Col 1:.20; Eph 1:7; 2:13.

Paul's focus in Colossians and Ephesians appears to be upon the result of God's gracious action in Christ.[38] In further usage, Eph 2:13 addresses gentiles directly and stresses that now in Christ Jesus *they* (lit., *you*) are the ones who then were far off, but who have been brought near (ἐγενήθητε, aor.) in/by the blood of Christ. Colossians 1:20 expresses the point that God intended through Christ to reconcile all things to himself, having made peace through (διά) the blood of his cross. Colossians 1:22 is Paul's interpretation of verse 20 and affirms that estranged gentiles are reconciled in the body of his flesh through (διά) death to establish them holy, blameless, and irreproachable before him. Christians now have a cross-imperative which stands before them.

In fact, a cross-imperative is attributed to Jesus himself in the Synoptic Gospels. Jesus does not say "take up *my* cross," but rather "let one take up [ἀράτω] *one's own* cross," albeit expressed in the third person with a permissive imperative ("his cross," τὸν σταυρόν αὐτοῦ, Mark 8:34; Matt 16:24; Luke 9:23). Whether this goes back to Jesus or to Synoptic tradition, it reflects a cross-imperative. In the Synoptic tradition, "taking up one's own cross" is given as the preface for the permissive imperative of following Jesus (ἀκολουθείτω μοι). To follow the "way of the cross" is to follow the way of Jesus. It is also interesting to note that Luke in Acts preserves "the Way" as an early designation of the Christian movement (Acts 9:2; 19:9, 23; 22:4; 24:14, 22; cf. 18:25, 26).

Pauline Emphases

The noun "cross" (σταυρός) and the verb for "crucify" (σταυρόω) in fact do not occur very often in Paul's letters, which is perhaps surprising in the light of the emphasis within Christian theology. The noun occurs ten times (out of a total of only twenty-seven times in the entire New Testament) and the verb but eight times (out of a total of forty-four times in the New Testament).[39] With the exception of three occurrences of the noun in Colossians (Col 1:20; 2:14) and Ephesians (Eph 2:16), all the other occurrences belong to letters of the Collection Campaign and are found primarily in Galatians and 1 Corinthians, both of which were written at a time when Paul was beginning to have trouble with the Judaizers or Nomistic Evangelists. As a side point, because they belong to the period of Paul's Collection Campaign, one may or may not presume a like conceptual stress or importance for Paul's Foundational Campaign among those same churches.

---

38. As has been seen, the present author accepts both Colossians and Ephesians as Pauline, and, they are attributed to Paul. Should one deny Pauline authorship, they would still apparently offer a trajectory of Pauline thematic conceptualization.

39. For the noun σταυρός, see Gal 5:11; 6:12, 14; Phil 2:8; 3:18; 1 Cor 1:17, 18; Col 1:20; 2:14; Eph 2:16. For the verb σταυρόω, see Gal 3:1; 5:24; 6:14; 1 Cor 1:13, 23; 2:2, 8; 2 Cor 13:4. The compound verb συνσταυρόω ("I am crucified together with") occurs in Gal 2:19 and Rom 6:6.

Beker reminds one that even though crucifixion terminology is comparatively rare in Paul, terminological importance often occurs in inverse proportion to frequency. He observes that the theology of the cross is rare in the entire New Testament, contrary to popular belief, and that "it must be distinguished in some ways from a theology of the death and resurrection of Christ and from that of the suffering of Christ."[40] There are distinct meanings belonging to these differing reflections, such that their distinct meanings should not be fused. Beker does not take the cross to be the center of Paul's thought, although a number of other scholars do.[41]

The atoning significance of Jesus's death is generally divorced from *Paul's* emphasis upon reconciliation. The theological emphasis of today is often concerned with notions of expiation, propitiation, and other doctrines of substitution or satisfaction. After centuries of debate, it is now difficult to read Paul without the overlay of one or more classical theories of the atonement. Theological barnacles have firmly attached themselves to the Pauline wood. The "dramatic" theory portrays the saving work of Christ as a cosmic drama of conflict and victory; the "satisfaction" theory presents Christ's death as a satisfaction tendered to God, which removes the barrier between God and humanity. The "moral influence theory" presents the cross as a demonstration of God's boundless love to be emulated by humanity.[42]

The satisfaction theory came to ascendency and was developed with the particular corollary of penal or forensic satisfaction. This emphasis upon Christ suffering the penalty deserved by humanity has proven to be rather problematic in contemporary theological discussion, as Green mildly suggests.[43] Indeed! The cross has been understood as a manifestation of God's wrath and Christ's mercy, portraying God as a sadist and Jesus as a masochist.[44] Green suggests that it is highly unlikely those who formulated the satisfaction theory would recognize the contemporary characterization of their view. This view has particularly been problematic in hymnody and popular interpretation, which in turn is derivatively based upon earlier Christian preaching. It is likely true that one of the greatest formative influences upon the average Christian's theology is that of "Christian" hymns and songs—for better, or for worse. The matter of the atonement will be treated at greater length in later chapters.

The idea of sacrificial death has often been unduly stressed in passages like Rom 3:25. Paul was familiar with the idea of sacrifice and used its imagery without scruple

40. Beker, *Paul the Apostle*, 198. That reminder, however, is not license for one to interject the term freely where Paul does not use it. Non-Pauline usage of both the noun and the verb occurs most often in the passion narrative of the Gospels. As might be expected, it belongs to narrative description.

41. Cf. Cousar, *Theology of the Cross*, 21–24.

42. See chapters 7 and 8. In view of other developed theories, the adjective "dramatic" or "dynamic" might be better than Aulén's "classical" designation.

43. Green, "Death of Christ," 203–4. Cf. Baker and Green, *Scandal of the Cross*.

44. While varying portraits of the "wrath of God" abound, the longest treatment of the wrath of God in the New Testament, once again, is by Paul and occurs in Rom 1. There, Paul describes God's wrath in terms of God turning sinful human beings over to themselves for *self*-destruction.

(Rom 12:1; 15:16; Phil 2:17). He may have given it christological overtones, but he *never* definitely called Jesus's death a sacrifice, according to Käsemann, because it was generally accounted as God's action. God does not offer sacrifice to himself.[45]

Pauline texts in reality provide no basis for the popular view of vicarious punishment of Christ (a view wrongly based upon Gal 3:13 and 2 Cor 5:21). Paul's texts do not speak of punishment, but fall under the category of reconciliation, which throughout the New Testament means the end of enmity. Romans 5:10 takes up the message of reconciliation. It describes the justification of the godless "as the gift of the divine peace to those who would otherwise remain enemies and who now through the *pax Christi* are led back into obedience."[46]

The historical reality of Christ's crucifixion is upheld by 1 Cor 2:8, where mention is made that the rulers of This Age crucified the Lord of glory. In the same context, Paul affirms that he preaches "Christ crucified" (1 Cor 1:23) and, in the light of divisions at Corinth, raises the question as to whether he himself had been crucified in their behalf (1 Cor 1:13). While the other references in 1 Corinthians support the historical reality of Jesus's death by crucifixion, they express something more. First Corinthians 1:17 speaks of "the cross of Christ" in relation to Paul's preaching of the gospel, while 1 Cor 1:18 speaks of the folly of "the word of the cross" in the light of Corinthian "wisdom." The gospel that Paul preaches is identified with the power of God. Paul wants the full power of God to be proclaimed. He does not want to offer any substitute in his ministry (e.g., baptism, eloquent "wisdom," false pneumatology) that would empty the Christ event or Christian living of its divine power.

When Paul says that he decided to know nothing among the Corinthians "except Jesus Christ and this one having been crucified [pf. part.]", 1 Cor 2:20), he is speaking about his own ministry, as the context makes plain. In other words, Paul uses this limited focal point to describe his own ministry at this junction. He is not describing the Gospel of God in itself. At a later point in the same letter, 1 Cor 15 makes clear that the resurrection is at least as significant as Christ's death, if not more so. In terms of questions and issues posed for Paul by the Corinthians, it is interesting that they apparently had no questions regarding the meaning of Christ's death. They did have significant questions regarding the resurrection (1 Cor 15). Nor does Paul "redirect" the Corinthians' concerns by suggesting they should focus on the meaning and effects of Christ's death. Paul's response to the Corinthians' question in 1 Cor 15 should be a clue to us concerning the nature of *Paul's* emphases.

In Gal 3:1 the reference appears to be Paul's preaching that had portrayed Christ as crucified. Jesus died a "cross" death (cf. Phil 2:8) and the proclamation of Christ died and raised belonged to Paul's gospel. The issue in Galatians is the proclamation of a false gospel that centered upon the keeping of the Jewish Law, especially

---

45. Käsemann, *Perspectives on Paul*, 43. First Corinthians 5:7 points not to the sacred rite, but to the result—for Christians, Easter has begun.

46. Käsemann, *Perspectives on Paul*, 44. See Martin, *Reconciliation*.

circumcision. Paul denies a "circumcision" gospel and maintains a gospel of what he terms "the scandal of the cross" (Gal 5:11). Both of these references (Gal 3:1; 5:11) bear testimony to the historical reality of Jesus's death as a "cross" death, which on the surface of things was certainly scandalous in that Greco-Roman world.[47]

The verbal reference to Christ being crucified in weakness (2 Cor 13:4, i.e., a "cross" kind of death in the flesh) also includes a reference to his post-resurrection life as a result of the power of God. Paul again is being called upon to defend his apostleship and his gospel before the Corinthians. Although he may at times have appeared to be weak among them, he warns them that his next visit will be in power (2 Cor 13:1–3a). Yet even in this uncertain context, Paul affirms life with Christ on the basis of God's power for both himself and the Corinthian Christians. Paul does not wish either the Corinthians or himself to be judged a failure. He encourages them to examine themselves to see whether or not they are remaining in the faith, whether Jesus Christ is living in them (2 Cor 13:5). If Christ lives within them and if they are "in Christ," it is the crucified *and* raised Christ of whom Paul speaks. For Paul, to live with Christ is to die with him. For Paul, to die with Christ is the necessary prelude to resurrection.

Colossians 1:20 affirms that God has reconciled all things to himself, having made peace "through the blood of his [Jesus's] cross." The historical reality of the cross is presented in the context of its theological interpretation of reconciliation and peace. There is no emphasis upon sacrifice, unless one assumes that every time Paul mentions "blood" he means sacrifice. From an Old Testament perspective, it was blood that signified life. God has brought life to those who were dead in trespasses "together with him" (Col 2:13), having canceled *whatever* legal bond that stood against us. This claim God set aside, "having nailed it to the cross" (Col 2:14).

Paul does not define the "bond against us" as to its nature or origin, other than to characterize it as having "legal demands." Does it reference transgressions and violations of Torah, hence, a "bond" held by God? Does it reference indebtedness to Sin in the weakness of "flesh," the end of which is death (cf. Rom 6:23, which uses a different metaphor)? Is Paul's emphasis simply that God sets aside any indebtedness, as he has spoken through his Gospel of resurrection symbolled by the cross? Is Paul's meaning that God simply serves notice to all opposing powers in the very place of death that they have no more claim? It is at least equally possible that Paul's emphasis is upon the lack of further *claim* rather than a focus of *payment*. It is a freedom metaphor. Of course, some might assume a "paid in full" satisfaction of debt by the death of Jesus on the cross.

---

47. There is a famous example of ancient graffiti which graphically depicts the scandal with scorn that was alluded to in the preface of the present volume. Scratched on a stone in a guardroom on the Palatine Hill in Rome near the Circus Maximus is the figure of a man with the head of an donkey hanging on a cross. The inscription, scratched in Greek, reads, "Alexamenos worships his god." See Elliott and Reasoner, *Documents and Images*, 105; Ferguson, *Backgrounds of Early Christianity*, 596–97. The "cross" was offensive and the idea of a crucified Lord was simply contemptible in pagan thinking. The difficulty of evangelism in a first century Greco-Roman world is highlighted.

What does seem plain in the context is that *God's own activity* is in our behalf "in Christ," all of which has freed us from the elemental spirits, the body of "flesh," from all indebtedness. While we were once "dead," God has now made us alive "with Christ" (σὺν αὐτόν), freed from every encumbrance and freed for appropriate relationships. "Death" brings freedom from all legal encumbrances and obligations (cf. Rom 7:1–6). God's "judgment" has been made plain, such that religious regulations and philosophies being held up before the Colossians have no substance. Rather, the "substance belongs to Christ" (Col 2:17, lit. τὸ σῶμα τοῦ Χριστοῦ).

The legacy of Christ's willingness to suffer a cross-kind of death is resurrection or life with God, as a result of any bond against us being forfeit and "nailed to the cross," the symbol of God's Gospel in Christ. The cross as symbol of our imperative and promise is the most significant place to proclaim a reminder for all to see. All claims against those in Christ are null and void, save the claim of God upon those who out of obedience live a cruciform existence with a view toward resurrection. In fact, to nail a "cancelled bond" specifically to the *empty* cross may become a vivid metaphor of both remembrance and direction toward a cross imperative. God also made a public spectacle of the "principalities and powers" (lit., "rulers and authorities"), having triumphed over them in Christ (or, "in the cross," Col 2:15). The powers have no more claim.

No one but God has claim upon those in Christ, for God has triumphed (by implication) over powers such as Sin and Death. At least metaphorically, one has died with Christ (Col 2:20), and one has been raised with Christ (Col 3:1–4). It is the "cross" that symbolizes that. Victory in God leads naturally to encouragement to live accordingly (Col 3:5—4:6). In like manner, Eph 2:16 emphasizes reconciliation and peace that has occurred through (διά) the cross, insofar as enmity or hostility between Jew and gentile has been brought to an end. One new person has been created in Christ, such that gentiles are no longer alienated from covenants of promise. Those once "far off" have now in Christ become near "in/by the blood of Christ" (Eph 2:13). Christ Jesus himself becomes the cornerstone of a living temple structure unto God, in which God dwells "in/by the Spirit" (Eph 2:20–22). That is a living symbol of worship.

When one examines the actual passages in which Paul uses words for crucifixion, one finds tacit acknowledgment of the historical fact of Jesus's "cross" kind of death. This was certainly a fact for which the early church and Paul himself had to account and had to interpret. The "cross" kind of death, along with the resurrection, certainly belonged to the centrality of the Pauline gospel. However, the Pauline emphasis begins to fall upon the cross as a mode of Christian living. One dies with Christ a "cross" kind of death, but one "having been raised" with Christ, one lives as one who has been "crucified with Christ." This latter aspect will be developed further under the character of Paul's "cross imperative" in a later chapter.

Distinctly absent from Paul's gospel, however, is any emphasis that would connect the cross specifically with sacrificial metaphors. This is not to suggest that Paul does not associate words pertaining to crucifixion with sacrificial terminology, as do most atonement theories within Christian theology. Overall, however, it is perhaps surprising how infrequently Paul does actually allude to crucifixion in terminology, especially in a theological rather than an ethical or imperatival sense.

Paul did use sacrificial metaphors to interpret Jesus's *death* in a general sense, but even here the cultic emphasis is not primary. Many other metaphors are employed. Even in a passage like Rom 3:21–26, only one out of the three primary metaphors (redemption, place of offering/provision, reconciliation) has to do with sacrifice. Atonement for Paul primarily has to do with reconciliation with a loving and just God and his inclusive Gospel. Paul does not suggest God put Jesus to death, but rather that Jesus gave himself up. He was obedient to the point of death. He did not shrink from death, if that was what was called forth—even death on a cross (Phil 2:8). The cross became a fitting symbol for Christianity primarily because of its connotations with regard to Christians who were called upon figuratively and literally to die with Christ.

"Death" for both Jesus *and* Christians was central to Paul's gospel. The cross became a fitting symbol for Christian living and Christianity itself, particularly in the light of the absence of construction of temples and places of worship. It was a material symbol that could stand for both death *and* resurrection. Indeed, it would have been much harder to find a symbol for the resurrection that could also suggest death. The best Paul could do with regard to resurrection, apparently, was to advance the metaphor of a seed, in order to symbol the resurrection (1 Cor 15:35–37). It is interesting that the Lukan account in Acts 17 reflects the Athenian philosophers' question, "What is this 'seed-picker' [σπερμολόγος] saying?," as Paul's sermon proclaims Jesus (a masculine noun) and the "resurrection" (ἀνάστασις, a feminine noun). The Athenian philosophers assumed a pair of deities, one male and the other female.

One last point. Interestingly enough, neither the word σταυρός or σταυρόω occurs in Romans (or 1–2 Thess and 2 Tim). Paul does use the compound form συνσταυρόω ("I crucify together with") in a singular occurrence in both Galatians and Romans. In Gal 2:19 Paul affirms that he died to the Law that he might live to God: "I have been crucified with Christ [pf.]." But he adds, "But *I* no longer *live*, but Christ *lives* in me; what I now live in flesh, I live by faith, that is, by (the faith) of the Son of God who loved me and who gave himself over in my behalf" (Gal 2:20, emphasis original). Paul's focus is his own present life and ministry "in Christ."

Finally, in Rom 6:6 Paul affirms that the "old man" has been crucified together with (Christ), in order that the body of sin might be destroyed, "such that we are no longer 'bonded' to Sin." The text occurs in a context which affirms freedom from Sin and the promise of resurrection (Rom 6:1–11). The passage ends with an imperative: "Consider yourselves to be dead ones on the one hand to Sin, but on the other hand living to God in Christ Jesus" (Rom 6:11). To perhaps paraphrase Paul's statement, "consider yourselves as ones crucified to Sin on the one hand, but those resurrected and living unto God on the other." It is helpful, thereby, to make specific inquiry regarding what has been termed a "theology of the cross."

A "Theology of the Cross"

A "theology of the cross" developed very quickly in the early church for two reasons, according to Tambasco.[48] It represented a puzzle and a scandal for believers who continued to experience suffering in their own lives. Paul drew out the positive, redemptive value of earlier Christian tradition (Gal 1:4; 1 Cor 15:3). Paul's understanding of "for our sins" is quite different from a view that God requires satisfaction or a legal justice of "balancing the scales." Paul does not employ the model of a penal substitute for all humanity. Christ does not undergo punishment for sin or give satisfaction in our place. It is questionable as to whether this view may be found anywhere in the New Testament. Tambasco describes Paul's model of Christ's death as a "representative journey" in which we are invited to participate by the risen Christ.[49]

Drawing upon the Old Testament and the Judaism of his time, Paul's convergent lines of thought speak of the varied effects of Christ's atonement. They arise from the blood of Christ, who dies for sinners.[50] There is the image of the martyr, the just person vindicated in death through effect upon the community of believers (4 Macc 17:20–22). The Suffering Servant of Isaiah 53, while not prominent in biblical Israel nor in early Judaism of the New Testament period, is focused upon in early Christianity and utilized to formulate a theology of Christ's suffering and death in terms of vicarious atonement that is representative and substitutionary for all humankind. Isaiah 53, however, is not at all prevalent in Paul. Martyr or servant theology could suggest the giving of one's life for a cause. However, this also developed in another direction, understood primarily within the context of temple sacrifice. Tambasco suggests that this enabled early Christians to understand Christ's atoning suffering as more than just moral example (cf. Rom 3:24–25; 5:9).

The phrase "theology of the cross" was first used in 1518 by Martin Luther, who understood that God could only be known through suffering and the cross. Luther's personal pilgrimage of salvation and discipleship grew out of a life marked by guilt and imposed suffering. In Luther's usage, it was a theological method of revelation rather than a specific doctrinal view of the atonement. One of the most vigorous contemporary advocates of Pauline thought as a "theology of the cross" has been Ernst Käsemann, who insisted that Paul should be understood both historically and theologically in the light of Luther's Reformation insight of a "theology of the cross" and "justification by faith."

---

48. Tambasco, *Atonement*, 65.

49. Tambasco, *Atonement*, 66.

50. Tambasco, *Atonement*, 66.

As a Lutheran, Käsemann sought to defend the insights of Luther and to defend the Reformed basis of Protestantism against what he saw as an incursion by a "theology of the resurrection." On the one hand, he affirmed that salvation always means resurrection from the dead, because that is the basic nature of God and the action of God toward his people. Yet he understood language that emphasized the "scandal of the cross" as a distinctively Pauline contribution which Paul utilized in the "polemical context of intramural challenge." [51] To see Christ's death as sacrifice for sins or as a vicarious, representative act for sinners or as redemption from slavery points to the benefits of grace. Paul stressed the anthropological and existential thrust of Jesus's death for the "ungodly" (Rom 5:6; 4:5). Käsemann attributed passages that carried atoning significance to the tradition that existed before Paul.

Paul's "theology of the cross" is polemical in the sense that it countered false understandings of the gospel within the church itself. It was thus no accident that it characterized Protestant beginnings, as well. According to McGrath, Käsemann thus sought to draw a precise distinction between Pauline theology and the pre-Pauline liturgical and doxological tradition which Paul inherited. Those passages referring to the salvific significance of Jesus's death on the cross were to be derived from earlier Christian tradition.[52]

Käsemann argued that Paul introduced radical new elements into the traditional material, that Paul's emphasis was upon the "here and now" of the crucifixion as a key element in his controversy with the Corinthian enthusiasts. Käsemann saw Paul as making two radical interpretive moves, interpreting the texts existentially and stressing Jesus's death for the ungodly. For Paul, faith means only one thing: Christ is Lord. The center of Pauline theology for Käsemann was a "theology of the cross," which points to the saving significance of Jesus's death in terms of the preaching of the event and the response of faith. In Käsemann's view, the cross and resurrection are to be related as "riddle and interpretation."

Käsemann was critical of those who only understood cross and resurrection as links in a chain, along with Christ's pre-existence, incarnation, exaltation, and return, respectively. Jesus's resurrection marked the beginning of the rule of Christ as Lord of the church, as the destined Cosmocrator, such that the resurrection became a chapter in the broader topic of the theology of the cross.[53] The cross was seen to have priority over all other events in the history of salvation. According to Käsemann, Paul's distinctive understanding of the saving significance of Jesus's death involved seeing Christ as (a) a criminal cursed by God (b) through whom God justifies the ungodly. Really? The significance of Jesus's death in Paul functions polemically to combat human arrogance

---

51. Käsemann, *Perspectives on Paul*, 32–59.

52. McGrath, "Theology of the Cross," 192–97.

53. Käsemann, *Perspectives on Paul*, 59. Cf. Cousar, *Theology of the Cross*, 14.

and self-righteousness, as he turned it in an existential and anthropological direction through the preaching of the event and response in faith.[54]

According to Käsemann, *prior* to Paul the cross formed the question which was answered by the message of the resurrection. In Käsemann's judgment, it is the cross that gives meaning to the resurrection and not the converse. While on the one hand the cross could be argued as the necessary presupposition for the resurrection, according to McGrath the cross is not a chapter in the history of resurrection, such that it excels the cross in significance. Although the resurrection gives meaning to the cross, according to McGrath, it is the cross that is the real center of gravity. Or, as he states, "*One might almost say that the resurrection is a chapter in a book on the theology of the cross.*"[55] Really?

According to this viewpoint, Paul reversed the way of looking at things, at least according to McGrath and Käsemann. It is suggested that this may be seen in the controversy with the spiritual enthusiasts in Corinth. According to this perspective, *in the Corinthian situation* it was not the cross that was the "riddle," with the resurrection its "interpretation." Rather, the problem was the resurrection. That could only be defined in the light of the cross. According to McGrath, building upon Käsemann, a misunderstanding of an already "realized resurrection" had to be qualified by what the present writer calls a "cross imperative," as the shadow of the cross had to continue to fall across Christian living. Believers become participants in the cross-death of Jesus through baptism, with the hope that they *shall become* participants in the resurrection.

For the present writer, there appears to be a mixed apologetic at work here that calls for better historical and exegetical clarity. When it comes to Paul's treatment of both cross and resurrection in 1 Corinthians, one is not dealing with a "theological book" in which one chapter has greater significance than another. If one wishes to use the metaphor of a "book and its chapters," then *for Paul* the book would be titled *The Gospel of God* (Rom 1:1–6) and it would contain a chapter on "The Cross," as well as one on "The Resurrection," among many others, including "Exaltation." It would not be titled *The Cross*. Generally speaking, the cross was a riddle for which resurrection offered proper understanding. It was the resurrection that heralded Gospel. There is a sense in which the Gospel of God will always be a "riddle" for human thought to grasp. The spiritualists and factionalists of ancient Corinth wrestled with the riddle of the Gospel as much as modern theologians and pietists.

Specifically speaking, the Corinthian situation appears to be one in which more than a single issue was afoot. In 1 Cor 15 Paul appears to be dealing with two issues associated with the resurrection. The basic issue appears to be a *denial of the resurrection* on the part of gentile Corinthian enthusiasts (1 Cor 15:12), based either upon gentile misunderstanding in need of clarification and support or upon an over-realized

54. Cf. Cousar, *Theology of the Cross*, 15.

55. McGrath, "Theology of the Cross," 195. Emphasis not original. See Käsemann, *Perspectives on Paul*, 59.

eschatological viewpoint. Paul makes it plain that apart from the resurrection there is no Christian faith (1 Cor 15:12–19). As a secondary, but related issue, Paul lapses into a diatribe defense of *the nature of the resurrection* (1 Cor 15:35–57). Paul simply reminds the Corinthians of the basic kerygma associated with the two poles of the gospel—namely, Christ's death *and* resurrection (1 Cor 15:1–11). His overall purpose appears to be encouragement to the Corinthians to remain faithful in the living out of the gospel (1 Cor 15:1–2, 58), and in Paul's understanding, that will involve a cruciform imperative. It will not involve human wisdom and a misplaced egocentric spiritualism.

With regard to the cross, Paul mentions its historical reality in the light of the power of the gospel. Paul's discussion occurs in a context in which he is addressing the factionalism and supposed "wisdom" of Corinthian enthusiasts who have challenged the authenticity of Paul's own ministry and nature of his very gospel (1 Cor 1:10—4:21). The problem is the gospel defined in terms of false "wisdom" that would deny a cross imperative. However, Paul can only affirm that the rulers of this age were not privy to the "wisdom of God" when they crucified *the Lord of Glory* (1 Cor 2:7–8). The phrase "Lord of Glory," as well as his emphasis upon "the power and wisdom of God," presumes both resurrection and exaltation; it thus implicitly interprets the cross event. Paul alludes to the cross in terms of a rebirth of imagery (1 Cor 1:22–23). The cross is no longer a stumbling block for Jewish Christians (as it once had been for Paul), nor should it be understood as foolishness to gentiles. Rather, and only in retrospect, Paul has come to see the cross as "the power and wisdom of God" (1 Cor 1:27) in the light of *both* the resurrection and cruciform living. By the time he writes 1 Cor, Paul has been engaged in ministry for some twenty plus years. He has been engaged in *living* a cruciform existence with the hope of resurrection.

Käsemann asserts that Paul found it necessary to sharply define "the sphere occupied by the reality of the resurrection" in his eschatology, doctrine of the sacraments, ecclesiology, and anthropology. As he suggests, the one who was crucified is the one who is risen, whose Lordship "marches with the present service of the one who was crucified."[56] Paul's controversy at Corinth revealed in the Corinthians a theology of the resurrection isolated from a theology of the cross which took precedence and which prompted a religious philosophy "in which the imitation of Jesus and the lordship of Christ lose all concrete meaning."[57] The cross is the signature of the one who is risen, it is that which gives Christ a name. It is that which distinguishes *the nature of* Christ's Lordship from the lordship of other religious leaders. Following Christ means becoming a follower of the actions of the crucified one, such that the cross defines

---

56. Käsemann, *Perspectives on Paul*, 57.

57. Käsemann, *Perspectives on Paul*, 57. One may wonder to what extent the church at large today has divorced the Gospel in exchange for a religious philosophy of "heaven," which ironically has been encouraged by a false "theology of the cross" that confuses the divine indicative with divine imperative. It divorces "glorification" from "suffering," such that the ongoing "Lordship of Christ" really has little concrete or earthly meaning.

Christology. However, as it defines Christology it also defines "Christian-ship," or, at least, it should. Once again, the emphasis becomes imperatival, which in turn created a certain discomfort for the Corinthians as well as modern or contemporary Christians.

Käsemann speaks against religious convictions, because convictions change. He suggested it is obvious that Christ is denied today by Christians most of all, "because his lordship over their organized religion and their dogmatic convictions has become illusory, theoretical and imaginary."[58] Jesus's cross demands interpretation which is directed against all religious illusion, as Käsemann reminds that no methodology and no hermeneutic can save people from "surrendering to illusion," whether in the form of mythology or ideology.[59]

It is with this in mind that the Pauline letters and especially the so-called deutero-Paulines speak of the cross and not just about the death of Jesus or about his blood (as a liturgical modification). Sacrifice, for whatever its deeper meaning, is something that can be ultimately manipulated by humankind. This is true theologically, as well, in terms of "doctrines" of atonement for example. The historical cross itself stands as a fixed event of foundation, along with the resurrection, which cannot be manipulated. While a theology of the cross can be manipulated, the foundational event is fixed in history. It is a stark reminder of faith called forth by the resurrection, a stark reminder of the fact that it is God alone who rectifies and who can bring good out of evil. It is God who rectifies because he is right. He is the only one who cann*ot* himself be manipulated. Theology about God can be manipulated, but not God himself, which may come as a surprise to much religion. Even a *theol*ogy of the cross can be manipulated as a changing conviction among adherents, as may be seen in various atonement theories.

Legitimate or not, most expressed "theologies of the cross" treat/view the cross as the *exclusive ground of salvation*. It declares that the cross is the *starting point of authentically Christian theology*, of authentically *Christian* theology. McGrath affirms that the cross "dominates and permeates all true Christian theology,"[60] that statements on ethics, anthropology, Christian life, revelation, salvation, etc.—all radiate from *the center of all Christian thought*, the cross. As Käsemann maintains, "Since Paul, all theological controversy has radiated ultimately from one central point and can hence only be decided at that point: *crux sola nostra theologia*."[61] Given the combined thought of McGrath and Käsemann, the cross stands at the center of all Christian thought and all Christian controversy.

---

58. Käsemann, *Perspectives on Paul*, 54. It is interesting that Käsemann's comment is now almost fifty years old as of the time of this writing.

59. Käsemann, *Perspectives on Paul*, 35.

60. McGrath, "Theology of the Cross," 192.

61. Käsemann, *Perspectives on Paul*, 59.

In Käsemann's perspective, the pre-Pauline tradition lacked such a radical emphasis upon the cross that appears to be typical of Paul himself. Two significant instances of Pauline redaction include Phil 2:6–11 and Rom 3:24–26. As McGrath states, echoing Käsemann, Paul's distinctive emphasis is upon the fact that "God wills to justify the ungodly through the scandalous crucifixion of Jesus as a criminal publicly cursed by God."[62] Really? While the "cross" may be scandalous in Paul's world and ours, Paul the Christian did not regard Jesus as a criminal publicly cursed by God (cf. Gal 3:13). And, Paul could speak as one who himself had been "crucified with Christ" (Gal 2:19; Rom 6:6). What is even more "scandalous" for many who espouse propitiatory "atonement" theology is the latter part of Rom 3:25, which suggests that God can indeed "pass over" previously committed sins without "damaging" his very nature. In the pre-Pauline tradition of 1 Cor 15:3–4, cross and resurrection are treated as events in a sequence, and they are treated together in like or equal manner.

McGrath recognized Käsemann's approach as "brilliant and original," yet called attention to some obvious points of criticism.[63] It is not as simple as Käsemann assumes, in that one cannot know precisely the nature, extent, and significance of Paul's reworking of earlier tradition. How can one be so sure Paul has reworked the tradition in the manner Käsemann asserts? Why should one assume the pre-Pauline tradition is less important than Paul's own redaction? Then, too, we have a tendency to think in terms of a longer time frame (such as may be associated with the development of the Synoptic tradition and Acts) when we hear the word "tradition." However, it should also be remembered that "pre-Pauline" Christian tradition is at best only four or five years older than the "Pauline tradition," such that a different set of temporal considerations should be envisioned as a correction to our own tendencies.

Käsemann's convictions as a Lutheran are plain, and in a sense he mirrors his own critique by turning discussion pertaining to the cross in an apologetic or polemical direction. If by his "links in a chain" analogy he means that cross and resurrection are understood as two things that only happened to Christ—pre-existence, incarnation, *crucifixion, resurrection*, exaltation, and Parousia, Käsemann would seem to be precisely right at this point in his understanding of Paul. And by nature of the case, crucifixion or death must precede resurrection. At least in his expression, Käsemann appears to be subject to an apologetic reductionism that does not adequately represent Paul in his total thought.

Cousar also reminds us that while Paul embraces the traditional material, he makes it his own. Reduced stress on Pauline redaction results in a broader interpretation of the theology of the cross than Käsemann offers with a focus on his polemics. A more broad functional theology of the cross in Paul's letters recognizes that it is not only "a weapon against triumphalism and legalism" but that Paul emphasizes it to nurture in his readers their identification as people of the cross. They are people

---

62. McGrath, "Theology of the Cross," 193.

63. McGrath, "Theology of the Cross," 194. Cf. Cousar, *Theology of the Cross*, 16–18.

who bear in their bodies the death of Jesus.[64] It serves to burst bubbles of pretense (polemic), but also to instruct one in calling and holy living. Once more, we are back to a "cross imperative."

An Interim Evaluation

Paul is generally claimed as offering foundational support for understanding the cross. While Paul certainly emphasizes the death of Christ, it is surprising that he seldom uses cross terminology. What may be even more surprising is *how* he uses cross terminology. Paul should be understood on Pauline terms, which will necessitate the cutting away of much assumptive theological underbrush. In the light of earlier or contemporary theological matrices, customary theology must be unpacked and examined in the light of what Paul actually says, not what he is assumed to have said.[65]

A Roman cross is certainly the mode of Jesus's death, which Paul understands theologically. As such, the cross represents the world's perspectives and values operative in the powers of evil. However, the historical cross of Jesus may not be divorced or isolated from Jesus's eschatological identity in terms of his resurrection, lordship, and the ultimate victory of God. Justification by faith, as well as the cross, may stand as significant aspects of Paul's theology, but neither represents its center. In Paul's understanding, the emphasis rests upon Christ's resurrection and exaltation by God. It is on the basis of reassurance of the resurrection that Paul calls upon those in Christ to become conformed to Christ and to accept the imperative of living under the cross. As Joseph Plevnik suggests, "Paul understood the end-time resurrection as a saving event in itself."[66] Paul formulated his "epistolic" theology in the light of the problems and needs of his communities, such that there are pastoral implications in his themes.

It behooves one to look again at Paul. First of all, it would seem that Paul focuses upon the meaning of Jesus's death and not specifically upon the mode. The mode of crucifixion itself was an historical "given" with which Paul and all the other early Christians had to work and interpret—and in some cases overcome.[67] As has already been noted, specific emphasis upon the cross occurs far less frequently in Paul than many assume, both within theological scholarship and within the emphasis of the church. It cannot be denied that Jesus suffered a cross-kind of death perpetrated by the Jewish leadership at the hands of the Romans, if one accepts the testimony of the Gospels and Acts. Crucifixion was an historical fact, well-known to both the early

---

64. Cousar, *Theology of the Cross*, 18. This bespeaks a cruciform imperative.

65. Cf. Wright, *What Paul Really Said*; Brondos, *Paul on the Cross*.

66. Plevnik, *What Are They Saying About Paul?*, 104.

67. It is actually very hard to appreciate the difficulty facing the first Christians in that Greco-Roman world that knew well the horror of crucifixion when they were compelled to proclaim a crucified Jewish provincial as a resurrected-by-God Lord of the cosmos. We do not adequately appreciate the hurdle of faith that the actual Gospel engendered for gentiles and Jews alike.

church and Paul. It could not be denied and perhaps could be stressed or downplayed by Paul or anyone else as the situation warranted. And surely, the cross becomes the supreme symbol for Christian identity over time. [68]

But for Paul, the cross was the way he symbolled the Christ event in terms of death *and* resurrection, the indicative and the imperative. Paul's encounter was with the risen Christ, as God himself chose to reveal the resurrected and exalted Son to him (Gal 1:12–16; Acts 9:3–6; *STA* 9:3–6).[69] The crucifixion of Jesus meant little to Paul the Pharisee—it certainly had no positive meaning, *until* Paul encountered the risen Christ according to the revelation of God. One moves beyond historical event and historical experience to supra-historical interpretation of the meaning of that eventful experience.

Ultimately, as has been seen, Jesus's death *and* resurrection for Paul marked the eschatological turning point of the Ages. To be sure, Jesus's death is not perceived to be simply natural, customary, or accidental. He was put to death and that occurred specifically on a cross. Paul's larger focus is the *meaning* of Jesus's death, not the *means* of Jesus's death. The title of a book like Cousar's, for example, *A Theology of the Cross: The Death of Jesus in the Pauline Letters*, ultimately deals with two different topics. The first is a "theology of the cross," which according to the present writer for Paul becomes most significant in the realm of the imperative. The second is "the death of Jesus," which is most significant in terms of the indicative.

Cousar's work focuses upon the "death of Jesus" as indicated by all of his individual chapter headings, and irrespective of Cousar's positions, that's where Paul's focus lies. As Cousar observes, one may appreciate the power of Paul's statements which use crucifixion language, but Paul's references occur in contextual proximity with other statements pertaining to Jesus's death. They should not be seen in isolation from alternative tandem statements which do not use crucifixion language.[70] In other words, statements of Jesus's death as crucifixion should not be taken exclusively.[71] With a due respect to Käsemann, to emphasize the cross as a Pauline imperative challenges rather forcefully the religious illusions, others of which he himself feels compelled to challenge.

In keeping with the other earliest Christians, Paul could only proclaim the cross in the light of the resurrection. To proclaim only the cross-death is to affirm that the priestly authorities and the Romans and the usual "Powers" won out. Even if the death be "sacrificial," death is still the usual and expected. According to Käsemann, Jesus's

68. It took time for the cross to emerge as the Christian symbol. It seems likely that as Christians themselves lived under the shadow of suffering for their faith (i.e., a "cross imperative") that the very ongoing collective experience of the faithful contributed to such. The sign of the cross becomes the visible metaphor of Christian faithfulness.

69. "STA" represents the underlying *Source Tradition of Acts* which is foundational to the book of Acts, as distinct from Lukan redaction. See Greene, *Ministry of Paul.*

70. Cousar, *Theology of the Cross*, 24.

71. Cousar, *Theology of the Cross*, 23. Cf. Gal 2:19–20; 6:14–15; Phil 2:8–11; 2 Cor 13:4; Rom 6:6, 8.

cross was first felt to be a "dark riddle which found its solution in the light of the Easter events."[72] Yet he finds at Corinth and in the book of Acts only a pre-Pauline Christology that emphasized enthronement and exaltation, which in reality is a reductionism by Käsemann.

Paul, on the other hand, opposed a viewpoint of a theology of redemption which was focused on self-interests of a false and enthusiastic anthropology and ecclesiology. Paul's own experience was one of suffering in the context of ministry, such that Paul saw himself and his converts to be "crucified with Christ." Paul thereby would be unalterably opposed to a "cross to crown" or "glory road" Christianity based upon self-interest and self-centeredness. He would also be opposed to an "old wineskins" Christianity that could not escape a pre-eschatological framework.

To re-center, Jesus himself, according to Synoptic tradition, emphasized taking up one's own cross and following him (Mark 8:34–35 par.). That is a cross imperative, whether the tradition goes back to Jesus or to the early church. Paul himself wrote of becoming "crucified with Christ" (Gal 2:19; cf. Rom 6:6). In the same context he could speak of being united in a death and resurrection like his. Paul's hope was to attain actual resurrection (Gal 2:19–20; cf. Phil 3:14). In Romans, Paul expressed this with a first-class conditional sentence in Greek: "Since we have become [pf.] united with him in the likeness of his death, but indeed we shall be [fut.] of the resurrection" (Rom 6:5). It would seem that Paul emphasizes both death *and* resurrection in conjunction with what could be termed a cross imperative.

It is only natural for the pre-Pauline Christology to emphasize enthronement and exaltation in the light of belief that God had raised Jesus from the dead. Yet Paul received his call to gentile missions not more than five years after the execution of Jesus—and more likely, only three or four years later. While Paul may have altered the early tradition, he was there at the "beginning" when the tradition was in flux. He was as much a contributor to the tradition as he was an inheritor of the developing tradition that was being hammered out in the give and take of everyday Christian living.

Misunderstanding at Corinth and post-Pauline development in Acts (which Käsemann terms a "through cross to crown" perspective) does not totally represent Paul's concern in all of his contingent situations, although his coherent "center" is more generally focused upon Christ's death *and* resurrection than it is specifically on the cross. This is supported by Paul's use of σταυρόω terminology as well, or, actually, the comparative lack thereof. Thus, the Pauline gospel is an ellipse having two centers and not a "bull's eye" target with a single center. It is elliptical at the point of the eschatological indicative; it is also elliptical at the point of the Christian imperative.

Käsemann appears to be overly apologetic in defense of Lutheranism, overly assumptive in terms of the developing Christian tradition (Paul included), and reductionistic in his overall emphases and conclusions which guide his concerns. He appears to exhibit some misplaced emphases. Paul had a Two Ages concept, in which

---

72. Käsemann, *Perspectives on Paul*, 55.

the resurrection and gift of the Spirit signaled the dawn of the Age to Come in the Age of Transformation. Death of any variety represented an enemy, characteristic of the Present Evil Age—an enemy to be overcome, which precisely was characterized by Jesus's resurrection and exaltation. Käsemann is right that Christ is for Paul the "destined Cosmocrator" as present Lord of the church. But he does not go far enough with Paul, for Paul emphasizes what God has done in Christ through resurrection and exaltation. His own rule in Christ is the vanguard of what Christ will finally do as exalted Lord, as the kingdom is given back over to God at the Telos (1 Cor 15:20–28).

The position of Bultmann and others would seem to be sound in its dual emphasis upon both Jesus's cross and resurrection, although he goes beyond Paul. Jesus is not proclaimed simply as the crucified one, but also as the risen one. "The cross and the resurrection form an inseparable unity. . . ." Bultmann moves beyond Paul when he asserts that "faith in the resurrection is really the same thing as faith in the saving efficacy of the cross."[73] It should be asked again, however, whether *Paul* anywhere says that the cross saves? And in the light of Paul's actual emphases, whose "cross"? Jesus's cross? The believer's cross? Does *Paul* say anywhere that the cross saves? Jesus's cross? The believer's cross?

Cousar presses a concern with other contemporary issues, such as a theology that balances the events of Good Friday with those of Easter in terms of avoidance of an easy-over triumphalism,[74] even as he acknowledges the decisive complexity of connection between the cross and resurrection. While there appears to be a reticence to embrace the triumphalism of the resurrection in some quarters today, Paul certainly had no hesitation to embrace the triumphalism of God's Gospel. Could it be that our theological priorities are different in the interests of dogmatic concerns and our desire to escape a cross imperative?

Christ's death lies at the foundation of Pauline theology and Paul explicates that with a variety of images. As Green suggests, Paul is more concerned with setting forth the benefits of the death of Christ for humankind than he is with the historical circumstances of Christ's death.[75] The nomenclature of "atonement" is used to develop the thought, although problems are presented. However, to focus on the benefits that accrue from Jesus's death is to focus upon the triumphalism of the Gospel of God. That Gospel comes with victory, but it is not without cost—or, direction.

The crucified Christ is certainly the framework for making sense of God's rectification, although religious convictions have often laid stress to the wrong "sense of God." McGrath, for example, asserts that the cross highlights the full seriousness of sin. It declares the powerlessness of a fallen humanity unable to achieve salvation. It

73. Cf. Bultmann, "New Testament and Mythology," 38, 41.

74. Cousar, *Theology of the Cross*, 90. This is also a concern of Käsemann.

75. Green, "Death of Christ," 203. This is, in part, because Paul's encounter and call was in the living Christ, raised by God and exalted as Lord.

expresses "human delusions of self-righteousness."[76] Jesus's death on the cross certainly does those things, even though McGrath does not develop how these things are accomplished. On the other hand, to assert Paul's distinctive emphasis is that it is God's will to justify the ungodly "through the scandalous crucifixion of Jesus as a criminal publicly cursed by God,"[77] represents a bald and rather jarring statement underwritten by theological and religious convictions, even ideology.

Paul would certainly support the idea of the scandalous nature of the cross (1 Cor 1:18), as well as the idea God chooses to justify the ungodly (1 Cor 5:6). That this represents *Paul's* "distinctive emphasis" is unproven and that Jesus was "a criminal publicly cursed by God" is simply wrong in terms of its hermeneutical orientation. The Romans may have viewed Jesus as a criminal, but God did not. And Jesus was certainly not "cursed by God," although Gal 3:13 has certainly at times been interpreted in that manner. Among other things, the content and tone of all of Paul's salutations would not support such an emphasis.

Ridderbos, for example, emphasizes the idea of Christ having become a curse for us (Gal 3:13) and God condemning sin in the flesh of his Son (cf. Rom 8:3; 2 Cor 5:21) as he calls attention to the forensic aspects of the cross. God both treats the sinless Christ as a sinner and makes him to be sin by delivering him to death on the cross.[78] This is substitutionary atonement and penal atonement in a most bald, objective sense, but it is not Paul. This is Ridderbos, but not Paul. If God *delivered* Jesus to death on the cross, then the death of Jesus is to be attributed to God as an unindicted co-conspirator, i.e., the cross belongs firmly to the indicative. God is made to be the direct agent responsible for the death of Jesus. That surely is not Paul's position. Where is the unequivocal evidence?

Paul's perspective is echoed by the sermons in Acts. The "Jews" (i.e., Jewish authorities) and the "rulers of this age" (Gal 2:14–15; 1 Cor 2:8) crucified the Lord of Glory. God exalted him (Phil 2:9–11). Traditional or not, it also represents Paul's distinctive emphasis. The logic of some ostensibly *Pauline theology* is amazing. In reality, it is more anthropology than theology. It is forensic legalism more than divine grace. It is based more on legacy guilt than upon divine redemption, on divine wrath against human sin than upon divine deliverance from enslaving and death-dealing powers. It essentially proclaims "God put Jesus to death, but God raised him from the dead." That becomes a rather crass and circular theological transactionalism.[79] Consider, however, alternative statements. "Human power brokers put Jesus to death;

---

76. McGrath, "Theology of the Cross," 193.

77. McGrath, "Theology of the Cross," 193. Cf. Käsemann, *Perspectives on Paul*, 36; Cousar, *Theology of the Cross*, 15.

78. Ridderbos, *Theology*, 168.

79. In basic substance, it is little different from Tetzel's advertised slogan that came with the sale of indulgences, "As soon as a coin in the coffer rings, a soul from purgatory springs." See Bainton, *Here I Stand*, 78.

but God raised him from the dead." "Personified supernatural powers put Jesus to death; but God raised him from the dead." Which is it? Of the three statements, Paul would affirm the latter two, but in no way would he affirm the first statement, which is nonsensical on the surface. The first statement would be affirmed, however, by the logic of much theology expressed in popular atonement theory which emphasizes the "judicial righteousness" of God. Such a perspective ignores the foundational eschatological nature of Paul's entire gospel, beginning with Paul's salutations, which in themselves set the tone for everything Paul writes.

Paul's "distinctive emphasis" upon the cross, which more often is simply expressed in terms of the *death* of Jesus, offers a plurality of images. Ultimately, however, "life under the cross" is life "in Christ." Paul's *theology* of life "in Christ" heralds a cosmological shift of the Ages in which the individual may have a share, paradoxically through a cross-imperative of living "in Christ."

Paul's cross imperative belongs to the Age of Transformation, while Jesus's death on the cross is representative of the Present Evil Age. Resurrection heralds the Age to Come.

2

The Significance of the Cross

Multiple Images

W HEN one considers the significance of "the cross" for Paul, then, a multiplicity of images is found. Paul had no single way of interpreting the meaning
of the cross. This was a difficult event for the earliest Christians, Paul included, to
comprehend and explain. It certainly required more than one avenue of interpretive
explanation. The crucified and obedient Christ stands at the center of Paul's theology
as the living foundation stone of resurrection and exaltation, as well as the foundation
stone of Paul's ethical imperatives.

It should be remembered, however, that it is susceptible to and capable of multiple interpretations. In fact, Paul appears to tailor his representation to the needs of
the particular, contextualized circumstances of his audience. This would suggest that
interpreters must be sensitive to the culture and/or circumstances, or, to the matrix
of Paul's statements. As Green suggests, contemporary interpreters should be guided
by apostolic testimony to the cross if faithful to Paul. They should be aware of the
way Paul draws on them. They should be fully sensitive to contemporary images and
metaphors that carry redemptive meaning. Contemporary interpreters should express
vital concerns with regard to the interplay among these three realities.[1]

Romans 5:6–11 is a significant passage, in which reconciliation midst other
themes is central. God demonstrated his love toward us. Christ died (act.) for us
while we were yet "sinners." ("Sinner" can be used like "Christian," i.e., identified with
Christ, identified with Sin/sin.) Romans 5:9 affirms we have been "justified" by his
"blood" (impersonal agency). As previously noted, "blood" occurs only twelve times
in Paul— once in Galatians, four times in 1 Corinthians, three in Romans, three in
Ephesians, and once in Colossians. We shall be saved "through him" (indirect agency)
from "wrath." Wrath is a Pauline word (twenty-one of thirty-six occurrences in the
New Testament), with twelve occurrences in Romans. We shall be saved by his *life*

---

1. Green, "Death of Christ," 204.

(impersonal agency). We have received (aor.) reconciliation through our Lord Jesus Christ (indirect agency). Second Corinthians 5:14—6:2 is also a significant passage, which deals with reconciliation.

A Multiplicity of Images

According to Green, Paul employs "several dozen metaphors" to express the benefits of the death of Christ, although he treats only a few of Paul's texts. Green, for example, focuses upon two texts—2 Cor 5:14—6:2 and Gal 3:10–14. Reconciliation stands at the center of 2 Cor 5:14—6:2 (vv. 18, 19, 20), but other themes are also present: vicarious substitution ("for us," 2 Cor 5:14, 15);[2] representation or interchange (2 Cor 5:14, 21); justification (implicit, 2 Cor 5:19, 21); forgiveness (2 Cor 5:19); and new creation (2 Cor 5:16–17). Both the cross and resurrection appear together as salvific events (2 Cor 5:15).

Reconciliation occurs infrequently. In Rom 5:10–11, it is humanity that is reconciled to God. In Col 1:20 it is the cosmos that is reconciled to God. In Eph 2:16 it is Jew and gentile who are reconciled to God and to one another. Green suggests that whether Ephesians is Pauline or not, its message at this point is "clearly Pauline," for the notion of "restored relationship" in Paul rather consistently embraces the dynamic presence of divine love. That love is active in the restoration of the divine-human relationship, as well as an enabling force for social restoration between persons.[3] In both 2 Corinthians and Colossians, the work of reconciliation is extended to the entire creation.

Paul tailors his terminology and logic to the context in 2 Corinthians, seeking to counter the triumphalistic perspectives of his opponents. He roots the message of reconciliation fundamentally in the sacrificial death of Jesus. He asserts that reconciliation means living no longer for oneself but for Christ and others, i.e., living sacrificially. He appeals to the Corinthians to be reconciled to God (2 Cor 5:20; 6:1–2), even as he himself hopes for personal reconciliation with the Corinthians (2 Cor 6:11–13; 7:2). Reconciliation is of prime concern for Paul in 2 Corinthians both personally and theologically, as he seeks to bring his Collection to successful completion.

Paul utilizes a convergence of images to expound the salvific character of the cross of Christ in Gal 3:10–14.[4] The larger context suggests the fulfilment of God's promise to bless the gentiles in Abraham which was made possible through the death of Christ. The *benefits* are presented in a combination of images: Christ is the *representative* of

---

2. While the phrase "vicarious substitution" is wholesale commonplace in theological discussion, especially in atonement and salvation theories, a phrase like "vicarious benefit" would be more akin to Paul's own thought.

3. Green, "Death of Christ," 204. See Appendix A of the present work, "Paul and the Death of Christ: A Survey of References."

4. Cf. Green, "Death of Christ," 204–5.

Israel in whose death the *covenant* reaches its climax; *justification* (Gal 3:11); *redemption* (Gal 3:13), which evokes exodus and exilic themes (cf. the corollary of *adoption* (Gal 3:26–29); *substitution* (beneficence "for us," (Gal 3:13); *sacrifice* (implicit, Gal 3:13); the *promise of the Spirit* (Gal 3:14); *triumph over the powers*. As may be seen, *triumph over the powers* emerges in Eph 2:14–15, where the Law appears as a barrier which is abolished by the death of Christ. In Galatians, the Law is characterized more as a force, much like the elemental spirits of the world, that holds one captive (Gal 4:1, 3). Paul insists the death of Christ has triumphed by demonstrating the Law's validity and execution of the blessing of the covenant.

As Green suggests, taken together, the message of Jesus's death *and* resurrection (shorthand, "the cross") in 2 Corinthians and Galatians (also elsewhere in Paul) raises two issues. First, attention is drawn to the *apocalyptic* significance of the cross. The cross has cosmic repercussions. This highlights our usual error, for we tend to see only the localized anthropological relevance and even that is seen in an individualistic sense. The emphasis upon "new creation" in 2 Cor 5:17 and Gal 6:15 is not focused upon the individual (contra *NIV*, *NAS*), but rather upon the role of Jesus's death in the termination of the old epoch and the presentation of the new. The death of Christ marks the end of the rule of the apocalyptic powers[5] and deliverance "from the Present Evil Age" (Gal 1:4). Such intrusion of the New Age had far–reaching consequences for Paul and all those who would follow the crucified *and* resurrected Christ.

Although Green mentions the embodiment of lives in the "new creation revealed in the cross"[6] and appears to reference the historical cross of Christ, surely that involves an emphasis upon cruciform imperative rather than the historical cross of Jesus merely in terms of death. Historically, it was resurrection and not the cross that heralded "new creation" in the Christ event. The obedience and faith revealed in Jesus's cross become paradigmatic elements for Christian living under the reminding sign of a cross imperative characterized by obedience and faithfulness.

There is transformation as a result of the Gospel of God. Old ways of personal relationships (boasting, one-upmanship, status seeking) and lines of separation (Jew-gentile, slave-free, male-female, Gal 3:26–29) are no longer operative. Secondly, Paul's understanding of the Gospel belongs to his ongoing reflection on the nature of Israel. The people of God, as a result of new creation, have a new identity through the inclusion of gentiles. However, to affirm that the death of Christ alone "marks the new aeon in which gentiles may be embraced, in Christ, as children of Abraham"[7] is not quite rightly put. While Paul's statement is one of cruciform living, "I have been crucified with Christ. It is no longer I who live, but Christ who lives in me" (Gal 2:19b–20b), we often offer a restrictive parody in terms of "Christ died for *me*." The meaning is far more than an *individualistic* ideology or soteriology.

5. Beker, *Paul the Apostle*, 189–92; Gal 4; Col 2:15.

6. Green, "Death of Christ," 205.

7. Green, "Death of Christ," 205.

Green is correct that the multiplicity of images used by Paul "raises a caution" against moving too quickly to posit for Paul a single or central theory of the atonement, or, to insist upon any single one as *the* central emphasis. For Paul the depths of the significance of the death of Christ "can scarcely be plumbed."[8] This merely highlights both the cruciality and the difficulty which early Christians, including Paul, had in coming to grips with the crucifixion of Jesus. It was a foundational event proclaimed by the gospel for which account had to be given. At first sight, it was "foolishness" and "folly," for by the world's standards it made absolutely no sense. Yet for the earliest Christians, Paul included, it had discernable and foundational meaning.

As previously indicated, Paul very seldom uses the expression "forgiveness," in that salvation for him does not primarily mean, as Käsemann affirms, the "end of past disaster and the forgiving cancellation of former guilt."[9] Instead, it is the positive possibility of new life, according to Rom 5:9–10 and 8:2, represented in the freedom from the power of Sin, Death and the divine Wrath. If Käsemann is correct, then most atonement theories have an improper focus. Romans 8:23 suggests that the chief meaning of redemption was liberation. Eschatologically speaking, the one who was obedient even to the point of death leads a new people who have renounced the claim of Adam to determine his own law for himself.[10] The focus is not upon divine wrath being directed toward individual guilt, but rather upon divine freedom directed toward an eschatological newness of life.

To sum up, theological reflection and liturgical creeds in the period before Paul (four to five years!), in the light of the resurrection, emphasized the death of Jesus as saving event. Paul picked up various ways of understanding, without giving preference to any particular one. That Christ "died for [ὑπέρ] our sins" is deeply embedded within the Pauline corpus (e.g., Rom 5:6, 8; 14:15; Gal 1:4; 2:20). The phrase is cited from pre-Pauline tradition (1 Cor 15:3). The historic event of the crucifixion is thus overlaid with a significant interpretive element. Yet if anything, the idea of sacrificial death is pushed into the background by Paul. He deepens and even corrects the tradition, giving it a new direction.

The tradition was not radical enough for Paul. His view of the saving significance of the cross is shocking and paradoxical, in that God's love is given to the sinner (the ungodly, the enemy). This is contrary to the Law. It is counterintuitive, generally speaking, but especially in terms of Jewish orthodoxy and orthopraxy—and customary identity of the people of God as Jewish. This is one reason Paul was so severely challenged by the Nomistic Evangelists who invaded Galatia and other Pauline churches. As Käsemann asserts, the common denominator is that justification of the ungodly is specifically the fruit of Jesus's death. "And this means *regnum dei*

---

8. Green, "Death of Christ," 205.

9. Käsemann, *Perspectives on Paul*, 44. These things tend to be associated with an introspection of the Western world (Stendahl).

10. Käsemann, *Perspectives on Paul*, 45.

on earth."[11] Eschatologically, it means the *regnum dei* on earth over humankind and throughout the entire cosmos, in and over humanity, but also over all the powers and principalities. Anything less is not eschatological. And Paul would say, anything less is not Gospel.

Focus Upon Jesus's Death

There is no question that Paul has a focus upon Jesus's death. It was an historical fact for which Paul had to account, even as did the other early Christians. Even so, Paul exhibits little interest in historical causation of who killed Jesus and why. The kerygma in Acts suggests the Jewish leadership had Jesus killed at the hands of the Romans (Acts 2:23), even though divine involvement in the life, death, and resurrection of Jesus is made plain (Acts 2:22–24, 32–36). The kerygma had a rather short time to develop prior to Paul's call to become an apostle to the gentiles.

By the time Paul writes 1 Cor 15:3 (almost a quarter of a century after the execution and resurrection of Jesus), the kerygma has come to interpret Jesus's death with reference to the "sins" of humankind. Is this a kerygma that dates to 33–34 CE or to 54 CE, to which Paul bears witness? Does this kerymatic tradition date to the beginning of Paul's ministry, or, to a time of Paul's Famine Visit to Jerusalem (Gal 2:1–10) or even to the time of the Jerusalem Conference (Acts 15)? Would it date to 33–34 CE or to 51–52 CE? Or, somewhere in between?

An insight which may be Paul's own, according to some, is the idea of Jesus becoming a "curse" for us in Gal 3:13. However, Paul in that text is simply using Jewish methods of exegesis to interpret Scripture in an attempt to explain *for gentiles* how it is that someone who met death by crucifixion could indeed be the Jewish Messiah and how the blessing of Abraham was now made available to gentiles.[12] With all due respect to Käsemann and the post–Reformation Lutheran perspective of "justification by faith" in a "cross theology," Paul's perspective centers more upon the cross and Jesus's death in terms of liberation from Sin and Death. As such, Paul focuses upon a

---

11. Käsemann, *Perspectives on Paul*, 46.

12. By the first century, "hanging on a tree" could refer to crucifixion. In the Dead Sea Scrolls, 11Q Temple suggests such. As Paula Fredriksen affirms, other than Paul's assertion, no Jewish source speaks of death under divine curse, whether hanging in general or crucifixion specifically. Fredriksen further clarifies Deut 21:23 from which Paul quotes. The reference does not describe a *method* of capital punishment, but rather a "post mortem" *display* and *publication* of the offender's death. See Fredriksen, "Who Was Paul?," 26. The propaganda of public display was a significant element of Roman crucifixion. According to the Gospel tradition, Jesus's body was taken down comparatively quickly and placed in a tomb. This action was likely taken for many reasons, but it would have effectively blunted the lingering Roman propaganda value of Jesus's death. While Gal 3:13 becomes a capital verse utilized in atonement theories, it may be that Paul simply affirms the very public spectacle of Jesus's crucifixion in terms of the reality of Jesus's real death. At any rate, Paul's topic in Gal 3:1–14 is not atonement and Gal 3:13 is not even a complete sentence in itself. Paul is dealing with the law-faith problem that arose in Galatia, as he affirms the blessing of Abraham is available to gentiles on the basis of faithfulness and not on the basis of law.

"cross imperative" and calls upon Christians to "die" with Christ, for that will mean the liberation of Christians as well. The emphasis is upon reconciliation with God and liberation from Sin through death. The two go hand in hand. Atonement theories which emphasize Jesus's sacrificial death "in our place" are simply not supported by Paul, theological barnacles to the contrary.

A basic error in dealing with the cross and/or the death of Christ is to approach it prospectively. Paul (and the early Christian tradition) approached the cross retrospectively. It is that for which the earliest Jewish Christians had to account and had to interpret. It was an historical "given." Paul and the early Christians did not try to understand the cross in the light of their situation, but rather they sought to understand their situation in the light of the cross. The Christian gospel is not that a bigger and better or more perfect sacrifice was needed to satisfy God's wrath or righteousness—that, hence, the cross was necessary to supply a perfect *human* sacrifice. It is not about how God thus took things into his own hands by sending his Son to die for human sins, such that sinners could then be forgiven in accordance with an ancient and primitive transactional system of sacrificial offerings.[13] Punitive and placatory atonement theories are not representative of Paul and are born out of a prospective approach seeking to understand the cross in later historical contexts, without first seeking to understand it in the light of its first century context.

Quite the contrary, Paul and early Christian tradition are called upon to interpret the death of Christ according to the models of their day, but only retrospectively in the light of the resurrection. Apart from the resurrection, there was really no need to "interpret" the cross. The death of Christ could be explained in any number of ways and responsibility for that distributed to Jews and Romans, as specified by the sermons in Acts, for example. A crucified Messiah was heresy to Paul the Pharisee, until he was arrested by the historical reality of the resurrection in his own call experience. In the long-term, overall scheme of things, the death of one more provincial messianic pretender would at best have warranted but another historical footnote (cf. Acts 5:36–37; 21:38; *Ant* 20.97–98; *J.W.* 2.117–18), but for the conviction "God raised him from the dead."

It was that encounter with the risen Christ in Paul's divine call that caused Paul to become a proclaimer rather than a persecutor of the Christian gospel. Paul became an apostle "in Christ." He was not a disciple "of Jesus." Yet in the light of the resurrection, both Paul and the early Christians were called upon to make sense of the cross-type death of Christ—retrospectively, not prospectively. It is not a case of God working toward the cross, but of God working in spite of the cross. It is a case of God demonstrating that he can overcome ultimate evil. It is a case of God's inaugurative, eschatological will being demonstrated in victory in the face of most grievous evil.

---

13. As some theology suggests, all that was needed was the perfect sacrifice, a requirement satisfied by the sinless Son of God. As the perfect sacrifice, there could be none better.

Theological meaning is attributed to historical event, rather than historical event being evoked by theological necessity. As Fisher Humphreys affirms,

> In our theology we should try to be empirically accurate rather than logically compelling. We ought to be satisfied to say, "This is what God has done," without adding, "And this was the only way he could have done it." . . . Many false turnings in theology can be avoided if we allow our theology to be empirical, simply reporting what God has done, rather than trying to prove it was necessary that God should have done a particular thing.[14]

God worked in spite of the evil of humankind and cosmic powers perpetrated in a Roman cross. God worked to bring his own eschatological victory out of the suffering and shame perpetrated on a Roman cross. According to Paul, we have a share in that victory, for all of the powers have been defeated in the resurrection. According to Paul, we have a responsible imperative to live accordingly.

Focus Upon Jesus's Resurrection

The real convincing point for Paul was his personal conviction that God had raised Christ Jesus from the dead. Paul's own visionary call experience became for him the convincing piece in the puzzle, for Paul underwent a "theological conversion." This "theological" conversion changed Paul from a persecutor of the early Christian movement to a foremost proclaimer of God's Gospel. It was the resurrection that convinced Paul that the time of fulfilment had arrived. It was the resurrection that served as the ultimate interpreter of the death of Jesus.

It was not just death, but a "cross" kind of death that had distinct eschatological ramifications, even divine victory over *Roman* power. The shift of the ages had arrived. The powers of the Present Evil Age were being overcome, which could only mean that the powers of the Age to Come were moving to fruition. Christ was understood as the "firstfruit" of a coming full harvest, wherein God would raise all of his people—both Jews and gentiles—to resurrection life "in Christ."

Focus Upon the Gospel of God

The Gospel of God included the realization of God's covenant originally established with Abraham, that through him all nations of the earth would be blessed on the basis of faith or trust in God. This Gospel becomes the fulfilment of Old Testament promises, such as the promise of a new covenant given to Jeremiah and descriptions of eschatological fulfilment as found in Deutero-Isaiah. The real powers that must be dealt with—which extended far beyond human indiscretions related to the Law—either had been conquered or soon would be conquered in Christ.

14. Humphreys, *Death of Christ*, 134.

Christ who had died had been exalted to heaven by God and would exact victory over all cosmic enemies of God, including the last enemy of Death (1 Cor 15:20–28). God's action, as always, was one of rectifying grace. The result was the peace of redemption. When Paul greets his churches in his letters, he always greets them with "grace" and "peace" from "God the Father and the Lord Jesus Christ." The eschatological change of the Ages is implicit in Paul's greeting, which heralds realities of the New Age. Those realities emerge as a result of the death *and* resurrection of Christ.

A Brief Excursus: The Crucified God

The question may be asked whether Paul presents a new orthodoxy of a "crucified" or "suffering" God. It need be remembered that we do not have a full statement of Pauline theology in the extant letters any more than we have a full accounting of any proclaimer's theology in what is written or spoken. Then, too, Paul is pre-Nicean, pre-Augustine, pre-Anselm, pre-Reformation, and pre-modern—he does not address later church controversies that arose after his time. His letters do not reflect ontological concerns which were at issue in church councils of the fourth and fifth centuries or even issues raised by the New Testament canon. Paul is his own witness within the matrix of earliest Christianity. For Paul, relationship between the Father and the Son was expressed strictly on a functional level.[15]

Nowhere does Paul call Christ "God" and nowhere does he reflect upon the unity between God and Christ as one finds in John (John 10:30; 17:20–26). Paul does not "fuse" the actions of Christ and God. As previously stated, any development of the Trinity (with a capital "T") is anachronistic for Paul and probably the entire New Testament. Paul's Christology highlights the obedience Jesus shows to God (e.g., Phil 2:8; Rom 5:19). Paul does not speak of a "crucified" or "suffering" God thereby.[16]

God Revealed in the Crucified Christ (1 Cor 1:18—2:5)

For Paul the crucified Christ and the resurrected Christ are one and the same person. Jews and Christians alike looked for verifiable signs or proofs, for "credentials." For Paul the crucified Christ (historical, eschatological) is the wisdom and power of God—i.e., there can be no human boast in the resurrection. What else was Paul to say? The "foolishness and weakness" of God? Indeed, he argues that even the foolishness and weakness of God are greater than whatever wisdom human beings can muster. The "wisdom of this age" is exposed for what it is, as it points to the incapacity of human wisdom.

---

15. Cousar, *Theology of the Cross*, 49.
16. Cousar, *Theology of the Cross*, 49.

With a rebirth of images, Paul points to the profound distortion offered by humanity—human wisdom which in the end is judged to be folly, while what is judged to be folly proves to be divine wisdom. That which does not make sense by human standards becomes that which saves. The preaching of the "cross" (i.e., Gospel) does not revamp human capacities, but demonstrates the eschatological action of God, whereby Christ crucified (historical occurrence with eschatological ramifications) becomes "for us" God's wisdom, righteousness, sanctification, and redemption (1 Cor 1:30), as one lives out of the cross—not as "moral example" but as eschatological reality.

Paul and the Classic Attributes of God

In contrast to the tendency of theology to define an attribute and then raise it to an infinite level in application to God, Paul stands in contrast to much Western theology. Paul speaks of the power of God in terms of oxymoronic weakness, failure, and the scandal of death by crucifixion.[17] Statements pertaining to God's *righteousness* have often been couched in an Aristotelian understanding of justice: equity and fairness suggests that each person receives what one deserves under the law. Against the backdrop of a guilt culture, both God's wrath and God's righteousness have been understood primarily in forensic and objective terms. On the other hand, Paul in Rom 3 suggests God's righteousness is manifested without any compromise in divine grace.

Classic theology has also rooted God's wisdom in a Greek philosophical tradition which is analytical and speculative in its epistemology. Paul declares that God's wisdom on the surface of it all appears foolish and contradictory, even absurd. Traditional theology tends to view the faithfulness of God in terms of God's immutability. On the other hand, Paul asserts that God keeps his commitments in ways so unexpected that God appears to be "illogical or inconsistent."[18] One who does not understand this is not able to understand grace. One who asserts that God's "justice" must be "satisfied" is not able to understand the nature of "grace," despite protestations to the contrary. For such a one, God cannot be just and justifying *sinners* at the same time (cf. Rom 3:26), unless someone received punishment or the price of justice has been paid. This is not to say "grace" does not have a cost. True grace always does.

From the event of the death of Christ, there emerges a framework for understanding God. God's attributes of power, righteousness, wisdom, faithfulness, freedom, and love become *dynamically* revealed in unexpected ways. They are better understood in terms of God's demonstrated activity, rather than as his "attributes." While the biblical God certainly may be said to be characterized by "attributes," it is the testimony of the entire Bible that God is known through his eventful actions, including the Christ event. In fact, God's nature before humans may only be perceived in his actions.

17. Cf. Cousar, *Theology of the Cross*, 46.
18. Cousar, *Theology of the Cross*, 47.

Divine purposes are revealed for the *people of God* and for *God's creation*. It is not first of all a matter of individual salvation. God's action in the Christ event first of all has a corporate and cosmic dimension, as is true of God's action elsewhere throughout the Bible, in which the individual becomes a willing participant. Romans 5:8 suggests Christ died as a result of a human indicative, but even through that shameful and scandalous event, God demonstrated his love and, faithful to his promises and expectation, he brought about the change of the aeons. Paul thereby does not portray a crucified God, but a vindicated God who is vindicated not by the satisfaction of wrath but by the satisfaction of personal love. Paul does not portray a crucified God, but a God who rectifies his entire creation through his own gracious action. The idea of a crucified God is idolatrous anthropocentrism of a moralistic vein, as well as muddled Trinitarian theology, which arises out of the tendency to exalt the human to the level of the divine.

Focus Upon the Glory of God

The ultimate focus of the Gospel of God in Paul is not anthropocentric, but *theocentric*. All glory will be given to God (1 Cor 15:20–28) when all cosmic powers are overcome with universal and eternal result for all of God's people. As Eph 1:3–14 stresses, the people of God are to live as a "praise of God's glory." That's it—"a praise of God's glory." Yet as one lives as a praise of God's glory, one gives up one's self-idolatry and lives as the creature God intended. One lives in right relationship with God, with one's fellow human beings, and with the cosmos. As one lives as a praise of God's glory, one has the opportunity to share in the glory of God—as creature, not as god.

Paul was a *man* "in Christ." That constituted both his Christian and his apostolic identity. The Son of God defined both Paul's gospel and Paul's role in proclaiming it. He could do no other. Paul's cross imperative has caused some to assert that Paul felt salvation was dependent upon him, that he completed the suffering of Jesus. In a singular sense, that was not the case. In a collective sense, all Christians were to follow Christ in a "cruciform" existence, with the hope of participating in the resurrection. There is a deep connection between the christological meaning of the cross and Christian ethics that is tied to the Pauline concept of "being in Christ." The faithfulness of Christ is demonstrated in his self-giving love revealed and realized in the cross.

The faithfulness of God is demonstrated in his self-affirming love revealed and realized in the resurrection of Jesus. It is the resurrection that Paul hopes to attain (Phil 3:12–16; 1:21–23), although the mode of attainment is through a cruciform existence (Gal 2:19–20).

Jesus's death and resurrection rest at the foundation of Pauline theology and Paul explicates that with a variety of images. He is much more concerned to treat the significance of the death of Christ in terms of benefits for humankind than he is to deal with its historical circumstances.[19] Still, it is theology in the service of history, not history serving the necessity of theology. The nomenclature of "atonement" is used to develop the thought, although problems are often presented or developed when the orientation of the basic word is not understood.

That Christ "died for our sins" is found in the oldest creedal tradition (1 Cor 15:3), which Käsemann locates in the Lord's Supper. This has obvious relevance for the sacraments. The existing tradition revealed a Christology that spoke of Christ as the second or last Adam. Traditional soteriology allowed sacramental participation in Christ's fate in terms of both his sufferings and his glory.[20] With regard to the Eucharist, for example, Paul puts the main stress upon the remembrance and participation in Jesus's death. One should, however, not misunderstand. A cross imperative involves more than just participation in ritual observance. Käsemann expressly denies that baptism, through which one dies with Christ, also enables us to participate in Jesus's resurrection. Baptism merely gives *expectation and hope* of the resurrection.[21]

Different variations suggest divine sacrifice and proof of God's love (Rom 4:25; 8:32), as in the self-sacrificing love of Christ (Gal 1:4; 2:20; 2 Cor 5:14–15). Love in Paul always means the manifestation of existence for others.[22] Jesus's death is "for us" in terms of its central theme, meaning "for our advantage." Some might say incorrectly, "in our stead" or "in our place." As Käsemann suggests, what is established is our inability to achieve self-salvation.[23] It is only God who gives life to the dead and calls into existence the things that do not exist. The faith that receives salvation receives it only as divine gift ever new.

As Käsemann affirms, the cross always remains a scandal and a foolishness for Jew and gentile. In a word, it "exposes man's illusion that he can transcend himself and effect his own salvation . . . ."[24] In terms of the first century world, when "Jew and gentile" are mentioned, that includes *everyone*. There is a sense in which the cross will always remain a scandal for theologians, for it will always expose our illusion that we can transcend ourselves by defining God and his actions. Remembrance of the cross is an encouragement to fulfilment of a cross imperative. It is a call and a challenge to faithfulness. Even though Paul might put it differently, we would do well to heed John's advice, "Little children, guard yourselves from idols" (1 John 5:21). That would include the theological idols of our own making.

19. Green, "Death of Christ," 203.

20. Käsemann, *Perspectives on Paul*, 57.

21. Käsemann, *Perspectives on Paul*, 58.

22. Käsemann, *Perspectives on Paul*, 39.

23. Käsemann, *Perspectives on Paul*, 39. Cf. Rom 3:24; 5:6–8.

24. Käsemann, *Perspectives on Paul*, 40.

Legacies, Illusions, and Paul

Joel Green observes that from the vantage point of a perspective shaped by the biblical narrative, "there is no Christianity apart from the cross of Christ," that "the cross became the chief icon by which to rally a robust Christian identity and to ground a Christian ethic."[25] The cross did indeed become the icon of Christianity. As the present writer would affirm, it became the foundation for a cruciform imperative. However, for Paul, there would have been no "Christianity" and no "apostle Paul" apart from the resurrection. With a rebirth of images, the cross became a powerful symbol of the wiping away of human sin, of paradoxical freedom from the powers that enslaved and killed, *and* of new life whose victory emerged even through suffering. The "cross" which always meant death in the ancient world, with a rebirth of images in the light of the gospel, came to symbolize resurrection life. How difficult it would have been to shift from one mind-set to the other! Paul's understanding of the cross is marked by a number of different emphases. The centrality of the topic has resulted in a number of theological legacies as well as theological illusions. Appreciation of Paul involves a number of considerations.

Some General Considerations

Although there are many points at which the present writer would disagree with Ridderbos, a strength of Ridderbos is that he does not offer a reductionistic presentation of Paul.[26] He offers a balanced, yet prosaic perspective of Paul's theology. He takes a conservative Reform position that is qualified by systematic theological adjectives. With regard to Rom 5:18, 19 (cf. Rom 5:8, 9), Ridderbos states that Christ's death is not considered from the viewpoint of "God's retributive righteousness," but from that of "Christ's voluntary and perfect obedience."[27] The Romans and the Jewish leadership become co-conspirators in support of a divine transaction. Such a viewpoint is not Paul, but an illusion which claims Paul in support.

Ridderbos continues the thought of substitution with regard to justification. Justification has both a substitutionary and corporate dimension. Christ's death and resurrection occurred for our sins with a view toward our justification. It took place "in our behalf and in our stead." God delivered him up "for us."[28] Or, further, Christ's death was the demonstration of God's eschatological judgment and justification as "the old aeon and the old man were judged in him, and justification unto life and

---

25. Green, "Kaleidoscopic View," 184. As he further states, Jesus's crucifixion exhibited the character of God's saving mercy, in that Jesus's suffering and death was "for us."

26. Ridderbos, *Theology*. His work extends to more than 500 pages and is prefaced by a thorough outline consisting of eighty topics presented in twelve chapters.

27. Ridderbos, *Theology*, 167, for example.

28. Ridderbos, *Theology*, 169. One should note what is and what is not supported by Paul.

the new creation came to light in him as the second Adam."[29] The perspective of Ridderbos appears to be totally anthropocentric. Romans 3:26 suggests justification is theocentric. And what is the "judging and justifying judgment of God"? Paul is concerned to affirm that God *is* right and able to make right those who are in Christ. God rectifies—and he does so freely through costly grace. That is the very reason Paul can commend to his churches, "Grace and peace to you from God the Father and the Lord Jesus Christ."

Ridderbos is more appropriately Pauline as he speaks of victory over the powers in the death of Christ. The cross and death of Christ have made an end to the bondage of Sin. Sin no longer has claim on one who has paid the toll of death (Rom 7:10). The thought is one has died to Sin (as an authority that exercises power, asserts its claim) and has freed oneself/escaped it by his death. The thought is not the sense of justification or reconciliation, i.e., that Christ died once "for the sake of" or "for the atonement of" sin.[30] Romans 7:4–6 suggests that by dying to the Law through the body of Christ, the Law is no longer that menacing, fettering power whose sanctions lend Sin its power. Paul has been crucified to the world, the life-context of the present aeon prior to Christ, as well as the powers (Gal 6:14).

As Ridderbos affirms, the same fundamental reality is portrayed in the language of died (crucified) to sin, the law, and the world. All represent powers of the old aeon. As he states, so also in the resurrection of Christ, the church has been set at liberty to live for Another, namely, for Christ himself (Rom. 7:4; 2 Cor. 5:15); or for God (Gal. 2:19).[31] Ridderbos stands on much firmer Pauline ground here in the present writer's judgment.

But the current state of Christians is that of a cruciform existence, living as a Christ-bearer with the future *hope* of resurrection. Colossians 2:13–15 indicates that "God in this great redemptive act with Christ forgave us our sins, nailed the Law to the cross, and in him triumphed over the powers."[32] Colossians 3:1–4 may be called, along with Rom 6, the *locus classicus* for the "objective," religious-historical significance of having died and been raised with Christ. While resurrection life after death affirmed Christ's identity and the advent of the new age (with victory over the powers), so it is that crucifix identity of Christians affirms the telic hope of resurrection.

"Death" will lead to life. The example of Christ affirms that hope for Paul. You have died (Col 3:3). If you have been raised with Christ, then you should seek to things above, i.e., the glory of heaven, where Christ sits enthroned at the right hand of God. The "things above" become evident only through cruciform living, or a cross-imperative. Paul thinks christologically and redemptive-historically, not in terms of

29. Ridderbos, *Theology*, 169.

30. Ridderbos, *Theology*, 208.

31. Ridderbos, *Theology*, 211.

32. Ridderbos, *Theology*, 212. Actually, Paul himself does not say "the Law."

anthropology.[33] And, once again, Ridderbos is foundational reading on the "theology of Paul."

The divergence of the understanding of God's justice in a popular, Anselmian view of the atonement varies from Paul's conception (see chapter 7). In the Anselmian view, as often interpreted, atonement has to be a "making up" or an appeasement of God's damaged honor—placation or satisfaction has to come from somewhere and it comes at Christ's expense. God's justice becomes the impartial activity of punishments or rewards according to a legal standard of law court experience with its insistence upon conformity to a legal requirement or satisfaction. *Theological allusions can lead to theological illusions, even delusions.*

Theological Legacies

We are the theological heirs of Irenaeus, Origen, Augustine, Anselm, Aquinas, Luther, Calvin, and a host of other theologians since their day, with regard to theology in general and atonement theologies in particular.[34] The idea of Christ as a *penal* substitute has been a frequent misunderstanding of Paul which arises out of the symbolism of blood as associated with sacrifices.[35] It has been assumed that the killing of an animal in sacrifice has been meant as a substitute offering for oneself, that God's justice demanded due punishment for human sin, that the death of the animal served as a vicarious punishment and appeasement of God, effecting atonement.

The theological term used to describe this view is that of *propitiation*. Such a position misplaces the emphasis found in sacrifice, placing it upon the death or killing of the animal. The death of the animal is neither the purpose nor the meaning of sacrifice. Leviticus 17:11 suggests the life is in the blood, which symbolically marks the dedication of one's life through the blood of the animal. The focal point is life, not death, as separation from God is overcome and one is reconciled with God. The life of the animal is released to be reunited with God. All of this is symbolled through a ritual rite.

While animal sacrifices were always to some degree inadequate as a symbolic substitution, substitutionary viewpoints suggest that Christ (as the divine one) could become the perfect, once-for-all sacrifice for our sins. Having taken on human existence and having taken on himself the punishment we all deserve, Christ satisfied God's judgment. The parallel of the death of Jesus with the usual pattern of animal sacrifice is maintained only by emphasizing the self-offering of Jesus himself toward placation of requirements of divine justice. And, need the reminder be given, in the

---

33. Ridderbos, *Theology*, 211.

34. With regard to atonement theories and theology, one may consult chapters 7 and 8 of the present work.

35. Leon Morris has been a strong advocate of this view. See Morris, *Atonement*. See chapter 8 of the current work.

literal sacrificial system, the flesh of the sacrificial animal was often eaten in conjunction with the ritual or post-ritual. The system reflected in the Old Testament also did not address those deliberate sins which cried out most for attention (Num 15). Paul himself could likely tell us a thing or two about both the literal and metaphorical use of sacrificial imagery, as well as offer an often needed corrective.

In the Reformation era, the "Pauline-Augustinian" presentment of the atonement is almost universal. Reformers on both the Lutheran and Calvinistic sides were generally agreed in representing the death of Christ as an atoning death. Lutheran and Reformed systems, including Anglicanism, held to the forensic idea of the death of Christ. In the Reformation era, Turrettin was the most distinguished writer on the atonement.[36] Chapters 7 and 8 of the present work offer summations of various views.

Yet atonement (or at-one-ment, reconciliation) is neither appeasement nor propitiation of sin by means of a penal substitute. The overriding issue is not punishment, but rather the removal of barriers that separate, impair, or destroy relationship. The better terminology would be *expiation*, or the removal of sin's effects, such that a person may be reunited with the will of God. Thus, when Christ's death is described as a sacrifice, it does not mean that Christ is punished by death, instead of us, in order to satisfy God's retribution. That is illusory fantasy. We rather see an obedience motif, as Christ offers perfect obedience to God as representative for all humanity, such that the sacrificial metaphor describes the blood of Christ released for a life fully joined to God. And we are called upon to take up our own cross, as we live a life before and unto God, in obedience, unto resurrection.

Theological Illusions

The history of the interpretation of Paul is the history of the apostle's domestication by the church and by theologians. According to McGrath, the theology of the cross has much to tell us here. It reminds us that "it is the cross, the crucified Christ, which lies at the heart of the Christian gospel, not a theory."[37] For Paul himself, both the cross *and* resurrection lay at the heart of the Christian gospel, or at least, the Gospel of God. The Gospel of God was an *event* proclaimed as advent, not a "theory." Practically speaking, though, a restrictive focus on the cross generally results in a doctrine of the cross that is tied to a doctrine of "the atonement," which the present writer refers to as "the eye of the storm." For Paul, the cross was personal and eschatological. In spite of all of his emphasis upon the cross, Käsemann expresses a reservation. "The message of the cross as such is not disputed; what is in question is whether it is right to make this the real, or even the sole, theme of Pauline theology."[38]

---

36. Turrettin, *Atonement of Christ*.

37. McGrath, "Theology of the Cross," 196. It should be noted, however, that many "theories" of the cross are set forth and arduously defended.

38. Käsemann, *Perspectives on Paul*, 47.

It is *a* "real" theme, but it is not the "sole" theme. Käsemann himself gives numerous other themes as well. This reservation appears to rest on irrefutable grounds, for there is a multiplicity of other themes in the letters of Paul.[39] References like 1 Thess 1:10, 1 Cor 6:14, 2 Cor 4:14, Rom 1:4 suggest that the risen Christ appears as the ground of salvation, just as significantly as the crucified Jesus does elsewhere. Or, as Käsemann expresses the point, Paul's theology stresses Jesus's cross and his resurrection equally, such that it consequently has two foci.[40] More accurately, one might say that *Paul* stresses Jesus's *death* and resurrection equally, rather than laying stress to the *cross* specifically. The cross was how Jesus died, historically speaking, such that it was assumed in the high context society of Paul's day.

Some contemporary proclamations of the "gospel" are nothing but illusions based upon sociological anthropology, yet which claim Paul as their origin. In reality they are illusory, based thoroughly upon a theological rationalism, the origin of which rests in a particular socio-religious matrix other than Paul's. One may posit and uphold a punishing God whose justice must be satisfied by putting his innocent and obedient son to death on a cross. But that is not Paul. Nor will the usual prooftexts chosen from Paul in defense of such a view adequately support the weight usually placed upon them, as may be later seen. These will be subject to exegesis in chapter 6. Paul does not portray a transactional Christ nor a transactional God reconciled to humankind through any kind of transaction of the cross. Paul does not draw his major metaphors for understanding the death of Jesus from the law court, but rather from within the history of God's covenant with Israel.

As Green affirms, Paul does not think of Christ's execution on the cross as punishment so as to satisfy the justice of God. Although the cross of Christ may be understood as substitutionary, it should be understood within the matrix of the Old Testament conception of sacrifice.[41] The rationale for the sacrificial system is not fully worked out in the Old Testament, although "identification" or "representation" may be basic, in the sense that the sin-offering in some way came to represent sinners in their sin. The life of the animal became forfeit, as the sinner's sin became identified with the animal.[42]

On the Day of Atonement in Lev 16, one goat was sacrificed as a sin offering for unwitting sins, while a *live* goat symbolically carries away the sins of the people into the wilderness. Sin was symbolically transferred to the body of the animal. The blood of *sacrifice* (from Latin, to make "holy" or "sacred") became the freedom of new life for the worshiper dedicated to God; it was not ingested (cf. Lev 17:10–14). The logic of what Paul says, according to Green, suggests Christ's dual role in his death—"his

---

39. One may consider the multitude of themes that characterize the divine indicative in chapters 7 and 8 of *Paul's Eschatological Gospel*, part one of the present work.

40. Käsemann, *Perspectives on Paul*, 47.

41. Green, "Death of Christ," 207.

42. Cf. Dunn, *Theology of Paul*, 218–23; Brondos, *Jesus' Death*.

substitution *for humanity* before God and in the face of God's justice, as well as his substitution *for God* in the face of human sin."[43] Such dual substitution does not appear to support Paul's conception of the active agency of God.

The Christian gospel must in part be the "message of the cross," for that is the manner in which Jesus died. The "message of the cross" appears to be virtually synonymous with the "gospel" in 1 Cor 1:18. Mertens acknowledges that Christian theology is "essentially, though not exclusively, theology *of the cross*."[44] However, as he further emphasizes, "the mystery of Christ is like a triptych: Jesus the believer, the crucified Christ, the risen Lord."[45] It is not atonement theories of systematic theology regarding the cross that lie at the heart of the Christian gospel, but rather the crucified Christ who died, who was buried, who was raised by God (cf. 1 Cor 15:3–5). It is not the cross itself, but rather the Crucified One raised by God who liberates. The "cross" becomes a sacramental symbol of the entire Christ event, rather than an event unto itself. For many theologians, anthropology defines theology. For Paul, his eschatological theology defined his anthropological soteriology.

Paul describes the Christ event as a "reconciliation" (καταλλαγή, καταλλάσσειν) or an "at-one-ment." Compound words based on the root –αλλ- in Greek carry the idea of "other" or "making otherwise." The imagery is one derived from relationships within the social or political sphere.

Paul always speaks of God or Christ reconciling human beings to himself and never of God or Christ being reconciled to humans. Paul points to the initiative that rests with God, not humans. We were reconciled to God through the cross-death of Jesus, such that *we* have been brought from the status of enmity to one of love and friendship (2 Cor 5:18–19; Rom 5:10–11). Paul extends reconciliation to the entire cosmos (2 Cor 5:19; cf. Rom 11:15; Col. 1:20–22; Eph 2:11–19). There is no suggestion of punishment, substitution, or placation. In terms of Gospel, atonement is not cultic. It is personal. We are reconciled to God through the cross-death of Jesus not because of substitution, but because God in Christ has conquered every impediment and power that prohibited the possibility of reconciliation. It is God who has acted to achieve rectification on the basis of his love and grace, thus extending his peace. In contrast to human actions, God's action is sealed by the resurrection and exaltation of Christ.

Pauline Emphases

There is a variety of terminology in the Pauline letters that references the death of Jesus. Pre-Pauline tradition bequeaths cultic language such as "expiation" (for some, "propitiation") and "blood" (Rom 3:25) and simple language like "died" (1 Cor 15:3).

43. Green, "Death of Christ," 208, italics original.
44. Mertens, *Essay in Soteriology*, 160.
45. Mertens, *Essay in Soteriology*, 185.

Paul contributes expressions as "gave himself" (Gal 2:20), "was crucified" (2 Cor 13:4) and "cross" (1 Cor 1:17). As has been seen, the texts which actually use crucifixion terminology are comparatively rare.[46] It is surprising that Romans has a single reference to Jesus's death as a crucifixion ("crucified with him") in a reference that is virtually indistinguishable from Rom 6:8, "died with Christ" (cf. Rom 8:13). The death of Jesus is referred to in six of the seven letters usually deemed to be authentic, but the high proportion of occurrences of crucifixion terminology itself is found only in 1 Corinthians and in Galatians. The time of writing of those two epistles was one of conflict and contention for Paul. Crucifixion language in Paul appears to be distinctive in polemical contexts, unlike other references to the death of Jesus in subsequent theological formulation, which appear in significantly different contexts.

With the advent of Christ, the fullness of time has come and the new creation has dawned. Paul deals with the entire redemptive action of God in Christ—not just sending, not just cross/death, not just resurrection, not just exaltation. The Christ event initiates the fullness of time (Gal 4:4). In particular, however, Paul's gospel has its starting point and center in the death and resurrection of Christ, for it is this event which "retrospectively" illuminates the incarnation and pre-existence of Christ and "prospectively" illuminates the continuing exaltation and anticipated Parousia.[47] It also prospectively illuminates a continuing cross imperative for Christians.

Paul's "in Christ" theology focuses upon a number of things, including Christ's death and resurrection. The ultimate focus for Paul, however, is *theo*centric in terms of both the Gospel of God and the Glory of God. God has blessed us "in Christ," that we might become a praise of God's glory (Eph 1:3–14). Paul does not envision a penal substitute when rather infrequently he describes Christ's death in sacrificial terms. Rather, he envisions God's gift and provision. Christ himself, in the name of all of us, lived a life of perfect unity with God and thereby reunites us all with God.[48] There is no sense of God being angry or having to be appeased, but rather a sense of God taking positive action and expressing a positive divine concern of redemption, rectification, and reconciliation.

Those who speak against a triumphant gospel in favor of a "theology of the cross" are more in tune with the subsequent historical realities and views associated with the legacies of Constantine and Luther. Constantine introduced "triumphantalism" under the "sign of the cross" and Luther assuaged his guilt in the face of a penitential system of his time under "a theology of the cross." Indeed, within the history of Christianity the "cross" has functioned in diverse ways. With Anselm it became a fundamental transaction, which in turn later resulted in the development of a penal substitution theory of divine satisfaction in subsequent scholasticism and fundamentalism.

---

46. Cf. Gal 2:19; 3:1, 13; 5:11; 6:12, 14; Phil 2:8; 3:16 (21); 1 Cor 1:17, 18; 2:2; 2 Cor 13:4; Rom 6:6.

47. Ridderbos, *Theology*, 54. Ridderbos is not reductionistic, as are many.

48. Tambasco, *Atonement*, 71.

For Paul, none of these things were so. God's personal action "in Christ" was an eschatological vanguard of fulfilment in the Age to Come which had dawned. The cross became an unlikely, reversal of images symbol for the entire Gospel, for how does one symbol resurrection? Yet it also became a paradigm metaphor for Christian faith and living, in terms of a cross-imperative that could define and sustain those who embraced what God had done in Christ, even in the midst of Christian suffering. And many suffered under "the sign of the cross," even to the point of martyrdom. And this included Paul himself.

David Brondos suggests that his own work calls for a radical rethinking of the Christian doctrine of the "atonement" and the salvific significance of Christ's death, as well as a profound revision of the scholarly interpretation of Paul's letters, especially at the point of soteriology.[49] Paul's underlying teaching echoes the same basic story of redemption found throughout the remainder of the New Testament—a story essentially Jewish in the midst of a Greco-Roman world. As Brondos indicates, it was later theologians who made the cross the center and starting point of Paul's soteriology, In earlier times, it was the whole story that was redemptive—"the cross was redemptive *only to the extent that it formed a part of that story.*"[50]

Later interpretations of Christ's death from Irenaeus (d. *circa* 202 CE) to the present time have supplanted Paul's own understanding of salvation and Jesus's death on the cross. Soteriological adaptations have been read back into the biblical texts by theologians, pietists, and biblical scholars alike, such that a different Paul is reflected than the one present in his letters. What is called for, according to Brondos, is a greater appreciation for the continuity that exists between the Jewish and Christian understandings of redemption. The result becomes the emergence of a Paul who looks very different in many ways from the common portrayal of the apostle. The present writer would certainly affirm Brondos's observation.

For Paul, who proclaims the Gospel of God, the cross is not in itself a real saving event or action apart from the resurrection (Rom 1:4). Even John Calvin realized that Paul's letters reflect the soteriological nature of Jesus's resurrection (Rom 10:9–10; 1 Thess 1:9–10), which is linked integrally with the crucifixion (2 Cor 5:15; Rom. 4:24–25; 8:34). Paul's focus in these verses is really upon the resurrection, more than the cross-death. Yet it is Christ Jesus who was put to death and who was raised, who now reigns as Lord. The resurrection does become the great verdict of God concerning the cross (Barth), as God brings life out of an evil death. God is not a co-conspirator in Jesus's death.

The resurrection, of which Christ is the firstfruit or first portion (ἀπαρχή, 1 Cor 15:20), offers assurance for faithfulness and assurance of future resurrection (cf. 1 Cor 12:22–32). First Corinthians 15:17 should be noted, for Paul affirms that if Christ is not raised then faith is empty and human beings are still in their sins. In Greek, it is

49. Brondos, *Paul on the Cross*, 194.
50. Brondos, *Paul on the Cross*, 195, emphasis original.

a first-class conditional sentence, affirming reality. Although the topic of 1 Cor 15 is resurrection, Paul makes no such assertion concerning the cross-death of Jesus. There simply is no "if Christ be not crucified, you are still in your sins" anywhere in Paul. While the cross-death of Jesus was an historical reality and a part of Paul's soteriological perspective, it does not represent Paul's whole soteriology. It simply doesn't. It is as Beker argues, even resurrection is not the *closure* event. Rather, it marks the inauguration of a new day that anchors God's future in the Parousia and the Telos.[51] The resurrection of the dead is assured by the Parousia (1 Thess 1:9–10; 4:14), as well as the current presence of the Spirit (Rom 8:11).

For Paul, both crucifixion and resurrection belong together. According to Cousar, "both are constituent of God's saving action" as events in a consecutive sequence in the pre-Pauline tradition (1 Cor 15:3–5).[52] Paul himself may mention only one, but the other is usually implied. The one who was crucified is the one who was raised and vice versa. Paul can speak of the crucifixion as God's power (1 Cor 1:18). However, as Cousar asserts, power and crucifixion may be spoken of together only as the death of Jesus is interpreted in the light of resurrection.[53] One may become the focal point without mention of the other (cf. 1 Cor 1:18—2:5; 15).

As Paul proclaims Jesus's death, he calls upon believers to live in the power of the cross. Paul has come to understand that it represents power in *apparent* weakness, for God's power has already prevailed in the resurrection. That which first appeared to be victory for all who crucified Jesus is ultimately demonstrated to be God's victory in the resurrection over all prior perpetrators of death. While the "powers" could orchestrate and manipulate a death as a usual and expected end, only God could bring resurrection and new life.

In response to Käsemann, Cousar states that it is plain that Paul's "accent" falls on the resurrection, i.e., the crucified one has been raised, rather than that one who is risen is the crucified one. Yet it is the resurrection that provides a ground for a realistic hope in God's future and "expresses itself in the cruciformed life of believers (2 Cor. 4:10–11; 13:4)."[54] Cousar's observations are cogent. This is effectively a cross imperative in Paul, as Paul repeatedly appeals to the crucifixion as the foundational norm for Christian identity and living. The exclusive symbol becomes the inclusive challenge of the entire story of the Gospel of God. To appeal to one part of the story is to allude to and assume the whole story in a high context society of the first century.

Paul Achtemeier acknowledges that the key question in Paul's theology is the question of a coherent center. He suggests the time-honored Reformation perspective of "justification by faith" is not the doctrinal center of Paul's theology, in view of its virtual absence in the majority of Paul's letters, as well as its subordinated position

---

51. Cf. 1 Cor 15:20–23, 24–28; Beker, *Paul the Apostle*, 156.

52. Cousar, *Theology of the Cross*, 103.

53. Cousar, *Theology of the Cross*, 104.

54. Cousar, *Theology of the Cross*, 107.

even in an occurrence like Rom 1:17. Might the death of Jesus on the cross be the coherent center of Paul's theology, a tradition pertaining to the fate of Jesus? Achtemeier acknowledges the rich variety of theological images Paul uses, all important to Paul's theological understandings—paschal lamb (1 Cor 5:7; cf. Exod 12:7, 12–13), sacrifice initiating a new covenant (1 Cor 11:24–25; 2 Cor 3:6; cf. Exod 24:5–8), a new covenant theme of righteousness through his blood (Rom 5:9; cf. Gal 2:21), a sin offering for those *already within the covenant* (cf. 1 Cor 15:3; Rom 4:28; 6:10), an act of obedience which annuls Adam's disobedience (Phil 2:8; Rom 5:19). Achtemeier concludes that "the crucifixion of Jesus did not constitute the central conceptual core of his theology," given the inconsistency and variety which Paul uses in expression. He suggests the same result of inconsistent expression would apply to other concepts, such as righteousness, Christology, and ecclesiology, should they be investigated.[55]

Instead of seeking a *conceptual coherent center* for Paul's theology, Achtemeier suggests one should seek a "generative center," defined as the central conviction from which Paul's theology grows. For Achtemeier, the *"generative center of Paul's theology, as it is his own understanding as apostle, . . . is his conviction that God raised Jesus from the dead."*[56] That is a perspective with which the current writer would agree, although the phrase "generative center" might be what the current writer refers to as the radiant, from which Paul's various theological trajectories emanate. Paul identifies Jesus as both Lord and Christ on the basis of the resurrection. He is one "marked out Son of God in power according to a Spirit of holiness by a resurrection from the dead" (Rom 1:4), through whom Paul has received both grace and apostleship. This has been little noted.

As Achtemeier points out, what sets the resurrection apart from such realities as the crucifixion of Christ and justification by faith is that this is the single event about Christ, the single element of Christian confession, that Paul singles out as having absolute, foundational importance. It is the resurrection that established Jesus as Son of God in power (Rom 1:4), which made him Lord of all (Rom 14:7), which gave him the divine name which allowed him to be worshipped like God (Phil 2:9–11). The reality of the resurrection is reflected in all of Paul's salutations in his identification of Jesus as "Lord" and "Christ."

Paul can make the point that if Christ is not raised, faith is futile, one is still dead in one's sins, and preaching itself is in vain (1 Cor 15:14, 17). It should be noted Paul asserts that apart from the resurrection, one is *still* dead in one's sins. In fact, 1 Corinthians represents the maturity of Paul's reflections some twenty years after his initial call. This is a post-crucifixion assertion that in itself should serve as a correction to much theology. The resurrection is both the key and goal of Paul's apostolic ministry, without which both Paul's ministry and the Christian faith would be without

---

55. Achtemeier, "Quest for Coherence," 132–37.

56. Achtemeier, "Quest for Coherence," 138, emphasis original.

consequence and probative force.[57] Paul's goal, as stated in Phil 3:10, was to know Christ and the power of his resurrection.

There obviously could have been no resurrection apart from Christ's preceding death. There would have been *no death on a cross* apart from the lethal opposition of Roman authorities supported by the collusion of the Jewish leadership, with which Paul also couples cosmic powers. The fact that *God* raised Jesus from the dead offers a clue of theological coherence behind Paul's contingent expression of other theological convictions. Achtemeier, for example, traces several implications. The resurrection of Christ makes possible his intercession on behalf of Christians (Rom 8:34), as well as final deliverance from the wrath of God that will accompany final judgment (1 Thess 1:9–10). The Jewish apocalyptic framework of the Two Ages was already at hand, having emerged from prophetic traditions that wrestled with the problem of evil in relation to divine justice and divine sovereignty. Yet for Paul, those Two Ages have now come together in a current Age of Transformation as the Age to Come gains ascendency.

How does one explain the suffering of the righteous in comparison with the prosperity of those who do not follow God's will? Going back to the time of the Maccabean martyrs, there had to be a coming time when God would set things right in a final judgment. For Paul, Christ's resurrection marked the necessary prelude to the time of final judgment. The resurrection provided the key to the inception of the New Age, as Paul adopted and adapted the apocalyptic framework that was already available within Judaism.

While the Old Age had not come to an end, the New Age had already begun with Jesus's resurrection. Paul's solution was to collapse the two into a period of overlap, which marked a third, intermediate Age of Transformation, if you will.

The forces of the Present Evil Age (Sin, injustice, and ultimately Death) had been defeated and were on the run before the breaking powers of the Age to Come (salvation, justice, Resurrection Life, Spirit). This Two Ages concept has relevance for both Paul's theological and ethical understanding, i.e., for the indicative and the imperative in the overlapping age. The fact that there is a gospel imperative heralds the idea of "already but not yet." It was an Age of Transformation.

The New Age with its promised general resurrection and the setting right of injustice, and even the entire cosmos in Paul's understanding, must already be underway with Jesus's own resurrection *by God*. Earlier Jewish martyrs had not been raised from the dead. The implication is that if *God* raised Jesus from the dead, then Jesus was the anointed one of God who would begin the sequence of apocalyptic events leading to the final Telos. Jesus was not the one "cursed" by God, but rather the one "blessed" by God. Jesus's death was not deserved for his own transgressions. He was obedient to God (Phil 2:8), he was free from sin during his life (2 Cor 5:21). He did not participate in the primal sin of disobedience, as had Adam (1 Cor 15:49; Rom 5:12). Not only was

57. Achtemeier, "Quest for Coherence," 139–40.

Jesus "blessed" by God, but through the Gospel of God the risen Jesus has become a "blessing" for humankind and the entire creation or cosmos.

As Achtemeier asserts, "at the core of Paul's thought about Jesus' death is the notion that it was for the benefit of others, . . ."[58] Indeed, this is Paul's echoed theme of ὑπὲρ ἡμῶν ("in our behalf"). It is the resurrection and not Jesus's death that is the generative center or radiant of Paul's theology. As Achtemeier suggests, the death of Jesus is a first level derivative, which Paul can understand in a variety of ways, as the contingent situation demanded. The resurrection is the *only* tangible action in the gospel story that could not be effected by or manipulated by humanity. It was an event or action that could only be effected by God himself.

If it were God's will that Jesus not remain dead, and if his death was not deserved for some disobedience to God, then it was those who put Jesus to death who had opposed God's will and who stood justly condemned. Aside from Roman power, those who condemned Jesus to death had acted to bring about the execution of Jesus in accordance with their view of Torah. At one time, Paul himself had been filled with zeal in the name of Torah and had persecuted the followers of Jesus. He apparently felt like he was fulfilling the will of God found in Torah. However, if the Torah were intended to communicate God's will and Jesus himself was the final expression of that will, then the question arises as to how those who understood Torah as the fundamental expression of God's will and national heritage oppose Jesus and bring about his death.

Paul came to the understanding that the Torah itself had fallen under the power of Sin. As a result, following God's will in the name of Torah had led to just the opposite, i.e., opposition to the final will of God in Jesus. Paul offers an objective description of the dilemma in Rom 7:13–25—the person who wished to follow God's will by adherence to Torah was led to oppose Christ, the final and personal expression of that divine will. For Paul, "law" means Torah and not "principle" or "rule." Paul can use the term in a variety of ways, although it is a second level derivative, according to Achtemeier, derived from the circumstance of Jesus's death.[59] God's will is clearly seen in the resurrection of Jesus; therein is the Gospel of God.

An Extended Conclusion

Death on a cross in itself was neither an eschatological event nor a divine event. Thousands of people died by crucifixion under the Roman Empire.[60] Crucifixion was a human (or *inhuman*) action, a Roman means of execution. Historically speaking,

---

58. Achtemeier, "Quest for Coherence," 142.

59. Achtemeier, "Quest for Coherence," 145.

60. Other than literary evidence, a single heel bone with a Roman nail driven through it discovered in a Jerusalem area tomb provides the major example of very meager archaeological evidence. It apparently belonged to a young man named "John." Cf. Elliott and Reasoner, *Documents and Images*, 103.

Jesus's execution on a Roman cross encouraged understanding his death as that of a common criminal or revolutionary, humiliated before his own people, and according to Jewish Scripture, even cursed by God (cf. Deut 21:22–23). Jesus died on a Roman cross, at the orders of a Roman governor. This is an historical fact attested even by ancient secular historians. It was a fact for which the early Christians had to account and explain. Paul does not appear to contradict the basic emphases of the kerygma in the book of Acts. In fact, some of it is attributed to him by Luke in the speeches of Acts (cf. Acts 13:28–30; cp. 2:23–24). The responsibility for the crucifixion is placed on human shoulders, "but God raised him from the dead."[61] It is the resurrection that informs and specifically defines the nature of Jesus's specific crucifixion. For Paul, Jesus's death is eschatological, yes, but he understands it as such only in the light of the resurrection. Paul's focus is on the risen Christ, not upon the historical Jesus. Paul approaches the cross retrospectively, in the light of the resurrection.

The Place of the Cross

At the least, two things are at stake in consideration of the place of the cross in Paul's gospel. First and foremost, how one understands the nature of God is at stake. The very nature of the "gospel" depends upon the nature of the God of the Gospel. *Paul portrays humankind being reconciled to a God who has seized the eschatological initiative in Christ to inaugurate the rectification and reconciliation of the whole cosmos (including human beings) to himself through his own rectification action.* While not Paul, John 3:16 provides in statement a perspective with which Paul would agree. On the basis of his own active love for his creation and his creatures, God has acted to provide a clear hope of the eschatological future. In this, there is a definite divine indicative expressed by a multitude of different metaphors, but there is also a divine cross imperative which opens new vistas of living. In any consideration of the cross, our understanding of the basic nature of God is at stake.

Also at stake in any consideration of the cross are our own theological perspectives. As Käsemann has reminded us, theological language involves "unfamiliarity, misunderstanding, and error."[62] To what extent is our theology characterized by an unfamiliarity with what Paul "really said"? To what extent have we misunderstood Paul? To what extent is our own theology in error in what it has attributed to Paul? Käsemann is correct that no tradition can be maintained in a glass case. One should not misunderstand. In this writer's judgment, one has the right and duty to "dialogue" with Paul and even to develop one's own theology *contra* Paul. Yet if we are to avoid a muddled theology, we should be clear as to what belongs to the legacy of historical developments, our own view, and what belongs to Paul. We should be humble enough to acknowledge points of misunderstanding or misappropriation and be willing to

61. Acts 2:24, 32; 3:15; 4:10; 5:31; 10:40; 13:30.
62. Käsemann, *Perspectives on Paul*, 35.

develop and grow. Paul can be for us a "catalyst for encounter" (Keck), even as he was in his own day.

Some Common Assumptions

There are some things commonly assumed for Paul that he did not teach, according to Brondos.[63] Paul did not teach that the world itself was "fundamentally different" in terms of being a changed historical reality or a realm of new ontological reality following Christ's death and resurrection. Paul's eschatology was inaugurative. For Paul as well as the other Christians of his day, the final transformation of the world still lay in the future; but it had already begun. Nor did Paul teach that actual deliverance from Sin, Death, and other powers of evil had occurred as a result of the cross. The very existence of a Pauline imperative suggests otherwise. There has been no general, completed transformation of humankind or human nature.

The reality of Jesus's death and resurrection through the rectifying activity of God proclaimed rather both the possibility and the certainty of a *future* freedom (from one's present condition of enslavement) in an Age to Come which had already dawned in a proleptic sense. Paul had no doubt that one could to some degree participate in the blessings of the Age to Come in the present. Indeed, the eschatological gift of the Holy Spirit as an ἀρραβών ("guarantee," "pledge") was present as a foretaste of the eschatological joy, communion, fellowship, and peace which would someday be fully realized. As Brondos affirms, Jesus's death has unique significance, but the early story "never claims that this event transcends history, puts an end to the world as it was, or produces some salvific effect for others."[64]

There would yet be a future judgment, for God's wrath with regard to sin and injustice continued. The early Christians of Paul's day were convinced that as they lived "in Christ" and in the power of the Spirit, they were being delivered and would be delivered from that wrath, until the time of the Parousia and the Telos, when God would judge Sin and Death and all other powers of evil once and for all. In the present, God's rectifying indicative "in Christ" offered a path of cruciform identity with Christ the Lord. That they could live as those who were being redeemed, reconciled, and rectified meant they would be delivered from the wrath of God. Those who were "in Christ" were those who had peace with God, not as a result of a "dead founder" viewed either as martyr or scapegoat, but because of a living Lord viewed through resurrection. Paul's salutations convey this—peace, which is predicated upon God's grace.

In and of itself, according to Brondos, the idea that God fulfilled a "requirement which humanity could not fulfill" in order for human beings to be saved, is equally foreign to Paul. In accordance with both Jewish and early Christian thought, God

---

63. See Brondos, *Paul on the Cross*, 191–94. David Brondos's monograph is devoted to the subject of this chapter. It provides for thoughtful reading and is commended.

64. Brondos, *Paul on the Cross*, 193.

is always free to grant forgiveness of sins to anyone he wishes. And, God is free and able at any time to abolish sin, death, and all forms and forces of evil simply by divine fiat. God may act whenever he chooses and however he chooses. That is what "divine sovereignty" means. It should also be remembered or noted once again that Paul does not emphasize "*forgiveness* of sins or transgressions" (only Col 1:14, Eph 1:7), nor repentance, for that matter.[65]

In radical statement contrary to much popular thought, Brondos affirms that, "In itself, Christ's death was not necessary for sin to be forgiven by God, or for human beings to be saved from the penalty or consequences of sin."[66] Paul does affirm that God broke the power of Sin to bring about death, through his gift of divine grace "in Christ" (cf. Rom 6:23)—through the resurrection (1 Cor 15). While all die independently of Christ and will be raised at God's pleasure, Paul does not affirm that it was impossible for God to raise the dead or inaugurate a New Age without Christ himself dying and rising first.

Paul can make use of the metaphor of dying and rising with Christ (Rom 6:1–10) as an encouragement to a Christian imperative of living free of the domination of Sin, of living out of God's grace "in Christ" unto eternal life (Rom 6:11–23). The experience of Christ is but the "firstfruit" of what one day will be the personal experience of the Christian, the one who is "in Christ." While what was true of Christ's own experience with regard to his own passion, death, resurrection, and exaltation is his alone and *not* true of anyone else, there is unique meaning that may be attributed to his death and resurrection that heralds the rectifying action of God in behalf of all. Consequently, Paul can commend "grace and peace from God the Father and the Lord Jesus Christ," to those in Christ, both Jew and gentile. That heralds the divine indicative. But it also calls for the imperative of living out that peace on the basis of grace under the Lordship of Christ. There is an implicit imperative inherent in Paul's statement of the gospel in his salutations.

It was, according to Paul, a belief in the resurrection of Christ *as experienced* by the earliest Christians including Paul himself, that caused the earliest Christians to re-examine and interpret the meaning of the death of Jesus, and thus define the meaning and import of the Gospel of God. Thus, Paul affirmed with others that Sin, Death itself, and the powers of evil had been overcome.

Retrospectively, Christ's faithfulness to his mission offered the saints of God an example of life to be lived in love and obedience. Christ's exaltation heralded his coming Parousia and God's Telos. It also heralded their own cross imperative in terms of grace and peace.

Paul's gospel involves death and resurrection. Apart from the resurrection, there is no "good news" associated with the "gospel." Apart from the resurrection, there is only the grave and the example of a martyr. Paul did not become a Christian to follow

---

65. Paul mentions "repentance" (μετάνοια) only four times—2 Cor 7:9, 10; Rom 2:4; 2 Tim 2:25.

66. Brondos, *Paul on the Cross*, 193.

the memory of a martyr. Paul's conviction was that of a risen Messiah-Son of God, who had been raised from the dead. Therein was Gospel—God's action of victory, for no one else other than God could raise the dead. The promise of his Pharisaic theology had been realized in the person of Christ Jesus as the firstfruit of eschatological promise and hope for all.

David Brondos maintains that "every doctrine of redemption is in essence a story," whether it be the Old Testament story or the New Testament story, both of which are contained in Christian scriptures.[67] In the first chapter of his book, Brondos briefly summarizes the various stories of redemption known in the Christian tradition. He finds that Paul's own account of the role of Jesus's death in the salvation of human beings to be quite different from that attributed to Paul by interpreters from earliest times to the present. Jesus's death did not save nor reconcile anyone to God, according to Brondos. As he states, "all of the traditional readings of the Pauline passages that ascribe saving significance to Jesus' death from patristic times to the present are foreign to the thought of Paul."[68] Brondos's statement is a strong one which flies in the face of much Christian "orthodoxy" regarding "atonement" discussion. In essence, he comprehensively denies that Jesus's death for Paul was an efficacious soteriological transaction.

According to Brondos, even Pauline scholars have succumbed to assumptions presented in many earlier and other stories of Christian redemption from Irenaeus to the modern day. Christ's death is seen to have salvific consequences, "effecting" salvation in some way. The claim that Christ's death, according to Paul, was *necessary* for human salvation runs throughout the theology of the contemporary church, as well as the writings of modern scholars.[69] One should, however, be driven to seek what Paul actually said on each point set forth. The issue is what Paul wrote regarding a given perspective, not a theological position or espoused ideology. One may debate with Paul and even espouse an alternative position, but one should spend time in the Pauline texts in order to discern what *is* Paul and what is our own.

As Brondos further suggests, Christ's obedience is what satisfied God and effectively put away divine wrath. Christ experienced the consequences of human sin (namely, death itself) in our behalf though not in our stead. God raised Christ from the dead, so as to ensure our redemption, opening the way for us to become dead to sin and alive to God through our own obedience in Christ.[70]

---

67. Brondos, *Paul on the Cross*, 1. Perhaps expressed with different focus, there is a story, historically bound, behind every development of doctrine. It is those stories that are often either unknown in their fullness, or, are on the other hand, ignored.

68. Brondos, *Paul on the Cross*, x. His extended statement becomes the introductory pretext for his majesterial work on *Jesus' Death in New Testament Thought*, 1:1.

69. Brondos himself mentions E. P. Sanders, T. L. Donaldson, James Dunn, Richard Hays, and N. T. Wright as examples. Cf. Brondos, *Paul on the Cross*, 9.

70. Cf. Brondos, *Paul on the Cross*, 194.

Brondos's contention is that while there may be some basis in Paul and the remainder of the New Testament for many of the associated ideas that make up the stories inherent in much Christian theology, in themselves these stories are fundamentally different from the one told by Paul and the first Christians. Later stories, even later canonical stories, should not be imposed upon Paul and his understanding.

For Paul, the cross was neither theology nor ethics, but Gospel. It was not something to be restricted to a cultic theological and religious transaction, nor was it a mere topic of discussion for isolated theological towers of scholasticism, nor was it to be a banner under which one might debate or carry out temporal ethical programs. Both theology *and* ethics are best addressed by Paul's conception of Jesus's death on a cross in terms of victory over the powers (liberation) and reconciliation (at-one-ment) to both God and humanity—and this on the basis of the resurrection. The overcoming of alienation and liberation from evil *is* the Gospel, both theologically and ethically. Paul's cross-imperative addresses both.

While theology may move beyond metaphorical language to "conceptual structures," the diversity of Pauline language for interpreting *the* atonement extends well beyond any single theory. One should not constrict Pauline categories in the interest of singular soteriological coherence. Logical precision does not do justice to the evocative expressiveness of Paul's metaphorical language nor to the mystery of what might be termed a divine event. If one judges Paul's soteriology to be primarily participatory in nature, Cousar suggests that "the judicial, sacrificial, and social categories are truncated."[71] However, one might affirm the reverse point is true as well. Primary treatment of Paul's soteriology as strictly sacrificial will also "truncate" social and participatory categories strongly present in Paul. There is a sense, given our human limitations, that we all choose our own reductionism.

Crucifixion and Resurrection

Are the crucifixion and resurrection of Jesus events in a sequence with independent roles to play? Or, are they to be linked, with the one always implying the other? How does the one impact or qualify the other? It is true that Paul's letters do not include a set of accusatory charges directed against the Jewish leadership and the Romans as are found in the book of Acts (Acts 2:23–24; cf. 2:36; 3:13–15; 10:39–40; 13:28–30), followed by a statement of God's vindication in the resurrection. In this instance, that does not mean Paul would necessarily disagree with the tradition which Luke reports long after the time of Paul. Paul's emphases simply fall elsewhere, given his contingent

---

71. Cousar, *Theology of the Cross*, 87. Cousar cites Hays, *Faith of Jesus Christ*, 212, to suggest that "justification" and "participation" belong together in a common theological sphere. Our salvation means participation in *Christ's* justification. Cf. Gal 2:17, where juridical and participationist categories are related.

situations at an earlier point in time. The connection between cross and resurrection is a significant issue.

Cousar makes two points, however, as he states that "a theology that rings loudly the joyful note of Easter without the sobering, dissonant sounds of Good Friday inevitably tends toward triumphalism." On the other hand, "a Good Friday divorced from Easter ceases to be good."[72] "Good Friday" and "Easter" are accumulated Christian terminology not found in the New Testament at all. The New Testament testifies to both the death of Jesus (Roman crucifixion) and the resurrection of Jesus. Cousar's comment reflects customary Christian theology and celebration that is well-stated. It resonates well with both Christian scholars and pietists alike. While "triumphalism" may carry many negative connotations—particularly in the light of Christian history—one should not be reluctant to speak of the "triumph of God." Without such, there is no Gospel of God.

For Paul, there was a day of crucifixion and a day of resurrection. For him, the two events together marked the Gospel of God in the Age of Transformation, affirmed by the exaltation of the living and risen Jesus as Lord and Christ—a Gospel that called for a "cruciform imperative" with a promise of resurrection. Without the reality of Easter (interestingly, *a word not found in the New Testament*), there is no resolution and no redemptive force—only suffering, defeat, and despair. This may not be the case for one who advances a penal substitutionary view. Jesus's resurrection is really unnecessary to the sacrificial transaction of the cross for such a perspective.

As previously suggested, whether the cross is a chapter in the theology of the resurrection or the resurrection is a chapter in the theology of the cross (Käsemann) is a question not quite rightly put. For Paul, the answer would be neither. For Paul, both are chapters in the Gospel of God, albeit very different chapters—the latter wrought by God, the former wrought by evil powers. Yet it is the resurrection that demonstrates the love of God and the fact that God was not an absentee God even at the point of the cross.

For the present writer, by way of example, the greatest truth depicted in Mel Gibson's *The Passion of the Christ* is the large heavenly tear that impacts the scene of crucifixion at the end of the movie. It speaks a metaphorical truth that could be interpreted in several significant ways, but it speaks a truth that stands in stark contrast to the continuous inflicted suffering that permeates the remainder of the movie. Paul held Jesus's death and resurrection together, as apparently did the early tradition (1 Cor 15:3–4). However, it is the resurrection that becomes the "generative center" or radiant of the Gospel of God.

Paul appears to be unconcerned with the question who killed Jesus and, as Cousar asserts, makes "no effort to attribute the death to political, social, or economic causes."[73] According to Cousar, God's character as a righteous and loving God is most

72. Cousar, *Theology of the Cross*, 90–91.

73. Cousar, *Theology of the Cross*, 109.

fully known in the crucifixion. While there is nothing in Paul that attributes Jesus's death to God (in the sense God killed Jesus) or that suggests the nature of God demanded the death of the Son, still, according to Cousar, "God is the primary actor in the drama of the crucifixion."[74] While God does not act to put Jesus to death, God may be the primary actor in the larger drama of the Gospel as he raises Jesus from the dead. One should strive to get the Pauline em*pha*sis right.

Paul's letters do not view "sin" as the simple, accumulative violations of moral law but as a controlling power over humanity. Paul's letters are rich in soteriological imagery. The cross effects an atonement with God. Death and resurrection belong together theologically; there is no reflection on an un-crucified or un-resurrected Christ. Both the cross-death of Christ and the cross imperative for those "in Christ" effect at-one-ment with God, for it is living unto God even in the face of suffering and apparent defeat that heralds full reconciliation and the enjoyment of grace and peace from a heavenly Father. It is living as a "praise of God's glory" that effects at-one-ment. It is a cross imperative that leads to resurrection life. In effect, one lives out a cruciform imperative as a "praise of God's grace" in the context of "peace" (reconciling at-one-ment, to be redundant) under the Lordship of Christ and in the light of his example. One thereby achieves one's identity as a "praise of God's glory."

Something objective was achieved in the death of Christ. According to Paul, Christ gave himself up for us *so that* we might live in him (cf. 1 Thess 5:9–10; Rom 8:3–4; 14:9; 2 Cor 5:15, 21). The possibility of one's participation in Christ's death and (and resurrection) is grounded in his first of all dying "for us." That is to say the imperative is grounded in the indicative. Attempts have been made in recent decades to find a Greco-Roman background for Paul's thought on the atoning death of Christ. It is more probable that Paul draws from the common quarry of Israel's scriptures and cultic sacrificial practices. One of Paul's concerns is to establish the universality of Christ's atoning benefits, which are not limited to Israelite cultic and memorial rites that need repetition and re-enactment.[75]

Some have found the binding of Isaac in the background of Paul's thought. There is also the interpretation of the cross of Christ mediated through the repetition of the Last Supper in the early Christian community. There is also interpretation of the cross as a general paradigm for Christian living, i.e., a cross imperative, within an eschatological community of the people of God. Paul's anthropological understanding was set forth in part one of the present work. The matter of Paul's cross imperative is specifically set forth in chapter 4 of the present volume. While a focus on the eschatological nature of the cross has already been presented, it yet remains to examine Paul's "cross imperative" more thoroughly.

It must be remembered that the cross and resurrection experience of Jesus and that of Christians are very different in more than one respect. The cross was a past

74. Cousar, *Theology of the Cross*, 109.

75. Cf. Hengel, *Atonement*, 51.

historical event for which one had to account. It was a shameful and very public event. The resurrection of Jesus was a glorious, yet hidden event of divine mystery, even though subsequently and publicly witnessed and proclaimed (1 Cor 15). For Jesus, both were *realized*, past events. For Christians, both one's own cross and resurrection are at present *unrealized*.

In the undisputed letters of Paul, resurrection of the Christian with Christ remains only an eschatological expectation and eschatological promise, as is the Parousia—an eschatological hope, if you will. The Parousia, Telos, and actual resurrection of Christians are still future for Paul. A cruciform imperative is life lived in the shadow of *our* crosses with the hope of our resurrection into God's final eschatological community. This is consonant with the attributed teaching of Jesus in the Synoptics to "take up *one's* cross and follow me" (Mark 8:34; Matt 10:38; Luke 14:27).

Paul does not make God to be the executioner of Jesus. He directly attributes the death of Jesus to the "Jews" (*aka*, Jewish leadership) and to the "rulers of this age" (1 Thess 2:14–15; 1 Cor 2:8). For Paul the Pharisee, messianic death on a cross was a scandal even under the Law. Paul as a Christian apostle has to account for Jesus's death, as did other Christians (as the sermons in the book of Acts illustrate). For Paul it is the resurrection that defines the death of Jesus as the fulcrum of God's redemptive event. Paul can use many different metaphors to interpret the meaning of Jesus's death retrospectively, some of them sacrificial and more of them non-sacrificial, but they issue forth as accrued result understood in the light of the inauguration of the Age to Come.

In a word, although the death of Christ is most often attributed to the divine indicative, Paul more correctly would understand the event of Jesus's death in terms of *foundational reality* underlying the indicative and as a *modalistic encouragement* for the imperative. The obedience metaphor, for example, employed with reference to Jesus in Phil 2:5–11 also becomes operative for those who place their faith in Christ (and what God has done through him), such that the same obedience ethic found in the action of Christ is made possible and called forth for those who are the people of God "in Christ."

From a larger cosmological and theological perspective, Jesus endured the worst that the power of Sin could effect, namely, death. God overcame both the power of Sin and the power of Death by raising Jesus from the dead. That same triumph is now available to those "in Christ," those who live out of the Gospel of God. While Paul's thought gives evidence of many streams and tributaries, the main stream of Paul's thought would understand the death of Jesus for believers in the light of the imperative rather than the indicative, if "indicative" is understood to mean "what God has done." Paul would understand the *death* of Jesus in terms of a foundation for the ensuing indicative and the *cross* in terms of an imperative for believers.[76]

---

76. The so-called "indicative" and "imperative" will be discussed in subsequent chapters. Briefly, to be clear, the indicative refers to what God has done in the whole Christ event and the imperative is what we should do in response to the divine indicative.

There are objective realities that issue forth from the death of Jesus, although effecting the death of Jesus is not something God did, at least according to Paul. Paul does not attribute Jesus's death to God, irrespective of some customary interpretations of isolated verses such as Gal 3:13 and 2 Cor 5:21. God did not directly act to bring about the "death" for any reason. For Paul, "death" or "Death" is seen to be an enemy of God that is conquered by God's eschatological Gospel of Life. Indeed, the Age to Come has dawned in the overcoming of death in the resurrection of Jesus. The death of Jesus marks the pinnacle of human idolatry and alienation under the power of Sin. The readings of Paul which make God responsible for the death of Christ are simply misreadings born of a thoroughgoing dogmatic rationalism and are drawn from systematic Medieval reflection and cultural accretions.

It was Paul's appreciation of the continuing power of Sin and Death in the face of a continuing weakness of the flesh that provided Paul with a theological foundation for an approach to a system of ethics. Paul's ethic was marked by eschatological tension that involved continuing renewed commitment. God's victory had been won and demonstrated in Christ's resurrection. The coming age had been demonstrated by sure inauguration, that marked the ultimate defeat of Sin and Death. It was an Age of Transformation. The powers of the Present Evil Age had been conquered, but they were not yet vanquished. Until Paul gained his share of Christ's resurrection, Paul's ongoing conformation was conformation to Christ's death through sufferings on a daily basis, hence, a cross imperative.

Such a perspective is very evident in Phil 3:8–16. Paul is still imprisoned and has faced life-death uncertainty (cf. Phil 1:18–26). To be found "in Christ" is to endure suffering (a cross imperative) but also to belong to God's New Age characterized by the resurrection (resurrection indicative). Paul admits that nothing he had achieved religiously speaking could compare with being "in Christ," ultimately, "gaining resurrection." Indeed, consequently, everything before Christ was so much "garbage" (σκύβαλα) compared to attaining the resurrection. Paul's words are practical, not moralistic posturing. Both a "cross" imperative and a "resurrection" indicative are clearly reflected in what Paul says specifically in verses 10–11. It is the resurrection Paul pursues (vv. 12–16) by all possible means. He obviously has not attained it, but the resurrection *is* "the prize of the upward call of God in Christ Jesus" (v. 14). It is that prize, that goal specifically, upon which Paul has his sights. Actual resurrection heralds God's New Age.

Some of the themes announced in this chapter will need to be unpacked with continued development in this work. The intent is not to be redundant, but to stimulate a growing reflection on significant aspects or matrices of Pauline theology. This cannot adequately be done all at once, although it is now appropriate to pursue Paul's Gospel polarities in the light of the overall nature of the Gospel of God.

3

The Gospel of God
Gospel Polarities

As is the case with so many treatments of Paul, John Knox slips into a dogmatic theological mode as he discusses the "Christian view" of Christ's death, seeing the crucifixion of Jesus as "the very crux" of the original divine event.[1] It was in the cross that God acted to save us. The cross represents the motive, occasion, and cost of the salvation event through which the new community in Christ was created. This is a sweeping assertion that attributes the motive of crucifixion to God. As Knox affirms, the cross points to the awful seriousness of our sin, the depth and quality of penitence required.[2] The cross is often seen as central to the divine indicative. In the present writer's judgment, however, what Paul emphasizes instead are the imperatival aspects of the cross more than identification of the cross with the indicative.

In terms of the Gospel of God, God did not cause nor require the cross as some necessary transaction to satisfy a legal requirement, although God did thoroughly transform a symbol of defeat and shame into a symbol of ultimate victory. And, in Paul, the cross becomes the mode of Christian living. As Knox himself realized, Paul has a paucity of references to repentance and forgiveness, even though he assumes that the substance of forgiveness and repentance is to be found at the very heart of Paul's gospel.[3] Such a focus upon forgiveness and repentance in Western theology inevitably carries with it a focus upon "guilt." In contrast to many, Knox does emphasize

---

1. Knox, *Chapters,* 125.

2. It should be noted that this is a focus quite different than all of Paul's salutations suggest, namely, God's "grace and peace." Paul likewise does not emphasize repentance (μετάνοια). As Knox affirms, however, the "*substance* of repentance and forgiveness" is surely to be found in God's grace. Knox, *Chapters,* 120.

3. One could perhaps argue that Paul writes to Christians, who already stand on this side of "repentance," such that he has no need to emphasize forgiveness and repentance. We are only privy to Paul's "literary" theology, his "epistolic theology," but all of Paul's letters are written to those already *Christian.*

the entire redemptive event—Jesus's ministry, teaching, death, and resurrection. Redemption takes the form of reconciliation. God acted to *reconcile* the world to himself and to adopt and embrace us as his children.[4] According to Knox, justification and reconciliation were "God's answer to our guilt," while redemption was his "answer to our bondage."[5]

At least in his letters, Paul focuses more upon justification and reconciliation. The former is most often understood as a legal term, while the latter is essentially a personal term.[6] This is more in keeping with Paul's emphases. Knox suggests that the division Paul made in separating the justice aspect of forgiveness from the mercy aspect was a tragic and fateful development within the whole history of Christian theology and even the intellectual history of the West.[7] However, Paul emphasizes grace and peace and reconciliation more in a family sense than he does in any forensic sense. And, as the current writer would suggest, God seeks to rectify the sinner, rather than "justifying" the sinner. God has an answer "to our guilt," yes, but even more, God has an answer to our need. As Brondos is wont to stress, the Christ event was for people's sake and not for God's sake, even as was the giving of the Torah.[8]

According to Knox, Paul's comparative neglect of the ideas of repentance and forgiveness in his letters deprived Paul of "the only possible theoretical ground for affirming the reality of ethical obligation within the Christian life."[9] Paul's opponents could ask what ground there was for ethical obligation, once one was in Christ. Paul himself could ask, "Why not sin in order that grace might abound?" (cf. Rom 6:1). Knox suggests that Paul was troubled by this question, but nowhere convincingly answered the question, such that he did not offer a convincing theoretical basis for insistence upon ethical living in Christ in terms of *obligation*, that the overall effect was to place law and grace in a totally antithetical relationship.[10]

---

4. Knox, *Chapters*, 127. Cf. Rom 8:15–17. The broadened focus of this sweeping assertion, which is certainly apropos, should be noted. The extent to which it accurately captures *Paul's* thought, rather than that of a contemporary Christian theology, is another question. Paul, for example, did not focus upon the "life and teachings" of Jesus or upon a direct emphasis upon "forgiveness and repentance" in his letters. See also Martin, *Reconciliation*.

5. Knox, *Chapters*, 129. A better quadriga might be redemption, rectification, reconciliation, and rehabilitation, perhaps in that order. And, God will not turn his back on those who are his children.

6. If "justification" is understood in terms of "rectification," then it may have a personal or familial connotation as well, rather than a merely legal or forensic one.

7. Knox, *Chapters*, 122. Support for such assertion might be questioned or at least more carefully defined.

8. See Brondos, *Parting of the Gods*. Such an emphasis is in keeping with Paul's use of ὑπὲρ ἡμῶν, "for our sake," "in our behalf."

9. Knox, *Chapters*, 126.

10. Knox, *Chapters*, 127. This could have been sensed by the Nomistic Evangelists. Generally speaking, it is not easy to maintain religious equilibrium without tending toward legalism on the one hand or antinomianism on the other. One might ask whether it was Paul or Knox who was "troubled" over the issue.

Some Initial Considerations

In reality, Paul's concerns are not those of individual salvation (repentance and forgiveness) in terms of Reformational Christianity with its consequent emphasis upon *ethical obligation*. To understand the indicative as "theology" and the imperative as "ethics" is an anachronistic reading of Paul that loses sight of Paul's own focus. His focus is upon the establishment of the new community of the church as the vanguard of what God has accomplished in the Christ event and what he will accomplish as he brings that event to appropriate conclusion in the Parousia and the Telos.

The church is the vanguard because it is the new community in Christ that heralds reconciliation and new creation. It is the new eschatological community because it participates in God's eschatological event. Paul does not focus so much on "ethical obligation" as he does upon "eschatological opportunity," "eschatological identity," and "eschatological responsibility." It is in the context of a cosmic, apocalyptic frame of reference that the Christian community is to be understood as God's eschatological beachhead community that demonstrates that the power of God has invaded the world.[11]

The question "What difference does the Gospel of God make in human living?" in Paul's perspective is an eschatological one and not strictly an ethical or individual one, although the Gospel of God does lead to renewal of living. What is usually designated as "ethical exhortation" is framed in the light of the whole redemptive event of God in Christ. Understood in this light, Paul's comparative lack of attention given to repentance and forgiveness should not be seen as a deficiency in Paul's theology, but rather should suggest that Paul's interest, attention, and understanding was directed elsewhere. Paul's understanding was not conditioned by, nor was his attention directed by, the legacy of later church history and Reformation theology.

The new life "in Christ" manifests itself unavoidably in the present time with multiple, concrete engagements in and with the world. Such life "in Christ" in terms of commitment to the Gospel of God involved concrete choices and relational interaction. Furnish is correct, however, that the terms "theological" and "ethical" tend to confuse rather than to clarify.[17] Instead, Paul's concerns are to preach the Gospel. Paul's concerns are *evangelical* (in the true sense) and *eschatological*. The Gospel of God is more than or greater than "theological" affirmations or "ethical" exhortations or even a combination of the two.

Yet the question remains, what difference does the Gospel of God make in human living? The imperative is living in the indicative by faith. The living out of the imperative moves beyond "ethics," however, just as the indicative moves beyond "theology." Faith working through love characterizes the imperative (Gal 5:6), but it is

---

11. Hays, *Moral Vision*, 32.
12. Furnish, *Theology and Ethics*, 110.

THE GOSPEL OF GOD

not simply a matter of human effort. New life in the new age means transformational living in the light of the gift of the Spirit and in the light of the cross and resurrection.

The whole of Pauline theology, including the so-called "Pauline ethic" is thus "eschatologically oriented and radically theocentric."[13] The power of God is the creative and redemptive power of love, revealed and made real in the death and resurrection of Christ. The inauguration of God's eschatological event indeed is able to reconcile, rectify, and summon to eschatological living out of the Gospel. While Furnish asserts that Christ's death-resurrection is the eschatological event, it would be more accurate to see death-resurrection as the inauguration of God's eschatological event which will also include Parousia and Telos (1 Cor 15:24–28). Indicative statements stand in closest connection with Pauline imperatives. Paul's view is rather one of actual new existence in a new age under a new Sovereign. The imperative is integral to the indicative, as one lives out the indicative.

Of some significance is Paul's use of indicative statements in order to exhort.[14] Pauline indicatives may frequently be used with an imperatival force. As examples, Gal 3:25–29 and 4:1–9 have stylistic characteristics of hortatory imperatives. Indicatives may be used as *protases* ("if" clauses) of conditional sentences followed by *apodoses* ("then" clauses) having an actual imperatival force, as in Gal 5:1. Romans 5:1–5 is a classic example of an "imperatival indicative." Romans 6 contains hortatory appeal beginning in verse 4 (cf. Rom 6:7, 11). Other examples include 1 Thess 4:7; 1 Cor 2:14–16, 6:11, 12:27; 2 Cor 6:16; Rom 7:4, 13:10, 14:8. Imperatival indicatives are thus one of Paul's primary means of exhortation, such that Paul utilizes the indicative with hortatory effect in an admonitory manner.

Paul may use obvious grammatical forms—such as imperatives, hortatory subjunctives, and verbs of entreaty—to urge his congregations to action. Yet as Furnish points out, Paul's exhortations should not be confined to such, for Paul makes use of many more subtle and less direct means to encourage his congregations to eschatological living.[15] In other words, interpretation of the Pauline imperative should not be restricted to the "ethical sections" with the more obvious forms of exhortations found therein. It should be noted, however, that they may be centered or concentrated there.

It is interesting that the interpretation of what Paul has to say often comes down to the interpretation of prepositions and Greek case forms. Galatians 5:24 may be customarily translated, "If we live by the Spirit, let us also walk by the Spirit" (*RSV*). In Greek, the verse is a first class conditional sentence which is brought to conclusion with a hortatory subjunctive. The initial condition assumes reality, "Since we live . . . ." The verbs in both halves of the sentence are present tense verbs in Greek, which suggest a continuing kind of action. The word for "Spirit" is in what most would term the dative

13. Furnish, *Theology and Ethics*, 223. Furnish's classic work, *Theology and Ethics in Paul* (1968), remains a sound work in this area.

14. Furnish, *Theology and Ethics*, 97. Furnish calls attention to a number of Pauline references.

15. Furnish, *Theology and Ethics*, 98.

case, here suggestive of either *means* (instrumentality) or *location* (logical sphere). The verse could be translated, "Since we are alive by means of/in the Spirit, by means of/in the Spirit let us also conduct ourselves." The first half of the sentence would suggest acknowledgment of the indicative of divine action, while the latter would suggest the responsibility of the imperative in Paul. The emphasis rests more with eschatological opportunity and realization of the eschatological age in a community context than it does with ethical obligation focused upon personal salvation. The imperative becomes the facilitation of God's new creation within a renewed community.

Indicative and Imperative

However, the imperative is most often construed in terms of ethics. In the post-Reformation period, the study of Pauline ethics continued to be dominated by Reformation debate concerning justification by faith and freedom from the Law in relation to personal salvation. Patristic writers, medieval scholastics, and Reformation theologians alike also made use of Paul's ethical teachings for treatises in moral theology. The first attempt to synthesize Paul's ethics was made by H. Ernesti in 1868. In the mid-twentieth century, Rudolf Bultmann related Paul's ethics to Paul's doctrine of justification by faith understood forensically. He introduced a distinction between the Pauline *indicative* (you are a justified Christian) and the Pauline *imperative* (then live like a Christian).

One may embrace the usefulness of the terms without adopting a full Bultmannian characterization. It bears repeating that the indicative is more than "theology," and the imperative is more than "ethics." The righteousness of the Christian is an eschatological phenomenon, dependent solely upon the event of God's grace. It is not achieved by human ethical acts, but rather by faith's response unto obedience according to the model of Abraham and Jesus.

Paul does not think in terms of an ethical transformation awakened from the slumbering powers of good that exist in humankind. Paul thinks in terms of the opportunity of new life brought about by God's accomplishment in Christ, which still involves human decision-making and personal responsibility, i.e., the obedience associated with eschatological faith. Scholarly treatment of "theology" and "ethics" in Paul thus makes use of the language of *indicative* and *imperative*, respectively. The *indicative* is the redemptive work of God wrought in the Christ event through the Holy Spirit, while the *imperative* is the responsibility placed upon humanity in response to the categorical demand of eschatological faith. Paul's statement that those in Christ have "died" to Sin (Rom 6:2) as a result of Christ's death and resurrection is foundational to any imperative which may follow.[16] The indicative pronouncement is directed toward rousing and stimulating human responsibility, i.e., the imperative to struggle

---

16. Ridderbos, *Theology*, 253–54.

against sin. [17] Paul's redemptive indicative of dying and rising with Christ should not be separated from the imperative. The context of both indicative and imperative is an eschatological one.

Not only does one see both the indicative and imperative in close connection in Rom 6:2, 12–13 ("Let not Sin reign . . . ."), but the same dual emphasis may be seen in Col 3:3–4 and 3:5—4:6, where Paul continues in an imperative mode. In Rom 8 Paul begins with the indicative in a declarative mode and conditional sentences (Rom 8:1–11), but then shifts to the imperative vein expressed through additional conditional sentences (Rom 8:12–13). In Phil 2:12–13 Paul indicates that God is the one who "works in you all to will and to work for his good pleasure" (v. 13), which is why the Philippians should continue to work out their salvation "with fear and trembling." While Paul's order may vary, the imperative is firmly based on the foundation of the indicative. As Ridderbos affirms, the imperative is grounded upon the indicative, makes appeal to it, and carries the intention of bringing the indicative to full development. [18]

Paul's concrete ethical teachings echo both Paul's Pharisaic Jewish as well as his Hellenistic matrices. Paul incorporates catalogues of virtues and vices that either should or should not characterize Christian life. [19] These are often marked by eschatological references (Gal 5:21). One also encounters *Haustafeln* ("household rules") in Col 3:18—4:1 and Eph 5:21—6:9, which Fitzmyer attributes to a Pauline disciple seeking to cope with social and ethical problems of a later day. [20] The present writer accepts both Colossians and Ephesians as late Pauline. Paul's theology and ethics could both be deemed to be "christocentric," in that Christ is the "image of God" (2 Cor 4:4). Growth in Christ (cf. 1 Cor 15:49; Rom 8:29) means that one lives one's life "for God" (Gal 2:19). However, for all his emphasis on Christ, Paul ultimately refers Christian existence to God the Father *through* Christ. [21] Once again, Paul's indicative and imperative are revealed to be eschatologically *theo*centric. Paul's theological understanding of the relation of God and Christ remains subordinationalist and functional, rather than systematically doctrinal and ontological. Paul's Christology is personal and not doctrinal.

There is thus a strong theocentric character to the new obedience which is called forth by the imperative. Nowhere is this more strongly expressed than in Eph 5:1, where Paul admonishes Christians to "become imitators of God as beloved children." We are to "walk in love, just as also Christ loved us . . . ." (Eph 5:2). We are to have the same mind-set as Christ and the same obedience unto death (cf. Phil 2:5–8). If we

---

17. Ridderbos, *Theology*, 254.

18. Ridderbos, *Theology*, 255.

19. Cf. Gal 5:19–23; 1 Cor 5:10–11; 6:9–10; 2 Cor 6:6–7; 12:20; Rom 1:29–31; 13:13; Col 3:5–8, 12–14; Eph 5:3–5.

20. Fitzmyer, *Paul and His Theology*, 101.

21. Fitzmyer, *Paul and His Theology*, 107.

have "died" with Christ to Sin, then we are to consider ourselves as "those dead to Sin on the one hand, but living unto God in Christ Jesus on the other hand" (Rom 6:8, 11). Having been slaves of Sin, one has now been freed *from* Sin but *for* servitude to Righteousness with a view toward sanctification. One has moved from a state of living unto death to a state of living unto eternal life (Rom 6:15–23). Definition of the new obedience in terms of righteousness and sanctification becomes the antithesis of the old disobedience which was characterized by impurity, lawlessness, Sin, and Death (Rom 6:12–23). Christians are "saints" (1 Cor 1:2; Rom 1:7; 15:25, 26; et al.) as the new people of God.

The new "redemptive-indicative" is no less a redeeming imperative that leads to a state of holiness. Paul can express this in cultic terms, as well, as he identifies the church as the people of God with the imagery of a "holy temple" of God (1 Cor 3:16, 17; Eph 2:21).[22] Believers, who live as "saints" of God, are to present their bodies as that which is *sacrificial, living, holy*, and *acceptable* to God as their "logical service" or "reasonable worship" (Rom 12:1).[23] Both the Pauline indicative and the Pauline imperative are thus radically *theo*centric. Ridderbos concludes that the theocentric point of view "*constitutes the great point of departure of the Pauline paraenesis.*"[24] Paul offers contingent exhortation directed to particular church situations, as well as general paraenesis reflective of his understanding of what God has achieved in Christ. He does not offer ethical maxims for the sake of general ethical concerns. Even his paraenesis is "baptized unto Christ."

Paul's imperative should not be understood as a division of responsibility, although both God and humankind have a share in the enterprise of salvation in the eschatological hour. Indeed, it is new creation of the entire created order and redefinition of Israel rather than individual salvation that is uppermost for Paul, although the individual has a share in that. If what God has done in Christ is truly eschatological, it could not be otherwise. The imperative brings the renewed life inherent in the divine indicative to real manifestation; the two cannot be separated. God is not mocked. For the individual, the new life requires a new obedience in order to achieve fulfilment. There is a different outcome for one who "sows to the flesh" versus one who "sows to the Spirit." The former leads to destruction (because it belongs in the realm of the "old" creation), while the latter leads to eternal life because it belongs to the realm of new creation in Christ (cf. Gal 6:6–8). One who is raised together in Christ will seek "the things which are above," and not "the things which are upon earth" (Col 3:1–2).

If one has been made alive in the Spirit, then one is to conduct oneself according to the Spirit (cf. Gal 5:25). "If you all died together [aor.] with Christ to the elemental

---

22. Cf. Ridderbos, *Theology*, 261–62.

23. It should be noted that Paul suggests four and not three separate descriptors for how Christians are to present themselves to God. The text should not be translated "a living sacrifice" nor "spiritual worship," as in the *RSV*.

24. Ridderbos, *Theology*, 260, emphasis original.

powers of the world, why do you follow principles as ones living in the world" (Col 2:20)? "But *you all* are not in the flesh but in the Spirit, if indeed the Spirit of God dwells in you all. But if anyone does not have the Spirit of Christ, this one is not of him" (Rom 8:9). In the latter reference, Paul phrases his thought with two first-class conditional clauses which assume reality of real conditions. New life afforded by the indicative is realized in the action of the imperative. Paul can express his perspectives differently in his contingent settings, but they have the effect of reinforcing each other.

Made alive by the Spirit, one lives out of God's indwelling Spirit unto new existence. Life made possible by the Spirit (indicative) is realized as one "walks in/by the Spirit" and "bears the fruit of the Spirit" (imperative, cf. Gal 5:16–25). Faith must become and remain active and vigilant, such that every Pauline imperative becomes "an actualizing of the indicative."[25] However, it should not be forgotten that both the indicative and the imperative have a provisional character of "already, but not yet." So far as the indicative is concerned, the Parousia and the Telos will complete the sure work of God already begun in Christ. So far as the imperative is concerned, there is continual renewal and expression of responsive growth and progress toward the realization of new life now taking place (Phil 3:12–16; Rom 5:1–5). New life becomes reality only through actual decisions of living out of one's faith "in Christ," of actualizing "grace" and "peace."

The new life that is made possible for one "in Christ" is totally the work of God. The origin of this life is found in the death and resurrection of Christ. If the indicative is defined as that which God had done, then the cross may not be placed under the indicative as a direct action of God. The resurrection may be described as a direct action of God, but the cross can only fall under what God allowed to happen and not what he caused to happen. At most, it would be admissible under the permissive will of God and not his deliberate will, to speak "systematically." Of course, the usual verses in Paul may be brought forward to support other positions which are often dogmatic and a-contextual. One immediately thinks of Rom 3:25, for example. Discrete Pauline references, such as Gal 3:13 and 2 Cor 5:21, along with Rom 3:25, will be treated in chapter 6.

One is made alive by the Spirit in a new birth. The new birth and the new life become reality as one embraces by faith what God has done in Christ. Beker is certainly correct in his assertion that Paul's Christology offers a theocentric-cosmic perspective that moves beyond Christocentric and anthropocentric moorings. Both the indicative and imperative must be understood in larger context.[26] What God has done "in Christ" comes as God's gift (indicative of grace), yet there is a coupled demand (the imperative). There always is, if one lives in the context of covenant relationship. In terms of Paul's metaphor, those adopted as children of God "in Christ" have the responsibility to live as such.

25. Ridderbos, *Theology*, 257.
26. Beker, *Paul the Apostle*, 277.

The new life is life to be lived under a new Lordship, such that a new obedience is expected. The new Lordship is as different as the new life. Romans 6:20–23 makes plain that the old life was life under the power of Sin, a life of disobedience to God according to the pattern of the first Adam, a life that led to death. Sin was able to work through the Law to bring about death. Sin was a corrupting influence or lord that found its base of operations in the "flesh," which Paul understood to be the weak (not evil) element of human beings.

The new Lordship was kinder and more gentle, a Lordship which offered the possibility of life in the place of death. On the one hand, it was not difficult to embrace the new obedience that accompanied the new Lordship and the new life. It came by grace and resulted in peace. On the other hand, because the powers of the Present Evil Age had been defeated but had not yet totally disappeared, there had to be a conscious struggle to resist and overcome their seductive claim. The Age to Come had dawned in triumph (Jesus's resurrection), but Paul realized he was living in the overlap of the Two Ages until the Parousia. The Telos was yet to come, when all malignant powers that enslaved and killed would be no more (1 Cor 15:23–28). In the present Age of Transformation, one must make the conscious choice to serve God in obedience through the power of the Spirit which now made possible such obedience (cf. Rom 6). One lives under a new Lord. We are back to "grace and peace from God the Father and the Lord Jesus Christ," which becomes reality in the presence and power of the Spirit, only by living out of the imperative.

The indicative is fundamental, for those in Christ have died to Sin (Rom 6:2). However, it is Christians who have "died" in Christ, not Sin that has "died." Sin is still present, even though its real power has been overcome in Christ's resurrection. For Paul, if there is a dying with Christ, there will also be a resurrection with him (Rom 6:5). In the overlap of the Ages, there is the necessity of stimulating Christian responsibility and actions. Thus, the imperative is given: "Let not Sin reign in your mortal body . . . and do not present your members any longer as weapons of unrighteousness in the service of Sin . . ." (Rom 6:12, 13). Dying and rising with Christ as a redemptive indicative may not be separated from the imperative struggle against Sin.[27] Because one has "died" and one's life is "hid in God," and because one serves a new Lord, one is to put to death those activities that are characteristic of the Present Evil Age (Col 3:3–10).

The imperative has its foundation in the indicative. As Paul makes plain in Rom 8, there is a "therefore" at the beginning of verse 12 that both calls forth and makes possible the condition ("if") given in verse 13: "*Therefore*, brethren, we are debtors, not to the flesh, to live after the flesh; for *if* you live after the flesh, you must die; but *if* by the Spirit you put to death the deeds of the body, you shall live." Paul was no Gnostic, who posited a radical dualism between one's spirit (seen to be good) and one's physical flesh (seen to be evil). Paul understood one's physical flesh to be *weak*,

---

27. Ridderbos, *Theology*, 254.

but at the same time he uses the term "flesh" to represent the way of living which characterizes the Present Evil Age.

To live "in the flesh" characterizes the domain life of the old human outside of Christ; it is to live under the domain of Adam. It is the actions of God that *make possible* life in the Spirit, but the effectiveness of divine action is maintained in the individual (or the community, for that matter) by continuing personal commitment to a new Lordship and the new opportunity. God has made possible the new life, but one must will to live out the new possibility. Human responsibility of a new obedience to a new Lord is called forth, although its possibility would not exist apart from God's indicative in Christ.

The imperative is thus born of the indicative and rests upon the indicative. It is the reasonable conclusion to the indicative, as illustrated by Paul's "thus" or "therefore" (Rom 6:12–23; 12:1; Col 3:5, et al.). This may come to clearest expression in Phil 2:12–13: "work out your [pl.] own salvation with fear and trembling; *for* it is God who works in you all [pl.] both to will and to work for his good pleasure." The divine indicative is introduced in the word *"for"* which provides the grounding for the imperative. The same is true in Rom 6:14, where "Sin will not have dominion over you all [pl.]; *for* you all [pl.] are not under the law, but under grace." In passing, one may note Paul's emphasis upon grace and God's good pleasure. God does not need our doctrinal formulations in order to "protect" his own holiness and integrity.

It is not human working with a right attitude that has called forth God's working in good pleasure, but rather the contrary point: because God has worked and works (indicative), humans can and must work (imperative). God's work is available, such that one should "walk in them" (Eph 2:10). Human obedience takes place according to "the working of God in Christ, who works in one in power" (Eph 3:20). There is no new contractural legalism, whereby God and humans have a derivative share of a new arrangement on the basis of contractural responsibilities. Rather, the imperative is grounded in the reality established by the indicative of grace and is intended to bring it to full expression in terms of peace.

One exhibits the fruit of the Spirit unto God-pleasing works as one manifests new life because one is in Christ as a result of God's rectification. It is the living out of new covenant obligations in the light of one's covenant identity in Christ, as a result of God's rectification. It is the living out of the new life of reconciliation. It is the realization of who one is in Christ, according to the power of God's Spirit (Gal 5:24). If one has been raised together with Christ, one is "to seek the things that are above" and live accordingly (Gal 5:1, 13, 16, 25; Col 3:1–12). The supposition of the indicative occasions the imperative (cf. Gal 5:25; Rom 8:9; Col 2:20).

Paul has an imperatival concern not only as a pastor and theologian,[28] but also as an apostle and evangelist. His theology was a theology to be lived. All of his letters are motivated by living concerns. The indicative for Paul did not mean escape from

28. As per Dunn, *Theology of Paul*, 626.

the world (asceticism), but a living in the world according to the resources of God in Christ (1 Cor 5:9–13). Paul's theology was embodied living, not that of an immortal soul escaping from a beleaguered material body or a hardened material world. Paul's theological affirmation (indicative) bears an intimate relationship to Paul's "moral" exhortation (imperative, in a narrow sense). The indicative had two key moments—the Christ event (especially the death and resurrection) and, secondly, one's incorporation into Christ, as represented in Rom 6:3–4.

The imperative can likewise be understood in terms of two matching emphases—the sustaining grace (rectification) of God and correlated human responsibility, as may be seen in Phil 2:12–13. These are divine and human perspectives of an ongoing process. The indicative is the necessary presupposition and starting point for the imperative. It is the "new creation" that makes possible a walk "in newness of life."[29] Paul's exhortations and moral observations are the inevitable working out of the indicative, although human responsibility and reception are called forth (Eph 2:8–10).

A new lifestyle must become manifest in new obedience to a new Lord, otherwise the former is denied in the individual or the collective body of the church. Both the indicative and the imperative belong to the matter and activity of faith. The indicative is God's realized possibility of new life, which must be taken upon the imperative and repeatedly realized anew. They make up the two sides of the same coin of "faith," as it were.[30] The imperative, then, is the appropriation of the indicative on a continuing basis. The imperative marks the continual actualizing of the indicative in the life of the individual or collective body of the church. Paradoxically, the indicative has to be accepted by faith once and for all and yet renewed time and again. As Paul suggests, one is to continually be "working out" one's own salvation (Phil 2:12). The imperative and indicative both become effective only "when faith is vigilant, militant, and sober."[31]

The occasional nature of Paul's letters may create a misimpression. The imperative calls for continuing rebellion against old enemies (such as Sin and Death), which faith must know again and again to have been defeated. The imperative is not just a series of vignettes—a kind of collage of snapshots, but rather a life lived continually on the basis of God's indicative. It is living, marked by a continual growth and progress (cf. Phil 3:12–16; 2 Cor 8:1–7; Rom 8:3).

Next to the theocentric nature of Pauline paraenesis, the totalitarian nature of the Pauline imperative may be stressed.[32] Romans 6–8 and Rom 12 are of decisive significance for understanding, once again. Just as Sin was a totalitarian master that claimed the whole of human existence, so also must all of one's actions and potentialities be placed at the disposal of God and be claimed by God. In terms of Pauline anthropology,

---

29. Dunn, *Theology of Paul*, 630.

30. Cf. Rom 1:17. See discussion of faith below.

31. Ridderbos, *Theology*, 257. Cf. 1 Thess 5:6, 8–11; 1 Cor 16:13; Eph 6:11–20.

32. Ridderbos, *Theology*, 265–72.

one's body, soul, spirit, heart, and mind must be subject to God's demand, even as the whole human being is affected by God's gift of the indicative. One's members are now to be yielded to God as "instruments of righteousness" (Rom 6:13). One is to be "obedient from the heart" (Rom 6:17). One is to experience the "renewal of the mind" (Rom 12:2).

Paul gives a multiplicity of commandments, admonitions, and advice that is frequently expressed in the plural. After all, he basically writes to the churches. He does not offer a system of ethical rules and precepts. This does not mean there is not a coherence beyond the particular, contingent settings. Paul does not offer a new legalism, but he is firmly cognizant of the foundational indicative. Love for one's fellow Christian and the good of the church as the new people of God, a vanguard in Christ, become for him dominant guiding principles. The church should exhibit in its living the new life dedicated to God, the new life no longer subjected to Sin, the new life defined in Christ, the new life which is a part of the new creation.

Is There a Pauline Ethic?

It is thus very difficult to separate and summarize the peculiarly "ethical" aspects of Paul's gospel because the indicative and imperative aspects of Paul's preaching are vitally interrelated. Paul himself has not posed many of the questions that we may ask, although elements of answers may be present implicitly or explicitly.

One cannot speak of a *systematic* ethic in Paul any more than one can speak of a "systematic theology." In common English, "ethics" is identified with standards or norms of morality in the practical affairs of life. It becomes a systematic standard judgment as to whether certain conduct is good or bad, right or wrong. The underlying Greek (ἔθος or ἦθος) would refer to that which is usual, customary, or habitual, hence, that which could be considered normative for a given societal group. Paul was not a moral philosopher concerned to appraise or promulgate ethical norms, principles, and theories. Paul has as little concern for a "systematic ethic" as he has for a "systematic theology."[33] Paul never attempts appraisal or presentation of ethical principles, norms, or theories. He offers no self-conscious, systematic analysis of the ground, motives, forms, or goals of Christian conduct. In a systematic sense, Paul has as little concern for systematized "ethics" as he does for systematic theology.

Paul was a proclaimer of the Gospel of God, who in that sense sought to set forth what it meant to be "in Christ" and to live "in Christ" in the light of that Gospel. Paul had no ethical theory and offered no code for Christian living. Rather, Paul set forth the dynamic interaction of indicative and imperative—i.e., how intended questions of conduct are transformed in the light of what God had accomplished "in Christ."

---

33. Furnish, *Theology and Ethics*, 209. We want there to be a concrete Pauline "ethic," a defined "ten commandments" of ethical behavior, for we perceive that to be so much easier than a life lived "in Christ" in the light of the Gospel of God.

Paul does have his own ideas of right and wrong, good and bad, many of which, no doubt, emerge from his societal upbringing or heritage in Judaism. When he exhorts, instructs, admonishes, or advises his readers, it is almost always done *ad hoc* fashion in relation to specific situations and cases. His concern is the same as that behind his preaching, namely, what God has done "in Christ" and what it means to live "in him."[34]

Is there a Pauline ethic? No single term or simplistic formula is able to do justice to the complexity of Paul's own ethical judgments and exhortations and the relationship between his theological and ethical perspectives. It is not possible to single out any one Pauline doctrine as specifically having to do with "Christian ethics" or the Christian's moral life. However, "Is there a Pauline ethic?" is not the right question. The right question is whether there is a Christian life to be lived and how that life is to be lived. This is subjective, in that it involves actual living, while the former may be too easily treated as an exercise in objective theory or codification. As Furnish suggests, the study of what is usually called the "Pauline ethic" is not a study of his ethical theory, nor is it a fixed code for Christian living. Paul had neither. The "Pauline ethic" is first of all representative of Paul's theological convictions. It is these convictions that underlie his concrete exhortations and instructions. His theological convictions shape his response to practical questions of conduct in contingent situations.[35] According to Furnish, Paul's ethic is to be found in the dynamic interplay of the apostle's theological, eschatological, and christological convictions. In the present writer's judgment, this translates to a cruciform imperative.

Paul did not seek to offer a simplistic formula or moral doctrine. While God's ultimate power has already been manifested in the present in raising Christ from the dead (thus overcoming malignant powers and re-creating life from death), the Parousia and Telos is yet to come. The eschatological paradigm for the entire creation is to be seen in the Christ event. God is the one who has and who will bring life out of death through his re-creative power. Paul's triangular focal points are thus to be found in his *theo*logical convictions, his *eschato*logical expectations, and his christological experience. All of this, however, is radically *theo*centric.

The power of the New Age itself is the demonstrated power of God to bring the dead to life (cf. Rom 4:17). That Christ has been raised demonstrates God's faithfulness as well as his power. That same faithfulness will yet be demonstrated in a New Creation and in the resurrection of those "in Christ." Paul sees hostile worldly powers set over against the power of God, exerting their own claims on human life. The power of God which raised Christ will also raise up those who are in Christ (1 Cor 6:14; cf. 15:43).

The eschatological orientation of Paul's whole gospel provides a fundamental perspective from which to view everything else. Pauline eschatology is not totally

---

34. Furnish, *Theology and Ethics*, 210–11.
35. Furnish, *Theology and Ethics*, 211–12.

futuristic—a problem for many who falsely understand eschatology as thoroughly futuristic. For Paul the eschatological action of God (in terms of his transcendent power) also has a *present* dimension predicated upon a *past* expression of the Christ event. The meaning and reality of the ultimate triumph of God's power are already manifested in the present. Christ is *now* Lord. The importance of the eschatological orientation for Paul's ethic is well exhibited in Rom 12–13. The Pauline interaction of present and future is closely tied to the interplay of indicative and imperative. Exhortations are rooted precisely in the future as it is already present to faith, though still hidden within this Age. The imperative becomes present testimony to the contemporary presence of the indicative or the Gospel of God.

Faith in God's power is focused and defined in *Christology* or commitment to Christ. Romans 6 is one of the crucial passages for determining the christological aspects of Pauline theology, generally speaking, and of the Pauline ethic in particular. Paul's understanding of the quality or character of the new life in Christ already given to the believer is derived from Paul's Christology. To be "in Christ" does call forth an *imatatio Christi* motif in Paul himself. It is not a case of Pauline audacity or arrogance. It really could not be otherwise, in the light of Paul's call and identity as an *apostle* of God in Christ, one sent with the authority of the sender.

As one considers the *imitatio Christi* motif, 1 Cor 11:1 points not to rules, but to personal relationships that are of primary importance in the Christian's deciding what and what not to do. The exhortation to "imitate" Paul points to a concern to "do good" to all men, in that Paul himself was guided by Christ. Paul makes clear the lot of those who are apostles in 1 Cor 4:9–13, even as he urges the Corinthians to imitate him (1 Cor 4:14–17). Paul reminds the Corinthians that he is their spiritual father (vv. 14, 15). The Corinthians should learn from Paul's life what it means to be in Christ and to live accordingly. There is a parallel in Rom 15:1–3.

First Thessalonians 1:6–7, 2:14 set forth a single clear and specific point to be imitated—patient and loyal obedience even in the midst of suffering. The Philippians are called upon to imitate the Paul who "presses on" (Phil 3:17). The Paul who "presses on" is the Paul who has renounced all past achievements and gains, who has shared in Christ's sufferings and who has been conformed to his death (Phil 3:10–11). *This* is the Paul the Philippians are to imitate, the Paul who seeks the resurrected life of God's new order in Christ, who yet presses on for the "prize of the upward call of God in Christ Jesus" (Phil 3:14).

The two themes that bind these *imitatio Christi* and *imitatio Pauli* motifs are (1) the need for humble, loving, selfless service and (2) the attendant need to be willing to suffer as Christ suffered in order to be obedient. One is conformed to suffering and even death in the service of others. Furnish observes that it is noteworthy that none of the passages single out any particular qualities of the earthly Jesus to be emulated.

Rather, Paul makes appeal to the *love* of the crucified and resurrected Lord expressed in humble obedience and self-giving.[36]

God's power is creative and redemptive, it is the power of love revealed and made real in the death and resurrection of Jesus Christ. Christ's death and resurrection as the eschatological event marks God's own powerful action of redemption. It is an action that rectifies and reconciles, but an action which also summons. Paul's ethic thereby is "radically and pervasively *theo*logical, *escha*tological, and *christo*logical."[37] Paul knew God not as a harsh judge, but as a loving and gracious Father. Paul knew Christ not only as a "living Lord," but also as a "loving Lord."

The indicative and the imperative thus represent an integral connection in Paul based upon God's eschatological action in Christ. It is Paul's view that one has been right-wised or rectified on the basis of faith, that one has entered an actual and total new existence. Obedience is constitutive of the new life. Abraham responded to God in faith and began a pilgrimage. The same is true for the Christian who responds to God in faith in the light of the Christ event. Christ's Lordship exercises powerful claim. Faith has the distinctive character of obedience and marks a deliberate response to divine claim in the light of personal identity, actions, and familial relationships.

The Mode of Faith

Faith's reference is first of all to the God who has raised Jesus from the dead (Rom 10:9b), coordinate with the confession that Jesus is "Lord" (Rom 10:9a). Faith is the acknowledgment that one trusts God's promises and actions, that one is committed to God "in Christ." Faith is the living acceptance of God's grace and peace under Christ's Lordship. One lives in obedience to God "in Christ." What does faith's obedience mean? The concept of obedience as it is found in Paul's letters must be pursued. The word groups of "subjection" and "persuasion" could also be pursued.[38]

Faith as Obedience

Christ's obedience and Adam's disobedience are contrasted in Rom 5:19. Christ's obedience was obedience unto death, as made explicit in Phil 2:8 (cf. Gal 1:4). Paul never specifically speaks of "obeying God," although it is implied by contrast.[39] Paul can characterize his whole ministry as an attempt to win "obedience" from the gentiles

---

36. Furnish, *Theology and Ethics*, 223. One should be mindful of the fact that Philippians is a "prison" epistle of Paul, written at a time in which he had experienced a severe imprisonment. Paul lived out a cruciform imperative in hope of resurrection. Cf. Phil 1.12–23; 3:12–21.

37. Furnish, *Theology and Ethics*, 224, emphasis original.

38. Cf. Furnish, *Theology and Ethics*, 186, for Greek word groups pertaining to ὑπακούειν and πείθειν.

39. Cf. Rom 2:8; 6:12, 16; 10:21; 11:30, 31, 32.

(Rom 15:18); he can also speak of the "disobedient ones in Judea" (Rom 15:31). Surprisingly, Paul nowhere speaks of obedience to the "commandments" of the Law or to God's "will" per se.[40] This may be because Paul understands obedience to be personally intrinsic and holistic, rather than external and occasional.

Paul avoids speaking of obedience to *the Law*. While Paul can use words like "do," "practice," "carry out," "keep," "serve," "submit to," Furnish states that nowhere does Paul suggest it is something one "obeys."[41] Formal obedience to specific requirements is not what Paul has in mind when he speaks of obedience. He means the surrender of one's whole life to God in obedience. The believer is freed *from* the Law's works and freed *for* the Law's fulfillment in a new sense.

Paul pens Gal 2:19–20 in the context of sharing once again his own experience of the Gospel of God for the Galatians, who were in danger of succumbing to what Paul saw to be a false, heterodox gospel. "For *I* through the Law, died to Law, in order that I might live to God. I have been crucified together with Christ [pf. vb.]; *I* live no longer, but Christ *lives* in me; but what I now live in flesh, I live by faith in the Son of God who loved me and gave himself in my behalf." As Paul has been crucified together with Christ, he lives by faith *in Christ*—not partially, but intrinsically. Galatians 2:20 is the *locus classicus* for the "mystical" conception of the new life in Paul. Yet Gal 2:20 does not point to a mystical depersonalization in which Paul's "I" is absorbed into the pneumatic "I" of Christ. Paul's thought is fundamentally anti-spiritualistic and anti-gnostic.

Life is *faithfulness* to the Gospel, as one lives life in communion with Christ through the Spirit in a new age. It is illustrative not only of the indicative (having died to Sin in Christ, having become alive to God), but also of the imperative (Christ lives through one, as one lives by faith in him). Faith becomes the manner by which one has a share in both aspects or elements. Paul thus presents what the current writer terms a "cross imperative" of a pilgrimage with Christ. Paul has been crucified with Christ, but now Paul lives that cruciform life on a daily basis in Christ. He sees his own life as a model of cruciform existence, both as an apostle and as one in Christ. Cf. Gal 2:20; 1 Cor 4:9–13; Rom 6:5–14.

While faith is almost thought of exclusively as a soteriological concept in Paul in the light of Reformation emphases ("justification by faith"), thus, indicative, it is just as important as a concept out of which believers live, thus, imperative. In fact, faith for Paul is the human response to the divine indicative of grace on an ongoing basis, through which Christians are infused with the power of God (Eph 5:1–2). As Dunn stresses, Paul's first and last references to faith in Romans carry the connotation of responsible living (cf. Rom 1:5; 14:22–23).[42] Paul introduces the purpose of his

---

40. Furnish, *Theology and Ethics*, 187.

41. For references, see Furnish, *Theology and Ethics*, 191.

42. Dunn, *Theology of Paul*, 634–35.

apostleship as "for the obedience of faith" (Rom 1:5), i.e., faith that is receptive and responsive and relational.

Faith is living out of trustful reliance upon the indicative of God in obedience to him. It is above all in Christ's death and resurrection that God's power is manifested (Rom 4:17). For Paul, faith means open participation in the redemptive power of God evident in Christ's death and resurrection. Primary in Paul's thought is faith as obedience, the surrender of life to God. It is proper acknowledgement of God as God, but it is more than that. It is an ongoing relationship which embraces the whole of living. On the other hand, the failure to acknowledge God as God rests at the heart of human sin and unrighteousness, for it marks a failure to live out of God's provision.[43] This is but a way of pointing to "faithlessness" and disobedience. In the failure to acknowledge God as God, one becomes self-idolatrous.

The noun "faith" is a consistent translation of the Greek word πίστις; "to believe" is a translation of the Greek verbal πιστεύειν. The common root is plain in Greek. It is perhaps unfortunate that the English language may create misunderstanding or misimpression through its use of nouns and verbs. In proper English, "faith" is a noun and "to believe" is its most common verbal equivalent.[44] The two words "faith" and "believe" do not look at all alike in English, but the transference is most often made from the verbal expression to the noun, such that "faith" becomes "believing something" or "expressing something" in terms of verbal assent. One "believes" (or accepts) a given doctrine, for example. This could not be further from Paul's understanding and usage.

In Greek the noun is πίστις, the adjective is πιστός/πιστή, and the verb is πιστεύω, such that the semantic relationship is immediately apparent.[45] For Paul, "faith" is a dynamic concept. There is an overall broad range of usage—belief, confidence, trust, faith/faithfulness, trustworthiness. Faith is "faithfulness." If so, "justification by faith" is not "rightness" on the basis of "belief" (as opposed to the basis of law), but rather "justification" on the basis of *faithfulness*, "rightness" on the basis of God's "faithfulness" (indicative), and on the basis of our own "faithfulness" (imperative) of living out of the Gospel of God. Rectification results from its basis in faithfulness, both God's and ours.

According to Lührmann, however, only Rom 3:3 and Gal 5:22 suggest the usage of "faithfulness," that πίστις for Paul means *conversion* to the God of the resurrection.

---

43. Dunn, *Theology of Paul*, 686. See, for example, Rom 1:18–23.

44. Romance languages often translate the noun and verb with different stems. The Latin rendered the Greek πίστις with *fides* and πιστεύειν with *credere*. By contrast, German utilizes the same word root, *Glaube* and *glauben*. In some quarters in English, the verbal form "faithing" is utilized, which while jarring and improper, may connote a truth on the one hand, or on the other, perpetuate a misunderstanding of mere "believing."

45. Louw and Nida place πιστεύω and πίστις under the semantic domain of "Hold a View, Believe, Trust." Specifically, they are placed under the subheading of "Believe to Be True" or "Trust, Rely." What is implied is "belief to the extent of" complete "trust," "reliance," and "confidence." See Louw and Nida, *Greek–English Lexicon Semantic Domains*, 1:365–79.

This is a very narrow understanding that appears to rest upon theological bias. The obedience motif reflected in Phil 2:8 surely reflects Jesus's own faithfulness. Becoming a child of God "through faith in Christ" (Gal 3:26) surely references more than mere "belief." "Putting on Christ" (Gal 3:27) surely involves more than "belief." Indeed, what is "faith" apart from "faithfulness"? In general, the phrase πίστις Χριστοῦ should likely be interpreted as an objective genitive, designating the content of faith, i.e., our "faith placed in Christ," our "faithfulness" called forth by the Christ event. On the other hand, a subjective genitive would suggest a faithfulness on our part akin to Christ's own faithfulness. This is not inappropriate to Paul, given the political context.

One may find a variety of traditions in the New Testament, such that there is no unified concept of faith. Faith becomes a self-definition of Judaism in the pre-Christian period. In the wider sphere of early Jewish Greek literature, "faith" referred to "faithfulness" or "trustworthiness." Philo follows Greek usage of "faithfulness." Abraham, for example, found God trustworthy. Paul, likewise, found God to be trustworthy, capable, and sufficient (cf. Rom 3:26). Josephus understands πίστις in terms of "faithfulness." Christianity could also understand in terms of "faithfulness," but in common self-definition "faith" was used in different ways to refer to salvation accomplished by God in Christ. The content of the gospel became the content of faith. "To come to believe" means to accept the proclamation of the gospel *and to live accordingly.* No opposition is seen between God and Christ, for faith is placed in the God who accomplished his salvation through the life, death, and resurrection of Christ.[46]

Lührmann suggests that the connection between justification and faith in Rom 3:21–31 is programmatic for Paul. The verb and noun for faith occur no less than nine times, while the Law (νόμος) is mentioned six times. Rom 1:16 is taken up again in Rom 3:21. Paul takes over a formula in Rom 3:24–26a, which describes salvation as a renewal of the covenant through the redemption that comes by means of the blood of Christ, which suffices for the forgiveness of sins. But even here, the effectiveness of ἱλαστήριον is achieved through faith (faithfulness?) in his blood (death) as a demonstration of God's forbearance and demonstration of God's own righteousness.

Justification is by faith in Jesus (Rom 3:26b), and Paul appeals to the story of Abraham in Rom 4 (cf. Gen 15:6). Yet this is not quite rightly put, for Paul's focus is upon God, not us, in verse 26b. God has demonstrated his own righteousness in Christ, even as he rectifies the one in Christ. According to Lührmann, Paul takes the content of Abraham's faith to be the belief that God gives life to the dead and calls into being that which has no being (Rom. 4:19). Abraham thus becomes the example of *conversion* (Rom 4:5, 24).[47] That is true only if Abraham is understood as a non-Israelite. Historically speaking, according to the Genesis account, Abraham was not an Israelite. Paul sees Law and faith as alternatives. Faith is made possible by

46. Cf. Lührmann, "Faith, New Testament," 753. Lührmann echoes an individualistic, Reformation legacy view of "faith," focused on personal salvation.

47. Lührmann, "Faith, New Testament," 754.

proclamation (Rom 10:14–15). The content is faith in God, who has achieved salvation outside the Law in the death and resurrection of Christ.

Faith and the Gospel

The view expressed by Lührmann appears to be suggestive of the older, especially Protestant, view of the Pauline bifurcation of Law and grace/faith with reference to personal salvation, wherein the two are categorized as polar opposites. Paul recognized the temporary nature of the Law (Gal 3:23–25) and the priority of faith in Abraham (Gal 3:6–9, 17–18), as well as the distinct limitations of the Law (Gal 3:10–14, 21–22; Rom 7:7–23; Rom 3:10–20). Paul's ultimate focus is upon the re-definition of Israel in a new creation in terms of the incorporation of gentiles apart from works of the Law.

It is a matter of an eschatological reversion to a first principle, namely, the faithfulness expressed by Abraham, an outsider in the beginning who became the forefather of Israel and Judaism long before the giving of the Law. The playing field has once again been leveled, such that anyone may be incorporated into the Israel of God on the same basis, namely, faith (Gal 3:25–29; Rom 4:7–25). It was faith that characterized Abraham in a pilgrimage with God, now understood as forefather of both Jew and gentile in Christ.

In Paul, according to Lührmann, both the noun and the verb display an affinity for the *Christos*-title. Paul took up existing early Christian language, such that faith for Paul meant the acceptance of the proclamation of the death and resurrection of Christ as a final salvific event (cf. 1 Thess 4:14; Rom 6:8).[48] For Paul, πίστις and πιστεύειν suggest conversion to the proclamation of God, who raised Jesus from the dead.[49] However, beyond "conversion," it is new creation and new life realized on the basis of new obedience in Christ, i.e., faithfulness. "The righteous *shall live* out of faith" (Rom 1:17; cf. Hab 2:4, emphasis not original). This is occasioned and accomplished in or by means of the Spirit, the ἀρραβών, the down payment or guarantee of the future fulfilment of God's Gospel in Christ. The Spirit is not an anonymous impersonal power of a theological doctrine, but it is the Spirit of God in Christ or the Spirit of Christ living in one as one lives out a faith pilgrimage. The church and individual Christians have a share in the Spirit insofar as one or the other lives by "faith" in Christ (Gal 5:25).

Rectification comes by faith (Rom 3:28; 5:1), as do the reception of the Spirit (Gal 3:2, 5) and the promise (Gal 3:14). Faith now characterizes the mode of human life in the world, such that understanding faith is crucial for understanding Paul's ethic

---

48. Lührmann, "Faith, New Testament," 753.

49. As Lührmann suggests, this was a "new God" for people previously pagan, but the "same God" for Jewish Christians. On the other hand, Brondos argues that most Jews would have found the God proclaimed by Paul and other Christians to be "strange, new, and unrecognizable." See Brondos, *Parting of the Gods*, 313–31.

that gains currency though its expression in love and obedience.[50] It is the obedience character of faith that allows the believer to participate in Christ's death and resurrection, while at the same time allowing for a "walking in newness of life" (Rom 6:4). For Paul, life in Christ is life in faith. That would apply to both indicative and imperative. Paul's conception of faith is closely allied with his conception of *obedience*. Yet it is obedience born of identity of grace and peace in Christ. It is in love that faith operates (Gal 5:6). It is in love that faith's obedient identity is found and confirmed.

Grace is the mode of God's giving of himself to human beings for their rectification and salvation. Human beings are right-wised "by his grace" (Rom 3:24). It is more usual for Paul to speak of rectification "by faith," such that he designates man's openness and reception of God's grace. Paul's own definition of what faith and believing means may be seen in Rom 5:17. However, Paul does not offer a formal definition of faith, but rather points to the example of Abraham (Rom 4:1–12; cf. Gal 3:6–14; Rom 9:6–13). God's own righteousness is his persistent faithfulness in being true to his covenant and covenant people—and to his creation. Abraham's faith involves trust in the redemptive purpose of the righteous God. God's redemptive purpose in Rom 4:17 is expressed as resurrection from death to life. Abraham's faith is not only trust, but also hope (Rom 4:18). It is God's power that permits Abraham to trust and to hope. Abraham was "as good as dead" (in terms of childbearing age) before Isaac was ever born.

Faith and Gospel may thus define each another reciprocally. The "word of faith" (Rom 10:8) is "faith in the Gospel" (Phil 1:27), it is "hearing of faith" (Phil 3:2, 5). Paul speaks of "obedience of faith" at the beginning of Romans, a phrase repeated in Rom 16:26. The righteousness of God is the content of the Gospel (Rom 1:17). Lack of belief or acceptance of what God has done is disobedience (2 Thess 1:18; Rom 10:16; cf. 11:30). Faith and obedience belong together interchangeably (cf. 1 Thess 1:8; Rom 1:8; 15:18; 16:19), as do unbelief and disobedience (cf. Rom 2:8; Eph 2:2; 5:6).

Faith as obedience is tied to the content of the Gospel and even more to the character of God in his own faithfulness as the author of that Gospel. One subjects or subordinates oneself to the righteousness or justness of God. Faith is the act of decision that is characterized by obedient response that *continually* participates in the grace of the Gospel. One is reminded once again of the terms "grace" and "peace" in the salutations of Paul's letters addressed to those who are participants by faith in the Gospel of God. Salvation for Paul is continued participation in God's re-creative Gospel.

---

50. Furnish, *Theology and Ethics*, 181–82.

Some Characteristic Elements of Faith

In 2 Cor 13:5 Paul encourages the Corinthians to prove they are in the faith. He writes to them to be sure they are δόκιμοι ("proven," "genuine") and not ἀδόκιμοι ("not proven," "counterfeit"), that they pass the test of truly being in the faith. Paul wants the Corinthian Christians to know that he himself is not ἀδόκιμος (2 Cor 13:6), i.e., that he is genuine. Pneumatic fellowship with Christ comes by the exercise of faith. Paul can alternate expressions "in Christ" (cf. 1 Thess 3:8; Phil 4:1; Rom 6:11; Col 2:6) and "in the Spirit" (Gal 3:25; Rom 8:4) with "in the faith" or "by faith" (Gal 2:20; 1 Cor 16:13; 2 Cor 1:24; 5:7; Rom 11:20). For Paul, faith is far more than "belief" or rigid belief usually termed "doctrines."

Paul makes use of the triad of faith, love, and hope (1 Thess 1:3; 5:8; 1 Cor 13:13; cf. Col 1:4–8; Eph 1:15–18). In Rom 5:1–5 the triad is interpreted in terms of rectification by *faith* (Rom 5:1), *hope* in the glory of God (Rom 5:2), grounded in the gift of God's *love* (Rom 5:5). The three concepts are fulfilled through rectification. In connection with Paul, Lührmann appears to downplay the meaning of "faithfulness." Paul uses Abraham as an example not only because he had faith, but because he believed in God's faithfulness and staked his life on it. Lührmann also emphasizes justification. He does not do full justice to the imperative of faith, even though he does emphasize aspects of the indicative. One is "justified" because one trusts in God's faithfulness in Christ, but also because one lives in faithfulness to the God revealed in Christ. Rom 3:21–31 is a key passage.

Hope is thus bound up with faith (Rom 6:8) and Christ himself is called the "hope of glory" (Col 1:27). He is the only one who has finally been raised. He is the only one who has been exalted above all the powers. He is the one who will deliver the kingdom to the Father. "Hope" can be understood as both action and object. One *lives* in hope. Hope, with faith and love, gives expression to the whole of Christian life (1 Cor 13:13; Col 1:4). One has a hope of calling (Eph 1:18; 4:4) that represents the new life in Christ wrought by the aegis of the Spirit. Hope becomes a source of confidence and strength (2 Cor 1:9, 10; 3:12). It does not put to shame (Rom 5:5; cf. 4:18).

For Paul faith, hope, and love constitute the essence of new life in Christ. Faith marks a trust placed in the great acts of God accomplished in Christ, that may be measured in actionable living. To live in faith is to partake of the "already" of the new life in terms of the eschatological existence and gift of salvation. It is, on the other hand, to realize the provisional nature of that new life in present temporality. In other words, one lives encumbered by weakness in the Present Evil Age, even while empowered by the reality of the Age to Come. Hope is expressive of that which is to come. Paul strives for that which lies before him (Phil 3:12–16), but he does so in the light of the gospel indicative that lies behind him. Love becomes the means by which one lives (imperative) both in the Christian community and the world at large. It is that which characterizes the divine indicative of reconciliation and re-creation, as well as the imperative of Christian living. Faith "energizes" through love (Gal 5:6).

Faith is also *confession* (Rom 10:9, 10), although one should not treat this aspect in a simplistic, non-contextual manner. Paul does not allude to creedal confession but to obedient confession (2 Cor 9:13). "Heart's faith" leads to righteousness. Salvation for Paul is a process and not a one time occurrence, as though one received an inoculation for immunization unto "deliverance."

"Faith in the Gospel" is "faith in Christ." Faith in Christ is faith in Christ as he is known to us—as the Christ who suffered, died, who has been raised, and who has been exalted. Faith "in Christ" is life lived out of the Gospel. For Paul, the character of faith as obedience is determined by apostolic authorization, for it is that which warrants the proclamation of the Gospel (cf. 1 Thess 1:5; 2:13; 2 Cor 12:12; Rom 15:18–21; Eph 2:12). To stand fast in the faith is to hold fast the tradition of the gospel in terms of both belief and action (2 Thess 2:14, 15; cf. 3:6; cf. Gal 1:6–9; 3:1–7; 4:9–11).[51] Faith stands over against "works" of the Law understood as a means of self-redemption and human boasting, just as it stands over against human knowledge and wisdom (γνῶσις and σοφία). God destroys the wisdom of the world.

In the Gospel, Christ has become the wisdom of God in whom one may boast (1 Cor 1:30–31; 2 Cor 10:17; cf. Jer 9:24). God is the source of life in Christ, whom God has made our wisdom (1 Cor 1:30). As Paul speaks of the cross in this context, he speaks of persecution (Gal. 6.12) and of being crucified to the world (Gal 6:14). He glories "in the cross of our Lord Jesus" (Gal 6:13) because that provides the foundation of a cruciform imperative of Christian living in terms of new creation of life in the Spirit apart from the negative aspects of the Law (Gal 6:14–15; 5:16–26). As one lives out of faith's obedience, "works," "knowledge," and "wisdom" are to be found, but these things are now conditioned and informed or defined by the Gospel and a cruciform imperative.

Faith can be qualified as conscious and directed, convinced and assured, even as it is characterized by knowledge, wisdom, and works based on the Gospel of God. One is to have the "mind" of Christ (Phil 2:5) and "renew" one's mind (Rom 12:2). It was the all-surpassing knowledge of Christ (the Gospel) that caused Paul to abandon earlier accomplishments (Phil 3:8–11). "Knowledge of the glory of God in the face of Jesus Christ" is not defined for Paul in terms of incarnation (as in John), but in terms of knowledge of the resurrection as both the cognitive ground and content of faith.[52]

51. In the deuteropauline Pastorals, adjectives are employed to re-enforce and develop this idea further—"sound doctrine" and "sound faith" (cf. 1 Tim 1:10; Titus 1:13; 2:3) and emphasis is placed on guarding the deposit (1 Tim 6:20; cf. 2 Tim 1:4). Development follows a Pauline trajectory, although it appears to be developed along creedal lines rather than lines of imperatival obedience. It betrays a more static concept than the dynamism of Paul, a sociological development which would be expected of the subsequent generation.

52. Ridderbos, *Theology*, 245. Cf. 1 Thess 4:14; Phil 3:10–11; 2 Cor 4:6; Rom 4:24; 10:9; Col 2:12.

The element of *trust* is not frequently mentioned explicitly in Paul's letters, but it is an element of Pauline faith. Without trust one cannot commit to Christian living, to obedience, or to the imperative. As one comes to be "in Christ," one no longer "trusts" in the flesh (Phil 3:3–7), but trusts in the Gospel. The exemplary faith of Abraham is marked by a living "trust" in God's promises (Gal 3:16–18; Rom 4:11, 17–21) and God's power, which in its Genesis context was the "trust" that God would bring life out of that which was as good as dead (Rom 4:19–21). Most characteristically for Paul, the trust of faith appears as the antithesis of Jewish trust in the Law, and as such, is marked by surrender to God's grace in Christ (cf. Gal 3:21–26; 1 Cor 16:13; 2 Cor 1:24; 13:5).

It is not that Paul supports the caricaturish characterization of Judaism as a "salvation by works" versus Christianity as a "salvation by grace." Rather, Paul understood a new and equal opportunity for *both* Jew and Greek apart from the Law. Faith in the Gospel applies to *both* Jew and Greek. Paul came to understand that the original qualification for membership in the people of God (the faith of Abraham) was now the eschatological qualification for membership in the people of God—it was still faith, but now faith in Christ, for the Jew first but also the Greek. If there had developed a misdirection through trust in the Law (cf. Phil 3:5–6; Rom 3:19–22; Gal 3:10–14), that was now corrected. His correction did not come by rejection of the Law, but by recognition of the limitations associated with it—limitations that had been surpassed in Christ.

Faith is the *certainty* of reconciliation coupled with adoption once accomplished and of having been adopted as children of God (Gal 4:4–7; Rom 5:1–2). Faith is that which knows with assurance that one will be included in what God has done and what he will yet accomplish in Christ. It involves all of life in the joys and expectations of God's indicative, as well as the anxieties and sufferings which may be expected as one lives out of a cruciform imperative. Faith is thus a state of life and living with confident assurance and obedience, even in the midst of unremitting struggle.[53]

Yet one lives in and shares in the power of God as communion with the living Lord. It is a communion with the Crucified One, now Resurrected Lord. It is cruciform living; it is a "cross" imperative.

New life takes place through faith in the working of God who raised Christ from a cross-death (Col 2:12). Faith manifests itself in power (2 Thess 1:11), such that believers fulfill their calling according to the power of God (2 Tim 1:7, 8), accompanied by the consciousness of one's own weakness (2 Cor 4:17). Human weakness makes plain the power of God. Christ himself was crucified out of/in weakness, but he lives by the power of God (2 Cor 13:.4–5). The one of faith learns to understand the present life in solidarity with Christ (2 Cor 4:11; 6:9; Col. 1.24; 2 Tim 2:10); one lives a life lived in weakness secured by the strength of God's indicative as evidence of coming glory.

Faith as *reliance* upon God's grace inevitably comes to expression in *love* in both the indicative and imperative, such that "faith working through love" (Gal 5:6, 13–14,

53. Cf. 1 Thess 3:8; Phil 3.12–14; 1 Cor 10:12; 15:1; Rom 5:3–5; 11:20; 14:4.

22–24) "bridges the whole sweep of justification by faith."[54] Faith as Paul conceives it is marked by the utter abandonment of self, which only the overpowering affection of self-giving love can generate. The real language of love is not words of endearment, but rather devotion expressed in commitment, surrender, and actions of sacrifice. Paul speaks of the willingness to suffer and to be silent rather than to retaliate (Rom 12:14–21). The real language of love is the love of one's neighbor as one loves oneself, which Paul says is the fulfilling of the whole Law (Gal 5:13–14). Paul's great conception of faith, according to Stewart, is the "willing, eager obedience of the bond slave to the Lord, and the adoring, self-abandoning response of the redeemed to the Redeemer."[55] It is also that which energizes through love, as it works Christian to Christian on a horizontal plane.

For Paul, faith did not render the Law invalid but rather established it (Rom 3:31).[56] The root of obedience for Paul rested in complete trust in God, as in the case of Abraham. Yet Paul realized that as long as Sin and Death retained power in the overlap of the Ages, the good purpose of the Law could be perverted into a force unto death (Rom 7:7–11). Being "right wised" or rectified meant right living, for it would represent creaturely trust in and reliance upon God on a continuing basis. This would mark the denial and refusal of idolatry (Rom 1:19–23). Paul could speak by way of contrast of the "law of the Spirit of life" as a shorthand way of referring to those who fulfil the requirements of the Law by living ("walking") out of the power of the Spirit (Gal 5:22, 25).

Whereas the written Law was subject to the weakness of the flesh under the powers of Sin and Death, the Spirit was not. Thus, the Law understood as guidelines for Spirit-directed conduct could be experienced as a liberating power for living when set free from the leveraged power of Sin working through disempowering flesh.[57] Sin finds its base of operations in the weakness of the flesh (Rom 7:8–12). Those who are in Christ have died to Sin (Rom 6:1–11), because the flesh has been crucified with its passions and desires (Gal 5:24).

Romans 4:13–21 may give Paul's "clearest and most powerful exposition" of what he understood by πίστις,[58] as he expounds upon Gen 15:6. Simple faith or trust is the proper response to the Creator God, "the one who gives life to the dead, and who calls things that do not have being into existence" (Rom 4:17–21). The tension-filled character of faith may be seen in Abraham, who though as good as dead (Rom 4:17–21) trusted with full certainty in God that he would be able to bring to pass that which he promised (Rom 4:20–21). And he lived accordingly in faithful obedience.

---

54. Dunn, *Theology of Paul*, 638.

55. Stewart, *Man in Christ*, 185–86.

56. See discussion in Dunn, *Theology of Paul*, 638–42.

57. Dunn, *Theology of Paul*, 647.

58. So Dunn, *Theology of Paul*, 377.

Paul himself experienced the tension-filled polarity of the "already" and the "not yet" in terms of his labors, assaults, dangers, and imprisonments, in his persecutions and distresses for Christ's sake. Paul realized the gospel was lived out in "earthen vessels"— "But we have this treasure in clay vessels (ὀστρακίνοις σκεύεσιν), in order that the surpassing nature (ὑπερβολή) of power may be of God and not from us" (2 Cor 4:7). According to the Gospel of God, God's power is made strong through human weakness. Indeed, the contrast between the power of God and human weakness is always great. For Paul, to know Christ and the power of his resurrection is to know Christ through fellowship in his sufferings (Phil 3:7–14).

Thus, it is a cruciform imperative that calls for the living out of obedient faith, such that as one becomes conformed to Christ's death, one may also attain the resurrection of Christ's life in God (Phil 3:11). Resurrection comes only through "death"; exaltation comes only through resurrection. And God alone can resurrect one from the dead. Christian life is not a patterned program, but a wrestling in the present with the vicissitudes of life, while living in obedience to God, as one stretches to attain all of God's final promises (Phil 3:7–14). From such trust comes the defining manner or mandate as to how one ought to live.

In contrast to Adam who succumbed to Sin and failed to trust in the Creator God, Abraham's response offers a paradigm of obedient trust—the human creature who fully confident relies upon divine promise because it was God who promised. The real contrast with Abraham is found in Rom 1:18–23. Just as it "was reckoned to him as righteousness" (Gen 15:6; Rom 4:8, 22), it is the "unrighteousness of men" (Rom 1:18) who suppress the truth in unrighteousness to whom are accorded the wrath of God (Rom 1:18). They are guilty of willful rejection, arrogance, and idolatry (Rom 1:18–23). They exhibit not just a lack of faith but the rejection of the One in whom faithfulness and faith rest (Rom 1:17; cf. 3:26).

Faith is not a "work" acquiring merit before God. It is not simply believing what the church believes. It is not "religion lite." If it is only mechanical assent to propositions and dogmas (otherwise known as "doctrines"), then it is only a degenerate faith. "Faith" for Paul was a living out of the confidence that God would fulfil his promises begun in Abraham and now eschatologically evident in Christ. Faith thereby becomes a force for living, in terms of action and attitude expressed in self-commitment to a God deemed worthy of trust.[59] As Stewart suggests, "Love turns the discipline of life into romance."[60] Indicatives do, indeed, become "veiled imperatives."[61]

59. Stewart, *Man in Christ*, 176.

60. Stewart, *Man in Christ*, 197.

61. Cf. Furnish, *Theology and Ethics*, 97; Stewart, *Man in Christ*, 199; Jacks, *Alchemy of Thought*, 315.

Polarity of Christian Life in the New Age

Because both the indicative and the imperative are yet in process and unfinished, Christian living in the dawn of the new age is filled with polarities. The Parousia and the Telos are yet to be; Christians have not yet attained to the literal resurrection. The time of Paul's ministry was a period of polar tension for both Paul and Christians. There was a polarity between the waning power of malignant forces of evil and the full realization of Christian hope and identity at the Parousia, the time of the resurrection of the dead (1 Thess 4:13–17).

Tension of Ages and Powers

The relation that exists between the indicative and the imperative is determined by the present redemptive-historical situation, by the overlap of the Two Ages or the intervening Age of Transformation. Both the indicative and the imperative have an "already" as well as a "not yet" aspect. There is a provisional character or qualification to be stressed with regard to Christian life/living in the Age of Transformation. The "powers" (including Sin) have not died, even though their power has been broken. It is the Christian who has "died" (Rom 6:2), such that one no longer lives in a state of sin under the power of Sin. Christ has not yet fully swept all of the malignant powers from the field of conflict, such that the kingdom has been turned over to God. That is yet to be (1 Cor 15:24–28).

The creation itself still waits with "eager longing" the revealing of the people of God (Rom 8:20). There are a number of such references in Paul which suggest that the Age to Come has dawned and the Present Evil Age has begun its demise. However, Paul understood himself along with other early Christians to be living in the overlap of the Ages, i.e., in the Age of Transformation. It was no longer that the Age to Come would come "someday" (as in Jewish thought), but that the Age to Come had dawned proleptically with Jesus's resurrection in the present. Final achievement and the fullness of the Age to Come would come to fruition with the Parousia and the Telos.

The Christ event, which assures victory (resurrection has broken the power of Sin, there is new creation in the Spirit), is not yet complete (Parousia, Telos). The imperative demands new obedience on a continuing basis, lest one fall back into subjection under the old powers which still have a presence. Christian living (and, hence, the imperative) is not a state of dormancy awaiting a heavenly transformation/translation, but rather an active, dynamic militancy against evil in present tense. It is not a "marching to Zion," but it is open warfare under the victorious banner of the cross and the resurrected Lord. One may note Eph 6:11–17, where one is called to put on the "whole armor of God." While metaphorical, the passage speaks a truth for actual living out of the Gospel of God. As Ridderbos indicates, the situation in Rom 7 becomes actual once again when faith slackens.[62]

The imperative thus becomes an ongoing lifestyle much more than a list or series of commands. It is a continual living out of the Gospel of God (Eph 6:18–20). It is a "working out" of one's salvation (Phil 2:12–13). This is one reason Paul gives exhortations, rather than ethical maxims. But again, Paul's word is "Grace and peace to all of you from God the Father and the Lord Jesus Christ." Those words come both as a statement of divine indicative and encouragement to a cruciform-imperative.

However much Paul may speak of having been set free from the power of Sin and Death in terms of positive indicative, as Ridderbos points out, those of faith have not left Sin behind as ground already conquered. Otherwise, Paul's ongoing exhortations in the imperative would have no meaning. Paul employs many metaphors in his presentation of both indicative and imperative.[63] In 2 Tim 2:3–5, for example, he employs the metaphors of a soldier, an athlete, and a farmer one after another. The military metaphor is a powerful one which Paul makes use of elsewhere. Paul can describe the life of the believer time and again in terms of battle and victory gained as a result of battle.[64]

God has won victory through the Christ event of resurrection, over the Pyrrhic "victory" of Sin in death. "Death has been swallowed up in victory; where, O Death, is your victory? Where, O Death, is your sting?" (1 Cor 16:54–55). Victory over malignant powers has been given by God, "victory through our Lord Jesus Christ," as expressed by indirect agency (2 Cor 15:56–57). Paul immediately follows this with paraenetic exhortation (2 Cor 15:58). Christ leads before in triumphal procession, having disarmed rulers and authorities (2 Cor 2:14; Col 2:15; Eph 4:8). At the same time, one is to put on the "whole armor of God" and be strong in his might, as one contends against rulers and authorities of present darkness—and even against spiritual hosts of evil in heavenly places (Eph 6:10–17).

The Christian life is one of moral freedom, exercise of faith, and perfecting of holiness, based squarely upon the victory of God in Christ. Yet it is one of continuing struggle to stand in battle on the basis of Christ's victory and to emerge victorious, even as Christ himself was victorious in God. On the one hand, one may envision the powers of evil harnessed to Christ's victory chariot in triumphal procession (Col 2:15); on the other hand, *while Christ reigns*, every last ruler, authority, and power

---

62. Ridderbos, *Theology*, 257.

63. For a thorough study of the character and context of Paul's metaphors, see Williams, *Paul's Metaphors*. Williams treats Paul's metaphors under twelve broad categories supported by more than eighty specific sub-headings. The number and breadth of Pauline metaphors is indeed extensive, as one might expect in description of an eschatological gospel and ministry. Paul's metaphors created a lively dynamism for his original audience. However, these are often *missed* or overlooked by a contemporary reader of his letters and perhaps often *dismissed* or misunderstood or mis-appreciated by the biblical literalist, who treats them moralistically or dogmatically.

64. Ridderbos, *Theology*, 267.

(including Death) have not yet been finally or yet totally destroyed (1 Cor 15:25–27). The Parousia and the Telos are yet to come. Paul does not proceed from the idea that the church has already reached a state of sinlessness in which it may rest. Rather, Paul looks forward *in the power of the Spirit* to final victory that is sure to come, albeit through struggle.[65]

Life in Christ and being joint heirs with him involves first a suffering with him in order that we may be glorified with him (Rom 8:17b). Paul expresses an "eschatological reservation," according to Hays, which qualifies Paul's understanding of Christian existence. The time of suffering and struggle at the turn of the Ages is a wrenching one, in which the community is called upon to participate in the suffering of Christ. With regard to Rom 8:1–17, those who celebrate the blessings are those who, paradoxically, suffer with Christ now.[66]

The Presence and Power of the Spirit

Christian life for Paul was one that was lived between promise and threat. There was a kingdom yet to be inherited and a judgment yet to be faced.[67] Christians have "died" with Christ and even been "raised" with him, yet there is the struggle to live in accordance with life in the Spirit. There remains for the person of faith a continuing struggle between the flesh and the Spirit. This is true for at least two reasons. First, even though the person of faith has received the Spirit, one also retains the subjugated human nature of the "flesh," a realm of ethical frailty or weakness. Still, Paul can affirm that those of Christ Jesus "have crucified the flesh with its passions and desires" (Gal 5:24). Secondly, even though the Age to Come had dawned, the Present Evil Age had not totally disappeared. The power of Sin was still operative, working through the Law and the weakness of the flesh to bring about death. Yet in at least one instance—Jesus's resurrection—the power of Sin to bring about Death had finally been overcome. That in itself was the gospel Paul preached and the ground of Paul's hope (Phil 3:12–16). That in itself is the Christian hope in general.

In 1 Cor 2:14—3:3, Paul can describe three classes of people—the natural person (ψυχικός, 2:14), the fleshly person (σαρκικός, 3:3), and the spiritual person (πνευματικός, 3:1). The natural ψυχικός person is the unregenerate person who is "in the flesh" (Rom 8:9) and who does not know the things of God. The πνευματικός person is the one whose life is strengthened and ruled by the Spirit of God. The one who is σαρκικός is one who is a baby "in Christ," still "fleshly" and also "in the Spirit," yet one who does not "walk" by the Spirit (Gal 5:16–26; Rom 8:1–17). The one who is indwelt by the Spirit of God has to grow in God's grace and learn to walk by the Spirit

65. Ridderbos, *Theology*, 272.
66. Hays, *Moral Vision*, 25.
67. Dunn, *Theology of Paul*, 672.

94

and not by the flesh. There is a cruciform imperative, but one based upon "grace and peace."

Dunn points to the "unavoidable corollary," namely, that *apostasy* "remains a real possibility" for the Pauline Christian during the whole time of the eschatological tension.[68] Believers may die, if they revert to life κατὰ σάρκα ("according to flesh"). But in Christ, there is now a choice and an equipping power. One may experience renewal towards wholeness in the face of Sin and Death, or, one will experience daily deterioration towards destruction by Death (cf. Gal 2:18; 1 Cor 3:17; 8:11; 10:9–11; Rom 8:13; 14:15). Evangelistic work may be in vain (1 Thess 3:5; Gal 2:2; 4:11; Phil 2:16; 2 Cor 6:1). One may "fall away" from grace (Gal 5:4) or, to use Paul's analogy, may be cut off from the olive tree of Israel (Rom 11:20–22).

One becomes a joint heir with Christ in terms of glorification, provided one suffers with him (Rom 8:17). One has the responsibility of holding fast to the gospel (1 Cor 15:2), of remaining established and steadfast in its hope (Col 1:22–23). There is a race to be run (Phil 3:12–14; 1 Cor 9:27), such that there is a call for carefulness and watchfulness (Gal 5:15; 1 Cor 3:10; 8:9; 10:12) and self-scrutiny (1 Cor 11:29–30; 2 Cor 13:5). There is thus a polarity of struggle between the Spirit and the flesh that remains for the Christian. This is the struggle of the indicative and the imperative and once again points to Paul's cross theology, for which some "cross theologies" are but a parody. The Christian, however, may be fully equipped by God for the battle with full assurance of victory in Christ.

Conclusion

Foundationally, in terms of the Gospel of God, the indicative of God's faithfulness demands the imperative of our faithfulness. The imperative is in part to become what we are in Christ—*Werde das was Du bist*,[69] or, at least, become what you have the opportunity to become in Christ. As the Westminster Confession affirms, the goal of religion must be "to glorify God and to enjoy Him forever." Once again, the disciplined obedience that emerges in the living out of divine love turns the imperative of the cross into romance far removed from doctrine and ritual.

As one lives in a union with Christ, one lives in a union with God, who is both the beginning and the end of new creation. As Stewart suggests, Paul experienced a triumphant certainty that God was "in Christ."[70] Paul's Christocentric living was Theocentric living, and this based upon divine initiative of "grace" and human response of

---

68. Dunn, *Theology of Paul*, 497. This reality in Paul may have contributed to the development of comforting doctrines such as "once saved, always saved," which may deny Paul's eschatological tension and his continuing imperative. For Paul, one would be "once saved, always saved" at the point of the resurrection and not the point of one's baptism. Paul understood salvation as a continuing process that extended through a lifetime, not as an inoculation or vaccination.

69. Stewart, *Man in Christ*, 190.

70. Stewart, *Man in Christ*, 171. Cf. 2 Cor 5:19.

"faith," which ushers forth in "peace." "Grace and peace to all of you from God the Father and the Lord Jesus Christ." As one lives out the Gospel of God in Christ, life itself becomes more lyrical.

4

Paul's Cross Imperative

R ICHARD Hays speaks of three closely linked themes that frame Paul's "ethical" thought—new creation in cohesion with the Present Age, *the cross as paradigm for action*, and the community as the locus of God's saving power. Hays interprets these in terms of "three focal images" of community, cross, and new creation.[1] The reality, as well as the possibility of new creation, has been ushered in through the Christ event, particularly centered in Jesus's death and resurrection. And, most certainly, a new community has been created and established in Christ—a community consisting of renewed individuals who now become a part of what Paul terms the "body of Christ." It is, however, a community that is characterized (among other things, such as the possession of the Spirit) by the cross as a paradigm for action. Paul's cruciform imperative becomes a paradigm for the entire life of the Christian community.

While the motif of a cross imperative may certainly show up where Paul refers to σταυρόω or σταυρός, it is not limited to those references. The cross for Paul represents a cross–death predicated upon obedience and suffering and death. Where Jesus's death is referred to it is *always* at least implicitly understood as a cross type of death simply because that was the reality of the historical truth. However, Paul only understood the meaning of the cross-event in the light of the resurrection. Thousands of persons died on Roman crosses. To say that the actual cross means anything more than actual death by Roman execution is to speak of either early Christian or Pauline theological interpretation. For Paul and the early Christians, the cross came to mean much more than just a Roman political execution. Because of the belief in resurrection, it came to mean victory rather than defeat. Because of the belief in resurrection, it came to be understood in terms of triumph over all malignant powers—civil and celestial, cosmic and universal—that threatened the well-being of humanity and the cosmos.

"Death" is the last enemy of human life and cosmic order. God's victory over Death in Jesus's resurrection was understood as the "firstfruit" of final victory, now

---

1. Hays, *Moral Vision*, 19–36, 196–98, emphasis not original.

guaranteed by the presence of the Spirit. Because of belief in the resurrection, there was now an inaugurated hope for the future (Rom 8:23–25). God had proved his faithfulness, as Israel's story beginning with God's promise to Abraham had now been fulfilled by a universal Gospel, the universalization of "Israel," if you will, which extended beyond ethnic limitations.

God's faithfulness was not demonstrated by the cross, a singular occurrence of death involving Jesus but holding future hope for all others. The cross was characteristic of the Present Evil Age. Rather, what is highlighted is the demonstrated faithfulness of God who brought life out of death, re-creation out of destruction, reconciliation out of rejection, rectification out of corruption, hope out of desolation, exaltation out of subjection. The cross, while not the goal of God, became the historical means for the demonstration of the intention of God, namely, the reclamation of his creation and the fulfilment of his promises to his people. As such, the cross became an ever-present marker and symbol of how Christian life itself was to be lived until the Parousia and the Telos.

Christians live in the shadow of the cross because it becomes the visible shorthand symbol of the whole Gospel of God. (Again, how would one symbol resurrection?) Christians are to have "the mind of Christ" in themselves, a mind-set that is willing to empty oneself rather than to grasp for power and position, a disposition of living that pours one's life out in loving service even as a slave (at base, a human tool), rather than being served. Christians are to have the "mind of Christ" that is marked by an obedience to God that may well lead to a "cross," whether that be seen as metaphorical or literal. "Obedience" within Judaism could be construed in terms of two great laws of total love for God and for "neighbor." Christians are to live by faith, but according to Paul that faith must energize by love—love for God and others, which is the fulfilling of the whole Law (Gal 5:6, 14).

This is what Paul means by his "cross imperative." It means freedom *from* powers that enslave, control, and kill, but it also means freedom *for* life in symphony with God's Gospel that energizes through obedient loving. It is loving without limits—even to the point of death. The Age to Come has dawned with its fulfilling resources and liberating powers. In the interim between the Resurrection and the Parousia/Telos, one lives out of God's indicative with the responsibility of maintaining the indicative through the continuing imperative in an Age of Transformation.

Paul can speak of being "crucified with Christ" (Gal 6:14; Rom 6:6). We must be "crucified with Christ" to become a participant in the indicative of God. Paul can speak of the need to "work out" one's salvation with "fear and trembling," as he collectively addresses the Philippian Christians (Phil 2:12). This is a cruciform imperative, the lens through which Paul understands his own apostolic suffering and Christian suffering in general.

Windows of Insight

Nowhere do we get closer to Paul than in Gal 6:11–18, where he writes with his own hand. Paul portrays those who want to make a "good showing in the flesh" ("to put on a good face," εὐπροσωπῆσαι) in order to avoid persecution for the cross of Christ. By contrast, Paul affirms that he boasts in the cross, through which the world was crucified to Paul and he to the world. Both emphases should be noted. The Gospel results in new creation of the Israel of God. That is not wrought by the rite of circumcision, but by suffering and persecution and by living out of the "grace and peace" of God.

Two passages in particular may elucidate Paul's thought. The first is Phil 1–2 and the other is Rom 8. In the Philippian passage, Paul mentions the "cross" only in Phil 2:8, where it is given without a definite article in the hymn associated with Christ: Christ Jesus became obedient unto death, even a cross-kind of death. Paul does not say "the cross." As significant as Phil 2:5–11 is, it is easy to allow the context to be obscured. That passage is introduced by a plural imperative (φρονεῖτε, "have this mind-set," v. 5) as well as followed by a plural imperative (κατεργάζεσθε, "you all work out," v. 12). Paul's purpose is to hold up the example of Christ Jesus before the Philippians as relevant to their Christian living and unity in Philippi (cf. Phil 2:1–4, 12–16).

Paul's own imprisonment, which carried possible implications of death, also enters his discussion (Phil 1:12–26; 2:17). Both Paul and the Philippians have been granted the opportunity to suffer in behalf of the Gospel and in behalf of Christ. Not only was it granted to the Philippians to come to faith in Christ, but also to suffer in his behalf with a suffering akin to that of Paul's own suffering (Phil 1:29–30). It is in the light of Christian suffering for their faith that Paul encourages the Philippians to live a life of joy even in the midst of suffering (Phil 1:27–28; 2:1–4; 14–16). The contextual suggestion is that of a cruciform imperative. However, Paul's encouragement is remarkable, based as it is upon the Gospel of God.

While Paul does not mention the cross of Jesus at all in the letter to the Romans, other than his singular metaphorical acknowledgment that "our old man was crucified together with [Christ]" (συνεσταυρώθη, Rom 6:6), it is suggested that Paul's cruciform imperative may implicitly inform what Paul says in Rom 8. If the Spirit of God dwells in one, one is certainly not under any kind of divine condemnation (Rom 8:1–11). One has been adopted by God as his child (Rom 8:12–16), as testified by the Spirit. However, Paul adds that we are heirs as well as children—"heirs of God and joint-heirs of Christ, provided we suffer together with [him], in order that we may be glorified together with [him]"(Rom 8:17). After he treats the help and aid given by the Spirit, he asks the question, "Therefore, what shall we say to these things?" (Rom 8:31).

Having affirmed the indicative of Jesus's death and resurrection (Rom 8:31–34), he affirms that no natural tribulation or dangerous persecution or any kind of power or entity, including Death itself, will be able to sever us from the love of God in Christ

Jesus our Lord (Rom 8:35–39). The reason this is so, of course, is that those in Christ are God's adopted children as part of his new creation. There is a cross imperative implicit in all of this that emerges alongside the indicative. God did not spare his own son from a historical death on a Roman cross, but he raised him from the dead.

By implication, the meaning that emerges is that those in Christ may not be spared from persecution or even wrongful death. However, they are to live out a cruciform existence in full awareness of their identity as children of God who will participate in God's new creation, in view of the fact that nothing—absolutely nothing!—shall sever them from God's love in Christ Jesus their Lord. One lives in obedience under the shadow of the cross according to the grace and mercy of God.

The cross does not belong to the indicative—it is not something for which God was directly responsible. It belongs rather to the imperative, to the kind of responsible living by God's people to be exhibited in the eschatological overlap of the Ages. God's people, who now incorporate both Jew *and* gentile, are to live even in the face of cruciform existence on the basis of obedient faithfulness. Hays illustrates the point in the light of Gal 6:2 ("Bear the burdens of one another and thus you all will fulfill the law of Christ"). The pattern of Christ's self-giving (Gal 1:4; 2:20) has been projected into an imperative for the community, which is to serve one another in love. This is to suggest that Paul reads the cross as a metaphor for the actions of Christians that are to correspond analogically to Jesus's own self-giving exemplified by his death. Hays affirms that the metaphorical interpretation of the cross in Gal 6:2 is consonant with Pauline usage elsewhere.[2]

One of the major problems within Pauline studies and Christian theology based on Paul, generally speaking, is the confusion occasioned by placing the atonement under the sacrificial category of propitiation/expiation/mercy seat rather than with the category of reconciliation. This has been combined with a preoccupation with "sins," borne of a guilt-ridden ecclesiology and anthropology, particularly as found in Western Christendom. This in turn has resulted in attention being given to a few Pauline texts that have been assumed to give support to such viewpoints, with other Pauline texts either being ignored or subordinated to the texts in question.

In other words, the death of Jesus and specifically the cross have been interpreted as belonging primarily to the indicative. The Pauline emphasis upon the imperative has been too little noticed or too easily ignored. That there is a cross for those who are Christian is plain in the tradition attributed to Jesus (Mark 8:34; Luke 9:23; Matt 16:24), and it is at least implicitly (the present writer would suggest explicitly) present in Paul.

The Christian's cross may be just as "historical" as Jesus's cross—there have been Christians who literally died on crosses. However, it is Jesus's cross alone that has eschatological meaning in a foundational sense. As a result of the eschatological death *and* resurrection of Jesus, humanity is delivered from bondage to Sin, Death, and the

2. Hays, *Moral Vision*, 27–28.

Law. That opportunity of liberation, however, is characterized by Paul as a cruciform existence of suffering that ultimately leads to life. So does the tradition attributed to Jesus point in the same direction. This means that the "Christ-bearer" (Deissmann) is also a "cross-bearer."

To be united with Christ is to be united with his resurrection *and* death—it is not just a "bound for glory" gospel. As one unites oneself with the death of Christ, then Sin will no longer be able to "lord" it over one (Rom 7:4; 8:1, 3). "Reckon yourselves to be dead unto Sin" (Rom 6:11). If one wishes to speak of "doctrines," there is a "doctrine of *necrosis*" (Greek, νέκρωσις, "death") evident in Paul's thought which is seldom if ever recognized and emphasized.

According to Brunner, faith itself is a *passion* and a *suffering*, that means complete reversal of one's whole existence.[3] Christ completed the work God gave him to do, such that nothing is "lacking." We are called to fellowship with his sacrifice and suffering in the present in what the present writer terms a "cross imperative." As indicated, this is not alien to Jesus's own teaching as reflected in the Synoptics, whereby Jesus calls upon those who would follow to take up their own cross (Mark 8:34 par.).[4] To be baptized unto Christ is to be baptized unto Christ's suffering, to "die" with him, in order that one may be "raised" with him (2 Cor 4:10–12; Rom 6:1–6).

As Dunn suggests, because the gospel is a gospel of the crucified one, the ministry of the gospel itself becomes a living out of a "*theologia crucis* rather than a *theologia gloriae*."[5] Dunn applies this to Paul's understanding of apostleship, but it is a statement that applies to Christians generally speaking. There is a "cross imperative" for Christian living in Paul.[6] It might be said, however, that a *theological gloriae* is only realized through a *theological crucis*.

Paul's cross imperative is chiasmic. Just as Christ was obedient even unto death on a cross and was exalted as Lord in resurrection (cf. Phil 2:8–11), so also will one who lives a cross-like existence unto death thus experience life in terms of resurrection. It is this for which Paul hopes and encourages (cf. Phil 3:8–16). Paul no longer glories or boasts in any of his human qualifications in the "flesh" (cf. Phil 3:1–7). This is perhaps best seen in Gal 6:12–17.[7] Paul addresses the Judaizing issue associated with the Nomistic Evangelists in both Philippians and Galatians. However, he strongly incorporates allusion to crucifixion language in Galatians. Paul writes with his own

---

3. Brunner, *The Word and the World*, 70–71. Brunner indicates that "faith" is misconstrued if understood merely as an intellectual process. Cf. Stewart, *Man in Christ*, 189.

4. Should this belong to the early church rather than Jesus, it illustrates a cross imperative in early Christian tradition, which was also present in Paul.

5. Dunn, *Theology of Paul*, 580.

6. One may consult Gorman's works on "cruciformity," for example, to see a strong emphasis upon this mode of living. See Gorman, *Cruciformity* and *Inhabiting the Cruciform God*.

7. This is as authentic as it gets in Paul's letters. Paul writes with his own hand. There is no interpretive amanuensis involved. Paul's deep concerns and central understandings are keenly in evidence. This becomes a touchstone passage that reaches across the centuries.

hand (Gal 6:11) as he suggests that the Nomistic Evangelists who seek to compel a legalistic circumcision seek themselves to avoid suffering persecution for the sake of the cross of Christ (Gal 6:12).

While Paul formerly gloried in human qualifications "in the flesh" (cf. Phil 3:4–8), Paul now wishes to glory "in the cross of our Lord Jesus Christ, through which/whom the world (κόσμος) has been crucified to me and *I* to the world" (Gal 6:14). What matters in Christ is a new creation (Gal 6:15). But how is that achieved? Only through the imperative of a cross kind of living, which may involve everyday suffering and which is able to give up what may *appear* to be life in the interest of that which really *is* life.

In the ancient world, temples were the visible abodes of the divine presence and could be seen everywhere. In general, a temple was the house of the deity represented by the statuary of the god or goddess that "dwelled" therein. In that same world the cross proclaimed the death of a criminal. Jesus's death on a cross was thus seen to be scandalous. Käsemann affirms that everyday reality should be the true place of divine worship by Christians. Through Jesus's cross the world is crucified to him, and he is crucified to the world. At least for an apostle, Paul suggests that he bears the death of Jesus in his body, always being given up to death for Jesus's sake, that the life of Jesus may also be manifested in mortal flesh (2 Cor 4:10–11). As Käsemann stresses, what Paul says of himself is true for every Christian—one is only a disciple as long as one stands in the shadow of the cross. Our relegation of the cross to the category of atonement instead of reconciliation has had consequences for appropriate theological understanding of both the cross and resurrection, and of both the indicative and the imperative.

As Käsemann observed, our theological thinking focused upon a *theologica crucis* has become a blood-full conviction of divinely caused substitutionary suffering, while theological thinking focused upon a *theologica gloriae* has become a series of bloodless convictions of dogmatic beliefs that turn the church's piety into an illusion in which the cross is but symbolic decoration in art, on tombstones, and as jewelry.[8] And even then, except in Catholic circles, the image of the cross has been emptied of the image of the one who died upon it. Had there been the erection of literal Christian temples dedicated to Jesus, the statuary contained therein would have had to have been a crucifix, as unlikely as that may have seemed to first century people.

In a word and in contrast with other first century temples, Christ lives in no temple other than the body of Christians who are living a cruciform existence within the full grace and peace of God under Christ's Lordship. This means that everything in Christian devotion must locate its foundational criterion in the cross.[9] While Käsemann himself emphasized the centrality of the cross, he could also address its misapplication.

---

8. Käsemann, *Perspectives on Paul*, 38. Indeed, his point seems to be even more clear in a contemporary age.

9. Käsemann, *Perspectives on Paul*, 39.

Paul takes over a traditional view in Rom 5:12–21 and portrays by way of contrast the disobedience of Adam, the archetypal human, and the obedience of Jesus, Adam's eschatological antithesis or counterpart. Obedience is the sign of "regained creatureliness" that was lost by Adam. God rules over those who adopt the insignia of the cross as their own, for it is from the cross that resurrection comes by the power of God. Cross and resurrection are distinguishable, but connected. As Käsemann suggests, resurrection is not mere revivification, but it is *regnum dei* "which raises us above rebellion and death."[10] Paul appropriated the tradition in circulation about Jesus's cross, offering his interpretation in terms of the doctrine of rectification based on the cross. God destroys our illusions and delineates new obedience, freeing from the way of the Law and delivering from the rebel's despair.[11] We are freed *from* the Law and freed *for* a cross. Paradoxically, in the Gospel, it is the way unto life.

Clearly, the death of Christ occupies a position at center stage in Paul's theology. Better stated, death *and* resurrection lie at the intersection of the indicative and the imperative. Paul draws upon an abundance of images from Israel's scriptures and the common faith of the early church. He uses them to relate the message of the cross more directly to his audiences in their diverse backgrounds and circumstances. Green asserts that the cross of Christ "lies at the intersection of the major avenues" of both Paul's theology and his imperative of faithful living prior to the Parousia.[12] This is not quite rightly put, for otherwise Paul would make much greater direct use of cross language. It is not specifically the historical cross of Christ itself, but rather what that came to represent in terms of subsequent events of the indicative and the provisional model held forth for the Christian imperative.

The "Christ hymn" of Phil 2:6–11 offers the most fully developed paradigmatic significance of Jesus's death. It is contained in a context of exhortation of mutual support (Phil 2:1–18). The Philippians are to have the "mind of Christ" (Phil 2:5) as their exemplar in obedient faith.[13] As Hays suggests, Paul presents a metaphorical understanding of Christ's self-emptying and death. The function and power of the metaphor invites those in Christ to understand one's own life and vocation as that which corresponds to "the gracious action of the Lord whom they acclaim in their worship."[14]

The trajectory of Christ's obedience even unto death becomes the model for Paul's own apostolic career and those in his churches. The righteousness from God based upon faith in Christ involves sharing (κοινωνία) in his sufferings, even becoming conformed to his death (συμμορφιζόμενος), in the hope of sharing in the resurrection or Christ's vindication (Phil 3:9–11). The resurrection is the sign of hope of

10. Käsemann, *Perspectives on Paul*, 42.

11. Käsemann, *Perspectives on Paul*, 42.

12. Green, "Death of Christ," 209.

13. Hays, *Moral Vision*, 29, suggests that Paul employs a doxological hymn in the service of moral exhortation.

14. Hays, *Moral Vision*, 30. See further discussion in Hays.

vindication by God, while the cross becomes the presiding metaphor for Christian living in obedient faithfulness, *as was true of Jesus*.[15]

It is not only Paul's vision of the *moral* life that is founded upon the "twin themes of conformity to Christ's death and the imitation of Christ"; rather, that is Paul's vision of Christian life as a whole.[16] Hays affirms that if Rom 3:21–26 is read with Rom 5:15–19, a consistent picture emerges that portrays Jesus's death as an act of faithfulness that reconciles humanity to God and simultaneously establishes a new reality of life in which we are set free from the power of Sin. We are enabled to be conformed to the pattern of his life.[17] Obedience and faithfulness to God are defined paradigmatically by Jesus's death on the cross.

The obedience and self-sacrifice of Jesus that is enacted in his death on the cross becomes the prototype for the "obedience of faith" that Paul's preaching aims to inculcate in those who live by faith.[18] Further, Paul understands the cross as a pattern for the life of those who likewise exhibit the "faith of Christ" (subjective genitive) by "faith in Christ" (objective genitive). Hays understands the reference in Rom 3:22 to πίστις Ἰησοῦ Χριστοῦ as a subjective genitive.[19] Scholarly debate over the nature of the genitive in both Rom 3:22 and 3:26 will continue.[20] In the current writer's perspective, Rom 3:22 suggests a subjective genitive—"the righteousness of God (which accrues) through (indirect agency) the faith of Jesus unto all who come to (like) faith," while Rom 3:26 affirms God "justifies" the one who has faith in what *God* has done in Jesus.

Gospel and Cross

And what has God done? The answer to that question involves the whole indicative. In the immediate context, God has manifested his righteousness (rectification) apart from the Law, he has provided redemption/release by his grace, he has passed over previously committed sins (pre-cross and pre-faith of Jesus). The passing over of previously committed "sins" becomes the necessary prelude for victory over "Sin" in Christ. He has demonstrated his righteousness in the eschatological age (through the overcoming of the powers in the resurrection), he has established his ability to make

15. This, indeed, may be a primary reason Paul and his theology is less popular in a day and age of a "health and wealth" gospel.

16. As per Hays, *Moral Vision*, 31. Hays calls attention to Rom 6:1–14; 8:17, 29–30; 15:1–7; 1 Cor 10:23—11:1; 2 Cor 4:7–15; 12:9–10; Gal 2:19–20; 5:24; 6:14.

17. Hays, *Moral Vision*, 32. It should be stated that the pattern of Jesus's life was cruciform.

18. Hays, *Moral Vision*, 31. Cf. Rom 1:5.

19. Cf. Hays, *Moral Vision*, 31, discussion and references.

20. On the debate over the genitive "faith of Christ" (πίστις Ἰησοῦ Χριστοῦ), see Howard, "Faith, Faith of Christ," 758–60, and the sources cited therein. See also essays by Hays ("ΠΙΣΤΙΣ and Pauline Christology," 35–60), Dunn ("Once More, ΠΙΣΤΙΣ ΧΡΙΣΤΟΥ," 61–81), and Achtemeier ("Apropos the Faith of/in Christ: A Response to Hays and Dunn," 82–92), in *Pauline Theology IV*.

righteous (to rectify) those who respond in faith, and he has done so without compromising his own righteousness.

Quite the contrary, God has established his own righteousness in the eschatological age as the playing field has been leveled for both Jew and gentile on the basis of obedient faith. While that faith may be marked by suffering during the overlap of the Age of Transformation, it will also be marked by vindication in resurrection. God, the Rectifier, has established foundationally everything needed to make human rectification possible without any compromise of his honor or righteousness. Lest one forget, the exercise of such freedom of action is one mark of divine Sovereignty. The power of God's indicative is in place, along with God's power (the Spirit) to empower a realized imperative which may be cruciform as need be.

Those who belong to Christ have crucified the flesh (i.e., the self-centered and sensual self) with its passions and desires (Gal 5:24). Paul can assert that "I have been crucified with Christ" (Gal 2:20) and that "our old self was crucified with him" (Rom 6:6). The same thing is meant by crucifixion of the flesh in Paul's rhetorical question, "How can we who died to sin still live in it?" Paul asserts that "we have been united with him in death," "buried with him by baptism into death," or "I myself have died with Christ" (Rom 6:2–4). While this may be accorded to the indicative, it also belongs to the imperative.

Christ the Risen Lord yet remains as the Crucified One for those "in Christ." They must now live as though they themselves are crucified ones, such that the powers of the old age no longer rule over them. As "death" to Sin becomes a reality in Christian living, one not only joins with Christ in a crucifixion death but also becomes joined with him in terms of a future resurrection. Colossians 3:9 metaphorically views the change as having taken place, "you have put off the old nature (τὸν παλαιὸν ἄνθρωπον) with its practices and have put on the new nature (τὸν νέον)," As Ladd observes, this is but another way of saying that the old self (ἄνθροπον) has been crucified with Christ (Rom. 6:6).[21] Ladd understands the issue rather moralistically.

The death of/to the flesh is an event appropriated by faith that involves two aspects. Believers must recognize from the point of view of the indicative that the flesh has been "crucified" with Christ (Rom 6:11). There has been a death, a "crucifixion with Christ." On the other hand, from the standpoint of the imperative, this must be put into practice on a daily basis—one must "put to death the deeds of the body" (Rom 8:13). Both are surely spoken of by Paul in an effective figurative sense. One must "walk in the Spirit and not gratify the desires of the flesh" (Gal 5:16; cf. Rom 8:4). It is life in the Spirit that makes possible this continual putting to death of the ways of the flesh. Once more, the crucifixion of Christ becomes the defining marker by way of remembrance and by way of identity for those in Christ who seek to live by the Spirit. Paul's theology of the cross involves not only an indicative but also an imperative. It is

21. Ladd, *Theology*, 517.

not circumcision nor Torah, but the cross that becomes the identity marker of those in Christ.

Paul also underscored by his own apostolic experience how much suffering and powerlessness was integral to living the Christian life, in spite of the reality of the resurrection. Paul translated the meaning of the cross into a life that was no stranger to weakness, opposition, and suffering (1 Cor 2:2–3; 2 Cor 11:23–29; cf. Col 1:24). The demands of Paul's own apostolic ministry, born of encounter with the risen Lord, are grounded in the centrality of the cross as a cruciform imperative of obedience.

Paul has his own understanding of the "way of the cross," which is a way of suffering that identifies with Christ's suffering. His personal theology carries with it a narrative quality that joins contemporary experience with the story of God's activity from Abraham to the Telos. In Green's judgment, the centerpiece is "the narrative of Jesus' crucifixion," even though Paul exhibits little interest in the historical details of Jesus's passionate suffering "*qua* historical data."[22] That includes the cross. This writer would mention that Green's point would also include the cross as historical event, in the sense that he makes his point.

However, it is obedience and not death which "atones." It is to be expected that obedience to God in a fallen world that stands in opposition to God will call forth suffering. Jesus was obedient to God—and, as a result, he suffered death, even death on a cross. Christian life will be lived out under its own cross, in the light of Jesus's cross. It may well involve suffering, but it will certainly involve obedience.

It is thereby clear in Paul that those in Christ carry the victory of Jesus into the whole world, but the church can only do that in so far as it takes up Jesus's cross after him.[23] Discipleship is following the one who was crucified, following him into the whole world and obediently living out the results of the Gospel of God in the period between the resurrection and the Parousia/Telos. Jesus's cross came before the resurrection. The disciple's "cross" is to be found between the resurrection of Jesus and the Parousia.

However, when one considers other references in Galatians, the focal point is different. Galatians 5:24 points not to Christ's crucifixion, but rather to the crucifixion of "the ones of Christ Jesus" who have crucified "the flesh with its passions and desires." Paul writes personally, with pen in hand, when he charges that those who insist upon a gospel of circumcision are only seeking to avoid persecution "for/in the cross of Christ" (Gal 6:12). Paul uses both the noun and the verb in Gal 6:14, as he strongly affirms his commitment to boast not "in flesh," as was characteristic of his false opponents (Gal 6:12), but "in/by the cross of our Lord Jesus Christ." Significantly, he also affirms that on the basis of the Gospel of Christ (which involves crucifixion), the world had been crucified to him and he to the world. The references in Gal 5–6 thus point to the "crucifixion" of Christians and Paul as a way of living that conforms

22. Green, "Death of Christ," 202–3.

23. Käsemann, *Perspectives on Paul*, 58. Jesus himself knew that (cf. Mark 8:34).

to the "cross" type of death suffered by Jesus. The language of crucifixion becomes a metaphor to describe the nature of proper Christian living in the light of the gospel and in obedience to the gospel.

In the Christ hymn of Phil 2:6–11, Jesus became obedient even to the point of death, even a "cross" kind of death (θανάτου σταυροῦ, v. 8). The emphasis in verses 9–11 turns to exaltation—an exaltation that assumes resurrection. The present significance, however, is the fact that the hymn is introduced by a Pauline imperative: "Have this mind-set among yourselves which indeed (was) in Christ Jesus, . . ." (Phil 2:5). While Jesus historically died on a cross, Paul is using Jesus's example of humility and obedience as encouragement to the Philippians. As an apostle of God and bond-servant of Christ, Paul encourages the Philippians not only to imitate Christ but also to imitate him and to pay attention to those among them who do so because they have Paul as a type or model (Phil 3:17). He warns them, by contrast, that there are many others who "walk as *enemies of the cross of Christ*" (Phil 3:18, emphasis not original).

Once again, the emphasis is upon a proper Christian mind-set and lifestyle. One way to "walk as an enemy of the cross of Christ" is by denying one's own cruciform existence. Another way would be the substitution of the Law (circumcision) for a cruciform imperative, as apparently was true of the Nomistic Evangelists.

Cross and Christian Living

How does the death of Christ on the cross affect Christian living? Paul provides no single answer to the general question, but he does supply some parameters. A part of our problem of misunderstanding Paul is our reductionism, as well as ossification of time worn dogmas and doctrines that have occluded the dynamism of Paul's metaphors. The full implications of a theology of the cross become clear in actual living, not in continuing theologizing or maintaining a museum of theological doctrines. It is here that Paul's autobiographical passages give account of how he has been shaped by the cross and conformed to the pattern of living of the crucified Christ.

It may be helpful to acknowledge Paul's use of terminology once again. He has only five references to the crucifixion of Christ as a verb in all his letters, concentrated in Galatians or 1 Corinthians (Gal 3:1; 1 Cor 1:23; 2:2, 8; 2 Cor 13:4). His other three references refer to Paul or Christians in general (Gal 5:24; 6:14;1 Cor 1:13). The compound form occurs in Gal 6:14 and Rom 6:6, where it is stressed that we are crucified together with Christ. Paul's use of the verb is rather exclusively concentrated in Galatians or 1 Corinthians, letters belonging to Paul's Collection Campaign. In addition, he directly mentions the cross of Christ ten times—only seven, if one excludes Colossians and Ephesians.[24] Paul uses "blood" (αἷμα) but eight times with reference to

24. Cf. Gal 5:11; 6:12, 14; Phil 2:8; 3:18; 1 Cor 1:17, 18; Col 1:20; 2:14; Eph 2:16.

the death of Jesus, three of which are in connection with the cup of the Lord's Supper celebration (1 Cor 10:16; 11:25, 27).

In Romans 3:25, expiation by his blood is mentioned, while Rom 5:9 speaks of rectification by his blood. The latter is a reconciliation theme, as is made plain by Rom 5:10, which stresses future salvation on the basis of resurrection. Ephesians 1:7 speaks of redemption through his blood (including forgiveness of trespasses *according to grace*), while both Col 1:20 (peace) and Eph 2:13 (brought near) stress a reconciliation theme. It is interesting that all of the above references are found only in letters of the Collection and Post-Collection periods—Gal, Phil, 1 Cor, 2 Cor, Rom, Col, Eph. They are reflective of Paul's mature thought and collective life experience. Paul has been engaged in ministry for eighteen years or more.

Paul mentions the resurrection (ἀνάστασις) eight times—four times in treating the Corinthians' question about the resurrection (1 Cor 15:12, 13, 21, 42) and four other occurrences (Phil 3:10; Rom 1:4; 6:5; 2 Tim 2:18). Paul's attention given to the resurrection, however, finds extensive reference in Paul's use of the verb ἐγείρω ("I raise") with predominate usage in 1 Corinthians and Romans.[25] Paul does not mention the cross of Jesus in some places where he could well have done so, such as 1 Thess 1:9–10; 2:15; Gal 1:4 (cf. 3:1); Rom 1:1–6; 2 Tim 2:8.

McGrath discusses 2 Cor 4:7–15, Gal 6:14, and Phil 3:8–12. For Paul, Christ and his cross become the organizing paradigm of the suffering of the believer.[26] An organic relation is traced between three crucifixions—those of Christ, Paul (or the Christian) and the world. To know Christ is to know his sufferings. McGrath's comment is very apropos, as he asks how Paul's theology of the cross is described. He answers by stating that the cross stands for Paul as the immovable and fundamental *reference point* for faith. Faith begins here and continually returns here, for faith is nourished by the living, yet crucified Christ. The one who has faith shares in Christ's sufferings and death out of total commitment to the Gospel, with the promise of one day sharing in Christ's glorious resurrection. The latter point becomes the hope that sustains. One may receive glimpses of heaven and hear voices of angels, but the reality is that Christians remain earthbound and committed to Christ crucified in the midst of a suffering world. "The cross stands as the image of the Christian life in the world, just as it stands for the hope beyond this world, . . ."[27]

While McGrath's comment is tinged with customary Christian theology that Paul himself would express somewhat differently, the essential emphasis is entirely appropriate. One who is a Christian is literally committed to one's own crucifixion, if need be.[28] Paul as an apostle of God in Christ understood himself as "crucified with

---

25. Cf. 1 Thess 1:10; Gal 1:1; 1 Cor 6:14; 15:4, 12, 13, 14, 15, 16, 17, 20, 29, 32, 35, 42, 43, 44, 52; 2 Cor 1:9; 4:14; 5:15; Rom 4:24, 25; 6:4, 9; 7:4; 8:11, 34; 10:9; Col 2:12; Eph 1:20; 5:14; 2 Tim 2:8.

26. Cf. McGrath, "Theology of the Cross," 196.

27. McGrath, "Theology of the Cross," 197.

28. One may see this reflected in the early generations of the church, Paul included, in the traditions of martyrdom in the face of persecutions.

Christ" (Gal 2:19; Rom 6:6). He had suffered much in the service of the Gospel (2 Cor 11:23–29). If one is not so committed, one may be living with a false gospel as an "enemy of the cross of Christ," in Paul's perspective.

Transformational Living

Paul encourages the Roman Christians in a church he had never visited to be transformed by the renewal of their minds, as he begins to focus on new life in Christ in the Roman letter (Rom 12:1–2). In a larger sense, that is a call to repentance and commitment. Paul largely writes to churches and not to individuals, such that the pronouns he uses to refer to Christians are usually plural and not singular.[29] Christian living is focused on life in the world until the Parousia and Telos. Paul's gospel is focused on transformational living "in Christ," not upon gnostic escapism or ascetic withdrawal or theological isolation and insulation. Paul opposed what he saw to be alternative gospels. One may consider different aspects of life in Christ that characterize transformational living. The focus is upon the Christian imperative inherent in the Gospel of God.

The key to Paul's thinking with regard to daily conduct is the motif of love. The believer lives on the basis of God's love (grace) and is called to the task of love in everyday relationships. Love is the substance of the "law of Christ" (Gal 6:2), as well as the well-known summary of substance in terms of the Law of Moses (cf. Rom 13:8–10; Gal 5:14). Christians are bound in love *precisely* because that is the expression of God's redemptive activity in Christ and Christ's own self-sacrificial obedience unto death for the sake of others (1 Thess 3:12; 4:10; Phil 1:9; 2 Cor 8:7; cf. 2 Cor 2:4). Those who have their identity in God the Father and in Christ the Lord are to conduct themselves in like manner.[30]

Paul does not have a "rational standard" by which to ascertain the demands of love (God's will) in particular instances. This is a matter for the Christian to decide, although it is not a matter of situational ethics without any guiding parameters. Having faith in Christ means acknowledging that one belongs to him and not oneself. Belonging to Christ means belonging to the body of Christ, the community of those who have been redeemed and claimed by the one Lord. Belonging to Christ and the community in Christ becomes the orientation and presupposition for everything the one of faith chooses or does.[31] God's gift of love is met *in Christ*, with the concomitant expectation to extend that to one's neighbor. As one belongs to Christ, one belongs to the body of Christ. As one belongs to the body of Christ, one belongs to the vanguard of God's New Age. The cross for Paul was not what much contemporary Christianity

---

29. To realize this is to clear up a lot of common misinterpretation in passages like 1 Cor 3:16–17, where in actuality the collective body of Christians plural is representative of the temple of God.

30. Furnish, *Theology and Ethics,* 235.

31. Furnish, *Theology and Ethics,* 237.

has made it to be. Its significance for Paul was other than what is generally assumed by much atonement theory, for example.

The cross came to be understood by Paul as a boundary-shattering event, *precisely because of the resurrection and the resultant Lordship of Christ*. God's power had been demonstrated in an event that traditionally heralded weakness, but which now trumpeted divine power revealed eschatologically. Christ's shameful death on a Roman cross (a common occurrence) was transformed into a symbol of divine victory that became a paradigm for Christian living. The example of Christ set forth in 1 Corinthians suggests a selfless death to those inured with status-based divisions. One gains a fuller appreciation of the body of Christ (1 Cor 11:17—12:31), which is a manifestation of the new covenant in Christ's blood (1 Cor 11:25). Faithful identification with Christ in his salvific work opposes more fundamental ethnic, social, and sexual boundaries (Gal 3:26; cf. 3:27–29; Eph 2:11–22).

The cross enables new life and points beyond itself to disclose the norms of life that inaugurate the new era. The salvific will of God is realized through obedience, even if it means a cross.[32] Only the power of God can free human beings from the bondage to the powers of this Age. Paul affirms, *that as an event of grace*, the redeeming, reconciling, rectifying power of God has broken all the powers of the Present Evil Age in the death *and* resurrection of Christ. The event of grace has the appearance of weakness evident in common Roman execution on a cross, when by the grace of God it becomes an event of power whereby one who shares in Christ's death and resurrection is released from slavery to Sin/sin.[33] It is God's love that calls forth God's power, accomplishes his grace, and extends God's peace. Grace and peace are realized by living out the Gospel of God in a cruciform imperative.

It was Paul's appreciation of the continuing power of Sin and Death in the face of a continuing weakness of the flesh that provided Paul with a theological foundation for an approach of Christian living. Paul's ethic was marked by eschatological tension that involved continuing renewed commitment to God. Inaugurative eschatology would surely become fully realized in Christ (1 Cor 15:24–28). Paul lived and worked as an apostle with that hope and expectation.

God's victory had been won and demonstrated in Christ's resurrection. The Coming Age had been demonstrated by sure inauguration, one that marked the ultimate defeat of Sin and Death. The powers of the Present Evil Age had been conquered, but they were not yet vanquished. Until Paul gained his share of Christ's resurrection, Paul's ongoing conformation was conformation to Christ's death through sufferings on a daily basis, i.e., through living out a cross imperative, as he followed a risen Lord in the Spirit, as he found himself living "in Christ." To live "in Christ," perhaps Paul's most frequent phrase, is to live out of the Gospel of God.

32. Green, "Death of Christ," 209.

33. Furnish, *Theology and Ethics*, 180.

Manifestation of God's eschatological righteousness on the part of those in Christ, the church, will involve suffering and "death" just as it did for Jesus. That becomes a part of the vocation of the new people of God. As Hays suggests, those who live at the collision point of the Two Ages "live under the sign of the cross."[34] Indeed, the present Age of Transformation is the time of an imperative cross. That is so because the cross is the transformative sign of God's eschatological victory in Christ, for the powers that became signified by cross-action have been defeated by Christ's obedience even unto death and by God's triumph in the resurrection. There is a transformation of symbolic images. The cross which formerly meant a shameful, excruciating death now becomes an avenue unto life in God's hands and the visible symbol of the entire Christ event.

Hays is precisely correct when he affirms that, for Paul, Jesus's death on the cross is "an act of loving, self-sacrificial obedience that becomes paradigmatic for the obedience of all who are in Christ."[35] While Hays's focus is upon New Testament ethics, this aspect of Paul's interpretation of the cross is not just determinative for Paul's understanding of the church's ethical responsibility. It *is* Paul's *major* understanding of the cross, specifically speaking. The common popular view of "Jesus died for my/our sins" denies this major Pauline emphasis, even as it ignores or denies a gospel imperative.

The emphasis in Jesus's death on the cross effectively falls upon his own sacrificial act. Jesus gave himself (cf. Gal 1:3–4; 2:21). Seen as a paradigm, Paul himself has been "crucified with Christ" (Gal 2:19), as he has lived out a suffering apostleship. The cross becomes for Paul a symbol, a model, a paradigm, a foundation for faith and for his own apostleship. While not denying the uniqueness of Christ's death on the cross in terms of its eschatological significance, it does become a metaphorical paradigm for how Christians are to live and die. The cross becomes the paradigm for the life of faith lived in obedience to the one true God, who himself is righteous and who makes righteous (rectifies) the one who is in Christ Jesus, the one who himself exhibits faithful obedience at whatever cost (Rom 3:26). Paul has given himself as a sacrificial offering to God in the fulfilment of his call, even as he encourages those in Christ to do the same (cf. Rom 12:1–2).

There is a deep connection between the christological meaning of the cross and Christian ethics that is tied to the Pauline concept of "being in Christ." The faithfulness of Christ is demonstrated in his self-giving love revealed and realized in the cross. The faithfulness of God is demonstrated in his self-affirming love revealed and realized in the resurrection of Jesus. It is the resurrection that Paul hopes to attain (Phil 3:12–16; 1:21–23), although the mode of attainment is through a cruciform existence (Gal 2:19–20), or, shall we say, a cruciform imperative. Paradoxically, it is a cruciform imperative that marks the visible accomplishment of God's love and power, grace and peace. As it was in Christ, so it is now in God's people in Christ through the gift of the Spirit.

34. Hays, *Moral Vision*, 25.
35. Hays, *Moral Vision*, 27.

All those in Christ take upon themselves the same kind of obedience to God presented in the life of Christ, which was ultimately expressed in his death (Phil 2:5–11). Paul's own apostolic ministry represented a participation in the suffering of Christ, such that he understood his own weakness and suffering to be the representative of the suffering of Christ. To suffer with Christ, and to be united with him in a "death" like his, heralds also being united with him in a resurrection like his (Rom 6:.4–5, 8). This was true for Paul, as well as for Christians. This is the reason Paul as an apostle of God in Christ could encourage those in his churches to imitate him. It was not Paul's arrogance, but rather his submission to a cross imperative.

Social and Civil Relationships

Sacrificial and sacramental covenant living is transformational living that reforms all relationships to one degree or another, including social and civil relationships. The conception of salvation as an individual matter between man and God, apart from social relationships, is utterly foreign to Paul's preaching. The individual does not stand apart from the whole people of God nor from the world. The call to people to belong to their Lord is at the same time a call to belong to one another, to belong to the collective body of Christ. It is a call to live in the world in a way that is different from the world—to bear fruit of the Spirit, rather than to exhibit what Paul terms "works of the flesh" (cf. Gal 5:19–26).

Natural Relationships

All natural relationships of social and civil nature have been transformed in Christ. The playing field of customary social distinctions has been leveled through God's eschatological action of reconciliation in Christ. Reconciliation has occurred not only on a vertical plane, in terms of relationship with God, but also upon a horizontal plane. Reconciliation demands not only a right relationship with God, but also with all of those who are in Christ—"for as many of you who were baptized unto Christ, you have clothed yourselves with Christ. One is not Jew or Greek, one is not slave or free, one is not male and female; for *you* are all one in Christ Jesus" (Gal 3:27–28). Such relationship together in Christ results in each one individually and collectively being of the seed of Abraham, and thus heirs of God's promise and children of God through faith in Christ Jesus (Gal 3:26, 29).

Individual identities have been changed. Paul acknowledges that among those in the Corinthian church were those who had been very immoral persons—fornicators with prostitutes, idolaters, adulterers, those who had played homosexual roles, thieves, greedy coveters, drunkards, slanderers, those who seize by violence (1 Cor 6:9–10). All of these are identified as ἄδικοι, those who are unjust or evil, those who are unrectified. As framed by an *inclusio*, none of these will inherit the kingdom of

God. Yet here is Paul's point: "Indeed, some of you were these things; but you were cleansed, but you were set apart as sacred to God, but you were put in a right relationship with God by the name of the Lord Jesus Christ and by the Spirit of our God" (1 Cor 6:11).

As Paul addresses those who were gentiles in the Ephesian context, he affirms they were once dead in trespasses and sins, being subject to the rulers and authorities of this Age. In fact Paul dares to speak in the first person plural to affirm that "we all" were by nature children of wrath (Eph 2:1–3). Yet with sustained argument, Paul stresses the richness of God's mercy and grace and the greatness of God's love, such that God made us alive together in Christ. We have been saved by God's grace and kindness, given as a divine gift and received through faith. In this, we have no boast, because we are God's creation (ποίημα), having been created in Christ Jesus to walk in good works prepared by God beforehand (Eph 2:4–10). Together, along with Jewish Christians, gentile Christians are called to live out of a cruciform imperative.

Paul thus encourages these gentile Christians to remember the time when they had been without Christ and alienated from the commonwealth of Israel, a time when they were strangers to the covenants of promise and were living in the world without hope. Paul actually calls them ἄθεοι ("atheists"). Paul's "But now in Christ Jesus" (Eph 2:13) rings out loudly in the context, as the dividing wall of hostility and the Law of commandments in ordinances (δόγμασιν) have been set aside and are no longer impediments. One new human being has been created in the place where there had been two (Jew and gentile). Both have been reconciled to God in one body through the cross, the sign and symbol of the Gospel "in Christ." Gentiles are no longer strangers and aliens, but rather are now fellow-citizens and members of the household of God. Together with Jewish Christians, they are now a holy temple in the Lord (Eph 2:11–22).

Because of this, gentile Christians are to live in ways other than those by which the gentiles live. They are no longer to live with darkened minds, alienated from God. They have a new nature in Christ, marked by a renewed spirit in their minds. Paul calls upon them to live according to their new nature (Eph 4:17–24). As those who have come from darkness to light, they are to conduct themselves as wise men, as God's children, as imitators of God (Eph 5:1–20).

Their new identity and new lifestyle is to have transformative effect upon their interpersonal relationships. They are to be subject to one another out of reverence for Christ (Eph 5:21). The relationships between wives and husbands, children and parents, and slaves and masters are transformed in the light of relationship with Christ (Eph 5:22—6:9). In each instance, Paul addresses the weaker party of that societal culture first and places greater responsibility upon the stronger party. In the corresponding parallel material in Colossians, Paul commends a single imperative to each party of the paired relationships. The only exception is the more extended advice given to slaves (Col 3:22–25). Otherwise, wives are to be subject to their husbands, husbands are to love their wives, children are to obey their parents, fathers are not to provoke their children, and masters are to treat their slaves justly and fairly (cf. Col 3:18—4:1).

The transforming element, however, in all of these natural relationships is that they are all now governed by being *in the Lord* (Col 3:17–18, 20, 22, 24; 4:1). There is to be forbearance (Col 3:13). One is bound by the peace of Christ (Col 3:15), the word of Christ (Col 3:16), and identity in Christ (Col 3:17). The "Lord" or "Christ" is mentioned no less than ten times in Col 3:13–24, with an additional allusion to "Master" in Col 4:1, as Paul addresses masters. The Colossians have "died" and have been "raised" with Christ, such that their lives are hidden with Christ in God (Col 3:1–3). The Spirit now directs their ways.

Paul acknowledges that the testimony of Christ has been confirmed among the Corinthians, such that they are not lacking in any spiritual gift (1 Cor 1:6–7). Christ is the transforming wisdom and power of God for those called by the Gospel, whether Jew or Greek (1 Cor 1:24). Paul encourages them to examine their call and what they have become in Christ, for not many were wise or powerful or of noble birth according to worldly standards (1 Cor 1:26–29). They now have wisdom, righteousness, sanctification, and redemption available in Christ (1 Cor 1:30).

The spiritualist problem at Corinth, however, was that the Corinthians were not living out their identity in Christ. Some saw themselves as "spiritual" people, but in reality they were behaving as "fleshly" people (1 Cor 1:11–13; 3:1–4). There was factionalism, pagan immorality, and a lack of unified love and concern for one another. There was arrogance associated with spiritual gifts, which was manifested in terms of disruptive and misplaced worship. There was a lack of concern for those who might be weaker in faith, as manifested by eating meat sacrificed to idol gods even in the context of an idol temple. There was pride exhibited over the exercise of particular spiritual gifts. There was denial of the reality of the resurrection, apparently on the basis of other philosophical "wisdom" characteristic of Hellenistic thought. All of these things are manifested in the letter of 1 Corinthians.

Paul makes use of his "body" analogy to encourage Christian living. He makes use of this analogy in the Corinthian letter in conjunction with the distribution of spiritual gifts *and* spiritual identity in Christ. All Christians—Jews and Greeks, slaves and free—are characterized by the eschatological gift of the Spirit. The whole body is to function as a single unity, not as a collection of individual organs. There is to be no discord in the body of the church, but rather individual members are to care for one another. The suffering or honoring of one means the suffering or the joy of all (1 Cor 12:12–26). As Christians live together in the one body of Christ, they are to make love their aim (1 Cor 14:1). Love, rather than pride over an individual spiritual gift is characteristic of one who is mature in Christ (1 Cor 14:20), not those who are "babes." Everything done in worship should be done for the edification of the church (1 Cor 14:26).

Paul encourages the Roman Christians to think with sober judgment, especially in terms of self-evaluation. All are individually members of the one body of Christ, and thus members of one another, even though their gifts may vary according to the grace of God given to each (Rom 12:3–8). Paul offers a string of paraenetic exhortations under the rubric of practicing a genuine love (Rom 12:9–21). One who practices such love overcomes the evil of the Present Evil Age with good. This includes respect for divinely appointed governing authorities. Paul recognizes that the abiding commandments of the Law are summed up in terms of love of neighbor (Rom 13:8–9). Paul's encouragement is couched in the context of the nearness of the eschatological hour of fulfilment, such that one should live out of the fullness of Christ's Lordship (Rom 13:11–14).

Although Paul places himself among those who are spiritually mature and strong (Rom 15:1; cf. Phil 3:14–17), he exhibits a deep and caring concern for the spiritually weak and immature. A more mature Christian is not to become a stumbling block for one's weaker, less mature brethren (Rom 14:1—15.1). Paul's citation of Ps 69:9b in Rom 15:3 is an allusion to the passion of Jesus. The contextual discussion draws the point of comparison in the voluntary surrender of personal prerogatives for the sake of others. One should walk in love and not for the sake of food cause the ruin of one for whom Christ died (cf. Rom 14:15). Those who make up the body of Christ are to live in harmony and accord with one another, that God the Father of the Lord Jesus Christ may be glorified (Rom 15:5–7; Eph 1:6, 12, 14).

The customary distinctions of Jew and gentile have been set aside in Christ, such that God's truthfulness and promises made to the patriarchs might be confirmed (Rom 15:9–12). The gentiles have now become a part of God's eschatological people. Those in Christ, both Jew and gentile, abound in hope through the power of the Spirit of the God of hope (Rom 15:15).

Subjection to Civil Authority

Romans 13:1–7 is Paul's most important treatment of what the attitude of Christians should be toward civil authorities.[36] When one looks at the context of the passage, Paul offers a paraenetic perspective on Christian living (Rom 12:9–21), whereby Christian love is to be expressed without exhibition of hypocrisy, with the encouragement to overcome evil with good rather than being overcome by evil (Rom 12:21). Following Rom 13:1–7, Paul returns to other paraenetic exhortation encouraging love as the

36. The present writer does not accept 1 Timothy and Titus as Pauline. One may observe a trajectory subsequent to and based upon Paul and developing Christian positions regarding subjection to rulers in 1 Tim 2:1–4 and Titus 3:1. The passage in Timothy basically encourages prayer in behalf of rulers, while that in Titus enjoins obedient submission. It is a point often forgotten or seldom realized, namely that Paul lived out his whole life and ministry under the Julio-Claudian dynasty of Rome. The author of 1 Timothy and Titus, if deuteropauline, lived under a different dynasty, that of the Flavians or the Antonines.

fulfilling of the Law (Rom 13:8–10). He also offers a reminder of the eschatological hour, suggesting that the eschatological hour has drawn very near.

Thereby, with hortatory subjunctive, Paul encourages the Roman Christians, "Let us conduct ourselves respectably as in the day" (Rom 13:13). With paraenetic imperative, he encourages the Roman Christians to be clothed with the Lord Jesus Christ and to make no provision "for the flesh, unto gratification of passions" (Rom 13:14). For Paul, the "night" was far gone, the "day" was at hand, such that again with hortatory subjunctive Paul encourages the laying aside of works of darkness in order to be clothed with the "weapons" (ὅπλα) of light (Rom 13:12).

The contextual setting does not change the fact that what he says in Rom 13:1–7 is not directly tied to the issue of personal retaliation presented immediately before or to future eschatological expectation that follows the passage. There is a connection with genuine love and holding fast to what is good (Rom 12:9). On the basis of what he says, there is a working out of the liturgical service of God in everyday life as tied to the transformative sacrificial service called for in Rom 12:1–2. Unavoidably in that first century world, the service of God and obedience to God involved submission of oneself to the order established by God. Paul saw the rule of authorities established by God as a part of that order. He offered the reminder that rulers were God's servants unto good and were not a threat to those who did good, but only to those who did evil (Rom 13:2–4). In order to avoid God's wrath upon disobedience to his will through divinely-appointed authorities, as well as for the sake of one's conscience, one should pay required taxes and offer respect and honor to whom it should be due (Rom 13:5–7).

The fundamental definition of Paul's position rests in his understanding of civil authority being established by God as a means of order that calls for respect and obedience. In the end, Paul produces no other ground for obedience to civil authority than that the authority is ordained by God. However, the church should neither give "blind" obedience to every existing governmental power as "inviolable and sacrosanct" nor "withdraw itself prematurely from this order appointed by God. . . ."[37] As Paul writes Romans, he has experienced local civic authorities and provincial Roman authorities. He had not yet experienced the first hand might of Rome *in Rome itself*. It should be remembered that Paul writes to Christians *in Rome* in the early and "good years" of young Nero's reign. The change of emperors at the time Paul wrote (56 CE) may well have been deemed to be a good thing by Paul, in view of the fact the earlier Edict of Claudius that had banished Jews and Christians was no longer in force.

Submission to governmental authority may be generally seen as a part of Christian living as related to everyday reality of life, as obedient service to God (Rom 12:1–2). Paul speaks generally throughout Rom 12–14, such that particular governing authorities are not in view. Paul had been persecuted by governing authorities, although he had also been aided by them. He does not seek to define unseen and

---

37. Ridderbos, *Theology*, 324.

undetermined boundaries with *a priori* precision. However, he does write to *Roman* Christians living in the capital city of the Roman Empire. According to Acts 18, Paul first encountered Priscilla and Aquila as refugees of Claudius's Edict against disorder in Rome. The case against Paul brought by the Jews in Corinth was dismissed by Gallio, the Roman governor. There appears to be no reason to doubt the basic historicity of the Acts account, even though one should take Lukan redaction into account.

At the time Paul wrote Romans, his mission had been more facilitated by the "governing authorities" than it had been hindered. He also hopes for support of the Roman church/es in a subsequent ministry to Spain (Rom 15:24). Paul would have had a firsthand awareness of Claudius's banishment of Aquila and Priscilla. There may have been a subconscious concern on Paul's part that the Roman church/es remain on the side of order and not disorder. Paul would then be able to receive the support for which he hoped, such that no new edict of banishment be forthcoming from the new Roman emperor, Nero, following upon the now expired Edict of Claudius.

It should go without saying that Paul does not offer a fully developed "theology of church and state," that in fact, modern notions of the "state" would be foreign to Paul. All that Paul adduces for obedience to the civil authorities of his day is that the ground of their authority is currently ordained by God. And, underlying what Paul wrote, there would stand Paul's conviction of the eschatological hour. Paul was not a revolutionary zealot, as would be seen in Judea in 66–70 CE, even though he proclaimed a revolutionary Gospel that would soon be marked by the Telos and ultimate order of God's rule. Does Paul offer a general statement for all legitimate authorities for all time? Does Paul offer a general statement about the Roman Empire, generally speaking, and specifically, does he give a statement pertaining to the time of a new emperor (Nero) upon the throne? N. T. Wright reminds that the more specific one makes the passage, the easier it is to "relativize it and declare it irrelevant to other times and places."[38] Contextually, Paul suggests that God wants order even in the Present Evil Age, that he does not want chaos to reign. Justice is not served by private vengeance or by an overly zealous, over realized or overreaching eschatology or "holy anarchy." The overthrow of pagan power is not realized by Christians who might preemptively seek to become agents of revolutionary anarchy.[39]

Indeed, should this be Paul's underlying supposition, the wisdom of such a view would be proven correct in the face of the disastrous Jewish-Roman War of 66–73 CE, which was marked by the destruction of the temple and destruction of Jerusalem. Christians conquer, according to Paul, not by the sword but by the cross. It is God, not humankind, who is able to transform apparent defeat into sure victory. It is God who

---

38. Wright, "Letter to the Romans," 717. In the light of coherence and contingency, there is nothing wrong with honestly recognizing relativity and even irrelevance when it may truly be apparent. Paul did not write "theology" for "all times and places."

39. Wright, "Letter to the Romans," 719. Such a view might suggest that Paul would not have supported the Jewish revolt of 66–70 CE.

is able to transform an instrument of abuse and shame and state terror—namely, the cross—into a symbol of eschatological living and victory. It is God who must and who will deal with all powers and authorities through the risen Lord. While on the one hand God may establish human authority, on the other hand human authority under the power of evil may seek to usurp the authority of God. And, in the light of the Telos, all human authority is temporary.

While what Paul does say is limited, Rom 13:1–7 does effectively represent an undermining of totalitarianism and self-divinizing of arrogant human rulers. Rulers are not themselves divine, but rather rule only by authority instituted by God. Paul does not subscribe to the Roman gospel of a divine emperor. And given Paul's eschatological outlook ("you know what hour it is," Rom 13:11), their rule is only a temporary one meant to maintain order until the fulfilment of the kingdom of God in the Parousia and the Telos. Until that time, the church must live a life of balanced eschatological outlook as an "outpost of the commonwealth of heaven" (cf. Phil 3:20). If the kingdom of God is characterized by love, righteousness, joy, and peace in the Spirit, then it will not be realized by chaos, vengeance, violence, "holy anarchy," or hatred.[40] Paradoxically, it will be achieved by a cruciform existence, by a cruciform imperative, for it is a kingdom of grace and peace lived in hope.

Some form of civic authority which offers at least some order, regulation, and authoritative structure would appear to be a necessary part of any ordered society and an orderly world. Legitimate human authority on the part of rulers, however, is limited by the will and pleasure of God, who has instituted such authority—generally speaking, although not necessarily specifically speaking. Romans was written prior to Paul's final visit to Jerusalem. It would be interesting to see Paul's expressed thought after he had traveled to Rome as a prisoner and after he had appeared before Caesar's tribunal. It would also be interesting to hear Paul's perspectives on the subject, had he lived through the Jewish-Roman War and the persecutions under Nero and Domitian. In Paul's world of the mid-fifties CE, one might avail oneself of Caesar's justice, freedom, and peace. Had he lived, Paul may not have found that to be true after 70 CE. However, one who is "in Christ" should understand the limited rule and role of earthly authorities, which were and are at best penultimate. Ultimate authority rests only in God—with whom there is a greater equity, justice, freedom, and peace to be experienced.

An Extended Conclusion

The "cross" became the symbolic shorthand for the entire Gospel of God for Paul and other early Christians. Paul could proclaim the gospel, but Christians could only carry the victory of Jesus into the entire world as they took up Jesus's cross after him.[41]

40. Cf. Wright, "Letter to the Romans," 719–20.

41. Käsemann, *Perspectives on Paul*, 58.

Käsemann thus suggests that the cross was not a historically unique event for Paul. Indeed, the cross of Jesus in one sense was not unique, for many people were crucified in the first century, including Peter according to church tradition. The cross of Jesus was an *eschatologically* unique event, made eschatologically unique as a result of the resurrection, which continued to have its effect.

It is only through the proclamation of the cross that the Christian faith remains Gospel. It is through *that* proclamation that grace, promise, and covenant living remain, as Jesus's death remains present, not just in memory but in celebration and in commitment. The cross defines *Christian* living.[42] Indeed, it is through living a cruciform existence that one remains "in Christ," the crucified and resurrected one. Discipleship (a word not used by Paul) is following the one who was crucified into the whole world and living out the results of the Gospel of God in the period between the resurrection and the Parousia/Telos.

Divine Imperative

The "cross" was an imperative for Jesus, in the light of his own faithfulness and obedience to God the Father. His faithfulness and obedience were born out of his own willingness, not out of a divine sentence or necessity. The cross was both an historical reality and an imperative for living in Paul's understanding. Faithfulness underscored the nature of the cross for both Jesus and Paul. So, also, is there a cross-imperative for the Christian, likewise born of faithfulness and obedience characterized by willingness, now informed by the presence of the Spirit and the beckoning of a risen Lord.

Paul's "ethic," then, does not proceed from an evaluation of one's capabilities but from a recognition of the divine imperative. The Christian's new life in the Spirit represents both redemption and reconciliation, for until one is freed from malignant powers, one cannot be reconciled, nor can one fully experience new life. Where the command is heard, the power to obey is also given and received (Phil 2:12–13). This is what is meant by being "led by the Spirit" (Rom 8:14; Gal 5:18) and by "living" and "walking" by the Spirit (Rom 8:4–5; Gal 5:16, 25; cf. 2 Cor 3:6). In Paul's view, the uniqueness of the new life in Christ consists of the nature and power of the Gospel whereby one has been redeemed from Sin and Death, as one is re-created for righteousness and life. It does not consist in self-chosen concrete actions. It is not a matter first of all of self-*reformation*, but rather of *redemption, rectification*, and *reconciliation* on the basis of divine action and claim.

Martin Luther looms large and dominating in all subsequent reflection on the cross after the time of the Reformation. In modern times and scholarship, the work of Ernst Käsemann, who was a Lutheran, is significant as well. The perspectives of neither one are final. Nor are the perspectives of John Calvin. Christ as crucified and

---

42. Cf. Käsemann, *Perspectives on Paul*, 59.

Christ as Lord cannot be turned into an object, as something to be accounted for as a Christian ideology. "Faith" is not *believing* a doctrinal listing. That would be one way to live as an enemy of the cross of Christ. Rather, faith has to do with obedience and personal relationship that comes to fullest expression precisely in a cross imperative and a cruciform existence.[43]

When the "facts of redemption" are moved to center stage apart from a cruciform imperative, one is simply confronted with an ideology—a soteriological *theologica gloriae* ("glory theology") apart from a *theologica crucis* ("cross theology"). Käsemann gave a warning now long ago, as he observed that Christianity has made Christ unbelievable, and has discouraged as many people as it has attracted. "Today the church's bankruptcy in all its religious activities is so obvious that we can no longer afford to identify Jesus with Christianity."[44] Indeed, there is a difference between Christianity and Christendom, as the present writer is wont to stress.

According to Käsemann, Christianity is drowning in a chaos of its own making, simply because the cross imperative has been sublimated or denied. He points to a significant problem. If the central question is "Who is Jesus?," according to Paul the answer must ever be the crucified and resurrected one. As Käsemann long ago observed, "Everything else is a distraction. We must measure ourselves against Jesus, not measure him against our churches and dogmas and devout church members." The value of churches, dogmas, and piety, as Käsemann suggests, rests entirely on the extent to which they "point away from themselves and call us to follow Jesus as Lord."[45] This is an astounding statement that is thoroughly in keeping with Pauline emphases. We must allow the Gospel to remake us, rather than remaking the "Gospel" in our own image according to our liking. The Gospel is not something to be codified in doctrinal liturgy, but something to be lived in Christ. There are a lot of distractions in Christendom today. And, substitutions!

As a rehabilitated image, the cross has greatest significance at the point of the imperative, as one follows in the train of the Lordship of Christ. By contrast, theological arguments over the interpretation of the crucifixion of Jesus as indicative have resulted in disunity of the body of Christ on the basis of theological dogmas. We have simply missed Paul's emphasis of the cross as imperative under the Lordship of Christ. Or, we have chosen to ignore or deny it. While Käsemann objected to an ideology of a *theologia gloriae* apart from a *theologia crucis*, one may suggest that a lot of contemporary theology represents an ideology of a *theologia crucis* of varied atonement doctrines. Paradoxically perhaps, such a focus loses sight of God's victory in Christ as a *theologia crucis*, for Jesus "paid it all" without cost to the believer. The imperative is

---

43. See the work of Gorman on "cruciformity."

44. Käsemann, *Perspectives on Paul*, 53. This is an interesting comment, given its date of writing a half century or more ago. Have things improved since?

45. Käsemann, *Perspectives on Paul*, 53.

robbed of its power. And a *theologia crucis* becomes the popular message of a costless theological or ideological "glory gospel."

The cross is indeed a complex symbol in the thought-world of Paul. It is a symbol of redemption from the "curse of the Law" (Gal 3:13), of the demonstration of God's righteousness (Rom 3:24–26) and of God's love (Rom 5:8). As Hays suggests, "It is the mystery that confutes human wisdom and shames human power (1 Cor. 1:21–31)."[46] It is a symbol marked by a rebirth of images in the light of the Gospel. It was an object of shame which God turned into exaltation and victory. It represents victory over the malignant powers that plague the whole creation. It is all of these things, but it would be none of those things apart from the resurrection.

The power of the cross is only intelligible in the light of Christ's resurrection. Contrary to much contemporary emphasis, Paul does not preach only "Christ crucified" (cf. 1 Cor 2:2), but Jesus as "Christ" and as "Lord." Every Pauline salutation is a reminder of the resurrection (cf. 1 Cor 1:3, for example). Both the sovereignty and faithfulness of God, as well as his love, is demonstrated in the resurrection of Jesus. God's victory over the powers of the Present Evil Age, and especially the conquest of Sin and Death (cf. 1 Cor 15:54–57), is to be found in the resurrection. There is power in the cross because the one who was crucified there was raised as *Lord* by the power of God (cf. 1 Cor 2:8). The one who died is the one raised as Lord (1 Cor 11:26). Paradoxically, perhaps, it points to the power of God who raises the dead (2 Cor 1:9). For Paul, *that God* had proven himself trustworthy in deliverance from death and would do so in the future for those "in Christ" (2 Cor 1:10). The cross is not held up as heroic example or as a substitutionary offering, but rather as the gateway to eschatological living.

For Paul, the death and resurrection of Christ mark the beginning of a new epoch that reaches forward to the time of Christ's Parousia and Telos. The reality of the new epoch fundamentally changes the way one understands life in the present. The awareness that Christ's death and resurrection has instituted a new epoch enables one to envision God's new life in contrast to former ways of life. It enables one to embrace the power of God inherent in the resurrection.[47] Believers are motivated to act in gratitude for deliverance from slavery to Sin.

However, recognition of the new epoch means life in the present is determined by the cross. One effect of the cross is the possibility of a restored humanity—restored in terms of relationships to God, to itself, and to all creation. Why? Because as Paul suggests, one dies with Christ to Sin, Law, and flesh. For Paul, "cross" always points the way to resurrection and new creation—what was deemed to be true *by looking back* at Jesus's cross.

What was true for Jesus's cross looking back will also be true for the Christian's cross moving forward. For Paul, the cross is a chiastic symbol of reality. Just as Jesus's cross led to his resurrection, so the Christian's cross will lead to resurrection. It bears

---

46. Hays, *Moral Vision*, 27.

47. Green, "Death of Christ," 208.

repeating: for Paul, "cross" always points the way to resurrection and new creation. Yet, the definition of existence put forward by sinful humanity has been radically altered, because it has been redefined in terms of the image of its cross, both in terms of indicative and imperative. When that happens, both the theology and life of the church is reshaped.

As Cousar indicates, "The church whose theology is shaped by the message of the cross must itself take on a cruciform life if its theology is to carry credibility."[48] However, by changing out Paul's emphasis upon a cruciform imperative for a portrayal of the cross of Jesus as an ideological indicative of a free, individualistic salvation with no personal cost, then *Paul's* emphasis has been lost. This means that the entire focus of Christian reality and Christian living has been misconstrued—at least as Paul understood it. One may debate with Paul, one may set Paul aside in favor of theological or ideological alternatives. That is one's choice and personal alternative. But then, that raises the issue of "scripture" and interpretation. There may be different understandings of the Gospel. However, what one should not do is to offer an alternative substitute and then call that "Paul."

As Paul stresses freedom from Sin, he mentions Christ's resurrection as an event in sequence with his death (cf. Rom 6:4–5, 8–9). This is in accordance with the early kerygma set forth in 1 Cor 15:3–4, which occurs as a preface to Paul's discussion of resurrection given in response to a question posed by the Corinthians. Where Jesus's death or resurrection is mentioned, there is the presumption of the other. The power of Christian interpretation of the crucifixion is only afforded through association with the resurrection (1 Cor 1:18–25). Paul's conception of the Gospel of God extends beyond the cross to resurrection and exaltation. To limit the gospel to the beginning of the sequence is to offer a caricature and a truncated soteriological, anthropological reductionism. Yet to focus on resurrection and exaltation, apart from God's victory in the cross, is to ignore the cross imperative of Paul for all Christians.

For example, Cousar affirms that "God's presence in the cross lends credibility to God's power in the resurrection."[49] In reality, it is quite the opposite in the retrospective understanding of Paul and that of the earliest Christians. God's power in the resurrection lends credibility to God's presence in the cross event. The cross and resurrection belong together, even though one or the other can become the focal point without the other being mentioned. However, Paul's cruciform imperative is supported by the resurrection which posits a realistic hope in God's re-creative future and expresses itself in the present as a cruciformed life of believers lived in the power of the Spirit and lived by faith (2 Cor 4:10–11; 13:4).

While Paul's narrative Christology may vary from letter to letter, the letters as a whole point to Christ's obedience unto death and subsequent resurrection and

---

48. Cousar, *Theology of the Cross*, 186. Of course, on the other hand, Paul's message of the cross may be altered to match one's ideological theology.

49. Cousar, *Theology of the Cross*, 105.

exaltation as the focal point of the Gospel, with the resultant freedom from Sin and its consequences. Allusion to part of the story assumes the whole story. Repeated appeal is made to the crucifixion as the foundation and norm of the Christian *life*. Both the present writer and readers know the complete story from start to finish. Although attention may be immediately drawn to Jesus's death, one is not unaware of his resurrection.[50] Indeed, it is faith in the resurrection that enables one to come to faith in the cross of Christ as the basis of Christian living. There is quite a difference in affirming "Jesus died so I could go to heaven" and "Jesus died so I could live a Christian life." Paul subscribed to the latter but not to the former. That life involved overcoming the powers, reconciliation with God, and empowerment even in the midst of suffering, as well as the promise and hope of future resurrection. It involved rectification, redemption, reconciliation, and resurrection. It involved life in Christ.

It is never forgotten that the one who lives now as Lord is the one who was crucified. On this basis alone, one is called to a cruciform imperative as one lives under the Lordship of the crucified yet exalted Christ. However, the meaning of the cross cannot be contained in the crucial but narrow doctrinal category of "justification" or "atonement" as usually understood. God rectifies and God reconciles, creating relationship. That is his dynamic activity, which far exceeds static conceptions of divine transactionalism.

In Dunn's perspective, Paul's "theology of the cross" becomes determinative for his gospel, in his measurement of other would-be gospels. On the other hand, because of his "cross imperative," Paul measures other gospels by the living results they produce. According to Dunn, the "fulcrum point" or "the central soteriological moment" is the cross.[51] This is not the case for Paul—for Paul it is the resurrection. While Paul certainly holds the "death and resurrection" of Christ together, as has been seen, he mentions the "cross" comparatively seldom (ten times), with some usages definitely applying to the imperative and not the indicative. The "cross" becomes a shorthand way of referring to the whole Gospel, both the indicative and the imperative, both crucifixion and resurrection.

Dunn has a chapter in his theology of Paul on "Christ Crucified." In a concluding section, he suggests that it may well have been Paul who attached the "cross" so firmly to the "gospel," such that Paul's influence may have caused Mark to shape his "gospel" (Mark 1:1) so as to "climax in the cross." Many have recognized Mark as a "passion narrative with extended introduction."[52] To put it differently, while engaging in like speculation, it may be Paul who stamped the "gospel" so firmly to the "cross," in that he adopted a "cross imperative" for Christian living based upon Jesus's death and the necessity for Christians to "die" with Christ. One is also confronted with a similar cross tradition in Mark 8 and suffering tradition in Mark 10.

50. Cousar, *Theology of the Cross*, 107.

51. Dunn, *Theology of Paul*, 233.

52. Dunn, *Theology of Paul*, 232. Cf. Kähler, *So-Called Historical Jesus*, 80.

Theological Declarations

While Furnish's classic work is primarily a treatment of Pauline ethics, he focuses upon Paul's theology in terms of themes found within Paul's preaching. The broad themes are found in his chapter headings—"This Age and the Age to Come"; "The Law, Sin, and Righteousness"; "The Event of Grace: Death and Resurrection"; and "Faith, Love, and Obedience."[53] There are obviously other themes that could be pursued in Pauline theology, as any such work on Paul would demonstrate.

What is salient in Furnish's treatment is the eschatological focus of these themes and the fact that they mark eschatological realities that underpin either Paul's theology or his ethics, the indicative and the imperative of the gospel Paul proclaimed. It is Paul's eschatological gospel that he proclaims and that infuses both his theology and ethics expressed in firm convictions in the light of contingent circumstances. It is very difficult to separate and summarize the peculiarly "ethical" aspects of Paul's gospel because the indicative and imperative aspects of Paul's preaching are so vitally interrelated. Paul himself has not posed many of the questions that we ask, although elements of answers may be present implicitly or explicitly. Paul is engaged in Christian living, not in isolated reductionism for theological discussion.

As Furnish expresses it, the context and some content of Paul's exhortations are gained from the apostle's "theological" affirmations, so that "the theological declarations may already carry within themselves the moral imperatives."[54] However, it should be said that Paul's imperatives were not just "moral" imperatives; they were eschatological imperatives of divine victory in which Christians were to fully participate. The dialectic of indicative and imperative is related to the present and future for Paul. While still not fully disclosed within "this Age," those "in Christ" have "put on" Christ (Gal 3:27, declarative indicative) and are to "put on the Lord Jesus Christ" (Rom 13:14, eschatological imperative). And therein is the cross imperative.

There remains a sense of imminence of the coming of the Lord throughout Paul's ministry which heightens imperatives of ethical action in terms of love and service. Paul does not forget the eschatological hour. Eschatological anticipation based on the resurrection and exaltation of Christ thus becomes the basis of Pauline "ethics." The guarantee of the Spirit becomes the pledge of future life. There is no anticipation apart from the cross. Anticipation of the resurrection can be an encouragement to those lost in perplexity or grief, who need to recover a hopeful vision. Yet the reality of a cross imperative may curb the enthusiasm of an overly realized eschatology or the corruption of a false gospel, as well, as seen in a Corinth or a Galatia. Christian living is confirmed by the presence of the Spirit that directs the new people of God in a this-worldly orientation based upon the model of Jesus's death and the hope of resurrection.

53. Furnish, *Theology and Ethics*, 112–206.
54. Furnish, *Theology and Ethics*, 110.

Richard Hays is correct in affirming that Paul offers little information about the man Jesus, but overstates the case when he asserts Paul's references point over and over again to the cross.[55] Contrary to much Christian theology, Paul's focus is not on the cross alone but on the cross *and* resurrection. Paul's focus is not so much upon the actions of Jesus, but rather upon the action of God. Paul's focus is the Gospel of God, of which his action in Christ is the content. "Grace to all of you and peace from God the Father and the Lord Jesus Christ."

The eschatological fulfilment of the Two Ages is marked by both ambiguity and paradox, in that suffering and joy endure together in the current Age of Transformation. There is a time of cosmic conflict, although the promise of God's ultimately making things right enables the Christian community to live confidently and faithfully, especially in view of the present gift of the Spirit. The church should expect conflict and opposition, just as both Jesus and Paul experienced the same. In other words, the church should expect its own cross. The sense of imminence of the coming of the Lord heightens rather than negates the imperatives of ethical action.

Paul proclaims the redemption of all creation, not escape from material worldly reality. Interestingly, Paul seldom uses eschatological judgment as threat to motivate obedience and more characteristically points to the sanctifying work of God's Spirit. The church is God's eschatological beachhead of power in the world, to be understood within a larger cosmic and apocalyptic frame of reference.[56] That power is exercised in paradoxical and apparent weakness by the world's standards or even the standards of a worldly-church. God himself is at work to prepare Christians for the Telos. What should not be missed, however, is that the church should be the beachhead of God's grace and peace now let loose in the world as a result of and reality of the Christ-event.

Regardless of his underlying intentional theology, Käsemann's comment is insightful. For Paul,

> Jesus' glory consists in the fact that he makes his earthly disciples willing and able to take up the cross after him; and the glory of the church and of the Christian life is that they are thought worthy to praise the one who was crucified as the power and wisdom of God, to seek salvation in him alone and to turn their existence into the service of God under the token of Golgotha. Here the theology of the resurrection is a chapter in the theology of the cross.[57]

In terms of positions taken in the current work, a theology of the resurrection has its focus in the indicative while a theology of the cross has stronger alignment with the imperative. They are, however, not in competition with each other. Together, they constitute "chapters" in the Gospel of God.

---

55. Hays, *Moral Vision*, 27.

56. Hays, *Moral Vision*, 26–27.

57. Käsemann, *Perspectives on Paul*, 59.

With alternative focus compared with Käsemann's statement, the resurrection is a chapter in the Gospel of God. The obedience of Jesus that led to a cross-death and the actions of the rulers and powers of this Age become the prelude for subsequent divine activity. All the more is this the case in view of the fact that the Christian's resurrection becomes a chapter of fulfilment following upon a cruciform imperative. So, also, is soteriology a chapter in a larger theology of divine victory in Christ, i.e., the Gospel of God.

Käsemann and others have viewed the cross as having priority over all other events in salvation history. The pre-Pauline tradition (1 Cor 15:3–4) is said to present cross and resurrection as events in a sequence. Paul is said to have reversed this understanding, making the cross to be the central focal point. However, it is not that the resurrection is a chapter in the theology of the cross, but if one chooses to use that analogy, both cross and resurrection are "chapters" in the narrative theology of the "Gospel of God." As McGrath states, those in Christ must first pass through "the shadow of the cross" before they share in the fullness of resurrection life. That shadow of the cross falls upon the entire range of Christian living.[58]

Believers are participants in the death of Christ on the cross according to Paul—they *shall be* participants in his resurrection. One is present reality, the other is future hope. Yet one may argue that it is the future hope (and the past reality of Christ's resurrection) that makes sense of a present crucifix life. Because believers are participants in the cross (imperative), they shall be participants in the resurrection. At present, there is a resurrection hope which is current even in suffering. And, *that* resurrection hope is sustained through faithfulness.

Above all, it is in Christ's death *and* resurrection that God's power is manifested (Rom 4:17). Paul carefully chooses Abraham's example as a paradigm of faith that trusts that God can bring life out of death. Abraham, being advanced in age, was as "good as dead" when God fulfilled his promise by giving him a son. Now, in the eschatological hour, Paul's fundamental conception of faith is marked by a full participation in the re-creative and redemptive power of God seen in Christ's death and resurrection. Primary in Paul's thought is faith as obedience. The obedience character of faith defines it in terms of the believer's participation in both Christ's death and resurrection. To embrace Paul's metaphor, this becomes a "walking in newness of life" (Rom. 6:4) in terms of both cruciform death and resurrection.[59]

The example of Christ is given in terms of a crucifix life of obedience (Phil 2:5). This marks an eschatological dimension beyond Abraham, necessary to overcome the tyrannical powers of Sin and Death. Living "in Christ" involves living "after Christ," i.e., living out a cross-type obedience. This, however, is only possible in the light of God's Gospel in the Christ event. It is no longer "faith as usual," but eschatological hope and trust in the operative power of God in the light of Christ's death *and* resurrection.

58. McGrath, "Theology of the Cross," 195.

59. Cf. Furnish, *Theology and Ethics,* 184–85.

Power of Obedience

The Christian's obedience is inseparable from the event of God's grace which makes it possible. The Christian already has a new life because he/she already has a new Lord, but the Lord exercises his power redemptively and not tyrannically. Paul does not equate obedience with the performance of "righteous deeds" moralistically or legalistically conceived. Knox mentions two kinds of "goodness"—that of the Law and that of the Spirit.[60] Legal goodness is sterile, and in the end, has no relational life. On the other hand, the goodness effected by the Spirit is God's goodness—it is God's gift, it is God's sacrament and not our achievement.

As Furnish suggests, righteousness is the presupposition of obedience and not its goal.[61] That it may be both, however, is not prohibited. Righteousness or rectification is the power of God in whose service one stands, not in *one's own* power to "do." Righteousness is God's rectifying power at work. It is *received* by the believer who gives oneself totally to the Lord. It is God's rectification action. "Righteousness" is not first of all a quality that adheres to God or man, but it is the activity of being right and acting right. In God's case, he acts right because he is right. In man's case, it describes one's reconciled relationship to God. Righteousness can only be known and demonstrated in relationship. Otherwise, it is static dogma. Insofar as the commandments of the Law are in accord with the meaning of God's grace as it has been revealed in Christ, they are still binding upon the believer. In Rom 13:8–10 and Gal 5:13–14 the Law's relevance for the Christian is defined in terms of its command to love the neighbor. If one is truly "in Christ," one already loves God. Love of neighbor thus fulfils the twofold summons of Torah.

However, it is not the Christian as a *performer* or *achiever* who fulfills the Law. "A person of faith" understood as a "religious person," is the exact opposite of what Paul means. This would be the equivalent of one who trusted in one's own piety or religious works (e.g., the Law). This was a fault of the Nomistic Evangelists, who according to Paul, proclaimed an alternative gospel. Rather, the Gospel is fulfilled by the power of God active as love in the life of the believer. Romans 13:8–10 and Gal 5:13–14 presuppose that the Law has no value as a norm independent of the believer's new life in Christ, under the dominion of grace and the control of love. The Law's commandments have meaning and force insofar as they express the commandment to love both God and neighbor. Furnish affirms that in the vocabulary of Pauline theology, "faith is obedience, and obedience is love."[62] Perhaps to re-phrase, that means "faith is love"—love of God, of Christ, of neighbor. As Stewart would eloquently suggest, life becomes "lyrical."

---

60. Knox, *Chapters,* 129.

61. Furnish, *Theology and Ethics,* 196.

62. Furnish, *Theology and Ethics,* 202.

Resultant Living

According to Wright, Paul does not offer a more extensive treatment of the meaning of the cross than he does in Phil 2:5–11 and Rom 3:21–26, even though he uses the word "cross" only once in these two combined contexts. Wright sees God's righteousness revealed in Jesus's death and resurrection, which has the effect of turning away God's wrath. God proves to be faithful to covenant, able to deal properly with sins and Sin, able to rescue the helpless, able to save us from ourselves, and able to demonstrate his impartiality toward Jew and gentile alike.

With regard to Rom 3:25, Wright points to the two phrases that qualify ἱλαστήριον—"through faith" and "by means of his blood." He accepts these as independent modifiers, as well as accepting cautiously "the faithfulness of Jesus" as a subjective genitive for "faith" in both Rom 3:22 and 3:26. However, his commentary remains in the arena of soteriological atonement and a cross indicative: "Jesus' faithfulness was the means by which the act of atonement was accomplished, . . ." The mercy seat becomes the advance symbol, such that "Paul sees the blood of Jesus as actually instrumental in bringing about that meeting of grace and helplessness, of forgiveness and sin, that occurred *on* the cross."[63]

However, it could better be said that the sin of man meets the grace of God, not *on* the cross, but *at* the cross, at the point of Jesus's death. Humankind under the aegis of Sin put Jesus to death, but God at that point raised Jesus from Death. The actions of humankind thus lead to the cross, the action of God thus leads from the cross in the victory of resurrection—a victory over all malignant powers, a victory that called for the installation of Christ as Lord (Phil 2:11; Col 2:9–15). For the Christian, however, as there was for Christ, there is a cross. This is made clear in both the Jesus and Pauline traditions. In Paul, it is a willingness to suffer with Christ in a cross imperative that leads to the promise of resurrection. This is not a call, however, for self-chosen martyrdom.

The Jesus tradition speaks of how foolish it would be to gain the whole world and yet lose one's life. The Jesus tradition speaks of taking up *one's own* cross (Mark 8:34–37). The kerygmatic emphasis of the tradition seen in the book of Acts accurately captures the dynamic of the cross event in the perspective of the early church (e.g., Acts 2:23–24; 3:14–15; 13:28–30). Paul shared that perspective and built upon it, as he stresses the eschatological key of victory over Sin personified.

It should be noted that there is often an unwritten assumption that Paul builds upon "earlier" Christian tradition. It should be stressed once again that Paul received his calling and commission within a five year window following Jesus's crucifixion. The "Christian tradition" prior to Paul did not have long to develop without its development being concurrent with Paul's own ministry. One could even argue that the

---

63. Wright, "Letter to the Romans," 478, emphasis added.

"kerygmatic development" seen within Acts is post-Pauline in its final formulation, and, perhaps, even "Pauline" in Paul's underlying contribution.[64]

It bears repeating. The cross for Paul has greatest value at the point of the imperative, as one follows in the train of the Lordship of Christ. By contrast, theological arguments over the interpretation of the crucifixion of Jesus as indicative have resulted in disunity within the body of Christ on the basis of theological dogmas. We have simply by and large missed or ignored Paul's emphasis of the cross as imperative under the Lordship of Christ.

If we follow the Gospel of God as Paul understood it, we can have no boast other than the claim to have lived a cruciform life. It is only that kind of faithfulness that meets and knows the faithfulness of God in Christ. It is in that vein that we are to present "our bodies" as a sacrifice, something living and acceptable to God as our reasonable service or logical worship (Rom 12:1). It is in that vein that we have hope of resurrection through the power of the God of the Gospel (Rom 1:4).

64. Cf. Brondos's work.

5

The Doctrine of the Atonement and Paul

"ATONEMENT," in many ways, remains the "storm center" in any theological discussion involving Paul and his theology.[1] In part, this is because Paul supplies key verses that are considered to be significant to any New Testament doctrine of the Atonement. These passages are subject to varied interpretations. In part, as well, it is a storm center because the earliest Christian kerygma had no choice but to deal with Jesus's death and resurrection. However, the kerygma did not offer singular definitions.

The two events, death and resurrection, indeed, characterized the kerygma of the Gospel of God, albeit with different focal points. In many respects, the alternative meanings of the death of Jesus expressed in terms of "the Atonement" remain at the center of Christian discussion, division, and controversy in the twenty-first century. While other theological issues may arise and may come and go, perhaps none is more pressing than the one with which the very earliest generation of Christians, Paul included, had to wrestle. What did the death of Christ mean? What indeed was the meaning *of the cross*? How does the death of Christ impact salvation "in Christ"? How does it define soteriology? The answers one gives not only determine one's understanding of Paul and the entire New Testament, but they also determine how one understands the very nature of God and his action in the Christ event.

Many resources may be utilized to pursue a study of the atonement as a theological doctrine. There seems to be no end to the number of perspectives, monographs, and articles on the subject in the Western world. What is presented herein is presented with a view toward understanding the perspectives of Paul by way of comparison and

---

1. The literature is prodigious. See, for example, Baker and Green, *Scandal of the Cross*; Beilby and Eddy, *Nature of the Atonement*; Brondos, *Paul on the Cross*; Brondos, *Jesus' Death*; Brondos, *Parting of the Gods*; Culpepper, *Interpreting the Atonement*; Carroll and Green et al., *Death of Jesus*; Cousar, *Theology of the Cross*; Finlan, *Options on Atonement*; Finlan, *Problems with Atonement*; Flood, "Substitutionary Atonement," 42–59; Grensted, *Doctrine of the Atonement*; Heim, *Saved from Sacrifice*; Hengel, *Atonement*; Hill and James, *Glory of the Atonement*; Humphreys, *Death of Christ*; Jeffery et al., *Pierced for Our Transgressions*; Morris, *Atonement*; Tambasco, *Atonement*; Tidball et al., *Atonement Debate*.

contrast.[2] The whole topic becomes an issue in the present context because of the citation of Pauline texts in support of one view or another. Paul obviously did not speak the final word on "atonement," given the continuing flood of materials, nor was Paul the only canonical New Testament voice. It is important to understand issues related to the historic views of the atonement. It is also, however, important to see what Paul *did* say and to understand why.

In spite of the attention already given to Paul's understanding of the significance of the cross and the death of Jesus in the light of his gospel, it is still appropriate to consider his gospel in a direct manner in relation to historic views of the "atonement" within Christianity. This is yet another matrix significant for a contemporary understanding of Paul's theology in relation to customary systematic theology. It is a topic, however, that moves beyond Paul, which is a reason why it could be placed in an appendix. However, the writer of the present work chooses to deal with the topic in several different ways.

This chapter will give a brief historical overview and then give extended exegetical attention to Paul's general thought. The following chapter will provide extended exegetical consideration of discrete references within Paul's letters deemed relevant to the matter of "atonement." Attention will then be given to historic legacies of viewpoints that are representative of the doctrine of the Atonement, in order to appreciate the issue within Pauline thought and its application in a contemporary theological world. Such developed perspectives incorporate understanding ostensibly drawn from Paul and other sources. Viewpoints of the church fathers and later Christian history obviously move beyond the time of Paul and the earliest Christians. However, it is appropriate to provide a developed historical summary as a foreground to Paul's thought.

Some of the issues pursued, and the manner in which they have been treated in Christian history, offer a rather jarring disjuncture to what appears to be Paul's own perspective. This chapter deals with a pressing issue—a "storm center" that is not altogether Pauline, but a storm center in which Paul is central. An appropriate understanding of Pauline texts in the following chapter may well address the issue with a degree of clarity and correction. If various historic viewpoints presented seem "jarring" in comparison with Paul's perspectives, it is because they are. Paul was not a systematic theologian offering dogmatic support for formulations of later centuries.

---

2. Baker and Green seek to present an appreciation of the concept of the atonement in the contemporary context of other cultures, such as an honor-shame culture rather than a legal-guilt culture. That is not the purpose of the present work. However, if current interpreters of New Testament social theory are correct, Paul included, an honor-shame culture must be taken into account in understanding Paul.

Preliminary Considerations

It should be stated at the outset that the questions "What does systematic theology say about the Atonement?" and "What does Paul say about atonement?" are two different questions. The first is a general question that involves both the entire New Testament and the history of Christian theology. The second is a specific, localized question that focuses upon *Paul's* understanding, regardless of how he has been pressed into service in the interest of the first question. The caveat is thereby given that in reading general treatments on the atonement, it is sometimes difficult to perceive Paul's position specifically, in the light of Pauline prooftexts used in general discussion. What *is* one to make of Jesus's death on a Roman cross? And, specifically, how did Paul understand Jesus's death. Appendix A offers a chronological listing (according to the author's Pauline chronology) of Pauline references to the death of Jesus.

While the single occurrence of the word "atonement" in the King James New Testament carried the idea of *reconciliation* (Rom 5:11), the word is used today in theological doctrine employed to describe an act that pays for or erases the guilt of one's sins and transgressions. This is a marked change. The center of contemporary Christian theology is thus often said to be Christ's sacrificial death on the cross. Sacrificial imagery is implicit or expressed via metaphor, even when not explicitly developed. It is said that Christ's death stands at the very "heart" of the Christian faith (cf. Heb 9:11–14).

It should be stated that theories of the atonement make use of all biblical verses perceived to be relevant, and thus by nature of the case offer a broader perspective than that which is limited to Paul alone. All theories of the atonement relate to the meaning of the death of Jesus Christ in terms of process and its ultimate effect. One confronts general atonement doctrine in Christian theology thereby, with appeal being made to Hebrews, 1 Peter, and other New Testament writings, for example. A reminder is given that Hebrews was attributed to Paul by many of the early church fathers—a point which may color many modern historical comparisons of understanding as it pertains specifically to Paul in the early witnesses.

Some type of "substitution" becomes a dominant note in much, but not all atonement theology. Substitutionary atonement may in fact describe a variety of proposed views that regard Jesus as dying as a substitute for others, "in their place" or "instead of them." Particularly does one find this expressed outside of Paul in 1 Pet 2:24 and 1 Pet 3:18. "Substitutionary atonement" is thus an umbrella term, of which the four best known variations may be described in terms of the *ransom* theory, a *variation* viewpoint characterized by Gustaf Aulén in his classic summary work as *Christus Victor*, the *satisfaction* theory attributed to Anselm, and the *penal substitution* theory which particularly emerges from the Reformation period following upon Aquinas's earlier revision of a definition of satisfaction.[3] These are by no means the only "theo-

---

3. See Gustaf Aulén's classic work, *Christus Victor*.

ries" of the atonement. A selection of representative theories and interpreters will be introduced in the current work and are set forth in chapters 7 and 8. "Substitution" may mean different things in different eras of Christian history. Context is important. The early church fathers, including Athanasius and Augustine, understood that Christ suffered in humanity's place, that through his death he liberated us from death and the devil. Their view, however, differs from the dominant contemporary "substitutionary" view of penal substitution.[4]

At the center of the Christian tradition from earliest times stood the centrality of Jesus's death (1 Cor 15:3) symbolized by the cross—indicated by Paul to be a stumbling block for Jews and foolishness to gentiles (1 Cor 1:23–24). There is perhaps no better commentary or confirmation of Paul's words than the rude graffito, found on the Palatine Hill in Rome, of a crucified man with an ass's head accompanied by a mocking description: "Alexamenos worships his god."[5] This reflects *upon* the worship of the early church. The mocker got right central facts of and symbol of the faith he despised and denigrated. However, fact of crucifixion does not equal theory; nor does mere fact equal faith.

Within Christian history, speculation on the subject of atonement develops mostly on the part of Protestantism during the Reformation and post-Reformation periods, with different models being advanced. In contrast to an earlier satisfaction viewpoint, the language of Aquinas could be quoted by the Council of Trent in support of an even more broad conception of the work of Christ. It no longer involved the affront to a ruler that required amends, but rather it became a question of reverent response to a holy and loving God. As Grensted observes, God was not to be approached with fear but with the worship and devotion of the believer. The idea of satisfaction "tended to pass over into the idea of sacrifice, regarded in part as an expiation for sin, but also as an act of homage and worship."[6] The association of sacrifice with homage and worship, rather than with punishment, should be noted.

As Grensted went on to observe, application of sacrificial language to the doctrine of atonement has been a characteristic of every period of doctrinal history. It never dropped out but could appear side-by-side with other views. Eucharistic doctrine had a part in the sacrificial development of understanding Jesus's death, such that the "sacrifice of the altar" was brought into direct relation with the "Sacrifice of Calvary." In all things except manner, the worshipper at the Eucharist feels oneself "brought into direct contact with the atoning work of Christ."[7]

4. For a defense of penal substitution in the early church fathers, see Jeffery et al., *Pierced for Our Transgressions*. For a rebuttal, see Flood, "Substitutionary Atonement," 142–59.

5. See Grensted, *Doctrine of the Atonement*, 32; Ferguson, *Backgrounds of Early Christianity*, 597; Elliott and Reasoner, *Documents and Images*, 105.

6. Grensted, *Doctrine of the Atonement*, 179. The emphasis upon homage and worship is significant.

7. Grensted, *Doctrine of the Atonement*, 180.

Paul, of course, recounts early eucharistic tradition in 1 Cor 11:23–26. This seems to be a significant point of reference and relevance with regard to Paul. Paul had to worship when he thought about the Christ event. He frequently breaks out in worship or doxology. If one takes Rom 3:25, Gal 3:13, 2 Cor 5:21 and other passages out of the realm of logic and places them in the realm of worship, then Paul's own metaphors take on an entirely different meaning. Matrix matters in any scenario of interpretation. The Gospel for Paul first called forth *worship* in the context of faith, hope, and love—not *logic*. Worship marks a redirection of humankind Godward. Logic remains earth-bound.

Examination of "*the* Atonement" not only moves beyond Paul but also beyond earliest Christianity, despite some protestations to the contrary. While Paul and others in earliest Christianity were concerned with "atonement" but not "*the* Atonement," Christianity from the late Middle Ages onward (and particularly from the time of Anselm, c. CE 1100) has professed a formulative concern for "*the* Atonement" within its systematic formulations.

Because several verses from Paul's letters figure prominently in atonement discussion, it is appropriate to consider the historical development of the atonement in relation to Pauline perspectives. This may be done by comparing and contrasting Paul's thought exegetically with developing doctrines of later ages. In view of the fact there are multiple, whole monographs on the topic of the atonement as well as a host of variations on the theme, the ultimate focus here remains upon the apostle Paul and the appropriation of Paul in support of various atonement perspectives. Examination of historical development involves a consideration of the general history and doctrinal development of the Christian church.[8]

The present focus remains upon the development of the doctrine with a view toward appreciating Paul. Thus, the "eye of the storm" may serve as a case study in itself as one ventures in search of Pauline theology. While one may choose to embrace systematic theology of any later age with regard to the meaning of the death of Jesus, *Paul* deserves to be heard on his own terms within his own matrices. One may question or dialogue with regard to the appropriateness of Paul's thought, but one should at least seek to hear Paul in his own context compared to interpretations that emerge from alternative contexts. The "theological barnacles" may be examined or even embraced in their own right, but they need to be removed from the underlying Pauline "wood," which in this writer's view certainly offers a different reality than what is most commonly presented.

---

8. For study of the larger matrix of Christian history and thought, one may consult the following: Marty, *Short History of Christianity*; Bainton, *Christianity*; Bainton, *Christendom*; González, *Story of Christianity*; González, *History of Christian Thought*; González, *Church History: Essential Guide*; Grant and Tracy, *Short History*; Kelly, *Early Christian Doctrines*; McGrath, *Christian Theology* ; Shelley, *Church History*.

A Brief Historical Overview

Atonement in Christian thought, like other theological conceptions within Christianity, begins with biblical events and develops by interpretation of those events. Born of history, Christian doctrine is also molded and developed by the forces of contemporary experience of the day, such that it emerges in a given historical context or matrix. The doctrine of atonement is no different.[9] The early church, Paul included, had to wrestle with the meaning of Jesus's death *once it came to express faith in Jesus's resurrection*. Apart from the resurrection, what reason was there for the early church to interpret Jesus's death in any significant manner? A dead martyr? Another messianic pretender? A discredited movement founder? Within days or perhaps hours of reports that Jesus was alive after his very public and shameful death, the earliest disciples had to begin to deal with the question: "If Jesus is alive, then how should we understand his death? How should that be explained?" The New Testament answers given to the question exhibit a richness of thought that is absent from subsequent ages. The issue, historically speaking, was an immediate one that had to be addressed by personal experience and the earliest kerygma.

The kerygma cited by Paul in 1 Cor 15:3–4 may be dated as early as 30 CE (literally very soon after Jesus's death and resurrection, cf. Acts 2:22–24, 3:13–26), or, twenty years later. It obviously antedates 1 Cor 15 (54 CE). Paul's initial work in Corinth would date to c. 48–49 CE (cf. ἐν πρώτοις, 1 Cor 15:3, "of first importance," as in the *RSV*, or, "at first," "in the first times"?).[10] The "gospel which Paul gospeled" to the Corinthians (τὸ εὐαγγέλιον ὃ εὐηγγελισάμην, 1 Cor 15:1) included the understanding that Jesus's death was "in behalf of our sins" (ὑπὲρ τῶν ἁμαρτιῶν ἡμῶν, 1 Cor 15:3). The reference is interesting, in that Paul uses the phrase ὑπὲρ ἡμῶν elsewhere in a number of places (e.g., Rom 5:8). Does the inclusion of τῶν ἁμαρτιῶν belong to the tradition or is it a Pauline addition (cf. "sinners," ἁμαρτωλῶν, Rom 5:8)?

On the whole, the New Testament bears witness to the factual *experience* of the Gospel. Jesus was perceived as a prophet during his lifetime, even as *the* eschatological Prophet expected within Judaism.[11] The event that transformed Jesus's death from being another chapter in the martyrological prophetic tradition within Israel was the affirmed reality of Jesus's resurrection by God. It was the *experience* of the resurrection that made a difference for Paul (Gal 1:13–17; 1 Cor 15:5–11). If God had raised and

---

9. Cf. Grensted, *Doctrine of the Atonement*. Although older, Grensted's work is thorough and informative, characterized by ready access to primary source reference citation. It is well worth reading.

10. Rather than "first importance," Paul may simply be alluding to the time of his first work in Corinth, the time when he proclaimed the basic nature of the Gospel, concerning which question has now arisen concerning the resurrection.

11. Cf. Acts 3:21–26; 7:37; Luke 13:31–33; Matt 11:3 par. Luke 7:19; cf. Deut 18:15–16. Israel had a tradition of rejecting prophetic voices sent to her by God (Luke 13:31–35; 20:47–51 par. Matt 23:32–39). See Greene, "Portrayal of Jesus as a Prophet in Luke-Acts."

exalted Jesus, if he were now alive after his very evident death, what did that mean? How was it to be explained?

At a minimum, the gospel (the "good news" proclaimed) included reference to Jesus's death and reference to his resurrection. These two elements were the foundational building blocks (cornerstones) of any gospel development. These two realities formed the twin centers of the ellipse of the Gospel of God. These two elements were perceived to be *historical* realities which came to be interpreted as *soteriological* realities.

The entire Christ event, as well as the fact of the cross as atonement, i.e., having some relation to sin, was interpreted in terms of a fulfilment of prophecy theme. The testimony of the risen Jesus (Luke 24:19–27; 24:44–47), "Peter's" speeches in Acts (Acts 2:16–36; 3:17–26), and even "Paul" in Acts (Acts 13:26–41)—all offer testimony to a fulfilment of prophecy theme, which set forth a rather simple, straightforward reflection of the meaning of the death of Christ.[12] Even Tertullian (d. 220 CE), writing as late as the end of the second century, likewise offers the still dominant note of appeal to prophecy as explanation of the cross.[13] Perhaps surprisingly, Tertullian, who was one of the creative forces of Western theology, makes no contribution to the development of the atonement.

Over time, the conviction grew that the cross was the central fact of the life of Christ to which his whole life led and that the cross held the key for the specific problem of sin. Jesus's own statement as attributed by Mark (Mark 10:45 par. Matt 20:28) suggested some type of transaction. Paul's language in familiar verses (e.g., Gal 3:13; 1 Cor 5:21; Rom 3:25) either echoed or contributed to this development. So did the language of Hebrews and 1 Peter. "Dots" were connected. Not only did *Jesus* speak of giving his life "as a ransom for many," *Paul* could affirm to the Corinthians that they were "bought with a price" (1 Cor 6:20;7:23). It is perhaps not surprising that the conception of a legal transaction with the devil became a characteristic of theologians of the Greek church, from Irenaeus to the eighth century.

The use of a phrase like "new covenant in my blood," present in the celebration of the Eucharist,[14] lent itself to a comparison with an old-covenant sacrifice, sealed by the "blood of the covenant" (Exod 24:8). The writer of Hebrews presented the meaning of the sacrificial death of Christ in terms of Priesthood and sacrifice, such that Jesus's death was understood in cultic terms. According to Paul (or a Paulinist?), God made peace "by the blood of his cross" (Col 1:20). Johannine language bordered on the mystical along with Paul in emphasis upon the Incarnation. "God was in Christ reconciling the world to himself" (2 Cor 5:19). "In the beginning was the Word, and

---

12. The references cited are found in Luke-Acts and may reflect earlier tradition, as however presented by Luke, c. 80–100 CE, i.e., later than Paul (d. 61 CE).

13. Tertullian, "Five Books Against Marcion," 3:19–20, 337–39.

14. Cf. 1 Cor 11:25; Mark 14:24; Matt 26:28; Luke 22:20.

the Word was with God, and the Word was God. . . . For God so loved the world that he gave his unique Son . . . ." (John 1:1; 3:16).

When one considers the response of the New Testament writers generally speaking in terms of a fulfilment of prophecy theme, the employment of Old Testament sacrificial metaphors and cultic imagery, the language of transactionalism, and the displeasure of God toward sin, one realizes that the building blocks of later atonement theories are to be found here. Finlan can speak of the cluster of atonement ideas "grown from the seedbeds of Paul and the letter to the Hebrews."[15] Paul, however, cannot be held directly accountable for the weeds that later grew in the Pauline soil. There are other influences in later matrices which call forth variations on the theme.

In actuality, and perhaps in the light of the situation in which they found themselves, the early thinkers of the church in a time after Paul were preoccupied with the problems of the nature of the Godhead (the "Trinity") and the Person of Christ. From earliest days, Christianity was a soteriology, such that redemption was an essential part of Christian experience and thought. However, other concerns in the early centuries after Paul suppressed developmental expression of atonement doctrine. Rival doctrines that arose pertaining to the Trinity or the Incarnation were tested by the *fact* of redemption; doctrines that were not compatible did not survive.

Prior to the time of Anselm, the so-called *Christus Victor* perspective became a dominant view of the Fathers, until it was supplanted by Anselm's satisfaction theory. In his book, Gustaf Aulén refers to *Christus Victor* as the "classic view" supported by almost every church father in the first 1000 years of church history, including Irenaeus, Origen of Alexandria, and Augustine. Indeed, the dominant theme was that of victory—God's deliverance of human beings from evil powers which held them in bondage and wrought personal destruction. The *Christus Victor* theory emphasizes the liberation of humanity from bondage to Sin, Death, and Satan by Christ's freely chosen, sinless submission to the power of Death, a power thoroughly overcome by God in the resurrection.

Christus Victor is not so much a systematic, rational theory as it is a drama—a kind of divine passion story of God liberating humanity from the bondage of Sin by his triumph over Powers. It is thus at base a narrative story. One sees aspects of narrative story in the various elements of the kerygma. Those who heard the kerygmatic "echoes" as they outlined the story could mentally recreate a more full narrative. One needs to remember that the early centuries were marked by an oral and aural culture, in which story and narrative would predominate. The vast majority of people could neither read nor write.[16]

15. Finlan, *Options on Atonement*, 36. It should be noted that Hebrews was considered to be written by Paul in some quarters of the ancient church.

16. Biblical scholarship in recent decades has become much more sensitized to the significance of narrative story present virtually everywhere in biblical writings.

A divine drama of victory would also describe Paul's own understanding. Story, more than theory, was important in the aural and oral culture of Paul's day and the immediate century following. Death, Sin, the Demonic are overthrown, for God's resurrection of Jesus broke the domination they once held over human life. Resurrection is a mark of the Father's favor, despite the apparent curse of the Law upon crucified men. The Law's ability to condemn is broken by God's action in the resurrection. In the basic thought of the time, the end justified the means, such that the subversive defeat of the Powers by the trickery of a divine conspiracy of Jesus and the Father was overlooked.

Christus Victor is rooted in the Incarnation, in that Christ entered into the realm of human misery and wickedness in order to redeem it by whatever means necessary. As supporting interpretation of the underlying story, when one works through the fathers, it becomes evident that more than a single theory could be held by a given church father at the same time. Paul himself could employ multiple metaphors. Indeed, the New Testament itself offers varied and alternative metaphors in support of *the story*, the divine drama of God's victory in Christ.

The question of how the cross fit into God's redemptive plan was addressed and answers were supplied from contemporary matrices of appropriation. However, speculation on the subject of the atonement seldom arose. Atonement was addressed, even in crude form, as some type of transaction between God and the devil. Grensted suggests that the fact that such a characterization of the atonement could stand for 900 years is testimony that the need for a serious discussion of the topic *had not yet been felt*. In the first two centuries after Christ, little attempt was made to go beyond New Testament *statements*. In the earliest days of the church, the language of the New Testament was used freely and devotionally in worship, without conscious effort being made to work out "theory." Grensted simply says, "Of theory there is none. . . . The age of doubts and questionings had not yet begun."[17] As he further states, the very crudity of the theory at the point of revival of theological learning "drove the Western church to speculate on the doctrine, a process which has at times threatened to obscure the fact."[18]

While Paul's mystical language found frequent echoes, for example, the penal and legal metaphors ostensibly found in Paul remained quite undeveloped. Wherein suffering is seen to atone for sin, it is righteousness and not suffering that is effective for deliverance. While emphasis may rest upon the fact of the cross, how suffering atones for sin is not answered. In mystical emphasis, the Eucharist brought one into mystical union with the passion of Christ. One shared in his passion, in order to share in his resurrection deliverance. The emphasis was upon a unifying love. Ignatius (d. 110 CE), for example, could emphasize the past fact of the passion of Christ in terms of its union in the heart of the believer: "Unless of our own free choice we accept to

17. Grensted, *Doctrine of the Atonement*, 11.
18. Grensted, *Doctrine of the Atonement*, 33.

die unto His passion, His life is not in us."[19] Ignatius wished to imitate the passion of his Lord. As Grensted suggests, there is no theory here but only the presence of great experience. The "mystery of the Atonement" is most vividly revealed in life.[20] One hears a mystical echo of a "cruciform imperative."

The meaning of Jesus's death mattered to the New Testament writers, Paul included, such that a plurality of metaphors were utilized to set forth its soteriological significance. Within the New Testament, Paul is recognized as the "quintessential theologian of the cross" in view of the fact that, outside the Gospels and Acts, apart from a single usage (Heb 12:2) Paul is responsible for both the use of the verb σταυρόω ("I crucify") and the noun σταυρός ("cross") in the New Testament.[21] The present writer has already stressed Paul's primary reference to the cross in terms of the imperative, not the indicative. Overall and metaphorically, Paul may have a dozen ways of interpreting/explicating the meaning of the cross.

In the Pauline tradition, Jesus's death was "for us" (ὑπὲρ ἡμῶν). Such collective salvific significance of his death became the subject of individualistic doctrines of the atonement. Even from the apostolic era, theories were set forth as to the effective nature of Jesus's death for our salvation. Centuries of speculation on the nature or mechanics of the atonement led especially to attempts to appropriate Paul's expression regarding the cross for systematic theology or fixed doctrines. In reality, Paul's treatment is to be found in occasional, contingent correspondence expressed in and for his own historical matrices. Abstract, lackluster, and overbearing statements have been read into Paul along rather narrow soteriological lines, as noted by Carroll and Green.[22] In the present writer's view, the underlying Pauline "wood" certainly offers a different reality than what is commonly presented.

The General Thought of Paul

General treatments of the atonement are based upon the entire New Testament, not only Paul. The focus in the present work is Paul. Vincent Taylor, in his older work *The Atonement in New Testament Teaching*, sought to treat Paul's use of the primitive Christian tradition and Paul's own distinctive teaching separately.[23] Taylor sought to trace and distinguish between the ideas Paul drew from the developing Christian tradition and those distinctive to Paul. Taylor found a number of elements or influences that Paul shared with that tradition. In addition, Taylor traced what he saw to

19. Ignatius, *Magn.* 5.

20. Grensted, *Doctrine of the Atonement*, 18–19.

21. Again, for convenience, for usage of the verb σταυρόω, see Gal 3:1; 5:24; 6:14; 1 Cor 1:13, 23; 2:2, 8; 2 Cor 3:18. For the noun σταυρός, see Gal 5:11; 6:12, 14; Phil 2:8; 3:18; 1 Cor 1:17, 18; Col 1:20; 2:14; cf. Eph 2:16.

22. Carroll and Green, *Death of Jesus*, 114. See also, Baker and Green, *Scandal of the Cross*.

23. Taylor, *Atonement*, 57–101.

be elements of Paul's distinctive teaching. Both sets of elements are rather broad in Taylor's treatment. The general observation must be made that the division is not altogether clear. We don't have a total isolated body of distinct Christian tradition, which, when set forth, is not in part inferred from Paul and from the Acts of the Apostles. Taylor, however, observes that even when Paul appropriates Christian tradition, he tends to place his own stamp upon it.

The centrality of the death of Christ stands out in the teaching of Paul, likely because this was also a central issue in the early tradition or kerygma, much as issues of the Trinity and Christology became significant *at a later point* in Christian theology. It was something for which the very earliest Christians had to account (Cf. Gal 1:4; Phil 3:18; 1 Cor 1:17–18, 24; 2:1). To proclaim a crucified Lord certainly ran counter to Corinthian "wisdom," for example. However, with the single exception of Heb 12:2, Paul is the only New Testament writer who uses the expression "the cross" of Christ. Paul alone uses the phrase "the death of Christ" (or "his death"). Paul exhibited his own uniqueness, but he also interacted with the earliest Christian tradition.

In reality, every aspect of the death of Christ known in primitive Christianity is also found in Paul. Some perspectives, such as the messianic character of Christ's death or the concept of the Suffering Servant, fall into the background in Paul (or, alternatively, rise in ascendency after Paul), while others such as the vicarious nature and sacrificial significance of the death are clearly expressed but without becoming distinctive of his thought. The basic elements in the development of Paul's thought are found in such concepts as the representative aspect of Christ's death, its relation to Sin/sin, emphasis upon the living Christ, faith-union with him, communion with him, suffering in his service, perception of the cross as the work of God (according to Taylor), proof of God's love, recognition of ethical and spiritual results. Irrespective of distinctive Pauline development, Paul's teaching is deeply rooted in the common faith of the primitive Christian Church.[24] Single ideas often become complex. Paul develops a distinctiveness among New Testament writings, but he does not develop a system. Paul's conception of the work of God in Christ revolves around rectification (justification) and reconciliation, the Law and Sin/sin, suffering and death, ministry and accrued blessings.

The Love of God in Christ

A correct perception of the work of God is absolutely essential to intelligent appreciation of Paul's teaching concerning the atonement. According to Taylor, "From first to last his doctrine of the Cross is conditioned by his doctrine of God."[25] No thought is perhaps more fundamental for Paul. God rectifies, reconciles, sanctifies. Taylor affirms that any theory of "the Atonement" which suggests an enmity of the Father

---

24. Taylor, *Atonement*, 74.

25. Taylor, *Atonement*, 77.

towards humankind which is overcome by the gracious work of Christ, must be deemed "a perversion of Christian teaching," if one is to be faithful to Paul's thinking. As he states, this work of Christ must be interpreted "as the manifestation of the grace of God, and not as a means whereby His favour is won."[26] If not a perversion, such a theory of divine enmity to which Taylor alludes is certainly an alternative to Paul's thought. God's action is born of love—not sentimentalized love, but love as an action of the will, deepened with a wealth of meaning worthy of God's own being. "Grace and peace to you all from God the Father and the Lord Jesus Christ."

Paul understands reconciliation as a growing fellowship with God that is characterized by growing obedience. It is the restoration of fellowship broken by sin. It is righteousness revealed against unrighteousness, that which is deserving of wrath rather than love (Rom 1:18). Yet, even God's wrath is not angry passion or manifestation of vindictiveness; it is born of God's will to redeem and restore broken fellowship. For Paul, the revealed wrath of God is God turning human beings over to their own self-destruction (Rom 1:24, 26, 28). God does not deny his own righteousness, but rather both his righteousness and wrath become the outworking of his revealed nature and desire of reconciliation (cf. Rom 1:17–18; 5:8). God does not *bestow* righteousness nor engage in *legal fiction*. While it is axiomatic for Paul that the work of God in Christ must be in harmony with his essential righteousness, in contrast to much common thought, it is a modern fiction that simply sees the righteousness of God as a righteous status imputed to humankind. God does not judge the guilty innocent nor does he judge the innocent guilty; rather, he judges the guilty "guilty" and seeks to rectify and redeem them anyway.

Paul nowhere offers any opposition between righteousness and love. Love is greater than righteousness, but it is founded upon righteousness and rectification. For Paul, righteousness is both a quality and an activity in the light of the Old Testament; it is more than the Greek concept of justice. It is who God is, but it is also what he does. God *is* right, but he also *rectifies* (Rom 3:26). God's love is implicit in righteousness, and his righteousness is explicit in his love.

The Law ("Torah")

Paul's attitude toward the Law and to Sin/sin deeply influence his treatment of the death of Christ. Paul's statements reveal remarkable contrasts. On the one hand, Paul speaks of the Law in appreciative terms. He affirms the Law is holy and just and good (Rom 7:12). Paul delights in the Law and sees the whole Law to be fulfilled in love of neighbor (Gal 5:14; Rom 13:8). The Law is fulfilled in the sacrifice of Christ (Rom 8:4). Still, Paul recognizes the limitations and temporary character of the Law. It was

---

26. Taylor, *Atonement*, 75–76. It might be suggested that God's favor need not be "won," but rather simply embraced in the Christ event. This is first of all conveyed in each of Paul's letters in his salutations.

something added long after the time of Abraham "because of transgressions" (Gal 3:19). The Law actually worked "wrath" (Rom 4:15). However, it has finished its task as a pedagogue (Gal 3:24–25). Paul can speak of the action of God in canceling it and nailing its obsolete bond to the cross of Christ (Col 2:14), the public place for all to see.

It was through his zeal for the Law that Paul learned the majesty of ethical demand, the vanity of human effort, and the need for complete dependence upon God. Law, for Paul, was not the cold and unrelenting spirit of Roman law. Rather, it was about righteousness—God's and ours. The Law was "holy and just and good" (Rom 7:12), but it had been co-opted by Sin and superseded in Christ. It was limited in its efficacy, even as the Old Testament sacrificial system based upon it had been. Had the Law been sufficient in redemption, then Christ would not have come nor would he have died in our behalf. There would have been no necessity, according to Paul (Gal 4:21). While Paul might maintain the validity of the Torah for Jewish believers, he recognized that there was not "so much as one" who was righteous on the basis of Torah (cf. Rom 3:10, 12; Gal 3:11). Paul's view of "the Law" may appear to be complex and complicated, but scholarly treatments of the topic are sometimes overdone.

Sin

Sin was a hostility toward God, as well as the evil acts in which it found expression.[27] In Paul, it was also a personified power. Its effect was wide-ranging (cf. Gal 5:19–21; 2 Cor 12:20; Rom 1:29–31; Eph 4:25–32; Col 3:5–9), affecting every side of human nature.

Paul accounted for the presence of sin in human living in different ways. He traces sin to the disobedience of Adam (1 Cor 15:21–2; Rom 5:12; cf. Wisdom 2:23–24.; 4 Ezra 3:31–33). That Adam's sin involved all his posterity became rather common thought in rabbinical teaching. In Rom 5:11, the Vulgate rendering of "in whom" (in quo) incorrectly translated the Greek ἐφ᾽ ᾧ ("because"). Paul could also explain the origin of sin in terms of the yetzer ha-ra' (the "evil impulse" or inclination within humankind). The concept is represented by the Pauline language of Rom 7:23 (cf. Eccl 37:3; 4 Ezra 3:21). Similar ideas may lie behind the Pauline use of the "flesh."

"Flesh" itself was not evil, but rather was the weak element in which the sinful impulse entrenched itself. It brings a wretchedness and moral inability from which one cannot deliver oneself. Yet a third explanation of sin rests in the idea of a personal agency associated with other hostile powers that threaten humankind's well-being. In Rom 5:12, 6:16 et al., "sin" is personified as "Sin." Paul understood a hierarchy of evil that attacks humankind from without. Paul does not seek to harmonize these different conceptions. By contrast, Christ is the personal agency through whom God condemns Sin/sin in the flesh (Rom 8:3) and delivers one from a body of Death (Rom

27. Cf. Moore, *Judaism*, 1:474–96.

7:24). Christ is the victorious Lord who conquers forces of evil and who leads them broken and defeated in triumph (Col 2:15), the one who heralds things to come (cf. 1 Cor 15:20–28).

Rectification and Resurrection

Although Taylor speaks in terms of "Forgiveness, Justification, and Resurrection," Paul says very little about forgiveness. It is never the object for which Christ died. The noun "forgiveness" (ἄφεσις) occurs only twice—Eph 1:7 and Col 1:14. The verb "I leave, I forgive" (ἀφίημι) occurs only once in Paul with the sense of "forgiveness" in his citation of Psalm 32:1 (Rom 4:7). Forgiveness may well be subsumed under grace for Paul, such that forgiveness is associated with remission of sins, with God's grace being associated with the salvation Christ brings.

However, forgiveness is more intimately connected with rectification (justification) and reconciliation. Justification is not just another word for forgiveness. True righteousness is not perfected achievement, but a righteousness or rectification of mind, thought, and will. Reconciliation involves an action of God in restoring and receiving human beings into fellowship with himself. Paul grounds both justification and reconciliation in the atoning work of God in Christ. We are rectified freely by his grace (2 Cor 5:19; Rom 3:24; 3:25; 4:25; 5:10; Eph 2:16; Col 1:20). God acts in harmony with his own nature as a God of righteousness, truth, and love. He is not limited *by* judicial action, nor *to* judicial action.

The Work of God in Christ

The work of God in Christ is a work of grace (Rom 5:8). Is Paul's doctrine substitutionary? The distinctive vocabulary is at best almost wanting. The preposition ἀντί ("in the place of") is not used. Nouns like λύτρον ("means of release"), ἀντίλυτρον ("ransom"), λύτρωσις ("liberation"), λυτρωτῆς ("liberator") are not used, nor is the verb λυτρόομαι ("I redeem, liberate") employed. Paul does use the noun ἀπολύτρωσις ("deliverance, setting free") in predominant New Testament usage (seven of ten occurrences, cf. 1 Cor 1:30; Rom 3:24; 8:23; Eph 1:7, 14; 4:30; Col 1:14). The noun ἀπολύτρωσις ("redemption") emphasizes the idea of deliverance or setting free from Sin/sin rather than substitution (cf. Eph 1:7; Col 1:14.). Paul employs the idea of "purchase" (ἀγοράζω, 1 Cor 6:20; 7:23; Gal 3:13; 4:5) rather than "ransom" (ἀντίλυτρον).

The one instance where Paul uses the word ἱλαστήριον ("place where sins are expiated," Rom 3:25; cf. Heb 9:5) does not suggest a *substitutionary* character, but rather a provisionary conception. Paul may describe vicarious activity (e.g., Rom 6:10–11), but that is not substitutionary but participatory. The same may be said of 2 Cor 5:14, which Taylor interprets along the lines of "Christ died a death on behalf of all, and therefore all *died to sin* in the power of His death."[28] There is no suggestion of penal suffering which is transferred from our shoulders to Christ. Paul generally avoids the vocabulary of substitution and does not use the word "mediator."

Paul does not present a theory of vicarious punishment, even in 2 Cor 5:21. He also avoids conceptualization that suggests the salvation of humankind is already complete. Rather, he develops an idea of faith-union with Christ on a continuing basis—one is "in Christ" in an imperative as well as in an indicative sense. For Paul, the definitive yet representative action of Christ is that which makes possible and calls for action on the part of humankind. That action is born of reconciliation and a cruciform imperative. God does for humankind what humankind cannot do for itself; it is empowerment. It is that in which humankind may participate through the reality and power of faithfulness. It is not substitution, but inclusive accommodation or participation. There is an imperative that arises from the indicative.

So what does Paul mean when Paul speaks of God's work in Christ and says that "he was made to be sin on our behalf" or "became a curse for us"? (Second Corinthians 5:21 and Galatians 3:13 will be discretely treated in the following chapter.) For the present, Paul does not hold a theory of vicarious punishment, as excluded by his silence and his emphasis upon atonement as the work of God in Christ. Such a theory of punishment meted out to an innocent Son is also unethical, for only the guilty are ethically and equitably punished. According to Taylor, what Paul means is that Christ voluntarily came under deepest gloom, sharing with men "its awful weight and penalty."[29] This idea is implicit in Gal 3:13, although the idea is expressed in terms of paradox and polemical argument. Paul claims Christ has delivered us from the curse of Deut 21:23 (cf. Deut 27:26). Paul has spoken of a "curse" resting upon those under the Law, such that much more is in question than the tragedy of crucifixion.

Paul's words in Gal 3:13 and 2 Cor 5:21 are the closest he comes to the idea of sin-bearing, so much so that Stephen Finlan finds these verses to make use of a scapegoat metaphor.[30] Paul never actually uses this particular image, and indeed it may be questionable that he would do so in writing to the Galatians and the Corinthians. There were other issues at stake. There is nothing in Paul akin to 1 Peter 2:24 or John 1:29, a verse very much misunderstood in terms of "sins" plural rather than "sin" singular. Paul's conviction is that righteousness and God and his purpose to reconcile

---

28. Taylor, *Atonement*, 86, emphasis original.

29. Taylor, *Atonement*, 87. "Deepest gloom" would apparently reference Jesus's own voluntary submission to death.

30. Finlan, *Problems with Atonement*, 42–46. Finlan finds this expulsion imagery elsewhere as well. According to Finlan, a strong likelihood of expulsion imagery is also found in Rom 6:6, 7:4, and 8:3. The death of Christ is seen in terms of sin-bearing and curse-carrying. This imagery remained vivid in subsequent generations of Christians. The Epistle of Barnabas 7:10 and Tertullian (*Adv. Marc.* 3.7.7) identify Christ with the image of the scapegoat, while Justin Martyr (*Dial.* 111.2; cf. 40.4) and the Didache (*Did.* 16:5) refer to Christ as cursed one. It should be said that subsequent generations were better schooled in the Old Testament than were the gentile converts of Paul's first-century churches.

humankind to himself, *in the end*, required Christ to suffer the condemnation of Sin and come under its curse. Reconciliation is the main contextual theme in 2 Cor 5:21. These verses will be discretely addressed in the following chapter.

Romans 3:25–26 is the only passage in which Paul treats the subject further, and he does so without direct reference to sin. This is a passage replete with exegetical problems. The passage will be further addressed in the next chapter. At this point it should be said that a few of the problems associated with the doctrine of the Atonement "are really problems of the Incarnation."[31] Paul has an "intractable element of subordination" in the functions of God the Father and the Son. Paul, for example, does not say that in Christ God himself submitted to the consequences of human sin. We should thereby not speak of the "crucified God" if we echo Paul's perspective.

Were the sufferings of Christ to which he submitted "penal" in Paul's thought? Taylor admits that everyone desires a better word than "penal." He observes that until we find a better word, "we ought not to abandon it because it has been used in ways which revolt the conscience."[32] The deep gratitude perceptible in Paul's letters is rooted in the belief that Christ embodied the love of God by freely enduring suffering in behalf of humankind at supreme cost to himself. Paul does not employ the word "penal."

However, having come in the flesh, Christ suffered death in keeping with his love for humankind and in accordance with incarnation and obedience to the Father's will. He came under Sin's, not God's curse, of which Sin's curse is death. There is not a sense of the transfer of punishment. Paul does not speak of the death of Christ as "propitiatory" or a "means of propitiation," but rather as a means or place of covering sins, i.e., an "expiation," a "means of atonement," a "provision." That God has shown himself to be right and able to rectify the one who exhibits Jesus-faithfulness is plain (Rom 3:26). God *is* right and sets forth Christ as a means or place of atonement provision. To say Christ was made sin for us is to say that Christ submitted to the consequences of sin. An ethical and rectifying solution to the problem of humankind is supplied by God himself—freely and without coercion, and, adequately. What Paul writes in Rom 3:25 should be interpreted in the light of what he says in Rom 8. The same Paul set forth both passages not many verses apart.

Romans 3:25–26 is plagued by a number of difficulties in the perspectives of exegetes, because there are many theological positions to defend which color the exegesis. Paul on his part must speak of the cross as an historical event in time that could not be denied. Jesus died by Roman crucifixion. Taylor interprets the cross as eternal, that what happened on Calvary was simply the emergence of a timeless activity, although he admits one risks the danger of losing Christianity itself in a flood of speculative

---

31. Taylor, *Atonement*, 89.

32. Taylor, *Atonement*, 89. That need not mean that we should embrace it. Heim's work, *Saved from Sacrifice*, seeks to move beyond scapegoating violence.

abstractions.[33] Taylor suggests that as humans, we are creatures of time and simply cannot see things *sub specis aeternitatis*. He would be right on that score.

Human Appropriation of the Work of God in Christ

For Paul, the atonement is a work of God accomplished *for humans* and wrought *in them*. The Pauline doctrine is only complete when both aspects are combined. Christ rendered complete obedience to the Father for the salvation of humankind (Rom 5:19) as one whom the Father himself sent forth as a means/place of atonement (Rom 3:25) through faith (faith offered, faith embraced). One sees an undertone of what Paul means by faith in Christ. Faith is devotion to God through the one and after the example of the one through whom God has manifested and worked his redemptive activity.

Without faith, or "faithfulness," there is no atonement. It is not human striving, which would be destined to fail. It is divine action, already understood to be victorious. It is the sovereign act of God completed, not a process of human attainment. However, there is an imperative which does not deny the character of the indicative, but which brings it to individual and collective attainment. Without the indicative, one lives in the arena of human striving. Without the imperative, the link of new possibility of living is broken and the indicative loses its applicational meaning.

Paul's concept of faith-union is expressed by the phrase "in Christ" and its equivalents, which dominate the Pauline literature. Union with Christ is union with the incarnational Revealer of God and, hence, fellowship union with God himself. The concept is set forth in terms of various metaphors—crucified with Christ, suffering and dying with him, buried and rising with him, being "quickened" with Christ, being glorified with Christ.[34] Paul speaks of vital union with Christ in these and other ways; Paul was a man "in Christ." Baptism becomes a celebration of the death of Christ, as one "dies" with Christ, in Christ. The Eucharist becomes a celebration of communion with the resurrected life of Christ; it is more than a mere remembrance. The believer (the one of Christ-faithfulness) is brought into a vital relation with the crucified and resurrected Christ, the one who is now the exalted Christ. The work of God in Christ is not only a revelation of God's love, but it is also the provision of a living way whereby humankind may know the wonder of a reconciled and abiding fellowship with God.

Summary

In Taylor's judgment, Paul's debt to the primitive Christian tradition is often greater than is supposed. A reminder is offered, however, that—Paul was "in Christ" within four or five years of the death of Jesus. To gather Paul's statements under theological

---

33. Taylor, *Atonement*, 92. Really?

34. Cf. Gal 2:20; Rom 6:4, 6, 8, 8:17; Col 2:12–13; 3:1; Eph 2:5–6; 2 Tim 2:11.

headings (salvation, redemption, reconciliation, justification, et al.) even as done earlier in part one of this work is to offer the advantage of simplicity of study, but it should be emphasized that Paul's very practical theology is neither a closely wrought theological system nor a mere collation of unrelated ideas. Paul's theology was integrated, but not holistically systematic in the sense of reasoned logic. The vital link is the redemptive work of God in Christ, whereby God reveals and expresses his own rightness and his redeeming love for humankind.

The truth of incarnation is expressed without pressing a doctrine of Incarnation, for the focus is upon the personal obedience of Christ the Son. The Christ who died for sins is a "personal means of atonement," through whom reconciliation and fellowship with God is restored. True fellowship with God does not take place on an "I-It" basis, but rather on an "I-Thou" basis. The ever deepening and widening effect of faith-union in Christ means that ethical and spiritual growth is the goal of those in Christ, a process that receives the name *sanctification* in the words of the theologians and pieticians. *Theology* represents summary abstraction which includes an interpretative bias and precision that is not found in Paul. Paul's words revolve around personal experience and eschatological hope, with "spiritual growth" predicated toward that end.

There is no focus in Paul on sorrow, penitence, or longing after God. In spite of suffering, there was emphasis upon living "in Christ." Taylor suggests, in the light of the New Testament as a whole, that Paul's neglect of some topics was costly. In defense, given the genre of occasional personal letters which Paul adopted, one would not expect Paul to develop every topic found in primitive Christianity nor to develop fully and completely every topic which he introduces. Paul was not a systematic theologian. Paul addressed the specific needs of his churches in their various contingencies, but he did so with Gospel conviction.

And in a high-context society, Paul did not feel the need to spell everything out. He did not write for later, low-context interpreters. This is true for any doctrine of the *atonement* posited for Paul (an actual word he did not use) or any other conception in Paul.

The Distinctive Thought of Paul

The theology of the atonement (small "a") is a central, paradigmatic concept in the New Testament, which New Testament writers address in different ways. The earliest Christians were called upon to explain and interpret the death of Jesus in the light of proclamation of the gospel. Systematic theology aside, the theology associated with the atonement appears to arise in the New Testament as various New Testament writers seek to make sense of the crucifixion event. If Jesus was indeed God's long-awaited Messiah or God's Son, how is his death on a shameful Roman cross to be explained?

It is better to address the issue in terms of "crucifixion event" than "cross," because the "cross" becomes a symbol of much more than just Jesus's death.

According to Tambasco, Paul's vision offers "the foundational and most explicitly articulated theology of atonement in the New Testament."[35] And certainly the focus of the present work is upon Paul. According to Finlan, Paul thought of Jesus's death as having saving effect on the basis of a ritual event, an effective martyrdom, and a legal substitution. This bears further examination, but Paul's logic was often unexpressed in the high context society in which he lived. Left unexplained, according to Finlan, Christian doctrines of atonement have combined elements from each of the underlying metaphors, such that a new logic has been created.[36] This may well be the case.

The multiplicity of Pauline metaphors creates confusion. He can emphasize the love of God, but on the other hand, he may imply the necessity of Jesus's death as an offering to God. While he can stress the self-surrender of Christ and the generosity of God, Paul's metaphors may also suggest to some that God is somehow manipulated, appeased, or bought-off (Cf. 2 Cor 5:19, 21; Rom 3:21–26). Paul's metaphors have been so interpreted. Salvation was "bought with a price" (1 Cor 7:23). While Paul may not have initiated the sacrificial interpretation of the death of Jesus, he is the one who gives expressed documentation useful to such a view (cf. Rom 3:25; 1 Cor 15:3–4). While Paul may use a series of metaphors to engage the significance of Jesus's death, the popular conception of penal substitution was not one of them. While Paul may see Jesus's death as "penal" in a generic sense (i.e., he suffered penalty) and view Christ as a representative substitute of humanity in the view of many, Paul does not join the two concepts together into a theory of divine "penal substitution."

While metaphors may "reveal and conceal, highlight and hide,"[37] they express partial truth and should not be made to "walk on all fours." Paul realized that no single metaphor captured the significance of Christ's death. A part of the problem is that American Christianity in its popular expression has literalized singular metaphorical language to the exclusion of consideration of the nature of metaphor and multiple metaphorical expression. Neither a single sociological model nor a singular soteriological model expresses entire truth, and may even, indeed, be severely limited at best.

Paul made use of a wide array of metaphors to communicate the significance of Jesus's death. He does not emphasize conceptions of punishment and retribution. God's "wrath" for Paul is not the striking out of a vengeful or vindictive God, but rather his allowable outworking of tendencies present within a fallen creation itself (Rom 1:18–32). It is not a case of "the mollification of a God angered by masses of misdeeds"[38] in which Paul emphasizes individual sinful acts. Paul does not lay stress to either repentance or forgiveness. Rather, Paul emphasizes a relational problem,

---

35. Tambasco, *Atonement*, 10.

36. Finlan, *Problems with Atonement*, 8–9.

37. Carroll and Green, *Death of Jesus*, 262.

38. Carroll and Green, *Death of Jesus*, 264.

whereby the power of Sin needs to be broken in order to restore divine-human relationships (cf. Rom 6).

God and Jesus are not the only actors within Paul's storied account of the gospel. In Paul's story, Jesus is not only the victim but also the victor. In Paul's story, Jesus is not only the offering, but the priest—a point iterated by the writer of Hebrews. Both Paul and John can refer to Jesus as the "Passover Lamb" (1 Cor 5:7) in terms of God's provision—the "Lamb of God who takes away the sin [singular] of the world" (John 1:29). The Passover Lamb in Paul's day was at the center of a celebrative feast of deliverance. John's reference does not say "sins," contrary to popular belief. Nor is it a collective noun. In fact, careful study of John's Gospel will note that the singular sin evident in his usage of ἁμαρτία is that of unbelief.[39] Paul's usage of "sin" is quite different from that of John.

While it may be hazardous to speak of the will and purpose of God, God is the chief "actor" in the Pauline correspondence, such that Christ's self-giving marks identification and solidarity with the salvific will of God for his creation (cf. Gal 1:4). This has relevance for both Paul's theological anthropology and soteriology. Any attribution of a view of the atonement which divorces or segregates the activity of God from the concordant action of the Son is not allowable as an understanding of Paul's theology of the cross.[40] This is inherent even in Paul's salutations.

For Paul, God's wrath is not an essential attribute or divine property. Rather, it is the active presence of God's judgment against all ungodliness and wickedness (ἀσέβεια and ἀδικία, Rom 1:18), both now in the eschatological present (Rom 1:18–32) as well as the eschatological future (1 Thess 1:10; 5:9; 1 Cor 15:20–28; Rom 2:5, 8; Col 3:6). God's wrath is not the anger of divine retribution, nor that of vindictive retribution. With regard to the death of Jesus, Paul does not portray "an angry God requiring mollification" or a required death seen as "vicarious punishment."[41] Paul, instead, proclaims the boundless love of God that is immeasurable and without anthropomorphic analogue (Rom 5:5–8). Christ died in our behalf, the ungodly (ὑπέρ ἡμῶν, ὑπέρ ἀσεβῶν), we who were not right (δίκαιος), we who are "sinners," those under the power of Sin. The suffering of Christians in the present time has meaning in the light of the suffering of Christ (Rom 5:1–5).

It is *not* the case, however, as Carroll and Green assert, that "Christ took on the measure of our powerlessness and died *in our place*,"[42] at least as Paul understood Jesus's death. It is Paul's assertion that we have a share in Christ's life on the basis of resurrection hope, a hope that transforms even one's own current sufferings. If the meaning is that Christ became human and died on a Roman cross powerless in the face of Death, then Paul would agree. Paul, however, did not believe that Jesus died as

39. Cf. Greene, "God's Lamb," 147–64. It marks the lack or loss of faith.

40. Carroll and Green, *Death of Jesus*, 121.

41. Carroll and Green, *Death of Jesus*, 123.

42. Carroll and Green, *Death of Jesus*, 123, emphasis not original.

our substitute in the sense of "in our place." Paul interpreted Jesus's death as having benefit "for us" (ὑπέρ ἡμῶν), as it transformed the imperative of living a cruciform existence because that existence was now fused with hope of resurrection.

It is *not* a case for Paul that "*God* demonstrates his love by means of what *Christ* did," if by that one understands a direct causative relationship between a death sought by Christ and the expression of God's love (cf. Rom 5:8).[43] One may uphold with Paul the retrospective affirmation of God's purpose and activity in the expression of God's love in spite of the cross. For Paul, the cross belongs primarily to the imperative and not to the indicative.

Paul distinctly does contrast God's faithfulness with human unfaithfulness (e.g., Rom 6:26, 23; Rom 1:17–18; 3:9–20). Human beings are inevitable victims both individually and collectively, however, as they are actively ensnared in sins, enslaved to powers (including Sin) from which they have no power to escape.[44] Human acts of wickedness are but the expressions of Sin. Paul's own enumerated expression (lust, gossip, deceit, et al.) are but the illustration of Sin's expressions that in themselves call forth the active wrath of God as they mark the consequences of its active presence in the destruction of human community. It becomes a vicious circle, as God's wrath simply turns human beings over to their own self-destruction (Rom 1:24, 26, 28).

A humanity that turns against God ultimately turns against itself out of a corrupt mind (Rom 1:28) that embraces a lie (Rom 1:25), under which it lives and from which it cannot escape. In slavery to the power of Sin, humanity is both victimizer and victim. It worships the wrong lord, and, as a natural consequence, suffers identical, relational, communal, and cosmological harm—corruption and death. A world bent on destruction does not easily choose or accommodate a radical, revolutionary reordering, all the more so if it exists in slavery, as Paul understood it to be.

While death and destruction are the worst that the "powers," including Sin, could effect, the soteriological effects of the work of God in resurrection following upon Jesus's death marked an invasion of the usual religious and sociological systems. The divine affirmation of the Son marked a power of eschatological proportions that was rooted paradoxically in seeming powerlessness (cf. 1 Cor 1:18—2:5).

Within the purview of Paul's eschatological horizon, Jesus's death on the cross followed by his resurrection had both divine and cosmic repercussions. A new epoch had dawned with the resurrection that marked the defeat of the powers, including Sin. Jesus's crucifixion, in the light of the resurrection, elicited from Paul a multitude of metaphors even in a singular context (as in 2 Cor 5:14–21) to describe its significance: vicarious benefit (2 Cor 5:14–15); representation (2 Cor 5:14, 21); new creation (2 Cor 5:16–17); forgiveness (rare in Paul, 2 Cor 5:19, 21); sacrifice (2 Cor 5:21); rectification/ justification (2 Cor 5:19, 21, implicitly); and the controlling metaphor of reconciliation (2 Cor 5:18, 19, 20). Galatians 3:11–14 offers yet other metaphors—justification (Gal

---

43. Carroll and Green, *Death of Jesus*, 123; Cousar, *Theology of the Cross*, 45.

44. Carroll and Green, *Death of Jesus*, 124.

3:11), redemption (Gal 3:13), substitutionary, sacrificial benefit (Gal 3:13), promise of the Spirit (Gal 3:14), and in Gal 3:26–29, adoption.

Paul's argumentation and choice of terminology is often context specific. The situation at Corinth was different from that in Galatia. Paul's multiplicity of metaphors in contingent situations should caution one not to choose too quickly for Paul a single or central theory of atonement or a single-faceted interpretation of the meaning of Jesus's death.[45] Carroll and Green, having acknowledged the foregoing point, cite 1 Cor 1:22–23 as they assert "Paul summarizes his proclamation of the cross as the central tenet of Christian faith."[46] Further, they affirm that Paul identifies the cross as the "centerpiece of his kerygma." They see the cross specifically as the outworking of God's redemptive divine plan by design (Rom 8:32). The cross is "the ultimate object lesson" for God's "unorthodox notion of the exercise of power." Indeed, "In the cross, God defines power and wisdom in ways otherwise regarded as weak and foolish." Still further, "Jesus' death was an outworking of God's redemptive design." All of this is Christian theology. Some of it echoes Paul, but it also moves beyond Paul. The execution of Christ on the cross is not a "punishment" to satisfy "the justice of God" in Paul's thought or to promote an object lesson of divine power.

How *does* Paul understand the redemptive role of Jesus's death? More than one half dozen points may be made.

1. Paul does not think of Christ being punished by execution on a cross to satisfy the justice of God.

2. The cross can be regarded as substitutionary, within the matrix of the Old Testament conception of sacrifice. This may not be as much a concept of "substitution" as it is "identification."

3. The possibility of participation in Christ's death (and resurrection) is grounded in Christ's first dying "for us." Reconciliation leads to participation.

4. Christ's death has existential significance, in addition to its theological, christological, and soteriological significance. It is suggestive of a Christian imperative.

5. The cross becomes the standard of faithfulness prior to the Parousia of Christ, such that the church itself takes on a cruciform life in the light of a cruciform imperative.

6. The cross leads to new life, even as it establishes the norms of the new life. One lives "in Christ," precisely because *Christ lives* and has provided a model for living.

7. Jesus's death heralds an inaugurative event. It heralds the change of the Ages in the resurrection. It heralds the end of the old and the beginning of the new.

45. Cf. Carroll and Green, *Death of Jesus*, 127.
46. Carroll and Green, *Death of Jesus*, 128.

It heralds the Parousia and the Telos to come, as one now lives in the Age of Transformation.

Paul subverted the patronage-based Roman system of order through his theology of the cross, according to Carroll and Green. The Roman empire was symbolically constructed as one great household characterized by patronal friendship and values of honor and shame. Paul, however, does not portray God as a dishonored patron "in need of mollification." God does not respond with the bruised ego of a Roman patron who exhibits retribution or withdrawal of friendship. Rather, God acts first to restore relationship "without placing the recipients of his benefaction in his debt,..."[47] Reconciliation is a way of life lived for others, such that Paul subverts the ordering of power according to the politics of a Roman world.

Paul does not mention explicitly any direct Roman role in the death of Jesus, unless he includes Roman authorities under the category of the "rulers of this age" (1 Cor 2:8), as is likely in addition to cosmic powers.[48] The Jews are identified by Paul as those who killed Jesus and the prophets (1 Thess 2:15). Carroll and Green make the rather astounding assertion that we encounter more frequently in Paul's letters the claim that "God was the author of the death of Jesus, but evidently the apostle also knew a tradition that assigned responsibility to (Judean) Jews."[49] It is an astounding assertion to affirm that God was responsible in any direct manner for the plan to kill Jesus and to offer that as Paul's claim.

Conclusion

The kerygma of the Gospel of God, basically a narrative story, had its foundational focus in two interrelated events of Jesus's death and resurrection. At the center of Christian tradition from earliest times stood the centrality of Jesus's death (1 Cor 15:3). While later Christian development sought rational explanation of Jesus's cross-death, it was the resurrection that guided Paul's thoughts Godward in terms of worship. Paul's thought remained primarily at a confessional level, rather than proceeding toward a theoretical level. Paul could draw upon both Scripture and developing tradition, but he could also employ the power of metaphor in the explication of the Gospel story in service to both his gentile and Jewish audience. The key element for understanding the cross is the resurrection.

47. Carroll and Green, *Death of Jesus*, 131.

48. Contra Carroll and Green, *Death of Jesus*, and Cousar, *Theology of the Cross*, who assume Paul speaks of "spiritual powers" only, although they note the mention of Pilate in 1 Tim 6:13, of itself non-Pauline. In their brief discussion of 1 Thess 2:13–16, where Paul speaks of Jesus's suffering at the hands of the Jews, they see the earliest indictment of Judean Jews as agents of Jesus's death. See Carroll and Green, *Death of Jesus*, 189–90.

49. Carroll and Green, *Death of Jesus*, 190. They cite Rom 3:25 and 8:32 in support and refer to Cousar's work on the *Theology of the Cross*, 25–51.

The Pauline view is that of a drama of redemption involving a complex of demonic forces, i.e., "the principalities and powers." Paul places Sin (Rom 6:11), Death (1 Cor 15:26), and even the Law (Gal 3:10; 1 Cor 15:36) among this complex of powers. It is perhaps surprising to find the Law given by God, which Paul recognizes on the one hand as "holy and just and good" (Rom 7:12), to be placed in the category of a tyrannical enemy. Yet Paul came to see the Law as bringing about the revival of Sin and the result of Death (Rom 7:9). Christ saves us from the tyranny of Law, and hence, Sin and Death (Gal 3:13; Rom 7:4; Col 1:14). The Law, as an enemy agent, is overcome in Christ (Rom 10:4).

Paul realized that legal righteousness as upheld by the Law could never lead to salvation and life (Gal 3:21; Rom 3:20). That was a false, misleading, and misplaced emphasis, if indeed one was trusting in one's faithful adherence to the Law for salvation, for there was "not as much as one" who could be deemed to be rectified and righteous on the basis of the Law (Rom 3:7; cf. Ps 14:3). Paul also realized, as Aulén expresses it, that "divine Love cannot be imprisoned in the categories of merit and of justice; it breaks them in pieces."[50] The love of God in Christ delivers from all condemnation and hostile powers (Rom 8:38–39). And, it should be noted that God's love set forth in Rom 8 is neither a coerced nor a "satisfied" love. Love is not, first of all, forensic.

For Paul, the cross was a paradigm for Christian living, as the community of the people of God "in Christ" demonstrated the locus of God's saving power in re-creation.

---

50. Aulén, *Christus Victor*, 68.

6

Discrete Pauline References and Atonement

I T is generally assumed that Paul offers extensive reference to the cross of Christ and thus proves to be the foundational basis for the doctrine of "the Atonement." It is thereby incumbent to examine the supposed supporting passages contextually in this chapter.

Although the orthodox theologians of the seventeenth century claimed Paul's support for the satisfaction theory of the atonement, the essential point in support of that theory is actually missing from Pauline texts. Paul does not give support to the idea that divine justice has to receive satisfaction through any payment made by Christ for human sinfulness. For Paul, "it is the Divine Love itself that makes the redemption."[1] Salvation, redemption, and atonement are not separated by Paul, in the sense that Paul's concept of salvation is one of redemption on the one hand and one of atonement on the other. According to Aulén, God through Christ "saves humankind from His own judgment and His own Law, establishing a new relation which transcends the order of merit and of justice."[2] Such a statement without adequate context could imply a divine schizophrenia.

Even so, Paul does not generally use "cross" terminology. He can speak of Christ's work as vicarious, as "for our sake" or "in our behalf" (ὑπέρ ἡμῶν), but he tends to speak of Christ's blood combined with other metaphors: new covenant (1 Cor 11:25); communion (1 Cor 10:16); rectification (Rom 5:9); Passover sacrifice (1 Cor 5:7, and the Passover lamb was redemptive, not punitive); place of remission of sins (Rom 3:25, which could be understood as positive provision rather than propitiatory payment). God acts as the direct agent through the Christ event and person of Christ to reconcile the world to himself (2 Cor 5:18–19). God is the actor, not the passive recipient. God may be the aggrieved party—grieved like a father for a wayward son, but he acts to judge the cause and rectify/redeem the victim from victimizing forces

---

1. Aulén, *Christus Victor*, 72.
2. Aulén, *Christus Victor*, 71.

that act contrary to God's will. Even 2 Cor 5:21 (which contextually focuses upon new creation in Christ as ministers of reconciliation) lacks any suggestion of satisfaction of divine justice. God works through us (δι' ὑμῶν, 2 Cor 5:20) as he did through Christ (διὰ Χριστοῦ, 2 Cor 5:18) in a ministry of reconciliation.

In our behalf or for our benefit (not "in our place"), God made Christ "sin," who knew no sin, for the purpose that we might become the righteousness of God in him (2 Cor 5:21). In this oft-cited verse, Paul uses a remarkable and unusual expression that surely should be understood along the lines of what he states in Rom 8:3 or even 3:25, properly understood. As Paul affirms there is no condemnation toward those in Christ Jesus (Rom 8:1), he explains that "the law of the spirit of life in Christ Jesus has freed you from the Law of Sin and Death. For the inability of the Law while weakened through the flesh, God condemned Sin in the flesh because he sent his own Son in the likeness of sinful flesh, for the purpose that the righteous judgment of the Law might be fulfilled in us, the ones who walk not according to flesh but according to the Spirit" (Rom 8:2–4). Paul portrays life in the Spirit, provided by God, as producing fruit pleasing to God in contrast to works of the flesh (Gal 5:19–21) under the power of Sin. In actuality, work of the flesh under the power of Sin brought about the death of Jesus.

Discrete Pauline References

According to Paul, God did not condemn the Son by making him a sin-offering to placate his wrath and satisfy his justice. Rather, Paul offers a statement of incarnation whereby God condemns Sin in the very domain where its power reigned. The Law lacked power, because of the weakness of the flesh and because it had been co-opted by Sin and perhaps because it was not incarnate. In the context of Romans 8, Paul is affirming the matter of life in the Spirit compared to life in the flesh (Rom 8:5–11). It is the Spirit of God that brings resurrection (Rom 8:11). Discrete Pauline references will now be contextually examined in turn.

Galatians 3:13

Galatians is the earliest letter of Paul (53 CE) in which crucifixion language occurs and it is a letter born of controversy. Because of the letter's overall significance and the part Gal 3:13 has played in atonement theology, it requires a rather significant development of its overall context and content. It becomes rather foundational for understanding other Pauline references, including Romans. Of the eighteen occurrences of crucifixion language (σταυρόω, σταυρός) in the Pauline letters, one third of them occur in the comparatively brief letter to the Galatians. Galatians was called forth by severe controversy regarding the nature of the gospel that arose during Paul's Collection Campaign.

Perhaps surprisingly, it could first of all be said that Gal 3:13 has nothing to do with atonement theory in terms of what Paul says and why he says it. For Paul, Galatians 3:13 had nothing whatsoever to do with any theory of the atonement. The Galatian issue is circumcision and ritual food laws, as to whether these things should be imposed upon gentiles in the name of the Gospel of God in Christ. The verse appears in a context in which Paul addresses Galatian gentiles to remind them that the blessing of Abraham (gentile incorporation into the people of God) and the promise of the Spirit that now is through faithfulness and not law. As a result of incursion by the Nomistic Evangelists, Paul affirms that it is evident that no one will be rectified with God on the basis of law, for "the one who is right will live on the basis of faithfulness" (Gal 3:11; cf. Hab 2:4), just like Abraham, who is father of Jew and gentile alike.

Paul builds his argument, which will continue through the remainder of the letter. Christ's very public and shameful death was potentially a curse on the basis of Torah, especially if his body should have remained upon the cross as a pollution of the very sacred Passover Sabbath. Christ himself may have been cursed according to Torah, but he was not cursed by God as demonstrated by his resurrection by God and Paul's call and commission in Christ (Gal 1:16).

While Paula Fredriksen is concerned to address other issues, she suggests that the scandal of a "crucified messiah" is a trope of scholarship that refuses to go away but that should be retired. In the present instance, so should an interpretation that calls for penal substitutionary atonement. Paul does not say that Jesus died *in our place* or *under the curse of God*. According to Fredriksen, no Jewish text signals "hanging" in a general sense (or specifically crucifixion) as a death that occurred under divine curse. The text of Deuteronomy cited by Paul (Deut 21:23) does not describe *method*, but rather points to very public (and shameful) *display*. Nothing within Judaism "holds that a man who died by crucifixion was therefore cursed by God, . . ."[3] In terms of the Old Testament, it is action and ignominy of public execution and display that represents the curse and potential defilement of the land (cf. Deut 21:23; Jos 8:29; 10:26–27; 2 Sam 4:12). Removal of the body and burial would seem to obviate the potential divine curse because of land defilement. It wuld also curb public shame. According to the Gospel tradition, that is exactly what the followers of Jesus did, as given opportunity (cf. Mark 15:42–46; Matt 27:57–60; Luke 23:50–54; John 19:38–42). They took the body of Jesus down from the cross and placed it in a private tomb. What happened to the bodies of those crucified with Jesus is not addressed by the written Gospel tradition. Even in their grief, the followers of Jesus sought to preserve the

---

3. Fredriksen, "Who Was Paul?," 26–27. Fredriksen employs the example of the bodies of Saul and Jonathan hung on the walls of Beth-shan to point out that nowhere does the text say the two men died a death marked by God's curse (2 Sam 21:12). In addition, one might observe that Deut 27:26 (cf. Gal 3:10) occurs at the end of an antiphonal liturgical curse ceremony (Deut 27:11–26) that was coupled with blessings predicated upon faithful adherence to covenant (Deut 28:1–6; cf. 26:16–19). It was part of the liturgical expression of Deuteronomy theology.

sacredness of Passover, which for them now certainly took on a different meaning as they covered the shaming of the one whom they had followed.

The bodies of those crucified by Rome were often left to rot or have eye sockets pecked out by birds. Crucifixion often occurred in the nude. It was made deliberately painful and shameful, for it was a political statement made by Rome concerning who was in charge, especially when the victim was deemed to be a threat to Rome. The Gospel record is clear that Jesus was crucified between two insurrectionists or robbers (ληστάς, Mark 15:27; λησταί, Matt 27:38; Luke 23:32 has κακούργοι, "criminals" or "workers of evil") as "King of the Jews" (Mark 15:26; Matt 27:37; John 19:14–20; cf. Luke 23:37). The charge against Jesus was a political one.

To return to the Galatian letter, Paul's message to the Galatian gentiles is this: you do not have to embrace the alternative gospel of the Nomistic Evangelists by submitting to ritual matters of Jewish Torah in order to become a part of God's new Israel. As it was with Abraham, faithfulness of trust in the God of Israel even in fulfilment of a cruciform imperative in Christ is sufficient. Paul has already affirmed he has been crucified together with Christ (Χριστῷ συνεσταύρωμαι, Gal 2:19–20). He thereby suggests that he has already died a death, that Christ lives in him, and that the life he now lives in the flesh, he lives by the Son of God, the one who loved him and gave himself for him (ὑπὲρ ἐμοῦ, Gal 2:20). What Paul says in Gal 2:19–20 prepares the way and sets the stage for Paul's affirmation and argument in Gal 3:1–14. Christ redeemed us from the curse of the Law, namely, that every requirement (ceremonial and ritual) must be kept to avoid curse. Paul defines the "curse" of the law in terms of the necessity to obey all of the Law, for example, including circumcision. In demonstration of faithfulness, Christ redeemed gentiles from that curse by becoming (according to the Torah Paul cites) a curse offering in behalf of all (our behalf) demonstrating that faithfulness.

The issue in Galatia is not really even sins or trespasses. The only place Paul uses παράπτωμα ("trespass") is in Gal 6:1 in a context where he enjoins responsible redemption of the offender. He uses ἁμαρτία ("sin") in but three places—Gal 1:4, 2:17, and 3:22. The controlling metaphor for the entire letter is that of deliverance, redemption, and inclusion on the basis of the Gospel of God in Christ—not on the basis of ritual divine requirement of Torah, but rather faithfulness. The issue is not "sins," but gospel.

In Gal 1:4, Christ gave himself to deliver us from the Present Evil Age in accordance with the will of "our God and Father." Galatians 2:17 follows Paul's developing point that one is made right before God not on the basis of works of the Torah but through the faithfulness of Jesus Christ (διὰ πίστεως Ἰησοῦ Χριστοῦ). "Indeed, *we* have come to faith in Christ Jesus, in order that we may be rectified by reason of the faithfulness of Christ and not by reason of works of law, . . ." (Gal 2:16c). In Gal 3:22 Paul makes the point that the Scripture made all things a prisoner under Sin, "in order that the promise of the faithfulness of Jesus Christ might be given to the ones who express faith." By works of the Law no one will be "justified"; no "flesh" (σάρξ) will be made right on the basis of the works of the Law (Gal 2:16e).

As Paul combats an alternative gospel that he does not feel *is* a gospel, Paul's concern is a reconciliatory inclusion based upon faithfulness, as it was in the case of Abraham, and not a ceremonial legalism set forth by the later Torah of Moses. In the Abraham story, God accorded righteousness to Abraham on the basis of his faithfulness (Gen 15:6) prior to the establishment of the rite of circumcision as a sign of the covenant (Gen 17:9–14). Galatians becomes an appeal to faith and freedom and not an appeal to a limiting latitude of legalism expressed in ritual.

The issue in Galatia is that brought on by the Nomistic Evangelists, which Paul understands as an issue of Law versus faith in terms of the nature of the Gospel. This is evident as Gal 3 begins. Galatians 3:10 is in keeping with Paul's overall argument that all those who rely upon the Law are required to keep the whole Law and all who don't observe *everything* are under a curse (Deut 27:26). Faith does not rest upon the Law, however, for the Law came 430 years after God's earlier covenant with Abraham that was established on the basis of the faithfulness of Abraham and the promise of God (Gal 3:15–18). As a corollary, the Law does not rest on faith (Gal 3:11–12). This is the context of Gal 3:13. Christ redeemed us from the curse of having to observe everything written in the Law, such that as Paul says the promise given to Abraham based upon faithfulness might be made available to the gentiles as well as Jews, those to whom the Law was later given. Paul's general argument is developed throughout Galatians and even further in the early chapters of Romans.

It is in this context that Paul states Christ delivered us from the curse of the Law (i.e., that the entire Law must be kept) by becoming a curse in our behalf (by not avoiding death, even death on a "tree") in the light of the Law (cf. Deut 21:23). Did Christ become a curse deliberately, was that his goal? Did he become a curse as a victim? By whom or what was Christ "cursed"? It is suggested that Christ became a curse, according to the Law, as he was put to death by "the rulers of this age" (1 Cor 2:8). According to the Law, when Christ died by crucifixion "on a tree," he became cursed under the Law (Deut 21:23).

A. T. Robertson identified Gal 3:13 as an instance where ὑπέρ has the resultant idea of "instead," rather than the usual notion of "in behalf of" or "for one's benefit." He acknowledges that when one acts on behalf of another, one usually takes that person's place in some manner.[4] One senses the presence of doctrinal influence in Robertson's interpretation. We were considered "accursed," i.e., *under* a curse, such that Christ rescued us "*out from under*" the curse. The preposition ὑπέρ can also carry the idea of "for the sake of" or "about" or "concerning." The preposition has broad usage— "on behalf of," "to be for someone," "to be on someone's side," "in the place of," "instead of," "in the name of," "for," "because of." It can also be used as an equivalent of περί with

---

4. Robertson, *Grammar*, 630–31. See *BAGD*, 838–39. Robertson's point is assumptive, even if well taken.

the sense of "about" or "concerning." The broad usage of the Greek preposition argues against the limitation of singular dogmatism, although benefit and not substitution comes to the fore in general usage.

According to Jeffery et al., Gal 3:13 is a clear statement of penal substitution based upon the universal human predicament. The underlying assumption is that God needs someone to "curse" because of committed sins. Christ was cursed in our place, whereby we were thus redeemed. As Jeffery et al. state, the doctrine of penal substitution emerges plainly in Gal 3:10–13: "Christ endured God's curse in the place of his people, that they might be redeemed."[5] This is not Paul's topic. Paul's topic is actually the inclusion of gentiles on the basis of faithfulness, such that the promise of the Spirit is received through faithfulness and not works of the Law. Christ's redemption, according to Paul, delivered us from the *curse of the Law*, not the "curse of God" (cf. Gal 3:10–14).

In Finlan's perspective, redemption and curse-transmission are blended in Gal 3:13, as Paul combines purchase and scapegoat metaphors. The focus is upon *ritual* status and not *judicial* status. Christ's *judicial* status is not at issue, while that of humanity's *judicial* and *social* status is. Christ incurs a negative *ritual* condition, which offers humanity opportunity to take on positive *judicial* and *social* status. In Finlan's view, Christ becomes a scapegoat as he takes away our curse. Freedom is purchased for the captives of sin, such that human plaintiffs receive a favorable judicial result in the divine court.[6]

Second Corinthians 5:21 and Gal 3:13, according to Finlan, almost certainly make use of the scapegoat metaphor or image in interpreting the death of Christ. One might raise the question of the continuing usefulness of an image associated with the tabernacle and period of wilderness wandering by the people of Israel in the age of a permanent temple located in Jerusalem. Its usage on a gentile mission field might also be questioned. Surely, the Day of Atonement would have been observed in Jerusalem, but the actual scapegoat imagery had likely become merely symbolic and ritualistic at best. This is completely aside from the issue of the relevance of scapegoat imagery for gentile Galatians and Corinthians. In contemporary circles, the scapegoat has become a metaphor for victims and violence.

Galatians 3:13 occurs within the contextual matrix of Paul's defense of his gospel in the light of Nomistic Evangelists troubling his gentile converts in Galatia. The focus is upon faith—Jesus's faithfulness, Abraham's faithfulness, and the gentiles' faithfulness—all apart from "the Law." Paul understands the new Israel of God (now Jews and gentiles) in terms of faith and a cruciform imperative, not in terms of a ritual circumcision based upon Torah as advanced by the Nomistic Evangelists. These Nomistic

---

5. Jeffery et al., *Pierced for Our Transgressions*, 90–95. It is interesting that Jeffery et al. cite 2 Cor 5:21 only once as representative substitution, which they see to be the equivalent of penal substitution. See below.

6. Finlan, *Problems with Atonement*, 45. This does not appear to be Paul's topic either.

Evangelists, in Paul's judgment, likewise sought to evade a cruciform imperative of the cross (Gal 6:11–16). Ultimately, in Paul's understanding, Paul saw the Nomistic Evangelists as attempting to substitute an *unnecessary* ritual requirement that was disdained by gentiles for a quite *necessary* cross-imperative that called for living by faithfulness in the new creation as a member of the new people of God. One does not actually get closer to Paul anywhere than what he writes here, for he writes "in his own hand" (Gal 6:11).

Paul's focus in Gal 3:13 is not sins or atonement, but the living out of the Gospel in actual time. His emphasis is not upon transaction. His focus is not on penal substitution. Paul's focus is upon the availability and actualization of God's promise to Abraham now made to gentiles on the basis of faith, as indicated by the remainder of Gal 3. Christ was not cursed by God, but rather fell under the curse of the existing Law. In his argument, Paul affirms that the Law was given by angels through an intermediary (Gal 3:19–20). The Law itself also had an intermediary function, which since the *coming and freeing* of Christ, is no longer operative (Gal 3:23–29). Christ, by his death, although cursed by the Law, was free of the Law (Rom 7:1–6). A "death" makes a law no longer binding.

The resurrection of Christ is the fulfilment of God's promise in Abraham which now offers new life apart from the Law. When Paul in Gal 6:14 speaks of glorying in the cross of Christ or being crucified with Christ in Gal 2:19–20, Paul as much includes himself under the "curse of the Law," at least metaphorically and rhetorically. Insofar as he has died with Christ, he is alive to the realization of divine promise and free of the Law.

Paul commends peace and mercy (and grace!) to the new Israel constituted by faithfulness in Christ (cf. Gal 3:26–29). In addition, Paul essentially says to his nomistic opponents, "So, bug off! Let no one continue to bother me." Paul has challenged his gentile converts to remain faithful to the Gospel of God, as he has defended his gospel. Now, he defends his own faithfulness to that same Gospel of God. "From now on, let no one trouble me, for *I* carry in my [own] body the στίγματα of Jesus" (Gal 6:17).[7]

Galatians 3:1 exhibits one of the comparatively rare uses of the verb for crucifixion and it does so in terms of a perfect tense participle. Jesus Christ, Son of God (Gal 1:16), was publicly placarded as the crucified one (προεγράφη ἐσταυρωμένος, pf. part., Gal 3:1). In the personage of the Nomistic Evangelists, the Galatians have now been confronted with two alternative gospels. Alternative domains associated

---

7. The verb "carry" (βαστάζω) that Paul uses can suggest the idea of carrying, as of a child in the womb (cf. Luke 11:27). The Greek word στίγματα left untranslated above has been anglicized as "stigma," plural "stigmata." *BAGD*, 776, suggests Paul likely refers to the "wounds and scars" he had received in the service of Jesus. The word suggests a "mark," "scar," or "brand denoting ownership," such as a master might place upon his slave in the world in which Paul lived. Although Paul himself was circumcised, the stigmata of Jesus rendered the mark of circumcision irrelevant. *Merriam-Webster's Collegiate Dictionary*, 1225, suggests that *stigmata* are identifying bodily marks or pains resembling the wounds of the crucified Jesus.

with Paul's understanding of the Two Ages are evident (three for Paul, including the Age of Transformation). Personified, Paul places the Law together with the Flesh as actors in the Present Evil Age. On the other hand, the gift of the Spirit belongs to the realm of the Age of Transformation as a harbinger of the Age to Come, now that the Age to Come has dawned with the resurrection. To center upon fleshly issues such as circumcision, food laws, and festivals as legal requirements would, in Paul's judgment, mark a return and subjection regression to the powers of the Present Evil Age, even after the Galatians had experienced the Spirit of the New Age in Christ on the basis of faith in the gospel that Paul had proclaimed.

Paul confronts the Galatians. They are in danger of a regressive apostasy (Gal 5:4–7). "Did you receive the Spirit through works of Law or through preaching/hearing [ἀκοῆς] of faithfulness?" "Having made a beginning with the Spirit, do you now finish with the Flesh?" "The one who supplies the Spirit to you and who works acts of power in you, [is it] by works of the Law or by hearing of faithfulness?"

To be included within Israel is to become a child of Abraham, but this adoption is on the basis of faithfulness and not Mosaic Law that came 430 years after Abraham (cf. Gal 3:6–9; 3:17; 6:11–16). As for the support of Paul's argument, he makes an appeal to the Torah (Gal 3:6, cf. Gen 15:6; Gal 3:8, cf. Gen 12:3; Gal 3:10, cf. Deut 27:26; Gal 3:13, cf. Deut 21:23). Paul also makes an appeal to the "prophets" in his citation of Scripture (Gal 3:11), making use of Hab 2:4, a passage that will be significant in Romans (cf. Rom 1:17).

Paul's opponents, the Nomistic Evangelists, advanced a gospel supported by Mosaic Torah. Paul advanced a gospel based upon what God had done in Christ. According to his awareness of the Old Testament narrative, the Torah itself was not present in the beginning time of Abraham. According to his understanding of the Two Ages, the Torah would not be needed in the Age to Come that had already been inaugurated by the resurrection of Christ and the restorative gift of the Spirit (cf. Gal 3:14, 24–25).

The promise of the Spirit had now been given in Christ through faithfulness/faith commitment to what God had done (Gal 3:14). God "had graced" (κεχάρισται, pf., Gal 3:18) Abraham with promise. The history of Israel with Torah had indicated that no law could make alive. In fact, the Law under the power of Sin (Gal 3:22) was not able to make alive and could indeed advance basic sinfulness by transposing it to the category of transgression (Rom 7:7–12). The Scripture confined all things under Sin, in order that the promise might be given to those who exhibit faith on the basis of the faithfulness of Jesus Christ (Gal 3:22, sub. gen.) Thus, all who belong to the people of God (Israel) are children of God and members of Israel on the basis of faithfulness in Christ Jesus (Gal 3:26).

Back to Gal 3:13. First of all, Gal 3:13 should be left within the context of Gal 3:1–14 and the book of Galatians as a whole in the light of the central issues with which Paul addresses. In the light of the threat posed by the Nomistic Evangelists, the basic nature of the Gospel is at stake. What characterizes proper response to God—law or faith? What characterizes God's foundational response to humankind—provision or wrath?

Secondly, Christ died on a wooden cross erected by Rome. He thus succumbed to a forbidden and potentially defiling death, according to Torah. What Paul essentially says is that Christ's death was "for us" (ὑπὲρ ὑμῶν). Paul again thinks retrospectively of the New Age in the Spirit. We were redeemed from the curse of an ineffective and temporal law. The actual giving of the Law in Paul's understanding was that it was given through the mediation of angels, which caused Paul to reaffirm his Jewish monotheism: "God is *One*" (Gal 3:20). Christ was directly sent by God in terms of incarnation.

Paul realized in a polytheistic gentile environment that the greatest numerical difference was the difference between one and two. For Israel and for Paul, God was One (cf. Deut 6:4–5). God had acted through Jesus Christ (διὰ Ἰησοῦ Χριστοῦ, indirect agency) to raise him from the dead (Gal 1:1), to evangelize the gentiles (Gal 1:16), that they might become heirs of the promise originally given by God to Abraham through faithfulness in appropriating the gospel (Gal 3:26–29). Through the Spirit given, both Jew and gentile now confess "ABBA Father" (Αββα ὁ πατήρ, Gal 4:6), no longer as a slave but as adopted children of God (Gal 4:1–7). Having been freed from the controlling spirits to which all were enslaved in the Present Evil Age (τὰ στοιχεῖα τοῦ κοσμοῦ, Gal 4:3, 4:9), Paul challenges and questions those who wish to return to the "weak and impoverished" στοιχεῖα (Gal 4:9).

In reality, God acting through Christ has not only delivered one from the "curse of the Law" (Gal 3:13), but also from the στοιχεῖα. God's action marks the fulfilment of the promise given to Abraham raised to eschatological key. *The curse that rested upon the crucified Christ was the curse of Death that rested upon all human beings,* heightened because of its very public and shameful nature in crucifixion. It is Death itself that has been conquered in the resurrection.

Christ is the singular seed of Abraham (Gal 3:16), allegorically speaking, through whom the promise is fulfilled. Christ redeemed us from the curse of the Law (Gal 3:13) because he fell under the Law's curse at the point of his death, but on the other hand overcame the curse of the Law when God raised him from the dead (Gal 1:1). Because Paul has died with Christ in the Gospel (Gal 2:19; cf. Rom 6:1–11), Paul expects to live with Christ in resurrection. Paul can describe Death as the final scourge or enemy (cf. 1 Cor 15:54–57). Death is the curse of Sin; resurrection is the promise of Life. The blessing of Abraham is now present for both Jew and gentile through the Spirit.

The upshot of it all is that Galatians 3:13 does not have anything to do with atonement generally and certainly not penal substitutionary atonement specifically, as is so often assumed. *Galatians 3:13 has no direct application to "the Atonement" as commonly thought.* To accept it as such is to contextually and conceptually misunderstand or misrepresent Paul's point. It is a verse, however, into which atonement may easily be read and theological weeds may easily grow.

2 Corinthians 5:21

Mindful of his own sufferings and peril as an apostle of Christ, Paul writes to encourage the Corinthians and to attempt to mend some fences broken down as a result of his second and painful visit as well as his "letter of tears" (cf. 2 Cor 2:1–4). Paul affirms he is controlled by the love of Christ, convinced that Christ died for all and all have "died" with him (2 Cor 5:14). In 2 Cor 5:15 Paul affirms that Christ died for all and implies that all have been "raised" to live life anew; one no longer lives for oneself "but for him who for their sake died and was raised."

Paul has a "therefore" as he begins his argument set forth in 2 Cor 5:16–21. As a result of the resurrection, Paul no longer regards Jesus from a human point of view, as presumably he did as a Pharisaic persecutor of Christians prior to his apostolic call. Paul acknowledges his prior view (2 Cor 5:16). If anyone is in Christ, one is a new creation (2 Cor 5:17)—a theme also found in Gal 6:15. It was a theme that Paul had personally experienced.

A personal theme of Paul in 2 Corinthians is his attempt to be reconciled with the Corinthians. Paul suggests his openness toward the Corinthians and encourages their openness in the Gospel to him (2 Cor 6:1–13). Paul, as an *apostle* in Christ Jesus, has been entrusted with a ministry of reconciliation. He, thereby, is an ambassador for Christ, proclaiming a gospel of reconciliation. As Paul describes the Gospel of God in this context, God in Christ was reconciling the world to himself (2 Cor 5:19). Aside from the syntactical option of translating θεὸς ἦν ἐν Χριστῷ κόσμον καταλλάσσων ἑαυτῷ as "God was in Christ reconciling the world to himself" or "in Christ God was reconciling the world to himself," the basic intent of reconciliation is clear. In order to reconcile the world (Jew and gentile) to himself, God did not count trespasses against the "world." Indeed, to hold gentiles accountable for Jewish Law for which they did not have access would render God unjust, an issue which Paul addresses in Rom 1–3. For Paul, if God is seen as a judge, he is a just judge (Rom 3:26). Paul himself was called to be an apostle to the gentiles through whom his appeal could be made (Gal 1:16). Thus, in this Corinthian context at this point in time (55 CE), Paul defines the Gospel in terms of God's reconciliation in Christ that did not reckon prior trespasses, a Gospel of which Paul was an ambassador for Christ with a message of reconciliation. Paul works together with God (2 Cor 5:18–20; 6:1), with God who directly called him (Gal 1:15–16).

Second Corinthians 5:21 offers a soteriological statement at the end of a passage that stresses Paul's ministry of reconciliation. The verse has been interpreted to include a scapegoat metaphor which expresses an exchange of conditions. In the scapegoat ritual, the pure animal took away the community's sin, while the community took on the goat's purity. It was a ritual exchange. Second Corinthians 5:21, however, does not have to do with sacrifice or justification. The stunning reversal in the scapegoat ritual has nothing to do with acquittal in a legal sense, but with sin-transfer and banishment in a ritual sense, as order and purity are restored. Paul does not spell out the difference, which he need not have done in a high-context society.

Second Corinthians 5:21 appears to be a parenthetical comment of Paul in the above context. Paul in a single verse is not attempting to set forth a doctrine of the Atonement.

What does Paul mean by Christ being "made sin" for our sake? Christ was sinless and thus not liable to death. However, Christ died. The wages of Sin/sin is death, such that Christ bears the hallmark and outcome of Sin/sin. Paul's statement, although vague, is really little different from 2 Cor 5:15 in its general thrust, which indicates Jesus died "for our sake" and was raised "for our sake" (both with ὑπέρ). Contextually, "that we might become the righteousness of God in him" (2 Cor 5:21) appears to be a metaphorical reference to the hope of resurrection (cf. Rom 4:25). God's own righteousness has been revealed in Christ, even in the passing over of former sins (Rom 3:25; cf. Rom 1:17).

Paul, according to the current writer, penned both 2 Corinthians and Romans in 55–56 CE, although a number of months separate the two writings. Again, it is not likely both contextually and conceptually that Paul is addressing a doctrine of sacrificial atonement. If anything other than a parenthetical thought, the entire context is focused on reconciliation, such that atonement viewed in this context would represent at-one-ment. Indeed, the overall focus of 2 Corinthians is that of reconciliation, as Paul seeks to be reconciled with the Corinthians so as to ensure the success of his Collection and the integrity of the gospel.[8]

Second Corinthians 5:21, much like Rom 3:25 (treatment of which follows), occurs in the midst of a sustained argument that Paul is writing to the Corinthians in defense of his personal apostleship and ministry. It should be understood in the light of the matrices of Paul's second and painful visit with the Corinthians, his painful letter to that troublesome church (2 Cor 2:1–4), *and* his now ongoing Collection Campaign (2 Cor 8–9). The necessary theme that Paul *must* address is that of reconciliation with the church, for only reconciliation will resolve the prior pain and ensure the success of his collection ministry.

Paul's thought is not centered upon developing a systematic theology of atonement, but rather upon reconciliation. Consequently, he speaks of God's own "re-creation" in the Gospel through God's own reconciliation in Christ. "Re-creation" of relationship is exactly what Paul needed with respect to the Corinthians. In the Gospel, both Paul and the Corinthians have been entrusted with a ministry of reconciliation. If the Corinthians will not be reconciled with Paul, then they will have refused their

8. It should be stated that one of the purposes of Paul's Collection ministry was that of reconciliation and establishment of unity between Jewish and gentile Christians. Paul is centered upon reconciliation and hope for the success of his Collection ministry. This is vital for his future plans of ministry (cf. Rom 15:22–29). However, he does not yet know how the Corinthians will respond, such that he faces his third visit to that church with some fear and trepidation (cf. 2 Cor 13:1–10). Historical context is important.

own missional identity in Christ and their own growth toward maturity—they will have come to faith in vain and will remain only as immature children (2 Cor 6:1–13). In this context of imperatival reconciliation, 2 Cor 5:21 suggests in different words the truth of Phil 2:5–11.

Romans 3:25

Romans 3:25 is the *sine qua non* of atonement theory generally and penal substitution particularly, as it would apply to Pauline passages. Jeffery et al. paraphrase Rom 3:21–26, stressing that God has now demonstrated his justice by punishing all peoples' sins in Christ. God set forth Christ as a "sacrifice of atonement" (literally, as "a propitiation," v. 25), thus "turning aside God's wrath" as he himself suffered in the place of his people. They then "quote" Rom 3:25–26 in full in the following manner.

> God presented him as a sacrifice of atonement, through faith in his blood. He did this to demonstrate his justice, because in his forbearance he had left the sins committed beforehand unpunished—he did it to demonstrate his justice at the present time, so as to be just and the one who justifies those who have faith in Jesus.[9]

Their particular emphasis upon "justice" and "punishment" should be noted. The latter, in particular, is an imposition upon the text. With regard to the former, there are alternative renderings of δικαιοσύνη than "justice" that fit the particular context. They interpret the reference to "blood" as synonymous with "death," understood as a penalty deliberately imposed by God. God must punish sin, although he delayed judgment of former sins until they could be punished in Christ.[10] In their view, God has placated himself and turned his wrath aside by offering his Son as a propitiation of the selfsame divine wrath. They admit "wrath" is not explicit in the immediate context, although they read it into the text anyway. In their view, Rom 3:21–26 is undeniable in teaching that Christ was set forth as a propitiation to turn aside God's wrath by suffering that wrath in his place. "The undeniable teaching of Romans 3:21–26 is that the Lord Jesus Christ was set forth as a propitiation, to turn aside God's wrath from his people by suffering it [God's wrath] in their place."[11]

Paul refers to Jesus's death as a sacrifice in Rom 3:25, as he refers to the ἱλαστήριον, the lid of the Ark in Israel's Day of Atonement ritual. Paul's usage, however, may refer more to "means" than to "place." The focus is upon provision. Both elements may be in view in the sphere of the Christ event, such that the term suggests a place of provision. Jesus's death is related to the sin offering in 2 Cor 5:21 and Rom 8:3. Surely, Paul understood the nature of the sin offering in the Old Testament (cf. Lev 4:1–35), which

9. Jeffery et al., *Pierced for Our Transgressions*, 80.
10. Jeffery et al., *Pierced for Our Transgressions*, 81.
11. Jeffery et al., *Pierced for Our Transgressions*, 85.

was an offering for *unintentional* transgressions. Paul's understanding in the use of the metaphor must have other relational application.

In view of what he says in Rom 6:23, that the wages of Sin is death, Paul appears to simply reference the death of Jesus. Jesus died, but in Paul's understanding, the death of Jesus marks the end of Sin's power and reach. Death is all that Sin and the powers can effect—it is the worst they can do. God condemns Sin in its own lair in the death of Jesus precisely by raising Jesus from the dead.[12] God, in fact, does more than merely restore Jesus to life by resuscitation.

It is in the resurrection that Jesus's own death is "made sacred" by God himself. "Redemption" understood to be inherent in sacrifice is not just a "slave market" metaphor as commonly perceived, but rather has ramifications of God's deliverance in the Exodus and from Exile. That deliverance is once again God's provision which *now* transcends national limitations. It is God's provision in eschatological key, which delivers the entire cosmos, as well as the Jew *and* gentile. Creation itself is being reclaimed. Jew as well as gentile, gentile as well as Jew, now mark the re-creation of God's people as Israel.

Reconciliation is a theme for Paul that underscores God's initiative in redemption. Paul's concept of reconciliation has "personalized social, human and cosmic, spiritual and material, religious and ethnic meaning."[13] In other words, it is all encompassing in its eschatological scope. As God's own apostle in Christ, Paul's own "job description" is that of a "ministry of reconciliation" (2 Cor 5:18).

Jesus's death understood under the rubric of "the theology of the cross" in the end is a divine mystery that works against all of the conventions and expectations and characterizations of humanity—it appears as "foolishness" that reveals the "wisdom of God," according to Paul.[14] God acts on the basis of his own initiative out of his covenant love expressed to Abraham to redeem his beloved creation. Neither God nor Christ were seen to be objects for manipulation within Paul's expression of the gospel. They were each acting subjects, such that God's punishment does not fall upon Christ nor does Christ offer appeasement to God. Christian theology should not objectify either, but should hear and heed Paul's greeting to his churches: "Grace to all of you and peace from God our Father and the Lord Jesus Christ." It is a totally subjective blessing.

Romans 3:23–26 may perhaps be intentionally translated differently than it usually is rendered. For purposes of emphasis and clarity, it is given in italics. *"For all have sinned. Indeed, they lack the glory of God, being rectified freely by his grace through*

---

12. Is it too much to say that Paul's understanding is that by means of the resurrection God condemned Sin with "blood on Sin's hands"? It as though God said, "Enough, O Sin, Death is conquered and the scourge of your power is overcome."

13. Carroll and Green, *Death of Jesus*, 274.

14. In current context, one might assert that the wisdom of God in Christ transcends the "foolishness" and limitations of all humanly-formulated atonement theories.

the redemption [indirect agency], *that is, the redemption of the one in Christ Jesus, whom God put forth as a provision of mercy through* [his] *faithfulness, by his blood* [full life and death] *for a demonstration of his righteousness, because of the passing over by God's forbearance of previously accumulated acts of sins, with a view toward the demonstration of his rectification in the present season, for the purpose that he might be rectifier and rectifying the one who exhibits faithfulness in Jesus.*" While not offered as a formal translation, this translation is offered to bring out the force of Paul's meaning in the writer's perspective.[15] Paul's Greek is somewhat cumbersome (and pleonastic), although his basic point does not seem to be different from the perspectives Paul enunciates in Phil 2:5–11, set forth below.

Practically every aspect of Rom 3:25 is controversial, although the overall context is the revelation of the righteousness of God (Rom 3:21–26). Paul's own emphasis is ultimately seen more clearly in Rom 3:25b–26, where he asserts that God has passed over former sins and shown in the present time that (1) he himself *is* righteous and (2) he rectifies the one who expresses faith in Jesus in terms of the faithfulness of Jesus. Romans 3:25 expresses a sacrificial metaphor in the use of ἱλαστήριον and the mention of "blood." Faith in Christ is the place (sphere) of expiation where former sins are passed over. It offers divine provision provided by God. Aside from arguments about theories of atonement, it is important to appreciate God's clear participation, according to Paul. Rectification comes as God's gift (Rom 3:24). It is God who makes provision. God himself freely provides a place or sphere and means wherein expiation is possible, even apart from the Law; it is through πιστὸς Ἰησοῦ, "faith in Christ" or the "faithfulness of Christ."

A number of scholars debate whether Rom 3:25 is an interpolation or not, in view of the isolation of its sacrificial atonement imagery compared to the remainder of Paul's thought. It stands out as a *hapax legomenon* in Paul's thought. Once again, other than the employment of a sacrificial metaphor in a context where Paul uses several different metaphors, Paul would not set forth a *theory of atonement* in a single verse.

Even in the context of Rom 3:21–31, it is God's initiative and pre-emptive action that is stressed, as his righteousness is expressed apart from the Law and the Prophets by his own choice. God passes over previously committed sins, *freely* justifying us by his grace, by his own redemption provided in Christ Jesus. Paul's point is that God *is* just and that he rectifies the one of faith in Christ, whether that one be Jew or gentile (Rom 3:26). God's "rightness" is not compromised by doing right. Even here, Paul does not use cross terminology. He refers to Jesus's "blood," which surely must refer

---

15. Pamela Eisenbaum offers a personal translation of Rom 3:21–30, a passage that many see to be the center of Paul's argument in Romans. She follows that with her own paraphrase of the passage. Both are excellent, in terms of revealing Paul's intended meaning. See Eisenbaum, *Paul Was Not a Christian*, 248–49. As she summarizes Paul's intended meaning, "In essence, he is describing the ingathering of the nations at the culmination of history, assuring his Gentile audience that they will be part of redemption, while clarifying for them the ongoing inclusion of Jews in this same redemption . . ." See Eisenbaum, *Paul Was Not a Christian*, 249.

to Jesus's life as well as his sufferings and death. He directly states that God put forth Christ Jesus metaphorically as a place where mercy might be received (ἱλαστήριον) for those who have faith—both Jew *and* gentile. God provides. One should not miss the point that God's provision is personal and incarnational, not abstract.

The ἱλαστήριον (a *hapax legomenon* for Paul) was the place where the impurity which resulted from Israel's sins was ritually cleansed on the Day of Atonement (*Yom Kippur*) once a year. Paul says that God put forth Christ as a "mercy seat of faith." English translations are not adequate— "expiation" (*NAB*), "sacrifice of atonement" (*NIV, NRSV*). Paul does not equate Jesus with the sacrificial victim in this passage, for the sacrificial animal was never termed an ἱλαστήριον but rather an ἱλασμός (1 John 2:2). Never in all of Jewish and Greek literature is a sacrificial animal called an ἱλαστήριον—the word used throughout the *LXX* for the mercy seat (cf. Heb 9:5).[16] Ἱλαστήριον is the place of provision, not itself the expiatory or sacrificial victim. Christian scholars and piety have over-interpreted Rom 3:24–25 and made Jesus into the sacrificial victim, when actually Paul equates him with the mercy seat. Such victimization has blocked development of a fresh understanding of "what Paul really said."[17]

There is really no suggestion of placation, appeasement, or satisfaction, or other legal transaction—forget all the misplaced discussion over "propitiation" and "expiation." Many interpretations of Rom 3:25 exist and it is a difficult verse. How should one understand the words "through faith"? What do they mean? Where should punctuation marks be placed? Whose "faithfulness" is mentioned? While the participle of Rom 3:22 clearly refers to the faith of Jews and gentiles ("all those who have faith"), this writer in the light of the entire passage would interpret the "faithfulness" mentioned in Rom 3:25 as a reference to God's own faithfulness. It is, indeed, "all about God." The imagery of a "place where mercy is obtained" as provided by God is coordinate with "by his blood," in recognition of Jesus's life and death. The phrase πίστεως Ἰησοῦ (vv. 22, 26) is debated as to whether it is a subjective or objective genitive, i.e., whether it points to Jesus's own faithfulness or the faith one places in Jesus .

Romans 3:21–26 is a tightly packed passage that raises two questions about God. First of all, there is the question of the reliability and faithfulness of God. What about God's covenantal history with Israel, his own people? They, along with gentiles, are implicated in sin. Does their faithlessness nullify God's faithfulness (Rom 3:3)? Paul will revisit the issue of God's faithfulness in Rom 9–11. Secondly, what about God's "moral integrity"? If God makes his goodness readily available to sinners, how can he be a just judge? If salvation is available to sinners outside of God's stipulated covenant law, then why not do evil such that God's goodness may abound (Rom 3:8)? Is God reliable? Does God have integrity?

16. Finlan, *Problems with Atonement*, 40–41.
17. Finlan, *Problems with Atonement*, 41.

Those two questions have now been addressed by God's own actions in Christ. The rectifying activity of Israel's covenant God, formerly revealed in the Torah and the Prophets (Rom 3:21), has now been revealed personally in Christ in the present time. Paul's metaphorical description echoes God's covenant keeping and making from Israel's past ("redemption," Rom 3:24; "provision of atonement," Rom 3:25). God's original covenant set forth in Abraham (as revealed in Torah, Gen 12) has now been set forth *for all* in Christ, such that God's reliability and integrity in terms of Torah covenant is upheld (cf. Rom 3:31). God is right and is able to rectify (Rom 3:26). The problem rests with humanity (and the cosmos!), which is why God steps in to rectify in the first place. The problem does not rest with God; with God, rests the solution. Paul's presentation here is a pre-emptive precursor of his lengthy discussion in Rom 9–11.

Paul can use the language of redemption (ἀπολύτρωσις) in keeping with other early Christian thought. The general framework or semantic domain of "redemption" may be supported by a number of other terms in the New Testament.[18]

In a world of sacrificial cults, redemption might be accompanied by the offering of a sacrifice ("to make sacred"). Sacrifice, however, had no monolithic meaning within ancient Israel and the salvific meaning of sacrifice never came to full expression. Formulaic expression in terms of "Christ died for all" (cf. 1 Thess 5:10; Gal 2:21; 1 Cor 8:11; 15:3; Rom 5:6, 8) and "his blood" (cf. Rom 5:9; Col 1:20) suggest sacrificial imagery. Yet all sacrifices are not the same. We see in Paul "covenant sacrifice" (1 Cor 11:25), "Passover sacrifice" (1 Cor 5:7–8), "sin offering" (2 Cor 5:21; Rom 8:3), offering of "firstfruit" (1 Cor 15:20, 23).

The question might be asked as to why Paul would write a passage like Rom 3:21–26 to Rome, when Jerusalem was the place of Jewish sacrificial offering. Paul's lead-in argument would certainly be addressed to Jewish Christians (Rom 3:1–20), although the conclusion he reaches is that *no one*, Jew nor gentile, will be rectified before God on the basis of works of the Law. The Law's function is to reveal knowledge of sin (Rom 3:20). Paul has already established that there is not so much as one who is right with God, and he has done so on the basis of Jewish Scripture itself (Rom 3:10–18). What may not have been realized or emphasized nearly enough is that Paul writes against the backdrop matrix of the threat of the Nomistic Evangelists who have plagued his churches and threatened his own gospel virtually throughout his entire Collection Campaign.

The Nomistic Evangelists have been insisting upon the necessity of the Law for gentiles as a means of completing the salvation process of membership within Israel. The gentile Christians in Rome would thus be overhearing a basic argument that Paul, at least in part, is rehearsing against the Nomistic Evangelists whom he expects to have to confront in Jerusalem—the "unpersuaded ones" as he terms them (Rom 15:30–31).

---

18. Cf. Carroll and Green, *Death of Jesus*, 267.

The Nomistic Evangelists have been challenging Paul's gospel at the very point of Paul's affirmation of Abraham's faith response to God, insisting that after one comes to faith it is necessary to embrace the Law. In other words, after Abraham "believed" and it was "reckoned to him as righteousness" (Gen 15:6), Abraham then took the next step as was now required by the Law or Torah. He underwent circumcision by the direct command of God, as an *everlasting* and *required* sign of the covenant (Gen 17:9–14). Any male not circumcised would not be included in the people of Israel.

The argumentative difference between Paul and the Nomistic Evangelists particularly revolved around an internecine struggle over the place and interpretation of Torah in relation to the gospel. Paul emphasized Gen 12 and 15:6, while his opponents emphasized Gen 17 in addition. They conceded Paul's point of Abraham's faith (Gen 12; 15:6) as a matter of entry into the Israel of God, but Paul did not concede their point of the necessity of circumcision for gentiles in addition to faith (Gen 17). For Paul, there was now a universal non-ethnic Israel that included both Jew and gentile on the singular basis of the Gospel of God in Christ. The new Israel, which was the fulfilment of the promise originally given to Abraham, was independent of external rites. It was a "new creation" wrought by God's eschatological Gospel (Gal 6:15–16).

Paul himself had been directly called by God to carry the Gospel to gentiles (Gal 1:15–16). He could not embrace and emphasize circumcision to potential gentile converts if he were to have a successful mission to the gentiles, for they looked upon circumcision as bodily mutilation. In addition, while they were interested in and embraced a gospel that proclaimed salvation, resurrection, and eternal life, they were not likely interested in becoming a Jew in a gentile contextual and cultural matrix. At any rate, Paul became convinced that circumcision as a physical rite was not necessary for gentiles. We are not privy to all the reasons why, although Paul may well have come to his position through much prayer and contemplation in addition to his scriptural interpretation.

Thus as we have seen to this point, the three cardinal verses in Paul that are most often used to set forth his support for atonement theories (Gal 3:13; 2 Cor 5:21; Rom 3:25) really have little or nothing to do with the development of atonement theory in Paul. Paul would not have set forth atonement theory in single, individual verses. Perhaps most of all, the verses certainly do not support penal substitutionary theory as popularly proclaimed.

Romans 4:25

Jeffery et al. claim Rom 4:25 as a verse in support of penal substitution, as they connect it with Rom 3:21–26. They supply emphasis to Paul's statement, "*he* was delivered over to death for *our* sins," as well as explicitly adding the phrase "to death." While Paul appears to implicitly suggest Jesus's death by his use of παρεδόθη ("he was handed over"), they connect the use of the word to Rom 8:32 (παρέδωκεν, "he gave, handed over"). They likely do this because of the reference to God "not sparing" (οὐκ ἐφείσατο, Rom 8:32) his own Son. They ignore Paul's usage of the verb earlier in Rom 1:24, 26, 28.

The context of Rom 4:25 is not a treatment of atonement, but rather one of faith or faithfulness in the light of the gospel. Romans 4:25 marks the conclusion of Paul's argument that began with the faithfulness of Abraham (Rom 4:1–25). Essentially, Romans 4 is Paul's midrash on Gen 15:6, supported also by Ps 32:1–2. The central phrase for Paul's point is that faithfulness "was reckoned [to Abraham] with a view toward what God requires [δικαιοσύνην]" (cf. Rom 4:3, 9, 22).

Paul will assume his argument of Romans 4 as he begins Romans 5, as seen by his use of οὖν ("therefore") and the participial form δικαιωθέντες ("being rectified," "placed in a right standing"). Romans 4:23–25 marks the conclusion of his midrash, as he makes application for the Christians at Rome, both gentiles and Jews. Paul implicitly appears to understand promised and impending resurrection as the righteous reward of God based upon current faithfulness. Reward will be reckoned to those who are faithful to the One "who raised Jesus our Lord from the dead" (Rom 4:24). Romans 4:25 becomes a characterization of Jesus as Lord in the light of the Gospel of God. Jesus was handed over to Death because of human trespasses (τὰ παραπτώματα ἡμῶν), but he was raised with a view toward our being made right with God.

It should be noted that the cross is not mentioned. Jesus's death is only obliquely mentioned ("handed over") as a necessary prelude to resurrection and to the rectification of those who now express faithfulness to God and the Gospel. Faithfulness after the manner of Abraham is enjoined. The stage is set for Paul's significant development in Romans 5:1–11. In Paul's presentation, Rom 4:25 has nothing to do with atonement theory, but it has far more to do with actual reconciliation with God on the basis of faithfulness, as seen in what precedes and what follows the verse.

Philippians 2:5–11

Although Phil 2:5–11 is not usually considered in discussion of atonement theory, the passage has distinct value for Paul's understanding of atonement. Whether the passage is an early Christian hymn adopted by Paul or a Pauline composition is irrelevant to the present discussion. Paul embraced and set forth its content. In the context, Paul is stressing an imperative of obedience on the part of the Philippians akin to that found in Christ Jesus (Phil 2:5, 13). Christ took on human form, being born in the likeness of human beings. Paul speaks in terms of incarnation (Phil 2:6–7). Christ humbled himself, becoming obedient to death, even a cross death (Phil 2:8). As a result of Christ's obedience, an act pleasing to God the Father, God exalted Jesus to be Christ and Lord (Phil 2:9–11). It was not God who "humbled" Christ, but Christ who humbled himself, even to the point of death on a cross. It was God who exalted him.

What does this have to do with atonement, when there is no mention of sin in the passage? The passage and context offer clarification of Paul's understanding of the cross, in one of the few passages where he directly mentions the cross. The death Christ died was not a sentence of God, but it came as a result of incarnation and obedience. The cross originated in Jesus's self-sacrificial obedience. By contrast, it would have been disobedience to seize equality with God and evade death. There is no suggestion of transactional satisfaction or imposed sacrificial requirement. There *are* echoes of idolatry (cf. Rom 1:18–32) and Adam's disobedience (Rom 5:12–21) playing in the background.

There is no concept of placation or propitiation or expiation of sin or guilt or justification present in Phil 2:5–11. There is no concept of a required or needed sacrifice. All of that imagery is totally missing. There is no concept of legal "satisfaction" present. What is found is the rejection of idolatry, as well as vulnerability, and obedience which led to a cross-death. What is found is God's action of rectification of wrong which makes possible rightful worship of God. The greatest example of idolatrous wrong is rectified by God's action of resurrection affirmation and by the outpouring of grace that marks victory over the greatest perpetrated evil. There is no stress upon a misplaced emphasis of a stringent transcendent holiness or a judge who must pass sentence. There is only emphasis upon a Divine Father who is glorified in proper worship because of his rectifying action.

The entire passage and its imperatival context are also informed by Paul's awareness of the resurrection of Christ (as was Paul's entire ministry), as well as the Christian hope of attaining to the resurrection (Phil 3:12–16; 1:23). Living out of a cross-imperative is to live worthy of the gospel of Christ (Phil 1:27–30)—in obedient relationship with God and with the prospect of suffering, something Paul himself most certainly knew very well. At-one-ment, the basis of which for Paul is the theme of reconciliation, is predicated upon the action and model of Christ Jesus. "Atonement" is something to be lived, not a transaction consummated. One could infer a "moral influence" theory operative which could be termed ethical. In reality, *for Paul* other themes are operative—denial of idolatry, reconciliation, obedience, self-sacrifice, and a cross-imperative. God is at work in the Philippians as they live out their lives, working out their own salvation (Phil 2:12).

When one examines Paul's thought, his perspectives do not match any of the "three primary views" of the atonement exactly, although the third "classic" view of Aulén may have closest affinity in the light of its emphasis upon the enslaving power of Sin and the initiative exercised by God. It seeks to hold together God's rectification of sinners with atonement (reconciliation). Paul employs a host of images and metaphors in his soteriological language in seeking to express what is ultimately inexpressible. Paul makes a number of allusions to a variety of categories to express God's saving action. He can use cultic-sacrificial, juridical-legal, and participatory-personal categories to stress the depth of the meaning of Christ's death. He portrays death on a cross in an aspective sense, in his larger attempt to give a comprehensive and unified voice to the meaning of God's saving action.

Paul's Metaphors

Paul offers a chorus of metaphors, not a solo description. Paul is certainly not univocal in the imagery that he employs, although he is univocal in laying stress to the soteriological significance of Jesus's death and resurrection. The problem comes when one seizes upon singular imagery to the exclusion of Paul's richer language and when one literalizes in singular ways Paul's manifold metaphors. It becomes an exercise, by way of analogy, of taking sublime picturesque poetry and turning it into most prosaic prose. Such exercises both misinterpret and misrepresent Paul. His arguments are not always consistent with his metaphors, such that his metaphors may be misconstrued. According to Finlan, Paul's arguments defend the free will and generosity of God. On the other hand, Paul's metaphors imply some necessary type of ritual or transactional payment.[19]

Paul appropriates the concept of cultic exchange filled with spiritual content. He uses a transformation metaphor. He speaks of the love of Christ (2 Cor 5:10–14), of the one who died for all (2 Cor 5:15), whose death resulted in new creation and reconciliation (2 Cor 5:17–19), sealed by a reversal ritual (2 Cor 5:21). Paul's argument has a cultic setting, because he writes to people very familiar with and steeped in cultic practices. When Paul wrote 1 Corinthians in 54 CE, he could refer to Christ in terms of "our paschal Lamb" (1 Cor 5:7).[20] Passover was a time of celebration. In spite of that, people's trespasses are not counted against them (2 Cor 5:19), although not *because* they have been imposed upon another sacrificial victim.

It should not be missed, however, that Paul calls upon one to recognize one's own death in *that* death (2 Cor 5:14), i.e., a cruciform imperative. In Finlan's perspective, while Paul speaks of God's kindness and eagerness to save, "the *means* of salvation" had to be cultic or economic. It would involve some kind of sacrifice, scapegoat, or redemption payment.[21] Any contradiction was not acknowledged by Paul—his use of metaphors did not require that. Paul used varied metaphors and models to interpret the death of Christ—sacrificial purification, sin-bearing scapegoat, redemption payment by a heroic martyr, such that to force Paul into a single metaphorical understanding misrepresents both Paul and the use of metaphorical language. "All that is needed for a metaphor to be effective is one point of contact."[22]

---

19. Finlan, *Problems with Atonement*, 43.

20. The reference that he intended to remain in Ephesus "until Pentecost" may perhaps suggest Paul wrote 1 Corinthians in the late spring of 54 CE, at a point between Passover and Pentecost (cf. 1 Cor 5:7; 16:8).

21. Finlan, *Problems with Atonement*, 43.

22. Finlan, *Problems with Atonement*, 39.

In fact, given the theological misuse of Paul's metaphors as they have been turned into theories, one might gain better insight into Paul by turning his metaphors into similes, if one should need help in understanding.[23] To re-visit the afore-mentioned models or metaphors, Christ's death "is *like* sacrificial purification"; it is "*like* a sin-bearing scapegoat"; it is "*like* a heroic martyrdom that functions as a redemption payment." Perhaps clarity may surface by the use of similes in the place of misconstrued metaphors.

The Window of Romans 5:1–11

It is instructive, for example, to reconsider Rom 5:1–11 as a window through which to view other troublesome Pauline "verses," such as Rom 3:25, 2 Cor 5:21, or Gal 3:13, which have just been treated. Based upon what has come before in Romans, it is a self-contained pericope within Paul's sustained argument in Romans. It serves as a foundational vista for what follows (cf. οὖν, "therefore," in Rom 5:1, 12). First, one must pay attention to context. Paul affirms we have been rectified (aor.) on the basis of faith or faithfulness (Rom 5:1), that Christians are those who are faithful toward (ἐπί) the one who raised Jesus "our Lord" from the dead (cf. Rom 4:24).

Contextually, according to Rom 4:25, Christ was given over "by reason of" (διά) our trespasses (παρεδόθη διὰ τὰ παραπτώματα ἡμῶν) and he was raised "for the sake of" our rectification (ἠγέθη διὰ τὴν δικαίωσιν ἡμῶν). Therefore, we have been rectified ἐκ πίστεως ("by reason of faith/faithfulness"), with ἐκ suggesting origin or reason.[24]

Rectification comes to us through the Lord Jesus Christ and, for Paul, reflects the reality of the resurrection. It is through Christ the Lord that we have already received the right of entry (pf. ἐσχήκαμεν) into the grace in which those in Christ have already come to stand (pf. ἐστήκαμεν, Rom 5:2).

Free right of entry before God, indicative of full acceptance by God, has been granted on the basis of faith/faithfulness (Rom 5:2; cf. Rom 3:27, 30) and not on the basis of sacrificial nor placatory necessity. It has been granted freely by God's grace, a point Paul stresses more than once (Rom 5:2; 3:24; cf. 3:25–26). There is absolutely no expressed concern for the need of divine satisfaction or the protection of "divine honor" or penal substitution. Paul has mounted a long argument to establish that all, without exception, are actually guilty of sin (Rom 1:18—3:23).

Paul's focus is essentially twofold—(1) the sin of humankind and (2) the expressed grace of God predicated on his rectifying nature (Rom 3:21–26). These two realities have alternative expression in "the glory of God" (Rom 5:2) and the "lack of God's glory" (Rom 3:23). Those outside of Christ, including the "religious person" who seeks to provide his or her own salvation (Rom 1:18–32; 3:20, 23), continue to

23. A simile, of course, is a figure of speech "on the way toward metaphor," perhaps expressing *a truth at a lower level of abstraction and at a more limited level of misconstrual.*

24. For the use of ἐπί, see *BAGD*, 289; for διά, see *BAGD*, 180; for ἐκ, see *BAGD*, 234.

pursue other alternatives that lack or deny the "glory of God" (Rom 3:23). How do humans obtain the "glory of God"? Not by their own efforts or expressions, but rather by acknowledging God's glory in their living and their worship. This is stressed in a tri-fold manner in Eph 1:3–14.

God has now demonstrated his glory in the strongest terms imaginable, by raising Jesus from the dead and exalting him as Lord. God's rectifying nature (δικαιοσύνη θεοῦ, Rom 3:21) has intervened to make things right—because he is right and because he has the power to make right, he rectifies the one who has faith in Christ (obj. gen.) or who exhibits the faithfulness of Christ (subj. gen., Rom 3:26). God has demonstrated his rectifying nature by passing over previously committed sins (i.e., by not demanding payment or satisfaction or meting out judgment or allowing his wrath to take over, Rom 3:25), i.e., by the expression of his grace in Christ (Rom 3:24; 5:2). Here is the Gospel news! In Paul's letters, the emphasis is upon faith or faithfulness, not upon repentance and forgiveness of sins. God "passes over" previously committed sins and calls us to faith in him, i.e., to properly acknowledge his glory, i.e., to worship.

What does all this have to do with atonement? First of all, we have been considering what Paul actually wrote and not a theory of atonement imposed upon New Testament texts. Secondly, once one understands what Paul actually says, then all the elements that constitute at-one-ment fall into their proper place in a coherent whole. This may be seen in what Paul goes on to say in Rom 5:2–11. Thirdly, what Paul has to say calls for the subjunctive ἔχωμεν ("let us have") in Rom 5:1 rather than the indicative ἔχομεν ("we have"). It is widely acknowledged that ἔχωμεν has the better textual support, even by those who choose the indicative form of ἔχω ("I have"). Consider, then, Paul's argument which he sets forth in Rom 5:1–11.

God has acted in Christ to rectify freely those in Christ on the basis of their faith, even as he counted Abraham as right before him on the basis of faith (Rom 4:22–25). *Faith* is significant not because it is a sacred and meritorious human attribute, but because it is the element of faith that expresses *trust in God*. It is faith that creates the opportunity of relationship from the human side, even as grace and faithfulness support the creational opportunity of relationship from the divine side. The Gospel is an appeal from faithfulness for faithfulness (cf. Rom 1:16–17). One who expresses faith in God acknowledges God's glory, as God created humans to do and to be—not for God's sake but for their own sake, as David Brondos is wont to stress in the light of Paul's own emphasis.[25] This was true of Abraham, and should be true for those to whom rectification is about to be reckoned, as a result of Christ's resurrection by God (Rom 4:24–25; cf. Rom 3:26). In the light of what God has already done in terms of God's indicative, Paul moves to the imperative. This calls for a hortatory subjunctive in Rom 5:1—in the light of God's rectification through a living Lord, "let us enjoy the peace we have with God." The hortatory subjunctive becomes a dynamic imperative in its force, rather than a mere static affirmation.

25. Brondos, *Parting of the Gods*, 314–23. See Gen 1:26–31; Eph 1:3–14.

The problem has never been with God; it has always rested with humanity since the time of Adam. One can enjoy that peace, because one already has a right of en-trée with God and already stands within his grace. One should fully embrace it and enjoy its benefits. This calls for a continuing imperatival emphasis in terms of two further hortatory subjunctives. "Indeed, let us boast in the hope (ἐπ' ἐλπίδι) of the glory of God." Contextually, the manifest "glory of God" is his ability to bring life out of death—whether that be a descendent motif as introduced in the Abraham analogy, or the resurrection motif introduced in terms of Christ himself (now past) and those in Christ (about to be, Rom 4:24).

Presently, Paul himself can only boast in the *hope* of God's glorious resurrection This calls forth Paul's third hortatory subjunctive, "indeed, let us boast in sufferings, because we know that suffering brings about patient endurance, and patient endur-ance (demonstrates) hope, and hope does not disappoint because the love of God is poured out in our hearts through [indirect agency] the Spirit of holiness given to us" (cf. Rom 5:3–5). Paul's use of a hortatory subjunctive (first person plural) in Rom 5:1, 2, 3 over a direct imperative (second person) is entirely appropriate in writing to a church he had never visited and to Christians whom he did not personally know.

A hortatory subjunctive is essentially a milder, participatory imperative. It is also in keeping with Paul's dynamic gospel which far exceeds any static status quo. Paul's gospel pointed to God's Gospel in process—a Gospel complete, but not yet concluded in its final definition. Paul has some concern for careful diplomacy (cf. Rom 1:11–13). Paul wishes to encourage the Roman church, but he does not wish to offend. Also, Paul is still "healing" from theological threats and injury brought about by the No-mistic Evangelists, who have dogged his Collection Campaign. He is still "healing" from his breech with the Corinthians. He requires the mustering of his personal and theological strength prior to his travel to Jerusalem with the Collection, where he anticipates a battle yet once again (cf. Rom 15:30–31). If Paul writes Romans from Corinth, he is likely cognizant of how easy it is to offend, as had happened with the most troublesome Corinthian church. For Paul, a hortatory subjunctive was the "lan-guage of diplomacy."

Paul employs a γάρ in Rom 5:6 to stress by way of further explanation what he has just set forth in the earlier verses. He does so by a bracketed thought inclusion: "Christ . . . died," i.e., "*Christ*, while we were still weak yet at the proper time in behalf of people living in a godless manner [ἀσεβής], *died*." Earlier, Paul declared the revela-tion of the wrath of God unto self-destruction against "all ungodliness" (ἀσέβειαν) and "wickedness" (ἀδικίαν) of men (cf. Rom 1:18–32). After a parenthetical thought of elaboration (Rom 5:7), Paul resumes his thought by stressing that God demon-strated his own love toward us, because Christ died for us (ὑπὲρ ἡμῶν, not "in our place") while we were still sinners, those under the power of Sin and destined for self-destruction, those who lacked and who had no concern for the glory of God.

Reference to the "blood" of Christ in Rom 5:9 appears to be a reference to Christ's death, i.e., the release of life. God has worked his rectification through the death of Christ, such that we shall be saved through him (indirect agency, δι' αὐτοῦ) from divine wrath, both present (Rom 1:18–32) and future (1 Cor 15:20–28). The greater emphasis would seem to fall upon the present wrath. Romans 5:10 suggests that our rectification included no longer being "enemies" with or hostile toward God. Indeed, how can one trust in or have faith in one who is an enemy? Rather, *we* have been reconciled to God through the death of his Son, through God's Gospel of resurrection and exaltation, through God's grace and peace. Once one is reconciled, one can no longer be an "enemy" or remain hostile. New relationship is born. Thus again, "Let us enjoy peace with God" (Rom 5:1).

It should be noted here, as throughout the passage, that the initiative of rectification rests with God and is characterized by his loving and gracious action in our behalf. "To be saved" in both Rom 5:9 and 5:10 is the same future verb (σωθησόμεθα). Salvation appears to be based upon the present life of Christ as living Lord in both instances. We now boast in God *through* our Lord Jesus Christ (indirect agency with διά). *God* (direct agent) works *through* Christ (indirect agent) to accomplish his purposes. Our reconciliation has occurred—it is we who have been reconciled to God, not God who has been reconciled to us—and now that reconciliation is demonstrated through acknowledgment of Christ's Lordship in our living,— through his Lordship, through his present life.

Paul accentuates positive accomplishment in Christ. God has acted to rectify his entire creation, including us. He did so not by compulsion, but freely out of his love on the basis of his grace, as he chose to demonstrate his rectifying action by passing over previously committed sins. God has opened the door to his grace and peace in an eschatological age, such that the imperative stands before us to enjoy that peace as those who have already been reconciled to him and who will ultimately be saved by him. The love of God has been poured into our hearts as evidenced by the presence of the Spirit, which has already been given.

Consequently, Paul can offer hortatory encouragement to enjoy the peace (*shalom*, well-being) which God has effected in our behalf. We stand already (pf. verb) within God's gracious action and have full access to it. The themes of grace and peace are well known from Paul's salutations. Beyond all of this, Paul encourages boasting in the hope of the glory of God (likely a reference to resurrection, among other things). It is the love of God as experienced that produces a hope that does not disappoint, even in the midst of trouble or suffering. It is a genuine hope marked by patient endurance. It is a cruciform imperative underwritten by a Gospel indicative.

All of this is "positive," and all of Paul's expression here in Romans should most properly call forth a spirit of worship and the courage and commitment to live as a "praise of God's glory" (Eph 1:6, 12, 14). Ephesians echoes other themes found here in Romans, albeit in different words and with a degree of pleonasm. In this regard, if

Ephesians is not Pauline, it is written by one who at least existentially understood the Pauline gospel in a thorough and intimate manner.

Colossians 1:27 should also be mentioned, for Paul makes mention of the hidden mystery of the Gospel which now makes known "the wealth of the glory of this mystery . . . , which is Christ in you, the hope of glory." The Spirit of Christ has been given to the church, such that one may experience the love of God even in the midst of cruciform living, for the love of God will lead to resurrection life. We have the hope of glory, as we live a cruciform life as a praise to God's glory. "Christ in you" is the Spirit of both the crucified and the resurrected Christ.

One might, however, in the light of some atonement theories, consider an alternative interpretation based upon "negative" considerations. God's righteousness is offended by human sin and requires satisfaction or reparations (Rom 3:23). God put Jesus forward as a propitiating sacrifice to himself, such that he could then be free (or habilitated) to justify those who have faith in Jesus's blood sacrifice (Rom 3:25). Sinners (all people) are justified by God's grace, because the penalty of sin carried out in Jesus's death is imputed to him and righteousness is imputed to us (Rom 3:24). (Or, alternatively, this applies only to "the elect.") Jesus was handed over (to sacrificial death) because of our trespasses (Rom 4:25). We have peace with God specifically because of the death of our Lord Jesus Christ (Rom 5:1). Christ died in the place of sinners or the ungodly (cf. Rom 5:6, 8). We have now received the atonement (Rom 5:1–11). At last, we are acceptable to God.

The central question becomes that of what kind of God? A God who must protect his own honor at any cost? A God who merely pulls the levers of a theological transaction? Abelard's rhetorical question, paraphrased, still stands: If the sin of humankind beginning with Adam was so great that it could only be propitiated by the death of Christ, what expiation will avail for the act of divine murder committed against Christ?[26]

Paul's position was that God had adopted us as his children, such that Paul's word was "Grace and peace from God the Father and the Lord Jesus Christ." One needs to immerse oneself in Rom 8 until the truth of Paul's sublime chapter courses through one's veins. All of it. We need to *listen* without hammering it to fit. One's view of the atonement matters, because it is indicative of the nature of the kind of God that one worships and in whom one places faith. We should listen to and hear what Paul and not Paulinism has to say, for properly understood, we shall be the richer for it by fully realizing the freedom and hope we now have in Christ. By doing so, we shall learn to live as a "praise of God's glory" in the context of living life and in the context of the worship of God.

---

26. Cf. Culpepper, *Interpreting the Atonement*, 89.

Atonement through Christ's Death and Resurrection

When one allows Paul to speak for himself and when he is not co-opted in support of other New Testament writers or historical atonement theories, self-sacrificial reconciliation emerges as central. Satisfaction of divine honor and penal substitution do not express Paul's understanding of God's own nature, the action of Christ, or the nature of salvation. Jesus did not come to save us from God. Jesus was *sent by God* to save us *for God* and not *from God*. Paul's soteriology is personal, based upon multiple levels of relationship and reconciliation underwritten by love, which foregoes self-idolatry. It is not a transaction that grants a free pass. To understand it in the latter sense is to succumb once again to self-idolatry. To understand in the Pauline sense is a call to worship, because one has been freed to do just that. "Grace and peace to you from God the Father and the Lord Jesus Christ."

Paul's theological vision of Christianity begins to become clear when one places his thought back into the matrix of his ministry, when one does not focus upon individual verses taken out of context. The contextual matrix of Gal 3:13, 2 Cor 5:21, and Rom 3:25 has already been treated above.

Paul's vision of Christianity begins to become clear in passages like Phil 2:5–13 and Rom 5:1–11. In fact, Philippians is a very significant letter for understanding Paul's theological perspectives. It is not plagued by as much historical "baggage" as a letter like Romans. It also portrays Paul at his uninhibited and "naked" best, as he writes in the light of having faced the specter of death in imprisonment. Righteousness or rectification from God comes through Christ's death and resurrection. Paul's vision of Christianity is centered on a theology of atonement, understood as reconciliation, although not upon what may be considered the "popular view of atonement" based upon cultic practice of ritual satisfaction.

God's justice or righteousness (his rectifying activity) comes as both a power and a gift, being manifested as positive saving activity from God, rather than as a mere static attribute of God.[27] One experiences and appropriates God's rectification through faith, which is likewise understood by Paul as dynamic activity and not a static entity. For Paul, *cross* and *resurrection* form an interactive unity creating a single, complex whole unit, although a unit with two different poles and vastly different focal points.

Paul can expressly refer to either aspective element and in any order without necessarily mentioning the other. Yet if only one is mentioned, the other is nearby and understood. Soteriological reality accrues in both events of the singular, effective complex. Jesus appeared to have been overcome by Sin and even the finality of Death itself. Yet his resurrection marks the denial of allegiance to either of these personified powers. Christ's resurrection demonstrates God's Power over all the "powers," including those of Sin and Death. It also endows Christ with new power as Lord, as he

---

27. See, for example, the emphases of Barclay, *Paul and the Gift*.

becomes a life-giving personal force, through his exaltation by God. It communicates to humankind the possibility of leaving the realm of Sin and Death under the Law for a new life in Christ. It is the new life in Christ that unites us with God. The Spirit of God present becomes the "down payment" and "guarantee," as well as the force within the life of the Christian, even in the face of a cross or a cruciform imperative.

Paul, however, understands participation in the risen life of Christ in terms of a participation in his sufferings and death (Phil 3:10). This is more than just an imitation of Christ as a kind of programmatic agenda (1 Thess 1:6). Paul does not point to mere resemblance with Jesus's kind of death, but through his language of "fellowship of his sufferings" points to a real union with Christ. His very suffering and death become the source of our own.[28] The risen Christ remains the crucified one, such that Christ's death remains as an eschatological reality and not just as a past event of history. Christ's death becomes a pattern of life that is incorporated into his resurrected life.

As Tambasco expresses it, "We share in the death of Christ by sharing in his resurrection."[29] But it should also be stated that we also share in his resurrection by sharing in his death, according to Paul. "In Christ" we are joined together with him in *both* his death and his resurrection. Signally and symbolically, if not also sacramentally, we are joined with him and fellow Christians in the action of baptism (Rom 6:4–11) and celebrate that identity repeatedly in the Eucharist or Lord's Supper (1 Cor 11:26–31). One lives a cruciform life in community, as suffering is transformed into victory "in Christ," through the presence of the Spirit.

Issues with the Atonement

One is charged by Paul with the necessity of working out one's own salvation through a cross imperative, after one has been reconciled to God (Phil 2:12–13). However costly atonement must be, salvation is not cost-free for the believer. This is perhaps one of the greatest fallacies proclaimed in modern-gospel circles of "popular Christianity." It is inherent in the statement "Christ died for my sins so I could go to heaven" in much preaching, and in much hymnody. For Paul, who suffered much as an apostle, Christians must "suffer with Christ (Rom 8:17). One is "united with him in a death like his" (Rom 6:5). One has the "mind-set of Christ" in oneself (Phil 2:5). Connection with Christ involves co-suffering and co-death (symbolic or not, potential or real).

Salvation in Paul models a pattern of dying and being raised from the dead, following in the steps of Christ's effective death and resurrection. As the apostle to the gentile world, Paul's motif of Christ dying for others may echo the major theme of the "noble death" or "effective death" well known in Classical and Hellenistic literature and

28. Tambasco, *Atonement*, 64.

29. Tambasco, *Atonement*, 65.

philosophy. Martyr-deaths were seen to have vicarious saving power.[30] However, if such a view influenced Paul, he did not take it over unchanged. God is the one who is able to work through a Roman cross in order to move beyond it in order to restore life.

A Problem with Metaphors

Paul's metaphors interpenetrate as they interpret one another. Paul does not limit himself to a single image but employs a range of metaphors. They do not take away from one another, but rather enhance and embrace one another. Paul may use social metaphors, for example, to describe the beneficial *results* of Christ's death for believers—redemption or deliverance (a payment, monetary, or Exodus metaphor), justification (a judicial metaphor), adoption (a familial, relational metaphor), and reconciliation (a diplomatic, familial metaphor). Expressed differently, the results for humans are liberation, rectification, re-identification as children of God, and reconciliation. All of these aspects herald regeneration and new life, both now and in the resurrection.

Paul's immediate successors simplified and domesticated him. On the other hand, Paul's later successors overlaid his simplicity with their own sophistication and contextual apologetics. As is evident in the pastorals of 1 Timothy and Titus, Paul's radicalism is toned down and his conservatism heightened.[31] Second Timothy 4:1–5 in particular, Paul's charge to Timothy, given just prior to all of his personal details in the remainder of the letter, provided a model for the pseudonymous works of 1 Timothy and Titus. Those two letters in particular are interested in preserving "sound doctrine" (Titus 1:9; 2:1; cf. 2 Tim 4:3) or "sound teaching" (1 Tim 1:10; 4:6). After his death, Paul's actual teaching became less important than his usefulness as an authority figure who stood against any independent or aberrant teaching.

The figure of "Paul" became a mouthpiece for church leaders (the teachings of bishops, or "overseers," 1 Tim 3:2; Titus 1:7) who were attempting to quell certain alternative doctrinal expressions. Following the time of Paul, there is intent to claim the Pauline legacy in the face of alternative teaching, particularly in the geographical area and Roman provinces of Asia Minor. First Timothy, Titus, *and* Hebrews all appear in one way or another to be dealing with the problem or threat of "religious drift" (cf. Heb 2:1), and likely in the region of Asia Minor. One needs to be mindful of the contextual matrix of Paul's lengthy stay in Ephesus as the headquarters of his Second (and final!) Campaign.

Paul may use several cultic metaphors to describe the Messiah's death—scapegoat, Passover lamb (1 Cor 5:7), "place of atonement" (Rom 3:25) cleansed during Yom Kippur, covenant peace (Gal 3:14)—each of which has a ritual significance resulting from a cultic act. Redemption and acquittal metaphors may be added, such

---

30. Finlan, *Problems with Atonement*, 52–55.

31. This would appear to be a natural sociological development by a minority social group in a subsequent generation.

that four different kinds of transactions are conflated to describe the saving effect of the death of Christ—*sacrificial, scapegoat, judicial,* and *monetary.* Undoubtedly, in a high context society, Paul's original hearers understood that he was blending different metaphors for which they had ready recognition. According to Finlan, later Christian thought misunderstood scapegoat imagery as having judicial implications, redemption as carrying scapegoat or sacrificial implications, and sacrifice as having judgmental implications.[32] It should not be assumed that Paul's mixed audience of Jews and gentiles would each hear Paul's mixed metaphors with equal clarity. Some, undoubtedly, worked better than others in a given contextual matrix.

In typological interpretation, the Passover lamb was a type of Christ, such that Christ's blood offers protection from destruction (1 Cor 5:7). Paul may employ the typology of expulsion rituals—e.g., the scapegoat ritual (cf. Gal 3:13; 2 Cor 5:21), which would symbolize the expulsion of an evil. When the scapegoat concept is assimilated into the concept of sacrifice, then Christian notions of substitutionary atonement are imposed on these rituals.[33] In Leviticus, neither sacrifice nor the scapegoat involves punishment. Sacrifice fundamentally has to do with purification, as the inherent life-force of "blood" cleanses sin-pollution from the sanctuary. The biblical scapegoat is not a sacrifice, but rather a vehicle of expulsion or sending-away.

Paul's conflation or mixing of metaphors has led to misunderstanding of the underlying singular metaphors. In Rom 3:24–25, Paul mixed the models of ransom, acquittal before God, and purification provision at the mercy seat. In Jewish theology, the sacrificial animal was viewed as a gift which retained its purity, such that sacrifice had to do with purification. In the scapegoat ritual (cf. Lev 16:20–22), the animal begins as pure, but ends up totally impure; it would not thereby qualify as a sacrifice. The scapegoat is a curse transmission victim which is a sin carrier. When sacrifice is united with scapegoat themes in later Christian thought, then "burden bearing is turned into *penalty*-bearing."[34]

With regard to Paul's atonement metaphors, they were turned into doctrinal formulas, as Paul's subtleties were lost on his successors in subsequent Christian theology. They fused and froze Paul's metaphors in the light of their own matrices. There was little or no awareness of Paul's contextual or contingent matrices. Paul's scapegoat (insofar as it was present) and adoption imagery faded out, justification became subordinated, and sacrifice-redemption became conjoined.[35] This is aided by emphasis on alternative thought present in other writings, such as 1 Peter and Hebrews. First Peter 1:18–19 focuses upon ransom and sacrifice. Hebrews, thought by many church fathers (such as Origen) to be Pauline, makes sacrifice to be the more dominant image, portraying Christ as both a Platonic high priest and a sacrificial victim. The writer

32. Finlan, *Problems with Atonement,* 52.

33. See Heim, *Saved from Sacrifice.* Violence and even divine violence is highlighted.

34. Finlan, *Problems with Atonement,* 35–37, emphasis original.

35. Finlan, *Problems with Atonement,* 64.

of Hebrews likely writes in the wake of the destruction of Jerusalem and its temple, seeking to rescue history itself by reviving an "Exodus" model.

Sacrificial imagery won the field in expressing the meaning of Christ's death in the time after Paul, and Paul's more conservative and general perspectives were likely more useful in the conflicts of subsequent eras. One might even raise the issue of the difference of understanding the conceptualization of sacrifice in a gentile environment versus a Jewish one as the church became more gentile. Paul's own soteriology offered building blocks for various perspectives— *exchange, cosmic rescue, typological fulfillment, substitution, sacrifice,* even *penalty.* In the light of changing sociological, political, and religious necessities or matrices, the focus began to shift toward "sound words," "sound teaching," "sound doctrine," and a "sound, abiding faith" that endures through struggle (1 Tim 6:3; Titus 2:1; Hebrews; 1 Peter).

Alternative Matrices

Generally speaking, changing matrices brought new problems, as well as a different focus on the meaning of Christ's death. While Paul could personify Sin as an enemy to be defeated, John could focus on the singular sin of lack of faith in Christ (John 1:29).[36] In an age marked by challenges posed to faithfulness as Christians settled into the world, the focus shifted to human sinning (cf. 1 John; Hebrews). For Paul, "sins" were but the symptom of the larger problem of Sin. For Paul's successors, the problem *was* human sinning, in the light of Christian identity and "faithfulness" in their present world often defined by doctrines. The breaking of or the refusal to embrace doctrines of orthodoxy becomes itself sin, even as such action might define one as "Christian" or not. The metaphor of Paul's personification of "Sin" was lost in the social context of a Hellenistic Roman and Byzantine world. It was sublimated to the needs of faithfulness and definition of a Christian lifestyle within the social, political, and theological matrices of later ages.

Thus, in the time after Paul and in the light of the delay of the Parousia, Christians settled down for life in the world. This is reflected in New Testament writings such as 1 Timothy, Titus, 1 Peter, and Hebrews. In the centuries after Paul, the "patristic developers" (Finlan) begin to do something that Paul never did. While Paul found saving significance in the death of Jesus, employing multiple metaphors of meaning, Paul's understanding of atonement was never separated from his understanding of the resurrection. As the present writer would maintain, Paul's understanding of atonement was never separated from the necessary reality of reconciliation, not of God to humanity but of humanity to God. That was at least a part of the central focus of the Gospel of God which proclaimed so decidedly and decisively "grace and peace"—not for God's sake, but for humanity's sake.

36. See Greene, "God's Lamb," 147–64.

One who "died" with Christ in a death like his would also be resurrected with him. Hence, Paul's "cross imperative" heralded life lived now at whatever cost was life to be lived in the light of coming resurrection. Paul's cross imperative provided a means of coping with every human exigency of life in the context of hope of resurrection. As Paul's legacy was claimed and combined with other voices in a post-Pauline age, church theologians began to adopt a concept of a sacrificial and redeeming *transaction* that occurred at the cross, a transaction that literally cleansed sin and paid "the debt" of human sinning on both an individual and collective basis—once and for all. "Once and for all," however, is now a long time ago.

The history of Christian theology with regard to the atonement is first of all marked by a reductionism of the alternative metaphors used by Paul to interpret the meaning of Christ's death. Secondly, it is marked by the simplification of sacrificial metaphors hardened into doctrine in ages that no longer practiced literal sacrifice but narrowly interpreted biblical texts. Thirdly, it is characterized by a thoroughgoing legal rationalism, particularly in the Western or Latin Church. This has resulted in the soteriology which most Western Christians now take for granted, dominated perhaps by guilt and a view of penal substitution. Perhaps in view of the plasticity of his metaphors, Paul himself is not totally without fault in atonement thought progression (or shall we say, "regression"?). Paul's subtleties, and his awareness that no single metaphor was sufficient, were left behind in subsequent matrices of thought. As Finlan asserts, Paul's soteriological formulas regarding the death of Christ "provided the seedbed for those frightening and rigid theologies of atonement that came later, even though Paul's own insight greatly transcended that of all his children."[37]

Finlan thus suggests that Paul cannot be absolved of all responsibility, even though later interpreters have brought a more literal transactional interpretation to Paul's expression that God "did not withhold his own Son" (Rom 8:32), that believers "were bought with a price" (1 Cor 6:20). To these references may be added the more usual—"Christ became a curse for us" (Gal 3:13), that God "made him to be sin who knew no sin" (2 Cor 5:21). In one sense of the word, however, it would not seem fair to hold Paul responsible for the literalization of his metaphors by later interpreters facing the issues of a subsequent age. On the other hand, Paul made available bald metaphors without further clarification in the light of his high context society—metaphors subject to serious misinterpretation, perhaps in his day, and certainly in ours.

Holistic Interpretation

Culpepper and others suggest that the incarnation, life, death, and resurrection of Jesus must be treated as a unity. All are essential parts of the saving event of God in Jesus Christ. The cross-event is thus but one significant part of the overall Christ

---

37. Finlan, *Problems with Atonement*, 79. The term "children" should be understood loosely.

event, of which the initiative and the outcome rests with God. The understanding of that overall Christ event developed on the basis of belief in the resurrection. It was *theology ex eventu*. While Jesus's obedience to the Father reached its climax in the cross (Phil 2:8), this obedience to the Father in the death which he died "is meaningless and unintelligible when separated from the life which he lived."[38] It is also meaningless and unintelligible apart from the resurrection, a point realized even by John Calvin.

Paul holds Jesus's death and resurrection together in closest proximity. "For I gave to you in earlier days, what indeed I received, that *Christ died* in behalf of our sins according to the scriptures, and that he was buried, and that *he was raised* on the third day according to the scriptures, . . ." (1 Cor 15:3–4, emphasis supplied). Righteousness will be reckoned "to those who express faith in the One who raised Jesus our Lord from the dead, who was handed over because of our trespasses and who was raised because of our rectification" (Rom 4:24–25). Christ is the "one who died, rather the one who was raised," the one who intercedes in our behalf (ὑπὲρ ἡμῶν) at the "right hand of God" (Rom 8:34; cf. Rom 6:3–11).[39] "If Christ has not been raised, your faith is worthless speculation, you are still in your sins" (1 Cor 15:17). Christ is the "one who died and who was raised in our behalf" (2 Cor 15:15).

As Culpepper states, "Apart from the resurrection, the cross is the greatest defeat of the ages! Interpreted in the light of the resurrection, the cross is the greatest victory of all time!"[40] As, indeed, it must be, for who could raise the dead but God? Caesar could kill, but only God could make alive. As Culpepper further states, "It is the deity of Christ and the resurrection of Christ which make the cross of Jesus the cross of Christ, the power of God unto salvation for everyone who has faith."[41] The crucifixion of Jesus by itself was a heinous crime and a most ignominious demonstration of human sinfulness. From God's point of view, the cross represented the self-giving of divine love to the extreme, divine love "in agony."[42]

Culpepper indicates that the cross of Christ is God's judgment on human sin, a perhaps common assessment in the light of the overall New Testament witness. In the light of Paul's convictions, however, that should not be allowed to stand without revised augmentation. The cross indeed highlights human sin, but God's judgment in the resurrection countermands human sin (the cross) with divine love and victory demonstrated in the resurrection and exaltation. The cross is neither God's wrath nor his vengeance; rather, it is God's love that redeems Christ—and us. This might be illustrated by the greatest metaphoric truth in Mel Gibson's otherwise mono-thematic

---

38. Culpepper, *Interpreting the Atonement*, 135. See also the works of David Brondos.

39. "In our place" will certainly not work as a translation of ὑπὲρ ἡμῶν here, nor will it work in association with 1 Cor 15:15–19.

40. Culpepper, *Interpreting the Atonement*, 135–36.

41. Culpepper, *Interpreting the Atonement*, 136. The foundation of Culpepper's statement rests upon incarnation and resurrection.

42. Stewart, *Man in Christ*, 221.

movie, *The Passion of the Christ*—namely, the giant tear that fell earthward at the end of the movie.

The cross becomes central in atonement because of who was crucified upon it, as it becomes the climactic expression of self-giving obedience of the Son of God. Still, it is interpreted in the light of the incarnation and resurrection. In victory, the cross becomes the supreme revelation of the amazing depth of both Christ's love and God's love and grace for those who were helpless, ungodly, sinners, and enemies (2 Cor 5:14; Rom 5:6, 8, 10; Eph 5:2). It does not allow humanity to "veil its sin in a cloak of respectability"[43] through any of the means by which we seek to excuse or justify our sins, including the promulgation of theological doctrines.

Second Corinthians 5:21, God "made the one who did not know sin [to be] sin in our behalf [ὑπὲρ ἡμῶν], in order that *we* might become God's rectification in him," heralds a significant point often missed in much atonement discussion. God did not work rectification in a mechanical nor merely forensic way, but rather in a *vital* way that issues forth in life. As Culpepper suggests, Christ's identification with us in our sin makes it possible for us to identify with him in his righteousness.[44] It could also be said that our identification with him in death involves identification with him in life. Our identification with him involves a commitment to a cross imperative, for his righteousness is sealed by the way of the cross. It is not substitution, but rather participatory identification that marks out and characterizes *vital rectification*. It is not *substitution*, but *submission*. It is not divine placation, but divine provision. It is not defeat, but the advent of divine victory.

While it may be commonly stated that Christ died the death that we should have died, hence, a substitutionary death, that also represents judgment against sin in Christ's cross. Paul's position as suggested above moves beyond that. God vindicates his own rectifying nature and rectification action in the resurrection, such that the cross *exposes* sin for what is and Sin for what it does. God's judgment and rectifying action makes possible our own participation in Christ's death and resurrection, firmly anchored in God's love. God's action makes it possible to fulfill the just requirements of the Torah, as one becomes fully identified with God's loving and rectifying indicative. We walk not according to the weakness of the flesh, but according to the fruit of the Spirit, such that God makes alive our mortal bodies (Gal 5:16–26; Rom 8:1–11). In his shame, suffering, and death, Jesus identified himself with us. In turn, we identify with him in God's victory.

As Culpepper significantly states, Christ's death *for us* has redemptive significance in our lives "only when it leads us by faith to identify ourselves with him in his way of life . . . ."[45] This enables one to affirm with Paul, "For *I* through the Law died to the Law in order that I might live to God. I have been crucified with Christ; for *I* no

---

43. Culpepper, *Interpreting the Atonement*, 143.

44. Culpepper, *Interpreting the Atonement*, 145.

45. Culpepper, *Interpreting the Atonement*, 146.

longer live, but Christ lives in me; for what I now live in the flesh, *by faith* I live in the Son of God who loved me and who gave himself in my behalf [ὑπὲρ ἐμοῦ]. I do not set aside the grace of God; for if rectification (comes) through Law, then Christ died for no reason" (Gal 2:19–21).

The bond of legal demands, which could condemn but not save, has been nailed to Christ's cross (Col 2:14; cf. Gal 3:13; 5:1; Rom 10:4).[46] Paul affirms both a divine indicative and a cross imperative. God's decisive action in the Christ-event makes possible deliverance from all evil powers that may hold us in bondage and wreak death—Sin, the Law, Death, the demonic, and all cosmic forces.

The cross of the incarnate Son of God willingly accepted but not sought, as interpreted in the light of the resurrection, makes possible our own cross and resurrection. The death of Christ becomes effective *for us* only as it becomes effective *in us*, such that one is to work out one's own salvation with fear and trembling, while rejoicing even in one's sufferings (Phil 2:12; Rom 5:3–5). Effectiveness *for us* and effectiveness *in us* are both anchored firmly in God's love. Salvation must begin with reconciliation, if it is to be anything other than a crass, imagined transactionalism based with legalistic girders of support.

While humanity in sin put the Son of God to death, God by his mercy as we are delivered from bondage "used this epitome of man's rebellion against his Creator to open up a way of salvation for sinful man."[47] God used the very symbol of defeat *by* the powers as the supreme demonstration of the overthrow *of* the powers (Col 2:13–15). The bond of the Law, held by Sin unto Death, is canceled and nailed for all to see in the very place where Sin pressed its ultimate claim.[48] God's victory in Christ is real, but not yet complete (1 Cor 15:20–28). God's final victory will be on a cosmic scale (Rom 8:18–25).

Culpepper affirms that Christ died *for* our sins in order that we might die *to* our sins. Jesus went to the cross not to enable us to escape the cross, but in order that we might take up our cross and follow him. "His sacrifice of perfect obedience does not make our sacrifice of obedience unnecessary. Rather it makes it possible."[49] While it is true that the crucified Savior meets us as the resurrected Lord, he meets us *and beckons us*. Saving faith is not *merely* substitutionary for Paul; rather, it is participatory in Christ. Saving faith unites us with Christ in both his death and resurrection, such that his cross becomes our cross, his obedience our obedience, and his resurrection becomes the promise of our resurrection (Gal 2:20; Rom 8:28–30). Paul encouraged

---

46. The Law, as it were, defined a debt that was owed that in the end could never be paid. It could define, but it could not relieve.

47. Culpepper, *Interpreting the Atonement*, 147.

48. Roman crucifixion was carried out in the most public of places, such as beside major roadways, for it was a means of Roman propaganda. It was meant to make a statement "most publicly." God now makes his own major counter-statement, according to Paul.

49. Culpepper, *Interpreting the Atonement*, 155.

the Philippians to "have this mind-set in you all that was in Christ Jesus . . . . continuing to work out your own salvation," for "God is the one who is energizing in you all both to will and to work concerning good pleasure" (Phil 2:5, 12–13)

A Vital Atonement

Paul's vision of Christianity is centered upon atonement, in that the importance of Christ in bringing rectification from God through Christ's death and resurrection becomes his focal point. God's rectifying activity occurs through Christ. No concept is perhaps more pervasive in Paul than the concept of "being *in Christ*" (cf. Deissmann). As to what that means, perhaps many passages in Paul may be brought forward in a definitional way. Philippians 3:8–12 highlights what is significant for Paul and shows Paul's vision of Christianity. Romans 4:25 demonstrates that Paul holds the death and resurrection of Christ together as one great, single, complex event. Philippians mentions resurrection first as the key event that makes all of Christ's saving work to be effective. "the key event making effective all of Christ's saving work."[50] Its meaning is multifaceted. It demonstrates God's power to raise Jesus from the dead by overcoming the worst that all of the powers of evil could do. It demonstrates the imbuing of Christ with the new power of his risen state—he is Lord.

Yet as Tambasco observes, the resurrection endows Christ with new power as a life-giving force. It enables the risen Christ "to transform Paul and every Christian by incorporating them into his very life."[51] The result is the possibility of leaving the killing powers of the Present Evil Age (Sin, Law, Death, Flesh) behind, in order to embrace the life-giving powers of Grace and Rectification through the Spirit in unification with God. We are now "found in Christ" (cf. Phil 3:9), that we may "know him and the power of his resurrection" (Phil 3:10). This, however, involves a "fellowship [κοινωνία] in his sufferings, becoming conformed [pres. part. of συμμορφίζομαι] to his death" (Phil 3:10). Paul's goal is the attainment of the resurrection (Phil 3:11). Paul makes clear that the participation in the risen life of Christ (which would be participation under his Lordship) involves participation in his suffering and death.

In the cross-death of Jesus, Christ appeared to have been overcome by the powers of Sin, Law, and even Death itself. Yet God raised him from the dead and installed him as Lord and Christ (cf. Acts 2:36). The death Jesus died is a past, once-for-all event. Paul appears to have little interest in the historical life of Jesus, including the cross itself understood merely as past history. To be sure, it had to be interpreted and accounted for as a foundational event that could not be denied. Paul's interest, however, is in the meaning of Christ's death going forward, for it becomes a signal part of God's saving activity because of the resurrection which followed. It becomes a means of at-one-ment *going forward*. Christ's resurrection and death become a pattern of life

50. Tambasco, *Atonement*, 63.

51. Tambasco, *Atonement*, 63.

never ending founded upon Christ's life of love and obedience and God's rectifying love. As Tambasco affirms, we are able to pattern our lives on his by living "in Christ." even to the culminating expression of death. If we have a share in the resurrection, we first have a share in his death.[52]

Conclusion

A theology of the cross developed very quickly in the early church, for it was the puzzle and scandal that marked the beginning of the Christian gospel. That gospel, however, was focused upon the resurrection, apart from which there would be no evident gospel. If Christianity were not to be a myopic and naïve religion out of touch with reality, then the cross had to be explained in ways other than the crude graffiti scratched on a wall in the Palatine hill district in Rome.

The tradition that Paul echoes in 1 Cor 15:3–4, which he came to embrace *at some point in his ministry prior to the writing of* 1 *Corinthians in* 54 *CE*, interpreted both Christ's death *and* resurrection *in accordance with the scriptures.* Paul himself, however, hardly adopted a "balancing of the scales" model representing legal justice, nor did he portray God as a judge demanding satisfaction through the punishment of Christ in our place for crimes committed. As Tambasco suggests, Paul's model is better described as that of "a representative journey" in which humankind is invited to participate by the risen Christ.[53]

Easter vitalized a new community in Christ. Pentecost empowered the new community in Christ. Both events witness to God's mighty act of redemption and rectification in Christ. Still, midst the waning remnants of the Present Evil Age, the church as the people of God in Christ must guard against becoming nothing other than a self-centered, power-hungry, secularized business institution offering control and entertainment—rather than the living body of Christ. The church as the body of Christ (to use Paul's metaphor) is called to be the believing, witnessing, "working out salvation" community in which the rectifying and redemptive act of God in Christ is proclaimed openly through a gospel word and through living a gospel life. The gospel word and a gospel life both call for a cruciform imperative, which offers life to all, even at the cost of our own.

The sacred ordinances of the church, baptism as well as the Lord's Supper, both symbol and call for participation in the death and resurrection of Christ. As the singular, initiatory rite of incorporation, baptism may depict in dramatic symbolism the sacramental reality of Christ's death for us and our death and resurrection in him (Rom 6:3–11; Col 2:12). While individual baptism occurs only once, it is remembered and re-celebrated in the baptism of new members in Christ born into the Christian community. Subsequent baptisms of others become the opportunity for celebrative

52. Tambasco, *Atonement*, 65.
53. Tambasco, *Atonement*, 66.

renewal. Repeated celebration of the Lord's Supper marks a unified and collective repetition that commemorates the death of Christ *for us* in the past, provides constant acknowledgement of his living presence *with us* in the present, and underscores a hope of resurrection consummation *in us* in the future (1 Cor 11:23–26).

Taylor suggests that "the theology which will fail least lamentably in presenting the doctrine of the Atonement is one which makes full use of the idea of sacrifice."[54] Maybe that is true, maybe not, given a view toward the liberation of Paul and the clarity of the Gospel. In later historical settings where sacrifice was no longer literally practiced and where it was perhaps least understood and infused with pagan conceptions (including the modern world), Taylor's perspective is a facile position which carries an element of truth and an element of danger.

Historic legacies of the Atonement will be treated in the next chapter. The recapitulation theory of Irenaeus, a *Christus Victor* model of victory over evil powers, a satisfaction theory of Anselm, a moral influence theory, as well as other theories, even "penal substitution," in and of themselves represent only a portion of the truth or singular metaphors drawn and adapted from Paul's teachings. None of these can be made the whole truth of the atonement, either in Paul's day or ours. Singular metaphors or even singular realities do not constitute the whole cloth.

While Paul is not the only biblical voice in discussions of atonement doctrines, his perspectives do loom large in any overall discussion, just as his voice looms large by nature of the case in any discussion of New Testament theology as a whole. It is difficult to *hear Paul* in the midst of a chorus of atonement "chatter" which seeks to claim Paul in support of different perspectives of "the doctrine of the Atonement" developed within the differing matrices of Christian history. Those who hold different views—even non-biblical views—wish to claim Paul for "their side." "Atonement" is the "eye of the storm" and may define one's very vision of Christianity.

Tambasco offers a summary statement with regard to the means (plural) of atonement. God, out of divine justice sends Jesus as a means of atonement. He works atonement by a life journey of obedience that involved suffering and death, not through appeasement of an angry God. As a means of atonement, the resurrection necessarily makes Jesus the Lord who is present for all time. His own human journey becomes the participatory journey of his followers, in which the gift of the Spirit becomes paramount.

> The Spirit is the final means of atonement because it is the Spirit of the risen Lord forming us into his likeness, beginning already in the present. By the Spirit we begin our gradual transformation, our journey. The Spirit's infusion reverses sin and alienation, overcomes the destructive powers of law manipulated

---

54. Taylor, *Atonement*, 100.

by sin, and brings us to overcome all forms of death until, finally, physical death itself is overcome and we share in the final glory of the risen Christ.[55]

A narrow understanding of atonement in Paul has often constricted the more comprehensive nature of the atonement in Paul.

According to Robert Culpepper, the doctrine of the atonement must give expression to a "worthy concept of the Triune God."[56] On the one hand, such an affirmation marks an accommodation to development of post-New Testament systematic theology. Paul had a multi-metaphorical concept of atonement, but he did not have a developed doctrine of the Trinity.[57] On the other hand, such an affirmation marks a correction to a lot of atonement theory that pits the Father against the Son. The cross event, while not sanctioned by God (in the present writer's viewpoint), certainly in the light of the resurrection became a signature of divine victory.

Christians looked back to make sense of the event in the light of the Gospel. In the light of their models available, they came to understand the cross event as sacrificial and substitutionary, as well as participatory. Their conceptionalization was not mono-dimensional. Neither was Paul's, as all searched for and found meaning in the cross event. So much was this the case, that the cross became the very symbol for the Christian gospel. Yet again, how does one symbol the resurrection, the other center of the Christian gospel?

Indeed, it is time to free Paul himself from the doctrine-makers, to recover him from his sublimation within homogenized systematic theological rationalizations which are post-Pauline. There are historical matrices which called forth specific theological definitions /doctrines within historical Christianity. In the light of the specific issue at hand and a thesis set forth in this work, problematic views of the atonement have resulted from an over emphasis upon anthropological soteriology and from placing the Pauline understanding of the cross under the primary category of the divine indicative rather than under the divine imperative.

Category error of emphasis has wrought a compounding of theological falsification through centuries of theological development that left the understanding of the initial kerygma, Paul included, far behind. Through his various metaphors, Paul may have provided a seedbed of fertile soil for subsequent development, but he cannot be held responsible for the theological weeds which ultimately grew there, even some deemed "orthodox."

Unfortunately in a later period of Christian history, misperception of the symbolism of blood sacrifice led to the presentation of Christ as a *penal substitute*, whereby God effected a "balancing of the scales" for a sinful humanity. The shed blood of a

---

55. Tambasco, *Atonement*, 93.

56. Culpepper, *Interpreting the Atonement*, 131. He speaks for the later theological interpretation of the New Testament as a whole, not singularly for Paul.

57. Paul had a functional, subordinationist Christology. He had a functional, eschatological pneumatology.

sacrificial animal became understood as a vicarious punishment for sin in order to satisfy God's justice, an act of appeasement or *propitiation* of God for sin. As Tambasco summarizes, Christ could truly take the place of all humanity by taking on human existence. By shedding his blood, he underwent the punishment we all deserve and satisfied God's justice. He became "a perfect once-for-all sacrifice for our sins."[58] The difficulty with such a view is that it misplaces the em*pha*sis of the meaning of the death of the metaphoric sacrificial animal in the Old Testament sacrificial system. The focus there is upon life, as seen in Lev 17:11.

The idolization of the angry, avenging gods of "Justice" and "Righteousness" that must be placated is not Paul. Idolization takes these supposed "attributes" of God (a theological abstraction) out of the realm of the descriptive character of an active and loving heavenly Father, so characteristic of the views of Jesus and Paul. It makes them to be the gods unto themselves, whose fearful statuary stands in temples of fear behind an altar of placation and appeasement demanding their sacrificial payment. The cross itself, for fearful believers who dare to worship here, becomes the talisman that protects against the draconian vampire gods that have been satisfied by the blood of Christ. As the writer of 1 John warned with his last word, "Little children, guard yourselves from the idols" (cf. 1 John 5:21).

Paul said, even as he wrote to those who were called to a cross imperative, "Grace and peace to all of you from God our Father and the Lord Jesus Christ." *It is those words that set the tone for all of the remainder of Paul's theology set forth in his letters.* Did Paul have an "atonement theory"? No. Did Paul believe in "atonement"? Yes, absolutely. His faith emerged from his own personal experience and calling. His understanding of "at-one-ment" in terms of reconciliation rings out clearly in passages like Rom 5:1–11, Rom 8:1–39, and Rom 12:1–2. In earlier letters, it rings out clearly in 2 Thess 2:16–17, 3:3–4 and Gal 2:19–21 and 2 Cor 5:15–21.

A reminder is given again that the actual word "atonement" occurred but once in the New Testament in the King James Version of the Bible, namely, in Rom 5:11, where it appeared as a synonym for reconciliation. In the context of the early seventeenth century, it meant "at-one-ment." The church has debated various *doctrines* of the atonement through the centuries, generally understanding the meaning of the death of Christ in the light of sociological realities of the time of the particular interpreter. This process of accounting for the meaning of Jesus's death on a Roman cross began of necessity with the earliest Christians and appears with differing explanation within the New Testament itself. Paul himself becomes a representative of the very earliest expression available to us.

The focus of the current work is not upon the developed systematic theology of later centuries, but rather the apostolic and pastoral theology of Paul. With that in mind, it is helpful and instructive to have reconsidered Paul's thought apart from later Paulinism which has co-opted Paul in support of sociologically-based and

---

58. Tambasco, *Atonement*, 69.

rationalistically-derived atonement theory. This has been done by considering Romans 5:1–11, for example, as a window of opportunity. It may also be done by comparing Paul's thought with later developed historic views of "the Atonement," opportunity for which is now extended by the inclusion of "Historic Legacies of Atonement," as the next chapter of the present work.

To hold Paul responsible for later atonement theories which misunderstood his metaphors is akin to holding Paul responsible for the second century Gnosticism which sought to claim his teachings as their own. As Paul himself stated, where the Spirit of the Lord is there is freedom. When we "with unveiled face," i.e. freed from doctrinal accretions or "theological barnacles," behold the glory of the Lord, it is then we are afforded opportunity to be "changed into his likeness from one degree of glory to another." And "this comes from the Lord who is the Spirit" (2 Cor 3:17–18). Paul's gospel *indicative* is compassionate, and his cross *imperative* is challenging. His *incarnational freedom* is re-creative. His *resurrection hope* is encouraging. For Paul, all of these things meant an experience of *at-one-ment* with God, which is why Paul could convey greetings of "Grace to all of you and peace from God our Father and the Lord Jesus Christ" (Rom 1:7 et al.).

An increasing number of persons and faith communities find atonement theology to be irrelevant, seeing it to be either offensive, obsolete, or even overbearing in personal application of cruciform living. One may indeed question how much both Scripture and theology themselves really matter within the social context of Christendom's recitation of creed and emphasis upon greater socialization. A religious association has taken the place of confessional living. Traditional models of redemption as represented by Irenaeus, Anselm, or Luther are seen to be obsolete. Feminist theologies generally find atonement imagery, as well as the divine drama of the cross itself, to be offensive. Some even view it as "divine child abuse." Some prefer to speak in broader terms of soteriology, foregoing "atonement" language entirely. Perhaps one should seek to recover a more appropriate personal perspective of "at-one-ment" that heralds reconciliation over the more bald theological conception of "the Atonement."

Paul himself recognized the offense of the historical cross of Christ, but he found in Christ's self-offered death the secret of a renewed life based upon the sacrificial imperative of his own cross (1 Cor 1:18–31; Rom 12:1–2). And for him, that brought "grace and peace from God the Father and the Lord Jesus Christ," even in the midst of suffering. Paul knew a "cross-Gospel." He did not know a "gospel-less cross."

7

Historic Legacies of Atonement

As has already been suggested, various theories of "the atonement" have arisen in church history which attempted to define the *soteriology* of Jesus's death as related to human sinfulness. The fathers of the postapostolic period proclaimed salvation by the cross, even though they offered little concrete explanation as to how Jesus's death on a Roman cross provided salvation. By the time of John Calvin and the post-Reformation period, one encounters a developed view of "penal substitution" as a dominant note among others. Robert Culpepper, in his book *Interpreting the Atonement*, lists twenty-two subcategories or characterizations under the general heading of "Atonement theories" in his index of subjects.[1] It should be understood that all atonement theories are anthropological, in that they mark an attempt to make sense of Christ's death in relation to human soteriology.

Pauline texts have played a prominent role in the development of Christian theology generally speaking, as well as a very prominent role in the development of atonement theology, specifically speaking. This chapter offers a developmental summary of atonement theory within early Christianity as a means of understanding Paul in the subsequent contexts in which we find ourselves. This chapter will offer a summary of historic views prior to the Reformation, while the following chapter will focus upon the legacy of the Reformation. General atonement views are constructed from all relevant biblical thought, although the specific focus of the present work remains upon the relevance for understanding Paul. Although associated commentary will be given, the present emphasis is upon a summary of viewpoints. Overall assessment of atonement perspectives will be reserved for the conclusion of the following chapter.

L. W. Grensted published his work on the atonement, *A Short History of the Doctrine of the Atonement*, in 1920, adding to what he termed at that time "a literature already voluminous."[2] He sought to fill a gap by giving as much as possible the *ipsis-*

1. Cf. Culpepper, *Interpreting the Atonement*, 159.

2. Grensted, *Doctrine of the Atonement*, vii. The flood of literature on the atonement has not abated. While an older work, Grensted's work is still valuable, particularly for its collective citation of source materials in their original language.

sima verba of the original Greek and Latin fathers and later theologians. Gustaf Aulén in 1931 published his historical study of the atonement, entitled *Christus Victor: An Historical Study of the Three Main Types of the Idea of the Atonement.*[3] Aulén understood the *Christus Victor* model to be the earliest theory that emerged in the early church. Both resources are valuable in the presentation and development of historic views of the atonement.

The present work is not meant to be a thorough treatment of the topic of atonement. For that, the reader is referred to the above two works, among others.[4] This chapter is meant to devote more general attention to individual interpreters and positions than was appropriate to the previous brief overview given in the earlier chapter on the doctrine of the atonement and Paul. The purpose of the overview given there was to offer a prelude for consideration of Pauline references. The treatment here is meant to provide an introductory and developmental matrix for better understanding Paul in the light of subsequent atonement perspectives and doctrines within Christianity.

Again, the topic is an "eye of the storm" issue in relation to Pauline theology today.

It is thereby helpful to provide a more complete context for understanding Paul today, in the light of developmental history of atonement theory within the Christian church. Summary and clarification of doctrinal development is helpful and has direct bearing upon contemporary appreciation of Paul as well. The present writer has heard it said that one cannot be a Christian if one does not believe in a substitutionary atonement. One might consider how such a perspective may be supported or not through doctrinal development in Christian history.

Every interpretation of *the Atonement* is related to a central understanding of the nature of God and the essential meaning of Christianity. However, the early centuries of church life were focused theologically upon the development of identity in terms of Christology and the "Trinity." The early church had no developed doctrine of the Atonement, such that the real beginnings of a "thought-out doctrine of the Atonement" is found in Anselm of Canterbury.[5] Anselm (c. 1033–1109 CE) was thus the first to construct a formal theology of the atonement, more than 1000 years after the death of Jesus. His basic view could be considered to be the "popular view" even

---

3. Aulén, *Christus Victor*

4. Numerous works on atonement are listed in the first footnote in chapter 5 or in the bibliography. For a thorough-going defense of penal substitution, see Jeffery, Ovey, and Sach, *Pierced for Our Transgressions*. It is interesting that their chapters on historic views is entitled "Surveying the Heritage: The Historical Pedigree of Penal Substitution." Their intent is evident—to establish an early historical *pedigree* for penal substitution. It is interesting that they cite Grensted but once (219–20). A historical sketch of multiple views of the atonement may also be found in Culpepper, *Interpreting the Atonement*, 73–121.

5. Aulén, *Christus Victor*, 1–2.

today.[6] This is the view of satisfaction through penal substitution espoused by many, as filtered through Aquinas and the Reformation as the orthodox view at the beginning of the twentieth century. This view still retains a problematical dominance in several quarters. As Dyson Hague stated, Christ's death on the cross was seen as a purposed substitute for humanity— "voluntary, altruistic, vicarious, sinless, sacrificial," that appeared to be unconsciously brutal and yet "indescribably glorious." The death of Christ satisfied the demands of God's righteousness, as well as offering a "powerful incentive to repentance, morality, and self-sacrifice." The Scripture thus offered two theories of the "moral" and the "vicarious," thus bringing together the complete "spiritual, moral, altruistic and atoning aspects of the death of Christ."[7] This view still retains a problematical dominance in several quarters. Hague appears to have embraced an historical amalgam or "homogenized" view of the atonement at the beginning of the twentieth century.

The predominate "Latin" doctrine that developed eventually in the West was marked by a rationalizing structure that has had rather fateful consequences regarding an expressed image of God. It was this expressed image of God that prompted Aulén to address the issue, as he sought to expose several caricatures of God: the God of fatalism, which even attributes evil to God; the God of moralism, "where the spontaneity of the Love of God is being killed"; the God of shallow love, "where Love is considered self–evident, . . ."[8] In the place of these ancient and modern caricatures of God, portrayed in rather prosaic static terms rather than dynamic conceptualization, Aulén hoped that his work might be "a work in the service of the living God of the Gospel."[9] While there have been many variations on the theme, Gustaf Aulén's work addressed the three main types of atonement theory that have been prevalent in Christian history. In contemporary times, representative theories from the time of Anselm forward may be briefly summarized. Paul himself did not espouse a developed doctrine of "the Atonement," as has been seen.

The early adherents of some type of *Christus Victor* model spoke out of the cosmology and religious sociology of their era as they addressed the perception of the people. The model is variously referred to as "the patristic theory," "the classic view," or the "Christus Victor" view because of its portrayal of dramatic conflict, struggle, and victory.[10] Victory over the powers, recapitulation, and the metaphor of ransom all mesh well on the surface with Paul's thought.[11] As Baker and Green affirm, the fathers Irenaeus, Origen, and Gregory of Nyssa avoid even a hint of Christ appeasing God the

---

6. Tambasco, *Atonement*, 14.

7. Hague, "At-one-ment by Propitiation," 3:86.

8. Aulén, *Christus Victor*, ix–x.

9. Aulén, *Christus Victor*, x. Aulén's work is thus confessional.

10. Culpepper, *Interpreting the Atonement*, 74.

11. Cf. Gal 4:3–9; 1 Cor 6:20; 7:23; 15:22; Rom 5:12–21; Col 2:13–15; Eph 1:10; 2:14–16.

Father or the Father punishing the Son.[12] However, the *Christus Victor* model began to decline after the sixth century, a decline which Baker and Green ascribe to changing cosmology and the Constantinian synthesis of church and state, which relaxed the experience (and, hence, the theology) of tension in the lives of people.[13] Interestingly, the *Christus Victor* model was revived in the thought of the Western church in the twentieth century, although it has remained as the dominant model in the Eastern church through the centuries.

In defense of a penal substitutionary understanding, Leon Morris's classic apologetic work, *The Atonement: Its Meaning & Significance*,[14] enunciates the popular understanding of the sacrificial death of Jesus on the cross from a larger New Testament perspective. What did Jesus's death on the cross mean, soteriologically speaking? The early church, Paul included, had to wrestle with the meaning of Jesus's death in concert with the meaning of his Lordship. Although differing proposals have emerged, the church after twenty centuries still lacks an agreed upon characterization. The popular view of the atonement, however, filtered through the Reformation and post-Reformation scholastics, had its origin in Anselm. One may pursue several fathers, theologians, and perspectives at greater length. It should be recognized that most studies and statements of the atonement are concerned with the New Testament as a whole, rather than Paul only. Paul, specifically, is the overall focus of the present work. The present emphasis simply seeks to place Paul in context.

Early Fathers and Theologians

A representative sketch of significant fathers and theologians is presented in the material which follows. The purpose is to augment and expand what was presented in part one with specific attention given to the atonement. The intent is to offer an appropriate summary suitable for the purposes of the present work. The summary is meant to contribute to an awareness of the historical development of the doctrine of atonement, as that may be appropriated for understanding Paul.

Ignatius (c. 35–110 CE)

The mystic Ignatius, on his way to martyrdom, betrays an identification with Christ and his passion. This marks the center of faith for him. As Grensted suggests, no "theory" of the atonement sets forth its mystery as vividly as does experience.[15] Ignatius opposed those who attacked the historical reality of Christ's humanity, such that in defense he emphasized the cross and resurrection (Ing. *Trall.* 9; *cf.* Ign. *Smyrn.* 1).

12. Baker and Green, *Scandal of the Cross*, 149.

13. Baker and Green, *Scandal of the Cross*, 150.

14. Morris, *Atonement*.

15. Grensted, *Doctrine of the Atonement*, 18–19.

Faith and love on the part of humanity is dependent upon the cross, mediated through the Eucharist, which brings one into mystical union with the passion of Christ (Ign. *Trall.* 8; Ign. *Rom.* 7). Ignatius found peace as he made Christ's passion his own, for the love of Christ involved the desire to suffer with him (*Rom.* 6). Ignatius sought to become an imitator of his God.

Ignatius lived at the beginning of the "age of heresy" and the church's confrontation with Gnosticism. Gnosticism, based as it was upon knowledge (γνῶσις), had little use for the cross and its materiality. The intellectualism of Gnosticism underwent a change in the Apologists, who understood that while "truth" saves, it does not bring moral alteration to the heart of believers. Adherence to earlier Christian tradition resulted in a greater stress upon the historical reality of the cross.

Justin Martyr (c. 100–165 CE)

Justin Martyr in his *Dialogue with Trypho* states that God the Father wished Christ to take upon himself all the curses of humankind (*Dial.* 95). Justin may be said to exhibit a view of substitutionary atonement, but it is far from clear that he would support penal substitution. Justin in fact speaks of our healing rather than God's appeasement. Christ became incarnate for our sake as a partaker of our sufferings, such that he might bring us to *healing* (2 *Apol.* 13). More attention appears to be given by Justin to the incarnation than to the atonement.

Irenaeus (c. 130–202 CE)

In Irenaeus (d. 202 CE), the mind of the theologian is at work in the correlation of the atonement with the justice of God in conjunction with the kingdom of Satan or the devil. God's own character of love uses persuasion rather than force in appeal to reclaim humankind from the devil, whose rule is based on aggression rather than love.

One early view of the atonement is associated with Irenaeus and is generally termed "recapitulation." By the time of Irenaeus (c. 130–202 CE) in the late second century, the proclamation of the saving significance of the cross was coupled with explanations as to why Jesus had to die on the cross and its effect upon salvation. The context was one of conflict with the powers of the day and tension with the dominant political and social structures of Caesar's world, in which Caesar was acknowledged as Lord and even worshipped as a god. It was a time beyond the second Jewish-Roman War (132–36 CE) during the time of Hadrian (117–38 CE). Cosmology posited a cosmic conflict between God and multiple forces of evil. It was "not surprising that Christians framed their discussion of the cross and resurrection in terms of a cosmic conflict between God and the forces of evil, with the resurrection sealing Jesus Christ's victory over sin, the devil and powers of evil."[16]

While Irenaeus could understand Christ's death in terms of a ransom payment (*Haer.* 5.1.1), this does not form the core of his soteriology. The core is to be seen in Christ's rescue of humanity by rescuing human nature itself. Such a theory features the idea that Christ lived through each phase of human life with obedience and without sin, such that the damage caused by human sin is repaired. Christ is the second Adam of a restored human race.[17] Or, as Irenaeus himself stated the reality, "And therefore does the Lord profess Himself to be the Son of man, comprising in Himself that original man out of whom the woman was fashioned . . . , in order that, as our species went down to death through a vanquished man, so we may ascend to life again through a victorious one; and as through a man death received the palm [of victory] against us, so again by a man we may receive the palm against death"(*Haer.* 5.21.1).

Christ summed up all things in his work of recapitulation. As a man born of woman, Christ overcame the enemy who had led us away captive in Adam. The ultimate goal of Christ's work for Irenaeus was to make humankind divine—"our Lord Jesus Christ, who did, through His transcendent love, become what we are, that He might bring us to be even what He is Himself" (*Haer., Preface, Book* 5). This becomes a dominant note in the understanding of other church fathers as well—"he became what we are, in order that we might become what he is." This was interpreted along the lines of "he became human in order that we might become divine" or "he suffered death in order that we might experience eternal life."

Within the framework of a *Christus Victor* model of the atonement, Irenaeus wrote in the context of the threat of Gnosticism that humanity lost its *immortality* as a result of corruption wrought by the sin of Adam and Eve. He could use Paul's Adam-Christ typology (Rom 5) to emphasize Adam's part in the origination of a disobedient race, countered by Christ's origination of a redeemed humanity. Irenaeus employed the concept of "recapitulation" with emphasis upon incarnation, as he understood that Christ both summed up and restored humanity to incorruptibility and immortality (*Haer.* 3.18.7). Irenaeus employed the Logos concept in the context of Platonic realism in connection with incarnation, but he also emphasized Christ's death and resurrection.

In addition to the concept of recapitulation, Irenaeus pursued the meaning of Jesus's death as release from captivity (*Haer.* 1.1). He could speak of Christ's saving work in terms of a "ransom." The question naturally arose as to whom the ransom was paid. Origen of Alexandria (c. 185–254 CE), a strong allegorist, was the first to develop a detailed theory of a ransom paid to the devil. In Origen, the devil is conquered

16. Baker and Green, *Scandal of the Cross*, 143–44. This is certainly true for Paul in an earlier day. One should note Irenaeus is some 100 years after Paul and that the concern is with anthropomorphic soteriology.

17. Finlan, *Problems with Atonement*, 67.

through his own miscalculation and self-deception. Sometime later, Gregory of Nyssa (330–c. 395 CE) portrayed God as a "good fisherman," having conquered the devil through trickery. Unaware the divinity of Jesus was concealed under his human flesh, the devil was caught by the "hook of Deity" as he took "the bait of the flesh."[18]

Irenaeus states that "the word of God was made flesh in order that he might destroy death and bring us to life" (cf. *Haer.* 3.19.6). Irenaeus had a significant influence in the development of atonement theology, as well as significant influence upon Athanasius. One sees here an incarnational theme, as well as a deliverance theme.

Origen (185– 254 CE)

With Origen (d. 254 CE), the dominant conception is the defeat of the devil and evil spirits. Christ defeated the devil by rising from the dead, even freeing the spirits trapped in the prison of the devil's realm (1 Pet 3:19) . Resurrection is at the center of this theology. Christians are really made righteous (not just acquitted), for they can be transformed into the likeness of Christ (*Against Celsus* 8.17; cf. 1.68). Incarnational theology allows the Spirit to be incarnated into the lives of ordinary people, as Christians are transformed into the likeness of Christ. Human nature can be divinized because God entered into human nature in Jesus. This process is an outgrowth of incarnational theology and since the fourth century has been known as *theosis* (θέωσις). It has been a prevalent concept in Eastern Orthodoxy. While the incarnation need not be linked with atonement theology, incarnational theology either leans toward atonement or toward *theosis* in varied degrees in different fathers of the church.[19]

In Origen, the transaction of reclaiming the soul of humankind is explicitly stressed: Paul's language of "bought with a price" (1 Cor 6:20; 7:23) called forth definition. If there were a price paid, to whom was it paid? "Now it was the devil that held us, to whose side we had been drawn away by our sins. He asked, therefore, as our price the blood of Christ" (*Comm. Rom.* 2.13). As Jesus could not have given his life as a ransom to God, it had to be to the devil, the evil one. The devil named his price; God paid it. However, the devil was deceived, for he found he had no power (death) over Jesus who was raised from death. Death did not hold Jesus—God raised him from the dead. This prompted some later theologians to conclude that notably no permanent harm had been done to any party in this seeming transaction.

Eusebius of Caesarea (c. 260–339 CE)

Eusebius of Caesarea (d. 339 CE), a relative contemporary of Athanasius, understood the death of Christ as a sacrifice. Christ appropriated our sins, willingly accepted the

---

18. Gregory of Nyssa, "Great Catechism," 22. Cf. Grensted, *Doctrine of the Atonement*, 40.

19. Finlan, *Problems with Atonement*, 68. On *theosis*, see Finlan and Kharlamov, *Theōsis*.

punishment we deserved, such that his death was a substitutionary sacrifice. Eusebius works with an entire scriptural canon, including Isaiah 53, 1 Peter, and Hebrews. Eubesius's *The Proof of the Gospel* (*Demonstratio Evangelica*) was perhaps written 314–318 CE, prior to his *Ecclesiastical History*.[20] In commentary on Psalm 60, Eusebius states that the Lamb of God "who takes away the sin of the world" (cf. John 1:29) became a curse on our behalf. God made Christ "sin for our sake," offering redemption for all, that "'we might become the righteousness of God in him.'" Because of incarnation, the likeness of sinful flesh, he made our sins his own because of his "love and benevolence towards us" (*Dem. ev.* 10.1).

Eusebius suggests the only way he could make our sins his own was through our being regarded as his body (cf. 1 Cor 12). Jesus as the Lamb of God suffered our woes and labors according to the law of love. He was chastised on our behalf, suffered penalty he did not owe but which we owed, became the cause of the forgiveness of our sins, received death in our behalf, accepted scourging, insults, and dishonor, and was made a curse for us (*Dem. ev.* 10.1). The seeds of substitution—and for some—"penal" substitution may be seen here. However, Eusebius's controlling thought is ransom or redemption "for our sake." As he states, though he knew no sin, God made him "sin for our sake, giving him as redemption for all, that we might become the righteousness of God in him" (*Dem. ev.* 10:1). And, Eusebius affirms that Christ's resurrection proved that "in Him the Father was well pleased."

As Kelly states, Christ was "able to identify Himself with our sins and the penalties attached to them because, as very man, He shared our nature."[21] Eusebius is illustrative of the fact that neither the "physical" or "mystical" theory associated with incarnation nor the "ransom" theory associated with deliverance from the devil marked the main stream of Greek soteriology in the fourth century. The main stream is interpreted in terms of a sacrifice offered to the Father. However, it is accompanied by an incarnational theme, either "Godward" or "humanward."

While Jeffrey et al. claim Eusebius, biographer of Constantine, unequivocally for "penal substitution," Eusebius speaks in terms of Christ bearing our sins and iniquities in terms of making our sicknesses his own, suffering our woes and labors according to laws of love (*Dem. ev.* 10.1). The paradigm is one of mutual burden bearing out of love, a point not unknown in Paul (cf. Gal 6:2). Eusebius can speak of Christ being made a curse for us out of love, in order to ransom "the whole human race, buying them with His precious Blood from their former slavery to their invisible tyrants, the unclean daemons, and the rulers and spirits of evil" (*Dem. ev.* 10.8). The view espoused by Eusebius has an affinity for the ransom model in terms of a *Christus Victor* understanding. As Derek Flood points out, two key themes by which the early Fathers understood substitution are evident in Justin (to *heal* humanity) and Eusebius

---

20. If the dating is correct, this would have been more than 250 years after the death of Paul (61 CE).

21. Kelly, *Early Christian Doctrines*, 384.

(to *annul* death's dominion). In fact, he concludes that "Christ's atonement under-stood in the dual context of our *healing* and death's *destruction* are prevalent themes throughout the writings of the Apostolic Fathers."[22] The same themes may be found in Ignatius, Polycarp, the Shepherd of Hermas, Epistle to Diogenetus, and the Epistle of Barnabas.[23]

Athanasius (c. 296–373 CE)

Athanasius (d. 373 CE) retained atonement and leaned toward *theosis*. Salvation be-comes restoration which emanates from the Incarnation itself. As the only perfect image of God, Christ re-created and restored the divine image in humans (*Inc.* 13). Anthansius's theory is really not a ransom theory, but a rescue theory.[24] Christ entered human living to enable human beings to be divinized both by and into the divine nature.[25]

It is with Athanasius in the fourth century, however, that one first encounters a sustained and specific treatment of the topic of atonement. Heretofore, one usually encounters isolated statements with little extended explanation. Athanasius in the fourth century for the first time offers a sustained treatment on the topic of the atone-ment. While some seek to claim Athanasius for penal substitution, his understanding of Christ's substitutionary death remains in the realm of healing of humanity and the overcoming of the domain of death.[26] Athanasius spoke in terms of "corruption" from sin, which he understood as a natural consequence that led to death. Corruption and death are not externally inflicted punishments, but rather they are the inevitable consequence when one shuts oneself off from the source of help.

In the Greek thought world of Athanasius, sin is a corruption that leads to death, a model of natural consequence. When one sins, one breaks communion with God and cuts oneself off from the very source of life. The result is death, but death as the natural consequence, the inevitable consequence of sin. It is not an externally inflicted punishment. Sin is not merely legal transgression of law, but rather a deeper sickness of the soul for which mere repentance is not a sufficient antidote.[27] Neither interper-sonal legal measures, repentance, nor punishment suffices to heal the corruption of

22. Flood, "Substitutionary Atonement," 146.

23. Cf. Particularly, Barn. 5:1, 5–6, where cleansing by forgiveness of sins, destruction of death, and demonstration of resurrection are featured.

24. Finlan, *Problems with Atonement,* 69.

25. Finlan, *Problems with Atonement,* 69. Cf. *Inc.* 54.

26 .Flood, "Substitutionary Atonement," 147.

27. "Repentance" implies something humans do, which results in or contributes to a desired end or goal. It should be recalled that Paul does *not* emphasize repentance (μετάνοια). For Paul, the human problem is deeper than a human solution.

sin. What is needed is "regeneration" or an actual ontological *change* wrought in *us* by God.[28]

As Flood states, "the problem of the atonement is not an angry God, but a sick and dying humanity." The concept of Athanasius is that of sin as a *sickness*, not "the more familiar Western judicial idea of *sin as transgression, . . .*" As Flood states, "the key focus of Christ's substitutionary atonement here is in *conquering death* in order to bring us *new life.*"[29] Athanasius thus echoes a recapitulation view of the atonement (often attributed to Irenaeus)—Christ became as we are, such that we could become what he is: "only the Image of the Father could re-create the likeness of the Image in men" (*Inc.* 20; cf. Rom 6:5, 8). This could only be accomplished through overcoming sin's corruption (healing) and death's dominion (resurrection).

Flood suggests that what is found in Athanasius is an understanding of salvation in terms or *restorative justice* based upon our rebirth and healing *and* the restoration of God's rule in overturning the system of death. This is a paradigm of transformative rectification—as Paul would say "the overthrowing of Sin and Death" (Rom 8:2). It would mark abolishment of crippling appeasement and retribution, rather than its establishment based upon punitive justice.[30] The idea of Christ "enduring and exhausting" God's punishment as found in Jeffrey et al. is not found in Athanasius. It is certainly not found in Paul.

What is found in Athanasius is a nuanced understanding of salvation as healing and abolishment of both death and curse through the vicarious death *and* resurrection of Christ.[31] The punitive view of atonement does not abolish death, but sustains it; it does not emphasize healing, but rather hurting. As Kelly indicates, the dominant strain in Athanasius's soteriology is marked by the physical theory that Christ, by becoming man, restored the divine image in us. Blended with this conception is the conviction that Christ's death was a sacrifice for us that was necessary to release us from the curse of Sin/sin.[32]

Athanasius's language suggests Platonic realism of a universal in which individuals participate. The "Word" became human, yet that incarnation becomes in effect the redemption of those who stand in special relation to Him, those who are divinized by intimate union with the Holy Spirit. Athanasius's Platonism caused him to lose touch with Christianity at times, but he did emphasize Christ's humanity at the point of the cross. There was still a debt owed, such that all humankind was doomed to death. Thus, after revelation of the Godhead by Christ's works, it still remained for him to

---

28. Flood, , "Substitutionary Atonement," 148.

29. Flood, "Substitutionary Atonement," 148, emphasis original.

30. In Jeffery et al., *Pierced for Our Transgressions*, 173, the summary of Athanasius offered is that "God became man in order to save humanity from God's punishment for sin, and Christ accomplished this by enduring and exhausting this curse in our place, as our substitute."

31. Flood, "Substitutionary Atonement," 150.

32. Kelly, *Early Christian Doctrines*, 377. Cf. Athanasius, *Inc.* 9.

offer sacrifice for all, such that humankind could be rescued or delivered from the liability of ancient transgressions.

As the representative man, Christ on the cross accepted the penalty in his own body through his death. His death was a sacrifice offered to God on our behalf, a ransom for sins. Christ thereby healed us and bore the burden of our weakness and sins. As Kelly comments, "On the surface the doctrine is one of substitution, but what Athanasius was seeking to bring out was not so much that one victim was substituted for another, as that 'the death of all was accomplished in the Lord's body.'"[33] Just as death was inherited through kinship with the first Adam, so now in union with Christ's flesh and death we share in his victory, conquering death and inheriting life.[34]

Athanasius expresses the same combination of Godward and humanward ideas in terms of incarnation and deliverance from the devil as found elsewhere. He has two distinct ideas of death, in that physical death is a stage in corruption as a result of sin, of which spiritual death is the completion. Athanasius is not the precursor of later penal theories, for he does not regard death as penal suffering nor Christ's death as vicarious punishment (cf. *Inc.* 20). The view is that "he became man that we might be made God" (*Inc.* 54), a thought set forth by Irenaeus. Restoration of the divine in humankind means the true knowledge of God is recovered, which is life eternal.

Athanasius was more focused on the deification and consequent immortality of human nature in terms of incarnation. For Athanasius, "He was made man that we might be made God" (*Inc.* 54). Christ as human became subject to death as Humphreys affirms, "but even his death played a role in the transformation of human nature and was inevitably overcome by the incorruption of the divine nature in the form of the resurrection."[35] In the viewpoint of Athanasius, as "very Word and God," Christ was not injured by death, for he was impassible and incorruptible. At his "second glorious coming," Christ the Savior will "render to all the fruit of His own Cross, that is, the resurrection and incorruption. . . ." (*Inc.* 56). The confession of the church was focused upon the incarnation. Hague advances Clement of Rome, Origen, and Athanasius as "outstanding exponents" of the church's thought on atonement in the first four centuries, because their doctrine of atonement was not marked by spurious explanation through philosophy and sophistry—in his judgment.[36] Overall, Athanasius was more

33. Kelly, *Early Christian Doctrines*, 380. Cf. Athanasius, *Inc.* 20.

34. One should note the dual emphasis—a past and present union with Christ in flesh and death (e.g., the Eucharist) and a future share in resurrection. This emphasis accords with Paul's thought (1 Cor 15).

35. Humphreys, *Death of Christ*, 51.

36. Hague, "At-one-ment by Propitiation," 87.

concerned with the problem of Arianism[37] and matters pertaining to the Trinity than he was with formulating atonement doctrine.[38]

In the view of Jeffery et al., penal substitution was central to Athanasius's thought. This is *not* the case. Death for Athanasius represented corruption as a result of sin. Jesus as the Word assumed a body capable of death that he might become a sufficient exchange for all by abolishing corruption for all through the grace of resurrection. While Athanasius speaks of substitution, he does not speak of *penal* substitution. The summary of Athanasius's thought by Jeffrey et al. is simply slanted and inaccurate. Contrary to their expression, Athanasius did not link incarnation to penal substitution. It was not the case that God became man in the incarnation to save humankind from the divine curse of God's *punishment* for sin. Nor did Christ accomplish this "by enduring and exhausting this curse in our place, . . ."[39]

While Athanasius did speak of incarnational purpose in terms of substitution overcoming corruption (hence, restoration and renewal of even the entire creation), it is disingenuous to read *penal* substitution into Athanasius. He does not understand corruption in terms of judicial punishment solved by legal measures. As Flood indicates, Athanasius's thought involves the themes of *healing* and *overturning* the corruptive dominion of sin unto death. Athanasius has a model of natural consequence; we die and return to nothing, as a result of becoming separated from the source of Life. Sin is a sickness of the soul which has inevitable consequence. The problem is far deeper than legal transgression and judicial punishment. The problem of atonement is not that of punishment by an angry God nor the need of repentance, but rather the need of regeneration which overcomes the corruption wrought by the sickness of sin.

For Athanasius, the remedy was the Incarnation, whereby we are *recreated* in Christ. One is confronted with the view of recapitulation, credited to Irenaeus. God entered into our humanity, Christ participated in our death, that we might participate in his resurrection life.[40] The key focus for Athanasius is to be found in Christ's

37 Arianism, with Arius of Alexandria (c. 256–336 CE), posited that Jesus as the Son of God was begotten by God the Father at a point in time and is thus distinct from and subordinate to God the Father.

38. Athanasius's career revolved around the Arian controversy. The Council of Nicea (325 CE) formulated a creed which sought to address the discord brought about by Arianism. The emergent Nicene Creed was Trinitarian in formulation, but with regard to Jesus, it states belief in *"one Lord Jesus Christ, the Son of God, begotten of the Father, the only begotten, that is, of the essence of the Father, God of God, Light of Light, very God of very God, begotten, not made, being of one substance with the Father."* The debate centered around two concepts. The word ὁμοούσιος (from ὁμός) carried the idea of "the same being or essence," while the word ὁμοιούσιος (from ὅμοιος) carried the idea of "similar being or essence." And who said one small iota (ι) makes no difference!

39. Cf. Jeffery et al., *Pierced for Our Transgressions*, 173.

40. Paul expresses as much in Rom 6:5, 8–9, as he states "if we have become [pf.] united with him in the likeness of his death, indeed we shall be of the resurrection; . . . if we have died [aor.] with Christ, we have faith that indeed we shall live with him; because we know that Christ having been raised from the dead no longer dies, Death no longer lords over him." Paul's expression actually undermines much *penal* substitution sentiment.

conquering death in order to bring to us *renewal* and *new life*. What one finds in Athanasius is not "substitution" as surrogation punishment, but rather real ontological change in us effected by Christ's victory over death and the power of the devil. Death and corruption are utterly abolished. As Athanasius states, "He was made man that we might be made God."[41]

Gregory of Nyssa (d. 394 CE)

Gregory of Nyssa (d. 394 CE) gave classical expression to defeat of the devil more than a century after Origen. Gregory, like Athanasius, embraced a physical theory involving the Incarnation. For Gregory of Nyssa, the incarnation culminated in the resurrection. The incarnation was the sovereign means of God for the restoration of humankind to its original state before the Fall.[42] Gregory of Nyssa had a ransom theory that could better receive the label of "rescue." He takes the notion of ransom more literally than Irenaeus. The devil has rightful claim because people sold themselves into his power through sinning. God has no right to steal people from the devil, but he has every right to buy them back ("Great Catechism" 22).

Yet God operated by deception. Divine nature was hidden under the veil of human flesh, so that "as with a ravenous fish, the hook of the Deity might be gulped down along with the bait of flesh" ("Great Catechism" 24). He fooled the devil, who took the bait much as a "greedy fish." ("Great Catechism" 24). The devil was tricked into allowing the power of life into his own house of death. Conquest of the devil occurred not through transaction, but through a masterful trick.[43] One really has to be watchful in the presence of a God who so masterfully deceives. The triumph that sets the pattern for repair and reunification of a divided human nature is the resurrection. Such reunification is a "Platonic idea Christianized."[44] Gregory shows a concern for justice for all, the devil included. Augustine later compares the cross to a mousetrap, the bait being Christ's death or blood unjustly shed (*Serm* 130.2; 134.6; 263.1).[45]

Gregory of Nazianzus (c. 329–390 CE)

For Gregory of Nazianzus, the Cappadocian Father, one goal of atonement was the very destruction of sin as well as its curse. Far beyond the bounds of theories of

41. Athanasius, *Incarnation* 54. There are a number of references in Athanasius's work which have a bearing on the issue at hand, such that it is recommended that one consult the entire treatise *in passim*.

42. Kelly, *Early Christian Doctrines*, 381.

43. Cf. Grensted, *Doctrine of the Atonement*, 39–41. One has to wonder whether Gregory chuckled or smiled as he wrote about the "trick" God played on the devil.

44. Finlan, *Problems with Atonement*, 69.

45. Cf. Flood, "Substitutionary Atonement," 155; Kelly, *Early Christian Doctrines*, 391–92; Finlan, *Problems with Atonement*, 70.

satisfaction or legal retribution, the superior economy of grace overcomes the economy of wrath. In Gregory's thought, "Christ became condemnation-itself in order to abolish condemnation-itself."[46]

Gregory has a concept of sacrificial substitutionary atonement understood in a context of healing and new life. According to Flood, the superior way of restorative justice supersedes, replaces, and even destroys the way of retributive justice in Gregory. Gregory of Nazianzus, friend of Gregory of Nyssa, becomes his critic by denying the necessity of any ransom payment at all. He could not accept either God or the devil being paid off. He anticipated the later theory of "moral influence."[47] In addressing the matter of a ransom payment, Gregory raised the question to whom it was paid:

> To Whom was that Blood offered that was shed for us, and why was It shed?
> . . . if to the Father, I ask first, how? For it was not by Him that we were being
> oppressed; and next, On what principle did the Blood of His Only begotten
> Son delight the Father, Who would not receive even Isaac, when he was being
> offered by his Father, but changed the sacrifice, putting a ram in the place of
> the human victim? Is it not evident that the Father accepts Him, but neither
> asked for Him nor demanded him; . . .[48]

For Gregory, Christ became the curse itself to destroy the whole process of condemnation itself. God did not hold us in subjection, nor did he ask for Christ's death. Christ's sacrifice did not appease God's wrath, nor did it represent divine punishment—God neither asked for Christ's substitutionary death, nor did he require it, according to Gregory. Rather, he suggests that humanity was sanctified by the humanity of God through the incarnation. The tyrant of Death is overthrown through the cross, as Death itself is slain by the one who is the giver of life. God seeks to draw us to himself though the obedient mediation of the Son.[49]

Ambrose (c. 340–390 CE)

The patristic theme of the destruction of the curse of sinful flesh itself (which admits the possibility of re-creation) is also found in Ambrose of Milan, a representative of the Latin fathers. Jesus took on flesh in order to destroy the curse of sinful flesh, becoming a curse "that a blessing might overwhelm a curse . . . and life might overwhelm death."[50] Ambrose does suggest an idea of satisfaction, but he really does not move

---

46. Flood, "Substitutionary Atonement," 151.

47. Finlan, *Problems with Atonement*, 69

48. Gregory of Nazianzus, "Second Oration on Easter," 7:431.

49. Gregory of Nazianzus, "Second Oration on Easter," 7:431.

50. Cf. Jeffery et al., *Pierced for Our Transgressions*, 175.

beyond Athanasius and Cyril of Jerusalem. It is Augustine and subsequent Latin writers who will stress the idea of justice.[51]

Ambrose does describe Christ's death as a satisfaction of justice, as fulfilment of a sentence of judgment. One can thus see the seeds of Anselm's *Cur Deus Homo?* emerging in the early Latin church fathers. This is not surprising, given the Latin legal mind-set as contrasted with the mind-set of the Greek fathers. There is a claim of penal substitution and retributive justice, but it occurs in a context of ecclesiastical practice of penance which characterized the time.[52]

Augustine (354–430 CE)

Augustine has been influential in both Catholic and Protestant circles. In *Against Faustus* 14.6, he states that Christ bore the curse which accompanies death, bearing our punishment, "cursed for our offences, in the death which he suffered in bearing our punishment." While this has been claimed in support of penal substitution,[53] in the same context Augustine develops what he means. Death was condemned "that its reign might cease, and cursed that it might be destroyed" (*Against Faustus* 14.3). It is not the satisfaction of punishment, but rather victory over death that held humanity captive. Death, sin, and the devil are "condemned," "cursed," and "destroyed" through Christ's death, which cancels our guilt and does away with our punishment (*Against Faustus* 14.4). A portion of Augustine's thought appears to echo penal substitution.

Augustine uses a "mousetrap" analogy similar to the "fishhook" analogy of Gregory of Nyssa: The Lord's cross was the devil's mousetrap: the bait which caught him was the death of the Lord.[54] Because the devil acted unjustly in putting Christ to death (he had no debt or sin), he lost his rights to humanity as well, his real debtors. The devil became a victim of his own malice and injustice. Christ's "just blood" was "unjustly shed" (*Trin.* 4.13.17). God did not deceive the devil; he acted justly. The crucifixion, however, was an unjust act. The price paid to the devil proved to be his snare. Condemnation and retribution are not "satisfied" or "exhausted," but rather are themselves abolished and destroyed.

Augustine directly broaches the question of God's anger: was the Son reconciled and prepared to die for us, "while the Father was still so angry with us that unless his Son died for us he would not be reconciled to us? (*Trin.* 13.11.15). In answering his question, Augustine points to God's love in the light of Gal 2:20, Rom 8:31–32, and Eph 1:4. Augustine saw the Spirit of both the Father and the son working in all things

51. Grensted, *Doctrine of the Atonement*, 89–90.

52. Ambrose's understanding is thus different from the Calvinistic understanding of penal substitution. Calvin understood penance to be a "pestilent" doctrine (*Institutes* 3.4.27) and a "feigned sacrament" (*Institutes* 4.19.17).

53. Jeffery et al., *Pierced for Our Transgressions*, 179.

54. Augustine, *Sermon 263, On the Ascension.* Cf. Flood, "Substitutionary Atonement," 155.

"equally and harmoniously." Justified in the blood of Christ, *we are reconciled to God* by the death of his son. As Augustine continues, he speaks of deliverance from the power of the devil by righteousness. As he states, "it pleased God, that in order to the rescuing of man from the grasp of the devil, the devil should be conquered, not by power, but by righteousness; and that so also men, imitating Christ, should seek to conquer the devil by righteousness, not by power."[55] As Flood comments, the "Triune God" acted freely out of love for humanity to free humanity from Satan's hold that had resulted because of sin. The real problem then was not God's willingness to love and forgive, but rather "the objective reality of our brokenness being in need of a real cure."[56]

In Augustine, it is the healing of our sin that removes the cause of God's anger, as God himself heals the spiritually sick and restores the dead to life. God justifies [rectifies] the sinner through the man Jesus Christ. God heals not only to destroy sins, but to provide also the "means of not sinning." God becomes the Great Physician who heals a deadly wound.[57]

While the language of sacrifice, justification, and reconciliation was available to Augustine, he frames things in terms of his two central motifs—healing and liberation. We are saved from God's wrath by God incarnate loosing us from the devil's power (cf. *Trin.* 13.16.21). It is a substitutionary, restorative model of salvation and atonement (cf. *Conf.* 10.43.69). The wound of sin is healed and we are liberated from its bondage.

While contemporary advocates may speak in terms of God's own sacrifice for us, the central function of penal substitution remains the appeasement of divine anger through retributive punishment as a precondition of divine forgiveness. As John Piper affirms, "if God did not punish his Son in my place, I am not saved from my greatest peril, the wrath of God."[58]

Augustine held to a confluence of atonement views of his age. While Augustine held to the ransom theory, his main theory appears to have been the moral influence theory. Augustine also taught substitutionary atonement, but he did not emphasize penal substitution. While the moral influence theory is often attributed to Peter Abelard, Abelard in fact restated Augustine's view, which in itself articulated the doctrine

---

55. Augustine, *Trinity* 13.13.17. Cf. *NPNF*, 3:176. According to Augustine, *righteousness* was commended by death of the Powerful One on the cross, whose *power* was promised to us through the resurrection. Cf. *Trinity* 13.14.18. Both are commended to us in what sounds very much like a cruciform imperative combined with a resurrection indicative.

56. Flood, "Substitutionary Atonement," 156.

57. Augustine, *On Nature and Grace* 26.29; *Exposition on the Psalms,* 51.6. Cf. Flood, "Substitutionary Atonement," 157.

58. Piper, "Foreword," Jeffery et al., *Pierced for Our Transgressions,* 14. Cf. J. I. Packer, "What Did the Cross Achieve?" Although Piper's theology is based upon sources far beyond Paul and his view is only representative, how sad it is (in the present writer's view) to remain in such theological slavery so far removed from Paul's own perspectives of "grace and peace" and what they suggest about the nature of both God and Christ.

current in his time. Augustine had no doctrine of an angry God who needed to be appeased.

Grensted observes that one sees in Augustine the attempt to extend the idea of justice more thoroughly and consistently than in the Greek fathers. "It was absolutely just that man should be in the devil's power, yet the treatment of the devil was also just."[59] The Augustinian theory of the Atonement is upheld by writers of the Western Church in very much the same terms for the next seven hundred years.[60]

It is Augustine especially who marks transition from East to West. While the ransom theory remained common property, the Western mind-set was different in kind from the speculative mysticism of the East. The interests of the West were largely ethical and legal. As Grensted suggests, "the great Roman system of jurisprudence" had "left its mark upon it in the legalistic bias which is everywhere present."[61] The idea of abstract justice meant much to Rome, such that this carried over to Western thought on the atonement.

Transference of atonement to the nature of the Godhead is perhaps Augustine's greatest contribution to the discussion of the atonement, for the devil becomes insignificant. Anselm and his successors will propose Godward theories, albeit centuries later.[62] Augustine himself did not go beyond the current ideas of his age.

Not since the time of Paul does one encounter a vision of the stern realities of sin as one does in Augustine, even though their views differed. As with Athanasius, sin is far more than disobedience. It is a deep-seated and inherited corruption of the soul of the family of Adam. Augustine thus thought in terms of actual sins and "original sin."[63] The Fall was entirely man's fault, its latent ground being an act of pride. The gravity of sin in Adam ruined the whole human race. Augustine believed that the taint of sin was propagated from parent to child by the physical act of generation, such that even infants were infected with sin. The Savior was born of a pure virgin, in order to avoid the "taint of concupiscence."[64]

As a by-product of our fall in Adam, we have lost our original liberty such that we cannot avoid sin. We are saddled with both original guilt as well as sin's ongoing evil inflicted upon us. Augustine seems obsessed with unbridled sexuality and its ravages produced in human beings, but he does not equate original sin with sexual passion nor does he advance an idea of "total depravity." The problem of "original" sin could be deemed to be even greater than the presence of "actual" sin. Augustine was hampered by his legalistic language, a point that probably endeared him to later legalists.

---

59. Grensted, *Doctrine of the Atonement*, 45–46.
60. Grensted, *Doctrine of the Atonement*, 49.
61. Grensted, *Doctrine of the Atonement*, 88.
62. Grensted, *Doctrine of the Atonement*, 91.
63. Kelly, *Early Christian Doctrines*, 361–66.
64. Kelly, *Early Christian Doctrines*, 365, and Augustinian references there.

Writing about 400 CE, the context of Augustine's treatise *Against Faustus* is Faustus's own publication that attacked Moses and the Old Testament. Faustus charged Moses with blasphemy for his curse pronounced against Christ, who for our salvation hung on a tree (Deut 21:23). Faustus's charge implied that Jesus was cursed by God, thus charging him with sin. Augustine seeks to explain the veracity of Moses's statement, how Jesus could be cursed without having been guilty of sin. He cites Paul in support in his immediate contextual reply (cf. Gal 3:10, Rom 6:6, Rom 8:3, and 2 Cor 5:21). He sees no problem in Moses calling accursed what Paul terms sin—curse and sin go together, such that one cannot reject Moses without rejecting Paul.

Among other things, Augustine defends both the inspiration of Scripture, the incarnation, and the reality of Christ's death within the context. God hated both "sin and our death," such that he sent his Son "to bear and abolish it" (*Faust.* 14.6). According to Augustine, sin is "a bad action deserving punishment" and "death the consequence of sin."

> Christ has no sin in the sense of deserving death, but He bore for our sakes sin in the sense of death as brought on human nature by sin. This is what hung on the tree; this is what was cursed by Moses. Thus was death condemned that its reign might cease, and cursed that it might be destroyed. By Christ's taking our sin in this sense, its condemnation is our deliverance, while to remain in subjection to sin is to be condemned.[65]

The curse, according to Augustine, is pronounced against sin, death, and consequent human mortality. For Augustine, to deny Christ was cursed is to deny that he really died a human death. "Death is the effect of the curse; and all sin is cursed, whether it means the action that merits punishment, or the punishment which follows. Christ, though guiltless, took our punishment, that He might cancel our guilt, and do away with our punishment" (*Faust.* 14.4). "Bearing our punishment" is interpreted in terms of Christ's real, human death. It is this denial of Christ's real, human death which is the focal point of Augustine's argument against the Manichaeans.

> The believer in the true doctrine of the gospel will understand that Christ is not reproached by Moses when he speaks of Him as cursed, not in His divine majesty, but as hanging on the tree as our substitute, bearing our punishment [i.e., dying a human death], any more than He is praised by the Manichaeans when they deny that He had a mortal body, so as to suffer real death. . . . Confess that He died, and you may also confess that He, without taking our sin, took its punishment.[66]

---

65. Augustine, *Against Faustus* 14.3, 4:208.

66. Augustine, *Against Faustus* 14.7, 4:209. An echo of Paul's thought in Rom 6:23 is perhaps seen here. In terms of surface language itself—"our substitute, bearing our punishment"—one has building blocks for a doctrine of penal substitution.

Augustine goes on to observe that Moses could have just as easily said that "Cursed is everyone who is mortal" or "Cursed is everyone dying" as "Cursed is everyone who hangs on a tree!" As Flood observes, Augustine's thought does not revolve around a legal demand for punishment but rather the overcoming of death which had held mortal humanity captive. It is death, sin, and the devil that are condemned, cursed, and destroyed by Christ's death as he "took our punishment." Guilt and punishment were canceled.[67] According to Flood, Augustine sets forth the concept of God's spiritual healing and restoring to life. God is portrayed by Augustine as a Physician who heals and cures, not as a Judge who condemns. Augustine does exhibit the biblical language of sacrifice, justification, and reconciliation, as well as substitutionary, ransom, and victorious models of atonement as these would relate to human liberation and restoration.[68]

Jeffery et al. assume a straightforward statement of penal substitution for Augustine.[69] A sinless Lord Jesus Christ bore the curse of death deserved by a sinful humanity," "death" representing the consequences of actual sinful actions. According to Jeffery et al., "Christ died instead of us, thus delivering humanity from the curse of death itself, as death was "cursed, condemned and destroyed at the cross."[70] In their syllogistic theology, death is the punishment due to *us* for *our* sin. Christ suffered death *in our place*. Therefore, Christ suffered the punishment we deserve. If the premises are not valid, neither is the conclusion. They quote Augustine, who states that Christ endured death as a man and for man. He bore the curse which accompanies death: "He died in the flesh which He took in bearing our punishment, . . . He was cursed for our offenses, in the death which he suffered in bearing our punishment" (*Faust.* 14.6). Jeffery et al. are forced to admit, however, that while Augustine may say Christ bore our curse, died in our place, and suffered our punishment, Augustine does not say Christ bore *our guilt*.

Augustine emphasized Christ's sinlessness, thus according to Jeffrey et al. "insisting that the fact Christ was cursed by God does not imply he had done anything worthy of death." Jeffery et al. distinguish between guilt *incurred* by a person and guilt *imputed* to a person. They thereby uphold "later writers" who on the basis of Isa 53:6 and 2 Cor 5:21 reckon that Christ was punished because God reckoned him as being guilty for our sins. This heralds a "tension" in Augustine's theology—"if Christ was not guilty before God even by imputation, then God *unjustly* punished an innocent man." They still claim Augustine in support in spite of whatever inconsistency, for "it

---

67. Flood, "Substitutionary Atonement," 154–55. Cf. Augustine, *Against Faustus* 14.4, in *NPNF*, 4:208.

68. Flood, "Substitutionary Atonement," 156–57. Cf. references to Augustine cited therein.

69. Jeffery et al., *Pierced for Our Transgressions*, 179. Cf. Augustine, *Against Faustus* 14.4, 6, in *NPNF*, 4:209.

70. Jeffery et al., *Pierced for Our Transgressions*, 178.

cannot be doubted that he believed Christ bore our punishment—the essence of penal substitution."[71]

For Augustine, however, the reason Christ bore our death was that death's reign "might cease" and that death itself "might be destroyed" (Cf. *Faust.* 14.3–7). Augustine expresses a substitutionary view of the atonement in the context of other concerns (such as Manichean heresy that denied the real death of Jesus). Augustine can also express a "ransom" view of the atonement as well.

Augustine summed up the theological thoughts of the West in his time and passed them on, impressed as he was with his own genius and authority. The central thought of Augustine's soteriology understood redemption in terms of the "expiatory sacrifice" offered in our behalf by Christ's passion.[72] Christ's innocence of sin gave atoning value to his death, such that Christ is substituted for us. Christ took our punishment upon himself, destroying our guilt and putting away our punishment. The underlying, defining realities here are the death and resurrection of Jesus defined in terms of incarnation, not retribution but deliverance.

The subjective side of the incarnation and atonement had great value for Augustine, for Christ as our mediator had demonstrated God's wisdom and love. The objective humility demonstrated in the incarnation and passion, i.e., divine grace released by the sacrifice of the cross, is what first makes reconciliation with God possible. Imitation of Christ by us is the effect of that divine grace in our hearts. The various strands of Augustine's soteriology are brought together in his *Enchiridion* on faith, hope, and love (*Enchir.* 108).[73] We could never have been delivered by Christ the mediator, had he not been God as well. Christ had a unique birth, lived and died without sin, that we might be reconciled to God and be brought to eternal, resurrected life. The incarnation of God was required to restore and heal humankind, such that reconciliation and restoration mark its primary features.

It was not until Anselm's *Cur Deus Homo?* (*Why Did God Become Human?,* 1097 CE) that there was an attempt made to give more exact definition to a theology of redemption or soteriology. At a later point, Anselm clearly suggests God did not require the death of Jesus at all.

> What man would not be judged worthy of condemnation, if he were to condemn someone innocent and release the guilty party? . . . it is a surprising supposition that God takes delight in, or is in need of, the blood of an innocent man, so as to be unwilling or unable to spare the guilty except in the event that the innocent has been killed.[74]

---

71. Jeffery et al., *Pierced for Our Transgressions*, 179, emphasis original.

72. See Kelly, *Early Christian Doctrines*, 392–95, and the Augustinian references given there.

73. Cf. *NPNF*, 3.272.

74. Anselm, *Cur Deus Homo?,* 1.8, 10.

Likewise, Aquinas speaks of penal punishment meted only upon the guilty for personal sins. He further describes or defines "satisfactory punishment" as penance done in behalf of another.[75]

Flood sums up the situation. Along with the themes of healing and liberation, the additional theme of satisfaction begins to emerge in the Latin fathers. This is a theme which comes to full fruition in Anselm and Aquinas. The satisfaction model continues to shape the Catholic understanding of the atonement. Rooted in the concept of retributive justice, like the Calvinist model of penal substitution, the view focuses upon an effective change in God rather than a transformation of humanity.[76]

A Patristic Summary

In spite of the continued appearance of the ransom theory, the early Greek fathers held to a combination of "Godward" and "humanward" conceptions of the atonement expressed in sacrificial and ethical language. These two aspects were framed as a single whole, aided by mysticism characteristic of Eastern Christianity. In this respect, these writers prove to be the true successors not only of the apostolic fathers, but also Paul himself.[77] The Western Church, on the other hand, given its practical bent, was generally content to live with doctrines of the church laid down by the Greek fathers of the fourth and fifth centuries. A notable exception in this regard was the development of the doctrine of *the* Atonement, a development which was almost exclusively Western. In Augustine and subsequent Latin fathers, the theory of a transaction with the devil is retained, although the emphasis now falls upon the *justice* of the transaction. This is illustrative of the legal mind-set of Latin Christianity. The devil begins to take a subordinate role (he is self-deceived) and the mystery of the atonement rests with the very nature of God himself.

One does not find elaborate worked out syntheses present in the soteriology of the fourth and fifth centuries. Developing theology had focused on such matters of Trinity and Incarnation. A variety of unrelated theories, sometimes mutually incompatible, are found—sometimes in the same theologian. However, as Kelly indicates, "redemption did not become a battle-ground for rival schools until the twelfth century, when Anselm's *Cur Deus homo?* (c. 1097) focused attention on it."[78] Mystical theory linked with Incarnation posited that human nature was transformed, sanctified and elevated by the very reality of Christ becoming man. In its full form it tended to be combined with a Platonic doctrine of real universals. One also encountered a ransom

75 75. Cf. Aquinas, *Summa Theologica PS* Q87.A8, as cited by Flood, "Substitutionary Atonement," 153.

76. Flood, "Substitutionary Atonement," 154.

77. Grensted, *Doctrine of the Atonement*, 87.

78. Kelly, *Early Christian Doctrines*, 375. The twelfth century is a long time after the time and culture of Jesus and Paul.

theory of redemption, either of payment offered to the devil (Irenaeus; Origen) or forfeit required of the devil.

Substitutionary theory placed the cross in the foreground and portrayed Christ substituting himself for sinful humankind. Christ shouldered the penalty of payment required by justice, such that humankind is reconciled to God by Christ's sacrificial death. How this is so is not clear. The various theories marked the attempt to elucidate the meaning of the cross (or the death of Jesus) from different angles. They were predicated upon the idea that fallen humankind was in the devil's power and salvation includes necessary rescue from that power (cf. Luke's statement in Paul's defense speech, Acts 26:18). "Ransom" explanations take on the character of divine rescue, not divine wrath.

Kelly suggests that the one great theme which runs through almost all patristic attempts to explain redemption rests in the ancient idea of "recapitulation," which Irenaeus derived from Paul. Just as all humankind was present in Adam, so they may be found in the last Adam. Participation in the first Adam led to sin and death; participation in the last Adam offers ultimate triumph over Sin, the forces of evil, and Death itself. Kelly suggests that all of the fathers reproduce this motif, regardless of school, except when automatic deification by the Incarnation is found under the influence of Platonic realism. "The various forms of the sacrificial theory frankly presuppose it, using it to explain how Christ can act for us in the ways of substitution and reconciliation. . . . Christ is a fitting exchange for mankind held in the Devil's grasp."[79]

In Aulén's description of the *Christus Victor* view, the work of Christ is seen first and foremost as a "victory over the powers which hold mankind in bondage: sin, death, and the devil."[80] The idea of "ransom" should be understood in terms of a rescue or liberation. The crucifixion was not a payment of a ransom to the devil, according to Aulén, as much as it was liberation from bondage. The concept of the Trinity has part in the redemptive plan. *Christus Victor* is not a legal offering to God to placate his justice, but rather the decisive moment in a war against Sin, Death, and the Devil, in which ironically the Law is included. In the ransom theory, justice was accomplished, the "war was won," such that God was able to free us from Satan's grip.

Thus, imagery of sacrifice, ransom/rescue, expiation, reconciliation, and justice all appear in the writings of the early fathers, with perhaps the dominant strain being the restoration of the divine image within us. This was blended with the idea that Christ offered himself as a necessary sacrifice to release us from the curse of sin. His death was necessary to release us from death and corruption, human enemies existing as a result of sin. Why this was thought to be so is not clear. It is said that the ransom theory, the recapitulation theory, and the moral influence theory were the main views of the atonement through the first 1000 years of Christian history, although there was never a "required" position. The literal "ransom-to-Satan" view is not widely accepted

79. Kelly, *Early Christian Doctrines*, 376–77.
80. Aulén, *Christus Victor*, 20.

today. Origen, Gregory of Nyssa, and Augustine taught views in line with the standard ransom theory of their own day. Ultimately, it is the reality and hope of resurrection that calls forth all theories to explain Christ's death.

The fourth century marked the beginning of a geographic and linguistic divide within the Roman Empire, as one begins to think of the Latin West and the Greek and Syriac East. The Chalcedonian Christianity of the eleventh century, based as it was on much earlier foundation, experienced a major schism (East-West Schism, 1054 CE). The eastern Orthodox Church flourished in the Byzantine Empire and its theologians wrote extensively on Christian doctrine. The so-called moral influence theory can be universally found in Eastern theologians who emphasized strongly the importance of moral transformation as a process of deification or *theosis*. Theologians during the Byzantine period may have taught several atonement theories and been guided by several models simultaneously, such as the ransom/rescue and *Christus Victor* models of the atonement. When "ransom" is purged of its crassness and understood as "rescue," the two different models go hand-in-hand.

Theosis faded among the Latin fathers, as they were more interested in spelling out the logic of atonement transactionalism in legal terms. All of the Latin theologians from Tertullian to Augustine to Gregory the Great reflect a Roman disposition for the fundamental importance of law, a perspective carried even to the divine level.[81] Augustine (d. 430 CE) is the most influential Latin father. Augustine demonstrates the replacement of the ransom theory with legal theory. He restates the ransom/rescue theory, suggesting God tricked the devil, enticing him like a mouse into a mousetrap. The offering of a ransom payment turns out to be a trick, which triggers a *legal* penalty against the devil. Jesus's death can still be described as a sacrifice for sins or a penal substitution, although it appears legal remedy is needed for the salvation of humankind.[82]

It should be remembered that Augustine formulated the doctrine of original sin, which became dominant in Western tradition. Thus, because people are hopelessly sinful, a reconciliatory mediator is necessary. This mediator must be able to appease deserved wrath (*justa vindicta*) through presentation of a unique sacrifice. Christ, having no original sin and no sins of disobedience, fulfilled that role.[83]

Pope Gregory the Great (d. 604 CE) popularized Augustine's ideas, blending both legal and sacrificial concepts. For every sin there must be penalty. Gregory's logic demanded a "sinless man," a human sacrifice, as payment. Gregory's conception is most crudely literal, yet logical, as he stressed a combined judicial/sacrificial atonement conception characterized by divine violence. Also to be included is a doctrine of punishment in purgatory.

---

81. Finlan, *Problems with Atonement*, 70.

82. Cf. Kelly, *Early Christian Doctrines*, 392–93 and references cited there.

83. Cf. Finlan, *Problems with Atonement*, and references cited there.

As one moves to later writers in the Western Church, the influence of Augustine is found everywhere. As Grensted observes, "Little violence to historical sequence would be done if we were to pass straight from Augustine to Anselm. Throughout the long interval there is practically no advance."[84] One continues to meet with theories of a transaction with the devil, as well as statements in the direction of moral theory. A soteriological emphasis upon incarnation remains, as does an emphasis upon complete justice. Combination theories are to be found.

Peter Lombard could be considered as the last explicit supporter of the traditional view, even though he wrote in the middle of the twelfth century after the time of Anselm. Of his two predecessors, Abelard made greater impression upon him than Anselm. He could still refer to the cross as a "mouse-trap" (Augustine). The motive power of atonement as the love of God is derived from Augustine. He emphasized the love of God as the one eternal truth, although his thought led him to a "human-ward" rather than "Godward" conception of the atonement. "It is the heart of man that changes and is changed"; the attitude of God toward the sinner is not modified by the death of Christ.[85] Lombard's position did not provoke violent antagonism, as had that of Abelard.

The Beginnings of Scholasticism

As one passes into the long medieval period (c. 500–1500 CE), the "ransom-paid-to-the-devil" view of the atonement (credited to Origen) held sway with few exceptions. According to Hague, it was a non-thinking era, such that the Bible was imprisoned under a reign of ignorance.[86] But by the middle of that period, Anselm of Canterbury came to the rescue with his *Cur Deus Homo?*. According to Hague, Anselm's work was likely the greatest work on the atonement ever written, because it offered great conceptions of God and great conceptions of sin.[87]

As one moves from the earlier patristic period, a "new era of intellectual vigour" dawned towards the end of the eleventh century, with the strong speculative work of Anselm (d. 1109 CE), the greatest of the pioneers of scholasticism. He faced old theological problems afresh and nowhere had more lasting effect than in connection with the doctrine of the atonement. The theory which Anselm framed of a satisfaction offered to God has remained the dominant conception and has been the underlying foundation of much later thought from Thomas Aquinas until modern times.

---

84. Grensted, *Doctrine of the Atonement*, 96.

85. Grensted, *Doctrine of the Atonement*, 116.

86. Hague, "At-one-ment by Propitiation," 3:87.

87. Hague, "At-one-ment by Propitiation," 3:87–88.

Anselm (c. 1033–1109 CE)

Anselm proposed his view as an alternative to the then-current ransom theory which held that Jesus's death paid a ransom to Satan, thus allowing God to rescue those under bondage to Satan. Anselm saw the current theory to be inadequate. Indeed, why should God owe anything at all to Satan? Why should the Son of God have to become human in order to pay a ransom? With Anselm, at least as it pertained to atonement theory, the devil was left behind (*Cur Deus Homo?* 2.19). The focus shifted from "ransom" to "satisfaction."

The "popular" model was thus given structure and definition by Anselm at the beginning of the High Middle Ages, and he became a favorite of thirteenth century scholasticism as a result of his close reasoning. He was the first to provide a formal theology of the atonement. He sought to demonstrate by rational argument so as to reason why Christ had to take on human existence and why he had to die on the cross. Paul did not pursue "why" Christ became human, but simply affirmed he had. So had the early kerygma (Phil 2:5–11; Rom 1:1–4). Paul did not debate "why" Jesus "had to die on a cross." For Paul, it was the resurrection that made sense of the cross—Jesus's cross as well as Paul's own cross.

The satisfaction view introduced by Anselm thus marked a major shift away from the classical view. Anselm perceived the problem not as the devil's claim but as a wrong done to God that required an *infinite* satisfaction. He gave singular importance to a substitutionary motif whereby Christ's sacrificial death offered satisfaction to God for an unpayable debt owed to God by a sinful humanity.[88] A "legal" solution is evident.

This concept of satisfaction became the dominant view in the Roman Catholic Church and within later Protestantism. The satisfaction theory, drawn primarily from Anselm of Canterbury, has been the traditional view taught in the Roman Catholic, Lutheran, and Reformed traditions in Western Christianity. Anselm's development was a revolutionary but logical development of penance theology (cf. St. Cyprian), whereby God cannot pardon humanity without having his honor "satisfied" by one capable of rendering adequate "satisfaction." Anselm's conception is more on the order of a business transaction, whereby a debt of honor is satisfied. In Paul, the atonement was an emancipation proclamation and a reconciliation, not an account payment.

The word "satisfaction" has to do with "restitution," paying back what has been taken. Affront to God's justice must be atoned for, such that it suggests the legal concept of balancing out an injustice, a balancing of the books, if you will. Anselm understood sin as human failure to render to God his due (*Cur Deus Homo?* 1.11). It was "honor" that constituted what was due God in the complex of service and worship. Humankind's failure to honor God through sinning creates a debt that must be, yet cannot be, repaid by humans to God. Anything that humans may do by way of

---

88. Baker and Green, *Scandal of the Cross*, 151.

reparation is what is already owed God in the first place and so cannot make up the debt. God is infinite, his honor is infinite, and affront requires *infinite* satisfaction. Nothing humankind is able to do on its own can compensate for infinite affront to infinite honor. While much in Anselm could be pursued, humankind has committed the fundamental crime against the Lord God by robbing him of honor through human sinning. A debt has been created through human sin thereby which is infinite, such that it is impossible for human beings to offer adequate compensatory satisfaction.[89]

Thus, in the understanding of the feudal-lord system of the time, Anselm saw the situation as one of *honor*. We owe God a debt of honor that God requires of us (*Cur Deus Homo?* 1.19). It is not enough to merely restore to God what has been taken away through human sinning, but in the light of the contempt shown, one must restore *more than* what was taken away (*Cur Deus Homo?* 1.24). God cannot simply ignore the imbalance of the moral universe created by human sinfulness. God must act to preserve his honor and integrity; he cannot simply forgive without adequate reparations.

Only a sinless person could pay an excess human debt; yet one greater than human is required to make satisfaction for the debt of all. Hence, only Jesus Christ who is both God and human is able to achieve satisfaction for the total debt of humankind. The only way to satisfy the infinite debt of humanity was for a being of infinite greatness, acting as man on behalf of man, to repay the debt of justice owed God and thus satisfy injury to his divine honor (*Cur Deus Homo?* 2.6). Christ, being both God and man, lived a sinless life (thus incurring no debt) and was willing to endure death for the sake of love. His death satisfied the debt of honor owed by all others.

The Anselmian view was developed through succeeding centuries with modifications, although the basic foundation remained in place. Sin was understood as robbing God of honor and becomes a failure to give God his due, such that reparations to God are required for failure to honor God. We owe a debt that we are obliged to pay, but cannot pay, such that the penalty is death. The gospel of the atonement secures at once God's honor, as well as the salvation of the sinners. As Hague suggests, no one *ought* to make satisfaction for sin except mankind, but no one *could* make satisfaction except God himself. The conundrum was solved by Christ's death, as "the God-Man of His own accord offered to the Father what He could not have been compelled to lose, and paid for our sins what He did not owe for Himself."[90] Satisfactory reparations are thus necessary to avoid divine punishment.

In this perspective it is humans who are deeply indebted to God, such that the debt must be paid and be paid from the human side. However, sin is so heinous that only God could pay such a debt. Thus, God sends Christ, the God-man, who becomes a propitiatory offering for the placation of divine justice. Jesus owed God obedience,

---

89. Given the limitations of being human, nothing human beings can accomplish is, in fact, infinite by definition of the case.

90. Hague, "At-one-ment by Propitiation," 3:88. One sees the echo of Anselm's influence.

but he did not owe God death (required only of sinners). Jesus's sacrificial death thus becomes an infinite and compensatory good, as a vicarious reparation that satisfies God's honor.

Christ suffers the divine punishment deserved by humankind, such that God is enabled to forgive the immense debt of committed sins through Christ's death without any compromise of his divine justice. Christ more than pays the debt in a transaction involving only Christ and God, such that the excess merits of Christ may be imputed to human beings in a second, separate act of justification. Anselm underscored the "necessity" of the cross, even as he affirmed the objectivity of Christ's work.[91] Christ's achievement is independent of human response. Yet it only becomes effective on the basis of human response, in Paul's understanding.

Anselm's conception understood soteriology on the basis of medieval feudalistic authority, sanctions, and reparation. In the face of a fallen world of sin, God's justice was seen to be at stake. For Anselm, either God had to punish the guilty, or, they had to offer adequate satisfaction for offenses against God. God could not just forgive sin as though it did not matter, but he had to re-establish his justice. It was God's justice, not his mercy, that must prevail. Thus, God is portrayed as offering impartial verdicts as a judge in a law court. In popular view, this view of God portrayed God as either annoyed or angry or "officially engaged."

Because human beings as the guilty party could not offer adequate satisfaction for their sin and thus make amends, i.e., they could offer only a *finite* satisfaction for an *infinite* offense, there emerges the need for an *infinite* satisfaction. Thus, Christ as the divine and human one steps in to offer the required infinite satisfaction for the infinite offense. Jesus's act of obedience through his death on the cross thus offers infinite satisfaction that merits God's reward. In this process of atonement, in thought akin to ledger accounting of a business transaction, Christ's death surpassed the effects of the death of any sacrificial animal and more than "made up" for our sins.

Anselm's model thus revolved around excess meriting; since Christ did not need God's reward, the merit was passed on to us.[92] Anselm's theory was later subject to the refinements of Thomas Aquinas and John Calvin, who introduced the idea of punishment into the equation of demands of divine justice. Anselm's own satisfaction model contrasts with penal substitution, in that Anselm views satisfaction as an alternative to punishment. Penal substitution views punishment as the means of satisfaction. The satisfaction view of Anselm is foundational and perhaps only a step away from penal substitution.

Hague suggests that the Anselmic conceptions of God, of sin, of man, and of the soul were too transcendent for Anselm's age, even though his thought has never been

91. Humphreys, *Death of Christ*, 55.
92. Tambasco, *Atonement*, 14–16.

surpassed. "His mind was filled with the august greatness of God, the just penalty of sin, the impossibility of human atonement, and the atoning work of Christ . . . ."[93]

Positively, Anselm's model reveals a very serious view of sin. As Cousar comments, such a view as the Anselmian theory "has the strength of taking very seriously the nature of human sin and the inability of humanity to provide a remedy."[94] Negatively, on the other side, Anselm focuses only on the death of Christ, ignoring the importance of Jesus's life and the essentiality of the resurrection. In the popular imagination, when associated with punishment, God is portrayed as taking out our punishment upon Christ. There must be a legal "balancing," such that God's justice must either punish or demand satisfaction. Apart from *infinite* satisfaction or *infinite* offense, there must thereby be *infinite* punishment or condemnation.

The number of assumptions and presuppositions given to create and support such a view is amazing, including a number that are simply wrong and not supported by biblical thought, and perhaps, especially Paul. The view illustrates, however, what happens when one begins with socio-political anthropology of a given era and places the cross under a divine indicative, which is then interpreted philosophically.

Anselm thus offered a logical (and for his day rational) explanation for the death of Jesus according to the social structures of his day. Anselm offered a less than biblical view at odds with Scripture, although he sought to speak in ways intelligible to his era. Anselm allowed medieval conceptions of honor to define how both "human vassals" and the "Lord God" should act in the face of sin. His focus on honor caused him to fall short of any relational understanding of sin that is so central to biblical views. However, it should again be noted, as Baker and Green remind, that Anselm does not present a "wrathful God punishing Christ in our place; rather, Christ satisfies, or pays, a debt we owe."[95]

Anselm thus did not develop a penal substitutionary view of Jesus's death on the cross. Anselm affirmed the divinity of Jesus, but portrayed God as a feudal lord, one who held the power of life and death over vassals. Anselm's view treated God as both subject and object of satisfaction and lent itself to development of an image of God that could be construed as cruel and vindictive. Anselm's God was thus quite different from the Father of Jesus—or, of Paul. Feudalism, the penance system, and Greek philosophy served to reinforce the image of God as an angry judge. When stripped of its medieval dress, interpreters who came after Anselm in a subsequent era took his core ideas and presented the result as "*the* biblical explanation of the atonement for all times and places."[96] In Anselm's view, satisfaction flows in God's direction in order to restore his honor. In Paul, God's grace flows in humankind's direction with a power that offers life and overcomes all obstacles to peace and human well-being.

93. Hague, "At-one-ment by Propitiation," 3:88.
94. Cousar, *Theology of the Cross*, 83.
95. Baker and Green, *Scandal of the Cross*, 158.
96. Baker and Green, *Scandal of the Cross*, 161.

Abelard (1079–1142 CE)

Abelard, a near contemporary of Anselm, pursued the same issue as Anselm, yet challenged Anselm on the issue of forgiveness. God was free to forgive as he wished. He proposed what came to be known as the "subjective" view of the atonement. Abelard did not understand Jesus's life and death as a demonstration of God's love through a unique act of grace. Rather than victory over powers or ransom paid to the devil or satisfaction of a debt owed to God, Abelard understood the demonstration of God's own love to be that which moved sinners to repentance and to love God in return. A heart of love is enkindled by a gift of divine grace, characterized as justified and reconciled to God through Christ's sacrificial death. He understood Jesus's death to be a fundamental demonstration of God's love, which in turn evoked repentance on the part of humankind.

Abelard saw the cross as the manifestation of the love of God, such that the justification of humanity is the kindling of this divine love in the heart in the presence of the cross. To love is to be free from the slavery of sin, so as to attain to the liberty of the children of God. Our justification and reconciliation "consist in the singular grace shown to us in the Incarnation, and in the endurance of Christ in teaching us by word and by example even unto death."[97] Or, as Cousar states, "Contemplation of such an astounding expression of divine love as displayed in the cross is bound to breed in men and women a responding love, leading to forgiveness and a fresh obedience to God's will."[98] Such a necessity does not appear to have as strong an influence upon humans as assumed by Abelard. This would certainly appear to be the case in the light of contemporary apathy. In Paul's view, human emotional response would be no match for the universal powers that could wreak havoc and destruction in life. Indeed, there was an evident emotional response exhibited by those who condemned and executed Jesus.

Abelard noted that Jesus forgave sins even prior to the cross. He posed a significant rhetorical question: if the sin of Adam "was so great that it could be expiated only by the death of Christ, what expiation will avail for that act of murder committed against Christ?"[99] Abelard understood the work of Christ as reorienting human intention, such that one does all things out of love instead of fear. Abelard appeared to overly emphasize the ethical, "humanward" aspect of the atonement as primary rather than secondary. While emphasis upon the example of Christ as inspiration for endurance in suffering was not new, a causal emphasis upon love's example in the cross appeared to be the complete accounting of redemption. As Grensted summarizes,

97. Grensted, *Doctrine of the Atonement*, 104.

98. Cousar, *Theology of the Cross*, 83.

99. Abelard, *Exposition of the Epistle to the Romans*, as cited by Baker and Green, *Scandal of the Cross*, 162. Cf. Culpepper, *Interpreting the Atonement*, 89.

"Remission of sins and reconciliation are wrought in His blood, but the power is love, love in God working as love in us."[100]

Abelard's position resonates well with Paul's own perspectives, although it falls short at several points. He displays an over-confidence in the human capacity to bring about humanity's salvation that overlooks the "powers." He relativizes "sin," such that it becomes a surmountable rather than an insurmountable barrier. His theory is overly individualistic in its expression. According to Baker and Green, he speaks "loudly of God's love" and "very softly of God's judgment."[101] However, he also offered a challenge to the concept of a "vindictive, punishing God." Beyond these things, it appears that his view in terms of human plight solved by human solution is rather reductionistic and some might even say simplistic.

Abelard's theory was very popular in the liberal theology of the nineteenth and early twentieth centuries in the environment of the "universal Fatherhood of God and universal brotherhood of human kind." Congenial to psychological understanding, it becomes a case of "Love so amazing, love so divine, demands my soul, my life, my all." Neither the view of Anselm nor of Abelard really suggests any "change" in God, although they focus on different "attributes." Anselm focuses upon debt which must be paid and God's honor which must be satisfied (divine justice), while Abelard focuses upon the provocation of divine love which effects a change in the heart of human beings.

The focal point of the two theories of atonement is different, although both reflect rather large, sweeping assumptions. In the one, God's very nature is the inviolable barrier. In the other, human nature is the barrier, at least until one's heart is warmed. Paul by contrast portrays a humanity plagued by powers extraneous to one's self—an unsurmountable problem for humankind, from which God seeks to extricate humanity as well as the cosmos, through his rectifying victory in Christ.

Thomas Aquinas (1225–1274 CE)

Aquinas developed the thought of Anselm in the context of his own theological system (the *Summa Theologica*). For him, the incarnation was the crown of all creation, a reality that came about as a result of humankind's sin. The incarnation and the atonement were thus very intimately connected in Aquinas's system. While neither the incarnation nor the atonement were strictly necessary, the incarnation reveals God's great love and provides an example of obedience and other virtues, inspiring us with justifying grace which enables a newfound freedom from sin. We come to know God's great love through Christ's own example, who through his passion freed humankind from sin. Through remembrance of the price paid for redemption, and the appropriate defeat by the devil, humankind has the obligation to keep itself from sin.

100. Grensted, *Doctrine of the Atonement*, 105.
101. Baker and Green, *Scandal of the Cross*, 164.

Aquinas echoes earlier thought and takes over the best from the thought of Abelard, which had been conspicuously absent from Anselm. Christ's obedience throughout the incarnation, culminating in the cross, becomes not just sufficient but superabundant. This concept of "superabundance" of satisfaction becomes "the most characteristic contribution made by Aquinas to the Anselmic scheme."[102] Aquinas combined moral theory with the commercial theory of Anselm.

Thomas Aquinas, in what is now standard Catholic understanding of the atonement, considered the issue in his *Summa Theologica*.[103] The main obstacle to human salvation rests in sinful human nature, which damns human beings. Repair or restoration is needed through atonement. He advances the idea that punishment is good and appropriate as a moral response to sin. It is a "kind of medicine for sin," which aims at restoration. Christ bore a satisfactory punishment for our sins, not his, and he becomes a substitution for our sin so long as we join in will with him (*Summa Theologica* III.Q85.3; III.Q86.2). The function of satisfaction for Aquinas is to restore a sinner to a state of harmony with God. This is accomplished by repairing or restoring in the sinner what both original sin and personal sin has damaged. Aquinas's major difference with Anselm is that he saw the debt as one of a moral injustice to be righted, rather than a debt of honor to be repaid.

Salvation becomes a matter or merit, such that the passion of Christ was what was needed to pay the debt of sin, not only for himself, but for all. Christ gave more than was required for the entire human race. Christ's death thus becomes God's solution of satisfaction for past sins as well as for future sins, for Christ merited grace by his passion and death. Aquinas thus articulated the formal beginning of an idea of superabundance of transferable merit. He does not speak of "penal" punishment, but rather of punishment that is "medicinal." This "satisfactory punishment" essentially translates into penance, which for Aquinas had a twofold function. There is the payment of debt, but there is also remedy for avoidance of future sin. Christ bore satisfactory punishment for our sins—not for his, but for our sins. His "penance" paid the debt of punishment to us incurred by our sin. This involves the penitential system with regard to a change in the human will and faith in Christ's passion.

Unlike Anselm, who taught that we could never repay God through what we owed God as a matter of course, Aquinas claimed that we could make up for our debt through acts of penance, such that we can make satisfaction for our own sins. The deeper problem, however, is not our personal sin but rather original sin—an "infection" of human nature itself that could not be expiated by the satisfaction of a "mere man." Christ, as the "second Adam," does penance in our place, through love paying the debt of our *original* sin, i.e., the sin of Adam.[104]

102. Grensted, *Doctrine of the Atonement*, 153.

103. See Aquinas, *Summa Theologica* III.Q46–49. Cf. Grensted, *Doctrine of the Atonement*, 150.

104. Aquinas himself comments that Christ suffered himself "to be nailed to the tree for that apple which man plucked from the tree against God's command." Cf. *Summa Theologica* III.Q48, as cited in

Aquinas's thought involves incarnation, justice, the cross, and penance. Central attention to the passion of Christ and atonement is given in *Summa Theologica* III. Q46–49. Aquinas affirms that Christ's passion delivers us from the common sin inherited from Adam and from personal individual sin. Christ paid the penalty on our behalf for Adam's sin, while individuals have a share in his passion by faith, charity, and the sacraments of faith (*Summa Theologica* III.Q49.5). Aquinas accepted Hebrews as Pauline and cites Heb 9:11–12.

A Scholastic Summary

The thirteenth century was a typical age of scholasticism. Anselm's close reasoning appealed to such an age. After a long reign of Augustinian teaching during the Middle Ages, Anselm in the late eleventh century rejected Augustine's position in favor of his own satisfaction theory. The satisfaction view suggests that Christ, by his sacrifice on the cross, offered general satisfaction to the Father for the infinite honor debt that humanity owed God for its manifold sinful offenses. In his critique of other views, Aulén sought to demonstrate that the penance systems of satisfaction theory and that of penal substitution placed an undue emphasis upon humanity's obligation to offer payment to God as well as God's obligation to Law. A counter view of the late Middle Ages was the moral influence view, later rejected by most Protestant Reformers in favor of a theory of penal substitution.

The moral influence or example theory, often associated with Peter Abelard, holds that the purpose and work of Christ was to bring positive moral change to humanity through the teachings and example of Jesus. This view is actually one of the oldest views of the atonement. Adherence or representation may be found in the Epistle to Diogenetus, the Shepherd of Hermas, Clement of Rome, Ignatius of Antioch, Polycarp, Clement of Alexandria, Hippolytus of Rome, Origen, and Irenaeus. It seems to have been predominant in the second and third centuries. A revival of the moral Influence theory in the eighteenth century found support among German theologians, as well as the Enlightenment philosopher Immanuel Kant. It proved to be a popular view among more liberal Protestant thinkers in the nineteenth and twentieth centuries.

The point remains, however, that seldom has any writer changed the thought of an age as did Anselm with his *Cur Deus Homo?*. Redemption as a transaction with the devil goes by the wayside. Interest is shifted to the Godward side of the atonement, which almost without exception (Athanasius) had received attention only in terms of the matter of complete justice of any transaction with the devil (Augustine). Anselm dismissed any thought of the devil as a possessor of rights. How is justice served by

---

Grensted, *Doctrine of the Atonement*, 153. Death on a cross atones for the original sin of Adam who despised God's command by plucking an "apple" from the *tree*. What Adam lost, Christ regained, as it were, upon a *tree*. Aquinas is dependent upon Augustine in his thought.

releasing the guilty and punishing the innocent, however willing the innocent may be? Anselm saw the difficulty and supplied a solution.

Anselm sought a solution in the light of the justice system of his day and the penitential system of the church. The whole idea of penance was that satisfaction offered to God in this life *through the mediation of the church* could be accepted as an alternative to eternal death, understood as the proper punishment of sin in the world to come. Anselm thus offered a solution to the problem of atonement through the principle of satisfaction. As always, current politics affected the doctrine of redemption. For Anselm, God is no longer a Judge, but rather a feudal Overlord.

Anselm sought to argue his case from pure principles of logic that (1) salvation is not possible apart from Christ, (2) human nature (body and soul) is constituted to enjoy blessed immortality, and (3) that which is believed about Christ the God-man is true.[105] His book was primarily a defense of the incarnation, in the light of which he discussed atonement. Anselm presents his case in the form of a discussion with an interrogator named Boso. Positions of old theories of atonement are shown to be untenable.

The Anselmian formulation of satisfaction should be distinguished from the view of penal substitution. Both views speak of Christ's death as "satisfaction," but each offers differing understanding of how Christ's death was satisfactory. In Anselm's view, human sin has defrauded God of honor that he is due. Christ's death as the ultimate and infinite act of obedience brings God great honor—honor far beyond any that would be required. Christ's surplus can thereby repay humanity's deficit. Christ pays the honor to the Father *instead* of our having to pay an impossible debt. Consequently, Christ's death is *substitutionary*. For Anselm, satisfaction is an *alternative* to punishment, for "the honor taken away must be repaid, or punishment must follow" (*Cur Deus Homo?*1.8). Penal substitution, on the other hand, understands Christ's death as paying the penalty of death that had always been the moral consequence for sins (e.g., Gen 2:17; Rom 6:23), not as paying God for lost honor. In part, penal substitution represents a protection of God's consistent sovereign righteousness and abstract divine "justice" rather than his "honor."

Anselm distinguished between satisfaction and punishment on the basis of civil law, acknowledging that either would vindicate the loss of God's personal honor (*Cur Deus Homo?* 1.14). Which would it be? Humankind, destined for blessedness, cannot itself make the reparation necessary to attain blessedness. Satisfaction must be made for human sin which is greater than man can make, yet it must be made by man. Hence, it must be the work of a God-man, who is perfect God and perfect man. Both virgin birth and the Immaculate Conception enter into his discussion as it would pertain to original sin and the perfection of Christ, who died through willing obedience.

---

105. Grensted, *Doctrine of the Atonement*, 123. Cf. Anselm, *Cur Deus Homo?*, Preface.

It is the sinlessness of Christ which makes his offering both voluntary and worthy in terms of an adequate satisfaction for the wounded honor of God.[106]

In a generation after Anselm and 1000 years plus after Paul, Abelard rejected all ransom and satisfaction theories in favor of a moral influence theory (*Epistle to the Romans* 3:19–26). Abelard aroused *clerical* rage against himself, in that he did not believe in universal guilt. Abelard redirected attention to aspects of salvation that had been neglected for centuries, placing emphasis upon the whole of Christ's life and not just its tragic end. The message of his life was the message of his death. The whole Gospel story mattered. Jesus came to instruct us in God's love and to inspire us to receive God's grace to reconcile relationships. Did not Jesus's teachings and actions matter? Did not his ministry suggest forgiveness of sins and saving significance? Was not Jesus offering forgiveness and exalting God's rule even prior to the cross event?

Or, to borrow from Paul, was not God reconciling the world to himself in the person and ministry of Jesus prior to the cross (2 Cor 5:19)? Indeed, as the moral influence view focused on Jesus's life it brought to consciousness the part of the story omitted by the Apostles' Creed and much atonement theory.[107] Ironically, it highlighted the limitations of theological reductionism present in ever expanding doctrines and creeds put in place after the time of Paul.

Aquinas's modifications completely overshadowed Anselm's more vague satisfaction theory and remains as official dogma within the Catholic Church, having been affirmed at the Council of Trent (1546). A sketch of Reformation and Post-Reformation views is now in order.

The church with its official theology in a post-Constantinian Christendom has moved a long way from Paul.

---

106. On Anselm, with numerous primary references quoted, see especially Grensted, *Doctrine of the Atonement*, 120–43.

107. Continuing recitation of creeds which essentially omitted the life and ministry of Jesus between birth and death would have restrictive effect and impact within Christian communities in times to come, including the present day.

8

The Shadow of the Reformation

W HEN one comes to the Reformation, one comes to a signal event in the history of Christianity and Christendom that remains with lingering effect far more than the average Christian realizes. This is true, even though it occurred more than 500 years ago. With regard to the doctrine of "the Atonement," it has had profound affect as "one of the outstanding facts of the history of theological thought," as Grensted observes.[1] The contextual matrix is again important. It was a time of significant change. It was an age of indulgences that placed in bold relief the dangers of the Middle Ages doctrine of merits.

The penal substitution theory emerges with full force. It suggests Jesus received full and actual punishment due humanity, suffering the unbridled wrath of God on the cross *in their stead*. Penal substitution is thus a particular kind of substitution, in which the substitution is that of Christ's *punishment* instead of our punishment. Christ dies "in our place." Christ's sufferings become the substitute for personal penalty, an occurrence which preserves the divine Law, including its curse. The penalty of sin is avoided by humans, as Christ is substituted in the place of punishment.

The Reformers

Expression by the Council of Trent defined justification as including sanctification, thus continuing the medieval tradition of justification as a making righteous and not merely a pronouncement of righteousness. The Council gave approval to the doctrine of "infused righteousness," which marked an attempt to do justice to the humanward side of the atonement on the part of the medieval Latin Church. The Reformers, by contrast, "thought only of the Godward side of Atonement"; they ignored its direct influence upon the heart of humankind. Grensted suggests there is something very external in the penal theory that is avoided by the more mystical expression of the

1. Grensted, *Doctrine of the Atonement*, 191.

Roman theologians. The definition of faith in terms of mere assurance as proffered by the Reformers was "far less adequate to the facts of religious life than the correlation of faith and love."[2] The uncertainty wrought by sociological factors and ecclesiastical power concerns of the times have their part in faith's very definition.

Martin Luther (1483–1546 CE)

The socio-political sphere of Luther's day marked an age of change and progress from the time of the feudalism of Anselm. Abstract law and the personal dignity of individuals had begun to assert themselves in a day of focus upon "justice." The standpoint of legal justice is what characterized transaction of the atonement in the Reformation age. The singular necessity is to be put right with God, to be released from the verdict of guilty by what the Reformers came to express as "justification." Justification, however, was totally an act of God dependent upon the righteousness of Christ *imputed* to us by legal transfer. Justifying faith, however, was totally dependent upon the grace of God.

In direct contrast to the horror of sin, Luther like Augustine viewed salvation from sin in terms of the grace of God rather than works righteousness. Luther saw sin as a total corruption, not just as a failure to give God his due honor. Faith as original righteousness had been lost in the Fall, such that one stood guilty before the judgment of God. Luther was more of a mystic than a theologian in some sense, such that he could understand the justice of God's judgment in terms of his love and grace. As Grensted suggests, Luther offered that which was better than a theory but does not offer a theory of atonement. It is rather in Philip Melanchthon that one finds a developed form of penal substitution.[3]

Martin Luther broadly followed Anselm's position and remained within the "Latin" model of his day. However, unlike Anselm, Luther combined satisfaction with punishment. Jesus, as the perfectly innocent God-man, fulfilled the Law perfectly during his life and in his death on the cross bore the eternal punishment that all men deserve for the breaking of the Law. For Luther, the soteriological conflict was personal and dynamic. The cross marked a struggle between God's implacable righteousness and God's love—a struggle between divine attributes, if you will. Luther was filled with a sense of God's love. For him, God was not a cruel judge who sought to press the full penalty of the Law, but rather a loving and merciful Father. God's love was the ultimate motive of redemption, although penal justice (wrath) was still present as a subordinate motive.

Luther supplied principles upon which the other Reformers built, although his own view of the atonement was not worked out in detail. His most complete statement occurs in his commentary on Gal 3:13 (*Com. Gal* [1535]). The orientation is

2. Grensted, *Doctrine of the Atonement*, 177.
3. Grensted, *Doctrine of the Atonement*, 204.

one of legal justice, such that the death of Christ is seen as legal penalty for sin. Luther expresses the barest concept of substitution, in that sin and its penalty cannot rest upon both Christ and us. If it vests in Christ, then we are free. Luther's theory of atonement remains Godward throughout. Luther is filled with a sense of the great love of God. His singular contribution to humanward theory is his insistence that atonement must be appropriated by faith. Overall, Luther does not offer a developed theory of atonement.

Philip Melanchthon (1497–1560 CE)

Philip Melanchthon may be identified as "the quiet Reformer" and "the enigma of the Reformation."[4] He provides a developed form of the penal substitution view of the atonement. Briefly stated, justice demands the punishment of sin. The attitude of a just God toward the sinner can only be one of wrath. However, if uttermost punishment is meted out and endured by one who represents the sinner, then "justice is satisfied and God's mercy towards the sinner can have free play."[5]

The view of Paul, who always speaks of humankind being reconciled to God and never of God being reconciled to humankind, is here abandoned. The thought is one of an angry God, who demands and receives "justice." Even the sacrificial metaphor retained by Protestant theologians is here transformed. Sacrifice is no longer concerned with the highest of all acts of worship rendered as an honor to God, but it becomes rather "an expiatory offering, a shedding of blood that wrath may be turned aside."[6]

Melanchthon makes this quite explicit. Christ is mediator, propitiator, redeemer, justifier, and savior. It is by his merited obedience that God's justice and wrath are placated and the penalty is utterly paid. The love of God in Melanchthon is far less prominent than God's wrath against us. Melanchthon employs Anselmian demand for satisfaction, but not on the basis of lost honor. God demands *justice*. Human sin is wicked. Only a God-man can bear the infinite suffering needed to placate God for infinite sin. Christ is the one true Victim for sin. Christ's benefits are thus to bear guilt and eternal death, to placate the great wrath of God.[7]

As Melanchthon explicitly makes plain, the justice of God that calls for vengeance upon the sinner is the central fact. That vengeance can only be turned to grace by the expiatory sacrifice of Christ. It is the wrath of God against human sinning, not the love

---

4. Manschreck, *Melanchthon: Quiet Reformer*; Stupperich, *Melanchthon: The Enigma*.

5. Grensted, *Doctrine of the Atonement*, 204–5. As Grensted summarizes, "The thought is wholly Godward, and that of which the early fathers shrank is now boldly proclaimed. By the death of Christ God's attitude towards man is actually changed. Wrath is transformed to love. Mercy is the result of Calvary, or, at least, is freed by the Cross from the necessity of enforcing the stern obligations of justice."

6. Grensted, *Doctrine of the Atonement*, 205.

7. Grensted, *Doctrine of the Atonement*, 205–7.

of God, which assumes prominence in his teaching. For him, like Anselm, the atonement is the demand of justice for satisfaction. Satisfaction is no longer an alternative for punishment, but it is now the punishment itself. Justice is now "avenging justice."[8] God demands penalty. Humankind has sinned, such that a new representative of the human race should bear the punishment of humankind. The infinite wickedness of human sin called for infinite suffering that could only be borne by a God-man.

The position of Melanchthon can be summed up in his singular phrase: "'Christ's benefits are these: to bear guilt and eternal death that is, to placate the great wrath of God.'"[9] Underlying his thought structure, is the influence of Anselm and Anselmic argument. Missing is Luther's emphasis upon the love of God and his conviction of Christ's own identification with sinful humankind. Missing also is Paul's emphasis, "Grace and peace to all of you from God the Father and the Lord Jesus Christ." As Grensted states, in Melanchthon "it is difficult to avoid the feeling that the treatment of Christ by the Father has become ethically repulsive."[10]

Melanchthon has an objective, expiatory view of sacrifice based on his understanding of Old Testament conceptions. Sacrifice for him is propitiatory. It placates God's wrath on behalf of others by making satisfaction for guilt and eternal punishment; it is that which merits for others remission of guilt and eternal punishment.[11] Melanchthon's viewpoint is born of anthropology defined by punishment.

John Calvin (1509–1564 CE)

While Luther never expressed a consistent, single, and systematic presentation of the Christian faith, John Calvin more than made up for that. In Book II of his *Institutes of the Christian Religion*, Calvin set forth his doctrine of the atonement with thorough clarity, consistency, and simplicity.[12]

The entire human race has been involved in sin and corruption since the time of Adam and has thus cut itself off from God. The incarnation provided a way or means of propitiating God. It provided a way for the salvation of a lost humanity (understood individually). Christ became the Mediator who made us "instead of sons of men, sons of God; instead of heirs of hell, heirs of a heavenly kingdom" (*Instit.* 2.12.2). God can not suffer and die; humankind alone cannot conquer death. The work of swallowing up death and conquering sin necessitated a Mediator who was truly God and truly human. Divinity and humanity when combined in one person made possible the endurance of death as expiation of sin, even as it marked victory over death. The

8. Grensted, *Doctrine of the Atonement*, 207.

9. Melanchthon, *Loci Praecipui Theologici*, 603. See Grensted, *Doctrine of the Atonement*, 207.

10. Grensted, *Doctrine of the Atonement*, 208. Some might say there is a scapegoating violence portrayed here that is perpetrated by God himself.

11. Melanchthon, *Loci Praecipui Theologici*, 571. See Grensted, *Doctrine of the Atonement*, 208.

12. See discussion in Culpepper, *Interpreting the Atonement*, 96–103.

priestly ministry of Christ as both priest and sacrifice becomes the heart of Calvin's understanding of the atonement, which he set forth in the framework of the Apostles' Creed (*Instit.* 2.16).[13]

While God hated us in our sin (our own creation), God loved us in terms of what he had made (his creation). God's love is thus the ground of atonement (*Instit.* 2.16.4). The obedience of Christ abolishes the guilt of sin and purchases righteousness (cf. Rom 5:15). Though innocent, Christ died as both a sinner and a criminal (Isa 53:12; Mark 15:28). Christ met death, not because of his guilt, but because of our guilt. Our guilt was thus transferred to him, as he by his death was offered as a propitiatory victim to the Father.[14] Calvin combined forensic and sacrificial categories, affirming that the penalty of our sin was laid upon Christ as a propitiatory victim. As a result, the penalty ceases to be imputed to us.

John Calvin appropriated the ideas of Anselm and Aquinas, but changed the terminology to that of criminal law, in keeping with his training as a lawyer. Biblical teaching was reinterpreted in the light of law. Humankind stands guilty before God's judgment seat; the only appropriate punishment is eternal death. Christ, as Son of God, became man and stood in the place of humankind to bear the weight of the wrath and condemnation of a righteous God. He was made a substitute and a surety *in the place of* transgressors, even as a criminal sustaining and suffering all the punishment which should have been inflicted upon them (Calvin, *Instit.* 2.16.10).

Calvin proposed that Christ's death on the cross did not pay a *general* penalty for humanity's sins, but rather a *specific* penalty for the sins of individuals. Jesus's death on the cross paid the penalty at that time for the sins of all who are saved (*Instit.* 2.12.3–5). Christ's atonement was seen to have limited effect only for those whom God has *chosen* to be saved, hence, "limited" atonement. Calvin drew upon Augustine's earlier theory of predestination (*Instit.* 3.17). Calvin rejected the idea of penance and thus moved away from Aquinas's idea of satisfaction as a change in humanity (satisfaction was penance) to the idea of satisfying God's wrath.

This ideological shift by Calvin focused on a change in God, rather than a change in humanity. God is propitiated through Christ's death. Christ becomes a substitute who takes our place, who takes our punishment and satisfies the demands of justice by appeasing God's wrath such that God can *justly* reveal his grace. The key distinction of *penal* substitution is the concept that restitution is effected through punishment. As one becomes united with Christ through faith, one receives all of the benefits of the atonement, Christ's suffering and punishment. Calvin's development was affirmed at the Synod of Dort (1618–1619 CE).

Calvin was educated for a career in the field of law, such that it is not surprising to find that his view of the atonement is thoroughly legalistic. His model is that

---

13. Aside from other considerations, the writer of Hebrews presented Jesus in terms of high priestly identity, who offered himself once for all as a sacrifice. Cf. Heb 7:23–28.

14. Calvin, *Institutes*, 2.16.5–6; cf. Is 53:5, 10; Gal 3:13–14; 2 Cor 5:21; Rom 8:3.

of a substitute who bears the punishment of others in order that they may escape punishment and be forgiven. Calvin's view, although characterized as "substitutionary atonement," was also one of "substitutionary punishment." It was penal. Calvin's view of God expressed a tension between love and righteousness. Although God wanted to save human beings out of love, the demands of his righteousness had to be met as well. One could not break the Law without punishment.

By punishing Jesus as a substitute, God was placed in the position of being able to forgive. His "righteousness" was satisfied, the law had been met and sentence carried out, with the result God was now freed to love. The tension was resolved. Given Calvin's presuppositions regarding the sovereignty of God and the context of the penitential system, along with his own legal background, Calvin proposed a thoroughgoing rationalistic system of forensic atonement.

Calvin's theory of atonement has been foundationally influential among Protestants. The last six chapters of Book Two of the *Institutes of the Christian Religion* offer a vigorous and concise statement concerning atonement, if indeed six chapters may be considered concise. Orthodox Christology as defined by the Fourth Ecumenical Council at Chalcedon in 451 CE is represented. In brief, according to Humphreys, "by his active and passive obedience, Christ rescued disobedient men from the punishment their sins deserved and this reconciled them to God."[15] Calvin's view of God was that of a righteous judge who would not permit his law to be broken without punishment. The righteous curse of an angry God bars the access of sinful human beings to him.

As Humphreys notes, in Calvin's view "Jesus offered himself as a sacrifice to appease God's anger, to make satisfaction for sins, and to wash away sin and guilt. God was rendered favorable toward men by Christ's sacrifice."[16] And in further description, "God punished Jesus for man's sins. This made it possible for God to forego man's punishment and to forgive men."[17] Calvin spelled out his position in terms of the summary events of Jesus's life given in the Apostles' Creed. Calvin appears to move beyond Anselm in his heightened view of a punishing God. One might raise the question of what models of debt repayment were current in Calvin's day. Was there also a concept of "debtor's prison"? One might also weigh the difference between love and adoration versus a forgiveness of fear. How do these alternatives impact the actual worship of God? How do they square with Paul's portrayal of God and Christ?

Calvin blended legal and cultic language, as he offered a framework which was "legal" and a process which was "cultic." Language that originally belonged to the cultic sphere of worship was now transferred to the legal sphere of "justice" and punishment or legal penalty. A new matrix occasioned a new interpretation or application. The words "curse," "propitiation," "expiation," "wrath," and "sacrifice" are incorporated

---

15. Humphreys, *Death of Christ*, 56.

16. Humphreys, *Death of Christ*, 56.

17. Humphreys, *Death of Christ*, 57.

into sixteenth-century legal language. Calvin's general framework in the context of a rising respect for law of his day remained normative for Reformed Christians for the next three centuries. In modern law, acquittal of the guilty and punishment of the innocent would be regarded as perfect examples of *injustice*. Law changes, but it should be remembered, so has and does theology change. Today, there are even different models of penal substitution.

Calvin's doctrine of the atonement was a milestone in Christian theology, with perhaps the greatest fault resting in his interpretation of sacrifice with the conception of propitiation instead of expiation. Calvin saw the essence of sacrifice to rest in the punishment of sin in terms of a substitute. In comparison with the Old Testament, as Culpepper indicates, "Calvin's interpretation is a gross misrepresentation of the meaning and purpose of sacrifice. Not vicarious punishment, but the dedication of life is the rationale by which sacrifice is to be interpreted."[18]

While both Luther and Calvin could emphasize penal substitution, Calvin offered a more moderate and systematic treatment than did Luther. While present in Calvin, Luther placed a greater stress upon the victory of Christ. Calvin emphasized Christ as enduring the penalty of our sins within a high priestly matrix, interpreting Christ's death as a propitiation.

A shift from the understanding of Anselm is already apparent in the Reformation perspectives of Luther and Calvin. Even though they could employ other concepts, penal substitutionary thought begins to become dominant in the wake of the Reformers and their successors. Anselm did not present a wrathful God punishing Christ in our place, but rather one who paid a debt that we owed—thus leading to "satisfaction" of that debt. However, in the context of a criminal justice system that deals with the apprehension and punishment of the guilty, the shift in legal framework called for Christ to bear the punishment of God meted out for human sin. Calvin, for example, perceived of God as an angry judge, whose wrath must be appeased and favor obtained through the priestly, sacrificial work of Christ (*Instit.* 2.15.6). A reminder is offered that all perspectives related to the atonement represent an attempt to account for meaning inherent in Jesus's execution, most often characterized as Jesus's "death on the cross."

Hugo Grotius (1583–1645 CE)

Grotius's theory arose in opposition to Socinianism, a view which suggested God could have simply overlooked sin. God was understood to be a cosmic king and judge, as moral governor of the universe. On the basis of his legal training, Grotius sought to demonstrate that the atonement appeased God. God publicly demonstrated his displeasure with sin through the suffering of his own sinless and obedient Son as a

18. Culpepper, *Interpreting the Atonement*, 102–3.

propitiation. Christ's suffering and death thus served as a substitute for punishment humans might justly receive. God is ready to forgive, but he must do it safely in a manner that does not threaten his governance. Every act of sin is rebellion which denounces the Law. God cannot pardon rebellion but must uphold his law.

The governmental theory rejects the notion of penal substitution, while still remaining generally substitutionary. Christ's death does not apply to individuals directly, but to the church as a corporate unity. There is general substitution, and not a one-to-one substitution. One partakes of atonement by virtue of attachment to the church through faith. This contrasts with *punishment* theory which posits Jesus's death served as a direct substitute for the sins of individuals. It may be argued that God would be unjust to punish individuals even if they did not come to faith, such that those for whom Christ died are unconditionally predestined to eternal life.

Hugo Grotius in some ways returned to the general nature of Anselm's theory in his modification of Calvin's view. In what is known as the "governmental" view, Christ's suffering demonstrates God's displeasure with sin. As just Governor of the universe, God demonstrates what sin deserves. Christ's suffering has the effect of enabling God to extend forgiveness while at the same time maintaining divine order. In contrast to Calvin's views, Christ does not specifically bear the penalty of humanity's sins, nor does he pay for an individual's sins. In Grotius's governmental view, Christ suffered for humanity so that God could forgive humans without punishing them. Through Christ's suffering, God still maintained his divine justice.

The governmental theory is similar to the views of satisfaction and penal suffering. All three views see Christ as satisfying God's requirement for the punishment of sin. All three views acknowledge that God cannot freely forgive sins without exacting some type of satisfaction or (in its extreme form) punishment. However, the governmental view sees Christ's suffering as an alternative to that punishment. It does not affirm Christ endured the precise punishment deserved by sin or that his death paid its sacrificial equivalent. The satisfaction theory suggests Christ made the satisfaction owed by humans to God as a result of sin through the merit of his propitiatory sacrifice. By contrast, penal substitution holds that Christ endured the exact "worth" of punishment that sin deserved.

Grotius's view differs from the Calvinistic view, in that love and not justice is the dominant quality of God. As Culpepper indicates, "There is no quality of retributive justice in God which demands satisfaction for sin by punishment or an equivalent of punishment. The idea of an equivalence of sin and punishment drops out of consideration, . . ."[19]

---

19. Culpepper, *Interpreting the Atonement*, 107.

Francis Turrettin (1623–1687 CE)

Francis Turrettin (d. 1687) published his monumental statement of Calvinistic belief, *Institutio Theologiae Elenchticae*, in Geneva in 1682. It reflected a mature Calvinism that had been tested by a century of debate with Lutherans and Counter-Reformation theologians. He made appeal to "satisfaction" in a legal sense, in which the penal sense of God's justice appeared uppermost in his mind. Punishment must be meted out for sin, yet Turrettin found a place for the mercy of God which in the light of grace could exempt some and inflict others with a vicarious punishment. In fact, he sought to prove the necessity of vicarious satisfaction along Anselmic lines to a degree that went beyond Calvin.

Francis Turrettin was perhaps the greatest exponent of later Calvinistic orthodoxy. He made appeal to "satisfaction," but in a legal sense.[20] He seemed to confuse civil justice (law of equity) and criminal justice (law of retribution). The penal sense of God's justice appears uppermost in his mind. God as creditor, lord, judge, and ruler demands satisfaction. Punishment must be inflicted impersonally upon all sin, although not personally upon every sinner. There can be transference of punishment to a substitute. God by his grace can exempt some and inflict others as a substitute in their stead. He may do this, not as a weak judge, but as the Supreme Judge who is free from all liability and who is free to act with his own supreme wisdom and pity. He can thus determine the means by which his own justice is satisfied, even to the point of exempting sinners from their due and transferring that "due" to a sponsor.[21]

Turrettin sought to prove the necessity of vicarious satisfaction, again along Anselmic lines, in a manner that went beyond the hypothetical necessity set forth by Calvin. The necessity was based upon (1) God's avenging justice that demands infliction of punishment, (2) the nature of sin itself which demands punishment, and (3) the sanction of the law.

Turrettin found a place for the mercy of God, in view of the fact that under certain conditions vicarious punishment may have the character of legal satisfaction. Again, there is a difference between civil and criminal offense; criminal offense demands punishment. However, satisfaction may be made by (1) one of the same nature as the sinner and (2) consideration of infinite value or price that is greater than sin's infinite demerit. Christ met these two conditions that were necessary for payment of satisfaction as the God-man able to bring infinite value to infinite sufferings.

Further, Christ was of the right nature, had consent of will, divine self-determination, divine self-capacity, and was unstained by sin. The thought echoes that of Anselm and Aquinas in terms of infinite suffering endured for infinite sin. In Turrettin's view, substitution can be carried out lawfully and without any injustice, provided all the conditions are met perfectly in Christ, our sponsor. No injury was done to any,

20. Turrettin, *Atonement of Christ.*
21. See Grensted, *Doctrine of the Atonement*, 241–52.

for even Christ now lives forever. Any injustice perceived in relation to Christ's death is overcome by the resurrection. Divine law was also guarded with its most perfect fulfilment.

As a sidebar, Turrettin held to the rigid doctrine of predestination characteristic of Calvinism, including unconditional election and perseverance. He did not thereby hold to the universal efficacy of the atonement, rejecting the Lutheran position that Christ won potential redemption for all, to be received by faith. Thus, the reformed doctrine of election and predestination provide the real theological basis for understanding the atonement. It is interesting that while Christ's punishment through sacrificial death is more than sufficient to placate or propitiate God's wrath and to reconcile God to sinners because he offered the perfect sacrifice, the effects of Christ's death are only available to the "elect."

According to Grensted, Turrettin expresses the scholastic thought of the age and illustrates that the penal substitution theory is already on the defensive in terms of the criticism of its opponents and the human instincts and sensibilities of its supporters. Retributive justice appears to reveal a radical injustice within the very being of God.[22] Rather than retributive justice, by contrast Paul's focus is upon redemptive grace—a grace that leads to well-being (peace or *shalom*).

A Reformation Summary

The question of the atonement was not deemed to be the primary issue in the Reformation. Rather, the nature of justification became the center of discussion in a matrix of protest against the medieval doctrine of merits. That doctrine seemed inconsistent with the doctrine of superabundant worth (insisted upon by Aquinas), which the Reformers preferred to stress in terms of the sole sufficiency of the satisfaction made by Christ in the cross.

Justification as proclaimed by the Reformers had a purely forensic sense. A technical and Pauline sense of release from a verdict of guilty characterized justification solely as the act of God. The accused is acquitted and pronounced righteous, but on the account of another (Christ) whose righteousness is communicated to us by faith. Justification thereby had no relation to our own righteousness, but solely the righteousness of Christ imputed to us, as it were, by legal transfer.

The work of the Reformers profoundly affected atonement thought, but not always for the better. Luther and others held a deeper and more intense view of sin than that common in the Middle Ages. It was no longer a dishonor done to God which deprived him of his due, after the manner of Anselm's thought. Rather, it was a horrible corruption that wrought death, after the manner of the thought of Augustine and

22. Grensted, *Doctrine of the Atonement*, 245.

Athanasius. Abuses of the market for indulgences threw into bold relief the danger of the doctrine of merits that was a standard of the Middle Ages.

Luther, like Paul and Augustine, was filled with a sense of the supremacy of the loving grace of God as salvation from sin. The original righteousness of Adam had centered in faith prior to the Fall, an occurrence which had left humankind unsure, without certainty, and inclined to sin. The single great necessity was to restore the faith humankind had lost, for only faith was that which could justify. For Luther, the thought of God's grace dominated everything. Humankind could not establish its own righteousness, for the human will was enslaved to sin. Luther, like Augustine, rejected belief in man's free will to do right. Humanity's every act apart from grace was sin. Both Augustine and Luther suffered from the daemon of personal guilt, from which they each sought theological relief.

Luther was pessimistic about human nature, such that he does not speak of *actual* righteousness in justification but only of *imputed* righteousness. Sin is *imputed* to Christ; righteousness is *imputed* to human beings (cf. *Com on Galatians* 5:17). For humanity facing damnation, the Son as innocent substitute bears the divine wrath that everyone deserved. Luther's personal conflicts and conflict with Catholic authorities pushed him further away from admitting any goodness to human nature, such that the emphases in his soteriology became one of absolute depravity, universal guilt, and transferal of divine wrath to the undeserving Son. Rather than victims of evil as in the understanding of Paul, humanity is now the totally corrupted perpetrators of evil. Even though Luther could declare independence from what he considered to be corrupt clerical practices, he could not escape his own internal conflicts, distorted dogma, and personal rage.[23]

Calvin taught that God burned with anger at human sin, "but that God set up a sacrificial avenue for escape from deserved punishment." Damnation is everyone's deserved fate—even babies "are guilty . . . . their whole nature is a seed of sin" (*Instit.* 2.1.8). As Finlan observes, doctrines of atonement can retain *either* the *goodness of God* or the *full sovereignty of God*, but not both. As he states, "To assert the full sovereignty of God and also the full raft of punishing and substitutionary theology is to rob God of goodness."[24] This may be true in terms of the theological reductionism expressed in dogmatic theology. Paul, on the other hand, appears to have held together the "goodness of God" (salutations), God's rectifying activity (Rom 3:26), and his sovereignty (1 Cor 15:27–28) quite well. Paul emphasized a different view of "sin" than did later interpreters.

At any rate, both Luther and Calvin opted to stress the full sovereignty of God, which meant they took an anti-humanitarian stance with regard to both the potential moral goodness of humankind and the primary portrayal of God. Augustinian theology had posited the universality of original guilt, even for babies, as a result of Adam's

23. Finlan, *Problems with Atonement*, 79.
24. Finlan, *Problems with Atonement*, 76–78.

sin. By the time of the Reformation, this resulted in a doctrine of "total depravity."[25] Humans had totally corrupted themselves, and God who is morally good in theory, according to the legalism of righteousness, had to respond with vengeful wrath. He was compelled to do so.

Within subsequent scholasticism, there was little change in the main principles of the penal theory advanced by Luther and Calvin. As soon as the Reformers introduced the penal view of satisfaction, i.e., vicarious endurance of suffering inflicted by the avenging justice of God, little room was left for the obedience of Christ either in his life or his death. It was not even logically necessary that the victim of suffering be willing. "If justice is wholly penal, suffering alone is the fulfilment of its demands."[26] One sees both an imbalance of misplaced emphasis, as well as a monocausal reductionism. These implications especially describe the language of Melanchthon (d. 1560). It is Melanchthon who first offers a developed form of penal atonement.[27]

The thought is totally Godward, but now in the emphasis upon the death of Christ, "God's attitude towards man is actually changed."[28] Mercy is the result of the cross, for the necessity of enforcing a stern obligation of justice is no more. Wrath has been transferred to love by transfer of penalty from the guilty to the innocent. Christ suffered, was crucified, died, and was buried *that he might reconcile the Father to us* (Augsburg Confession), that he might become a victim of both original guilt and all actual sins. The careful view of Paul, who always speaks of humankind as reconciled to God and *never* of God being reconciled to humankind, is abandoned in the theology of Melanchthon. This change of view carried with it other ramifications. Sacrifice is no longer the highest of all acts of worship, but rather it becomes an offering of blood that wrath may be turned aside. It also becomes an example of scapegoating violence upheld by God himself.[29]

The Contemporary Legacy

In the light of the Reformation and Post-Reformation developments, one may consider other and later viewpoints expressed as contemporary legacy. Summaries of representative viewpoints are presented.

---

25. The *TULIP* acrostic for the five points of Calvinism, of course, includes total depravity: *T* (Total Depravity), *U* (Unconditional Election), *L* (Limited Atonement, *I* (Irresistible Grace), *P* (Preservation of the Saints).

26. Grensted, *Doctrine of the Atonement*, 223.

27. Grensted, *Doctrine of the Atonement*, 204.

28. Grensted, *Doctrine of the Atonement*, 205.

29. See Heim, *Saved from Sacrifice*.

Charles Hodge (1797–1878 CE)

Charles Hodge, a leading nineteenth century Princeton theologian and father of A. A. Hodge, popularized the theory of penal substitution.[30] Hodge defined punishment as "suffering inflicted for the satisfaction of justice."[31] One should carefully consider the understanding of the character of God that such a view suggests. Retributive justice or holiness is the most important attribute in the character of God. The essential element in atonement is the vicarious punishment of sin in Christ, our substitute, such that humanity's sins are imputed to Christ and Christ's righteousness is imputed to the elect.

In commercial law, it does not matter who pays the debt, while in criminal or penal law it is the sinner himself/herself who must pay. However, it is the right of a sovereign power to arrange for an innocent person to suffer the punishment of the guilty. God's justice, defined as a form of moral excellence belonging to the nature of God, cannot be compromised and must be satisfied. Sin demands punishment, such that the sinner stands under the wrath and curse of God.[32] If pardoned in consistency with divine justice, forgiveness can only occur on the foundational basis of "forensic penal satisfaction."[33]

According to Hodge, this is Paul's understanding in Rom 3:25. "God sent forth Christ as a propitiation through faith in his blood, in order that God might be just in justifying the ungodly."[34] All that the Bible teaches regarding the impossibility of salvation apart from the work of the incarnate Son of God points to the necessity of God's satisfaction regarding our salvation. Only Jesus's blood has sufficient power to atone. Christ's death was absolutely necessary for an atonement satisfaction, for nothing else had sufficient worth to satisfy divine demand inherent in the Law.[35] Hodge affirms that the scriptures teach the absolute necessity of Christ's death (cf. Gal 2:21; 3:21; Heb 2:10; Luke 24:26) in accordance with the very nature of God. The satisfaction offered through the death of Christ was effectual through its own inherent worth that far surpassed the ineffectual and inherent worthlessness of other sacrifices, such as bulls and goats.

God, however, acts to save sinners from the penalty of sin and alienation by orchestrating Jesus's suffering and death on the cross. In Hodge's understanding, God's justice demands satisfaction (i.e., payment penalty) and human sinners live in a state of bondage and subjection to the power of Satan as they live in fear of the wrath of God.[36] Hodge's commentary on Gal 3:13 is revealing. Jesus's suffering and death on

---

30. Hodge, *Systematic Theology*, vol. 2. Cf. Baker and Green, *Scandal of the Cross*, 170–84.

31. Grensted, *Doctrine of the Atonement*, 310. See Hodge, *Systematic Theology*, 2:473–75.

32. Hodge, *Systematic Theology*, 2:516.

33. Hodge, *Systematic Theology*, 2:488.

34. Hodge, *Systematic Theology*, 2:488.

35. Hodge, *Systematic Theology*, 2:489. Echoes of Anselm may be heard.

36. Hodge, *Systematic Theology*, 2:518–19.

the cross were divine inflictions declared upon him as a result of our sins. As a designated expiation for the satisfaction of divine justice, the elements of divine justice dictated that Jesus was made a curse for us. Hodge's position extends beyond Paul as he considers the matter of atonement. Christ's sufferings were meant as an expiatory satisfaction of justice and thus exhibited all elements of punishment as he bore penalty of our sins. Christ was thus made a curse for us.[37]

Hodge actually objects to the use of the word "atonement" to describe the all-sufficient work of Christ. In common theological usage, to atone is to reconcile. As has been seen, Romans 5:11 (*KJV*) marked the singular usage of the word "atonement" in the English New Testament, where it appeared as a synonym for "reconciliation" (Greek, καταλλαγή). In Hodge's judgment, the word gives rise to ambiguity and confusion. It expresses the effect, but it does not adequately express the nature of the work of Christ.

While "to atone" may be used to mean "to reconcile by expiation," the substitute use of the term as "the *means* by which reconciliation is effected" is very common in theological writings but is not a scriptural use of the word. The atonement of Christ is *what* he did to expiate the sins of humankind. In addition, the word "atonement" is not sufficiently comprehensive, as commonly used. According to Hodge, the concept excludes Christ's vicarious obedience to divine law, while focusing only upon the sacrificial work of Christ. Hodge also objects to the use of the word atonement because it departs from established usage of Reformation-era churches.[38]

Hodge finds the word "satisfaction" to be a time-honored word to describe the special work of Christ in the satisfaction of humankind. "Satisfaction" for Hodge means that Christ has done everything necessary to satisfy the Law and demands of God's justice, both in the place of and in behalf of sinners.[39] He distinguishes between pecuniary or commercial *and* penal or forensic satisfaction. It is the latter that references criminal sins against God. The satisfaction afforded by Christ was not pecuniary, but rather penal or forensic. Christ suffered "in our stead"; he "bore the wrath of God." Christ's sufferings were designed for the satisfaction of divine justice, interestingly enough, that "God might be just in justifying the ungodly."[40]

What is most interesting in Hodge are the chapters that lead up to his discussion of "Theories of the Atonement" (Chapter IX). This is preceded by discussion of the work of Christ in terms of "Priestly Office" (Chapter VI), "Satisfaction of Christ" (Chapter VII), and a discussion of "For Whom Did Christ Die?" (Chapter VIII). All of this appears under his Part III heading of "Soteriology." He pursues an investigation of terms in relation to Christ's priestly office—atonement, satisfaction, penalty,

---

37. Hodge, *Systematic Theology*, 2:517. There are also echoes of Isa 53.

38. Hodge, *Systematic Theology*, 2:469–70.

39. Hodge, *Systematic Theology*, 2:470.

40. Hodge, *Systematic Theology*, 2:474.

vicarious, guilt, redemption, expiation, and propitiation. Hodge assumes Hebrews is written by Paul, which skews the Pauline understanding of Jesus's death on the cross.[41]

The interesting point here is that after virtually setting aside "atonement" as ambiguous and non-comprehensive on the basis of biblical texts which suggest the usage of some type of reconciling expiation, Hodge moves to the realm of theology. He further objects to the use of the word atonement because it is not represented by the established usage of the churches of the Reformation. Having more or less set "atonement" aside, Hodge prefers the usage of the term "satisfaction." *He proceeds, then, to define all the other words without appealing to any specific biblical support, Paul or otherwise.*[42] The single biblical reference which appears in the entire section of Hodge's discussion is Acts 20:28 in a quote from Turrettin.

It is with a great deal of irony, thereby, that Hodge criticizes those who may "philosophize" about the nature of God's forgiveness of sin, those who may never arrive at a satisfactory explanation. When one simply asks the question of what the scriptures teach, one comes to a comparatively easy answer, according to Hodge:

> What do the Scriptures teach on this subject? the matter is comparatively easy. In the Old Testament and in the New, God is declared to be just, in the sense that his nature demands the punishment of sin; that therefore there can be no remission without such punishment, vicarious or personal; that the plan of salvation symbolically and typically exhibited in the Mosaic institution, expounded in the prophets, and clearly and variously taught in the New Testament, involves the substitution of the incarnate Son of God in the place of sinners, who assumed their obligation to satisfy divine justice, and that He did in fact make a full and perfect satisfaction for sin, bearing the penalty of the law in their stead; all this is so plain and undeniable that it has always been the faith of the Church and is admitted to be the doctrine of the Scriptures by the leading Rationalists of our day. It has been denied only by those who are outside of the Church, and therefore not Christians, or by those who, instead of submitting to the simple word of God, feel constrained to explain its teachings in accordance with their own subjective convictions.[43]

Really? Hodge gave the appearance of scriptural support, yet he was a systematic theologian concerned to establish general doctrines on a basis that moved well beyond Paul and the Bible itself. He was concerned with dogmatic Christian thought through

---

41. Here is a significant point. If one assumes that Hebrews is written by Paul—an assumption quite common in the early fathers (such as Athanasius) and promulgated in modern times by the book's heading in the King James Version of the Bible, *the assumption of priestly and sacrificial imagery of Hebrews will seriously skew Paul's own understanding of "atonement."* A reminder is offered that the headings of New Testament books are not original, Hebrews is totally unlike Paul's letters, and very few today would accept it as "Pauline." To assume Hebrews is by Paul is to skew *Paul's* view of the atonement in the direction of sacrificial substitution for sin.

42. Hodge, *Systematic Theology*, 2:470–79.

43. Hodge, *Systematic Theology*, 2:478–79.

the ages. However, through the citation of some biblical references and allusion to "the Scriptures," Hodge's position appeared to be biblical when in reality it was often only systematic ecclesiastical dogma. His controlling perspective, however, was the criminal justice system of his time—he was all about justice, wrath, and punishment.[44] While appropriating the mechanics of a biblical sacrificial system, Hodge imported a view of penal substitution that was foreign to the biblical understanding of sacrifice. As Baker and Green state, "the sacrificial system did not have for Israel the purpose of appeasing God."[45]

Hodge's perspectives are representative of many expressions of penal substitution that exist today on both a popular and professional level. His model of justice drawn from his own day offers an abstract concept of how God *must* react. Rather than relationship, the problem is one of celestial bookkeeping. Hodge's solution portrays God the Father as having to punish God the Son, if one thinks in Trinitarian terms. Jesus's resurrection is really unnecessary to Hodge's singular focus on penal substitution, which becomes "*the* explanation of the atonement for all times and places."[46]

Compared to Paul, Hodge operates with a reductionistic view of sin as limited to actions of moral failure or transgression of the Law. Jesus is said to have met the standard of justice and the Law by living a perfect life. Conflict with the powers of his day really have no relevance. The penal substitutionary view has been in development since at least the time of the Reformation and is the most popular view of the atonement in the *Western* world, exhibiting alternative and nuanced variations even beyond those of Hodge.

Dyson Hague (1857–1935 CE)

In the understanding of Dyson Hague, the root idea according to the biblical thought which calls for at-one-ment is estrangement, an alienation that culminates in idolatry and death. Sin is understood as iniquity and transgression, marked egoistic rebellion and positive defiance of God (Rom 5:15, 19). Sin reversed the relationship between humans and God, placing self upon God's throne. It led to the problem of idolatry. Sin's blight and passion alienated, enslaved, condemned, doomed humankind to death, and exposed humankind to wrath.

Thereby, according to Hague, the sacrifice of the cross becomes the explanation for the "enormity of sin," and the measure of the love of the "redeeming Trinity." Surely it is a kind of ignorance or misrepresentation that says "God loves because Christ died." It is the other way around, Christ died because God loves. "Propitiation does not awaken love; it is love that provides expiation." Christ's death on the cross as a substitute representative of human kind thus "satisfied all the demands of the

44. Baker and Green, *Scandal of the Cross*, 172.
45. Baker and Green, *Scandal of the Cross*, 173.
46. Baker and Green, *Scandal of the Cross*, 174–75.

Divine righteousness" and offered as well "the most powerful incentive to repentance, morality, and self-sacrifice."[47] Hague thus upholds both the moral and the vicarious theories of the atonement within the scriptural witness, even though his basic position is substitutionary and Anselmian. He does not adequately take into account the seriousness of Sin personified, as did Paul, nor the concept of divine victory in Christ.

Gustaf Aulén (1879–1977 CE)

Interestingly, Gustaf Aulén was born in the year after Charles Hodges's death. Gustaf Aulén examined what he considered to be the three prevalent types of the idea of the atonement in his book *Christus Victor: An Historical Study of the Three Main Types of the Idea of the Atonement*. He termed the Anselmian view the "Latin view," for which he offered criticism in the light of its strong juridical and rational character. The Latin view was in complete accord with the general nature of medieval theology with its doctrine of penance (which emphasized the necessity of satisfaction) and emphasis upon the Mass (interpreted as a sacrifice for sins).[48]

Abelard's subjective view of the atonement represented an alternative view, that stressed Christ as teacher and example. In an age which had begun to lay greater stress on Jesus's death in both its theology and devotional practice, Abelard attached no particular significance to the death of Christ.[49] The third view set forth by Aulén was termed the "classic" or "*Christus Victor*" view with roots traced back to Irenaeus, the early fathers and Luther, whereby Jesus's death represented the decisive moment in a great cosmic drama of victory over evil forces. The power of evil and the devil is overcome at the point of the cross, such that God is the chief actor in a salvation-historical drama as both subject and object of a great salvation-historical act.

The bold thesis of Aulén's work is that the history of the concept of the atonement has often been understood as a conflict or variation on the theme of the two prevailing theories of the atonement—the objective view associated with Anselm and the subjective view associated with Abelard. These two views come from the twelfth century. Aulén suggested that the neglected third view which experienced demise in a post-Constantinian world portrays Christ as struggling against forces and evil powers, who by means of the cross, defeats them and liberates human beings who

47. All quotes are from Hague, "At-one-ment by Propitiation," 3:85–86. Hague appears to support a blended view of the atonement—it was substitutionary and provided moral incentive. On the basis of New Testament evidence, Hague understands the death of Jesus as "substitutionary, sacrificial, atoning, reconciling and redeeming" (Hague, 82). As he further states, "The atonement is not a mere formula for assent; it is a life principle for realization. . . . it generates love to God, and love to man; . . ." It offers "the highest incentive to self-sacrifice," which could be construed as a cross imperative. Cf. Hague, "At-one-ment by Propitiation," 3.96. Hague does not stress *penal* substitution in the overcoming of human estrangement. His view is interesting, in light of the fact it appeared in *The Fundamentals* at the beginning of the twentieth century.

48. Aulén, *Christus Victor*, 95.

49. Aulén, *Christus Victor*, 97.

had been enslaved to them. The cosmic drama, that results in victory over all powers hostile to the will of God, results in a new relation of reconciliation between God and the world. From first to last it is a work of God himself set against the backdrop of cosmic salvation.[50] As Humphreys suggests, this view of Christ as a victor "speaks of a drama of redemption rather than a rationale of redemption."[51] This is a significant distinction, as it might apply to Paul's understanding.

The backdrop of such a view is that of dualism of God against the forces of evil ("the powers"). Aulén argues that this is the dominant view of the New Testament, the fathers, and even Luther. Hence, he termed it the "classic" view. Paul, for example, stressed Jesus's victory over demonic principalities and powers. Origen, possibly following upon Irenaeus, is often credited with the theory that the atonement was a ransom paid to Satan. In the development by the fathers, some of the imagery becomes grotesque or amusing, such as Augustine's comparison of the cross to a mousetrap that snared the devil, or, Gregory of Nyssa's comparison of the devil to a fish caught on the hook of Jesus's deity concealed in the bait of Jesus' humanity.[52] Ransom theories hold the incarnation and atonement inseparably together. They thus mark the idea that God is both the Reconciler and the Reconciled and have an affinity for the classic view.

Connection between the incarnation and atonement are not so clear in the Anselmian view espoused by the late Middle Ages. In Aulén's perspective, Luther revived the earlier classic view, although Luther's emphasis upon the "Law" and the "Wrath of God" illustrate the double-sided nature of the classic idea.[53] Aulén's work affirmed the universal, victorious character of Christ's work, as well as his sacrificial death in dealing with individual sins. The "classic" view of the atonement emerged in the very earliest period and remained the dominant teaching for 1000 years, until displaced by the Latin doctrine in the West. While the doctrine of the atonement was not a polemical issue in Luther's day, Luther marked a revival of the classic theme of the atonement found in the fathers, albeit with greater depth of treatment. However, post-Reformation theology and Luther's contemporaries and successors rather immediately returned to developing a "rationale of redemption."

As Aulén analyzed the three types of atonement theory and views, he pointed to a difference in structure, as well as differences in the ideas of sin, salvation, the incarnation, and the underlying conception of God. Aulén's intention was not to write an *apologia* for the "classic" view, but rather to examine historical threads of atonement conception. In view of their thoroughgoing rational structure developed to explain both Divine Love and Divine Justice in the light of atonement, Aulén referred to the first two types (the Latin and the "subjective") as theories or doctrines, which they

50. Aulén, *Christus Victor*, 5–6.

51. Humphreys, *Death of Christ*, 77.

52. Cf. Origen, *Comm. Matt.* 16.8; Augustine, *Serm.*130.2.

53. See Aulén, *Christus Victor*, 102–22.

became. On the other hand, the classic view has never been shaped into a rational theory, but rather has remained as an idea, a *motif*, or a theme expressed in many different variations, according to Aulén.[54] Or, as some have suggested, it depicts or references a drama rather than a rationale.

As suggested by Aulén, there appears to be a greater preoccupation with "Satan" in the fathers than in Paul. This classical model does provide a sense of the cosmic dimension of redemption and the victorious consequences of Christ's death. In a way, it supports Paul's apocalyptic and eschatological point of reference. This view sees the cross as the decisive moment of victory over all hostile powers in a drama between good and evil, whereby a sinful humanity and an enslaved creation is liberated from the power of the demonic. Jesus as the agent of God also becomes a self-offering made to God. God is both the author and object of reconciliation, such that God as the reconciler also participates fully in reconciliation. From first to last the atonement is God's work of rectification, which comes as a result of the defeat of the powers of Sin and Death in the resurrection.

Aulén may have overstated his case. Aulén sought to reformulate the view of the atonement that predominated in the church in the first thousand years of Christian history. The dualistic drama of redemption portrayed God in Christ both combatting and prevailing over powers which held humankind in bondage. According to Aulén, this view was recaptured by Luther but lost again in subsequent Lutheran orthodoxy. While victory over evil powers may be a primary biblical witness (certainly true for Paul), the whole of the biblical witness to the atoning work of Christ (e.g., Hebrews, 1 Peter) cannot be subsumed under this singular category.

Leon Morris (1914–2006 CE)

Leon Morris should be mentioned because of his extensive writing and lecturing with regard to the atonement and the cross of Christ in the latter half of the twentieth century. Morris recognized that the essential difference between Judaism, Christianity, and in fact all other religions was the cross of Christ. He understood the cross as "God's great saving act," as the means used by God to address the problem of human sin. God sent his Son to die for the salvation of humankind as a demonstration of God's forgiving love. His book on *The Atonement* (1983) marks an examination of some of the great "picture-words" employed to bring out the meaning of the cross. This he does in eight chapters, beginning with "Covenant" and "Sacrifice" and concluding with "Propitiation" and "Justification." His perspectives are drawn from both the Old Testament and New Testament as a whole, but of necessity they also must offer a presentation of his understanding of Paul. Treatment of the "Day of Atonement" and

54. Aulén, *Christus Victor*, 156–59.

the "Passover" are the subject of intermediate chapters, as are the "picture-words" of "Redemption" and "Reconciliation."

Morris sees wrath to be a grim reality with God not easily dismissed, for it is God's active opposition to all evil including human sin.[55] Divine wrath extends beyond "human wrath at its best." Morris is critical of those who would find God's love to be incompatible with his wrath. "God's wrath is identical with God's love. God's wrath is God's love blazing out in fiery indignation against every evil in the beloved." And, further, in present context, "the idea of the wrath of God is a genuinely Christian idea." Our sins are the object of God's wrath, such that we face "nothing less than divine anger."[56]

Overall, Morris remains attuned to the Law and wrath of God in that God's wrath stands against every evil thing including human sin. Sin incurs a death penalty, such that capital punishment allows no substitute. He suggests that modern court analogies, however, break down. God wills the penalty be borne, but in the cross or Christ's death he also wills to bear the penalty himself. Justification is a way of viewing the cross that affirms (1) a guilty verdict for those who have sinned, (2) Christ's taking/receiving the penalty of sin due the sinner, and (3) those who express faith in Christ receive a legal verdict of not guilty.[57] The grace of God represents a great price paid to redeem or set us free from evil and wrath. The cross lies at the heart of Christian faith, because it is through the cross and in no other way that Christ has brought about salvation.

As he deals with the concept of propitiation, he characterizes the term as a "personal" word applied to a person, while he characterizes expiation as an "impersonal" word having to do with a sin or a crime. He, in fact, engages in a debate with the position taken by C. H. Dodd ("expiation"). Morris suggests that nothing in Rom 3 suggests ἱλαστήριον should be understood as a "means of turning away wrath." He upholds the view that, at least in one respect, "Christ's atoning work dealt with the wrath of God against sinners."[58]

Morris raises the question as to whether justification encompasses "everything that matters" or is simply an "irritating piece of legalism"? He acknowledges that Torah was not perceived in the Old Testament as a burdensome requirement to make life difficult, but rather was "the wise provision of a loving God to ensure that his people had the guidance they needed to enable them to live well-adjusted lives, lives pleasing

55. Morris, *Atonement*, 173. He also mentions the "puny thing human love is at best," that does not do justice if "love" is applied to God. In the present writer's judgment, Paul did not understand "God's wrath" to be identical with "God's love." Paul did not see human sin as the primary enemy of God. He recognized human beings to be victims of the power of Sin, those enslaved and who stood in need of liberation and restoration.

56. Morris, *Atonement*, 174–76.

57. Morris, *Atonement*, 199–202.

58. Morris, *Atonement*, 167–70.

to God and which fulfilled the best purposes for men."[59] Covenant is a legal term, essentially a legal arrangement.

Justification suggests right standing of acceptance when one appears before God, with the ground of their acceptance being the work of Christ. God sent Christ as a "sacrifice of atonement" ("propitiation"). The "absence of punishment of sins" would not demonstrate justice, such that the cross demonstrates God's justice in that the death of Christ on the cross puts sin away decisively. In Rom 3:26 Paul suggests God forgives in a manner that accords with right, according to Morris, that he saves in a manner that is both powerful and right.[60]

For Morris, Paul expresses salvation in terms of justice or legal standing or status before God. We are "justified" by the blood of Christ (Rom 5:9), such that justification is linked directly with the death of Christ. To think only of justice, of legal standing or status before God on the basis of the substitutionary sacrifice of Christ, however, is itself a substitutionary reductionism compared with Paul's understanding of the rectification of humanity by God's favorable "attitude" and action in Christ.

According to Morris, Christ redeemed us from the curse of the Law as he suffered in our stead (cf. Deut 21:23; Gal 3:13). Christ's death was a redemption, a setting free by payment of a price (Rom 3:24–25; Eph 1:7). "The death of Jesus is the sufficient ransom for all the redeemed, in whatever age they may live." And further, "In the New Testament redemption is deliverance on payment of a price and when men's salvation is concerned that price is the death of the Son of God."[61] It may be said that "ransom" language smacks of appeasement of evil rather than power over and eradication of evil. Paul understood the "payment of a price" in terms of divine provision.

The cross reveals the magnitude of the price paid for our salvation, as Morris stresses. Christ's death was not just a martyrdom. It was "God's costly way of overcoming evil."[62] While the language of "payment of a price" need not be restricted to a literal sum paid to the devil as in the early fathers, the underlying suggestion for Morris remains in a legal realm of justice meted out through penal substitution. Morris's views appear to wrestle seriously with the historical event of the cross, but then they appear to interpret the event theologically in the light of Post-Reformation developments that focus on the legal necessity of the punishment of sins. His focus is upon a proper legal standing before God and not upon actual renewal. He advances a forensic justification. One does not come away from Morris with a sense of "grace and peace from God the Father and the Lord Jesus Christ," but rather with a sense of "courtroom" theology of vicarious punishment. However, Morris appears as a gentle

59. Morris, *Atonement*, 177–82. As Brondos is wont to stress in *Parting of the Gods*, it was for their sake, not for his.

60. Morris, *Atonement*, 195. For Paul, God's power is demonstrated in the resurrection, God's "rightness" in his act of rectification of the entire creation.

61. Morris, *Atonement*, 121–24.

62. Morris, *Atonement*, 130.

and not strident voice that strongly advocated for a penal substitutionary view of the atonement.

Other Viewpoints

Vincent Taylor acknowledged some time ago that a catalog of opinions of the atonement could be either dull or full of interest.[63] Very briefly, he summarized the four main classical views. The "ransom theory" is the oldest and offers the view that Christ died to rescue humanity from "sin, death, and Satan." He also acknowledged Anselm's "satisfaction theory," which suggests Christ died to "satisfy" the wounded honor of God. He pointed to Abelard's "moral influence theory" which suggests Christ's death kindles love for God in the human heart. The fourth classical perspective of the meaning of Christ's death is to be found in the "forensic theory," as represented by the Reformers and their successors, which affirmed that Christ suffered the judgment of God upon sin "in our place." Sacrificial concepts play in the background of all of the classical theories.

Taylor set forth his understanding of the atonement in four books (*Jesus and His Sacrifice* [1937], *The Atonement in New Testament Teaching* [1940, 1945], *Forgiveness and Reconciliation* [1941, 1946], and *The Cross of Christ* [1956]). Taylor interpreted the death of Christ in terms of vicarious, representative, and sacrificial suffering, with the Old Testament conception of sacrifice serving as the natural matrix for understanding Jesus's passion. In essence, Taylor understood that Jesus offered the perfect sacrifice of obedience, which when received by faith, makes possible the sinner's obedient approach to God.

After briefly summarizing the four main classical expressions, Taylor presented the views of ten modern theologians from J. McLeod Campbell to Emil Brunner.[64] He detected several tendencies: (1) rejection of theories of substitutionary punishment; (2) a desire to take seriously judgment upon sins; (3) close connection between Christ and sinners as a representative intercessor; (4) a close relationship between the action of Christ and the faith of the believer, i.e., union with Christ in terms of sacramental communion and worship; (5) a growing tendency to interpret the cross in terms of sacrificial categories of the Old Testament.

Fisher Humphreys, a Southern Baptist theologian, offered a brief treatment of other viewpoints of the atonement (the death of Christ) in his book under a chapter heading entitled "Theologians at Work."[65] For current purposes, these may simply be

---

63. Taylor, *Cross of Christ*, 71. In his lecture on the modern theories of the atonement, he limited the period of his attention to the years 1856–1935.

64. Taylor, *Cross of Christ*, 73–86.

65. Humphreys, *Death of Christ*, 49–85. He offers brief treatment of Athanasius, Anselm, John Calvin, and Aulén ("Vicarious Victor") as well, under the same heading. One may also see Culpepper, *Interpreting the Atonement*, 73–121.

mentioned. John McLeod Campbell emphasized "victorious repentance." P. T. Forsyth expressed a "vicarious obedience" model. Hastings Rashdall stressed a "moral influence" concept. Don S. Browning is associated with "psychotherapy." Humphreys's own view was expressed in terms of "cruciform forgiveness," which involved the transformation of persons.

There are a number of other viewpoints regarding the atonement—which overall, is a New Testament issue and not merely a "Pauline" issue. It is an issue, even as Leon Morris observed, with which the church has struggled for twenty centuries. Humphreys himself suggests that it is better to find a basic model for understanding Christ's death from human experience that makes the victorious element clear and then demonstrates how the effects of that victory overcome the tyrannies to which human beings are subject.[66] Humphreys personally adopted a model of healing of interpersonal relationships along the lines of a psychotherapeutic model, which he terms a "theory of costly forgiveness." The theory arose in the nineteenth century, although it is rarely treated discretely, being most often blended into other theories such as the moral influence theory going back to Abelard and others. Specifically, Humphreys proposed a model of cruciform forgiveness based on biblical teaching.[67]

Again, what is interesting for the present work is that Paul himself seldom alludes to "forgiveness" or "forgiveness of sins," small "s" and plural. His emphasis is to be found elsewhere, notably in emphases upon God's rectification activity, freedom from all the powers, and transformation of life in terms of a cruciform imperative. A theology of atonement is certainly a topic of paramount concern in contemporary discussions of systematic theology, to which Paul has been claimed as a primary witness. Today, the issue of atonement (twenty centuries old, according to Morris) lives primarily in the domain of theological polemics and apologetic. It is often promulgated without adequate exegetical base in New Testament Scripture or adequate awareness of historical development. And, it is generally "doctrinal Paul" who is martialed in support or denial of a given viewpoint.

Derek Flood offers a view he terms "restorative justice" as an alternative to the "retributive justice" of a penal substitutionary viewpoint. His viewpoint is presented in a context of critique of the work of Jeffery et al., *Pierced for Our Transgressions: Rediscovering the Glory of Penal Substitution*, a work which in Flood's view has taken statements of cited church fathers "out of their contextual framework," and placed them into "one foreign to their thought."[68] He argues for clear distinction between "substitutionary atonement" as held by the fathers and the subset of "penal substitution" which is alien to their thought. While substitutionary atonement speaks broadly of Christ's vicarious death in terms of bearing our sin, suffering, and sickness, our

66. Humphreys, *Death of Christ*, 80.

67. Humphreys, *Death of Christ*, 80–115.

68. Flood, "Substitutionary Atonement," 142. For a rebuttal of Flood's analysis, see Williams, "Penal Substitutionary Atonement," 195–216.

injustice and brokenness, penal substitution specifically speaks of the demands of judicial retributive punishment and the appeasement of God's righteous anger.[69]

In the Reformed understanding of penal substitution, it is God's justice that has to be met by substitutionary *penalty*. In the Catholic understanding of substitutionary atonement based on an Anselmic concept, it is instead God's wounded honor that called for substitutionary *obedience*. While Anselm taught substitution, he did not teach penal substitution. In Flood's judgment, the mere identification of *substitutionary* themes (supported by the New Testament and the fathers) and even *penal* themes does not constitute endorsement of the Reformed understanding of penal substitution, especially when taken out of context.

In Flood's view, the core pattern behind many diverse patristic views was that of substitutionary atonement, understood in the contextual framework of *restorative* justice and not *retributive* justice. This means that one should not automatically assume a view of appealing retributive justice at the mention of substitutionary atonement in a given patristic writer. For the fathers, substitution is the functional mechanism through which atonement works. The common denominator behind varied patristic perspectives "is their starting point of a restorative conception of salvation and justice, rather than a retributive one."[70] The majority of the fathers had a conceptual narrative framework of restorative justice on both an individual (restoration of one to new life) and a systemic level (restoration of the order of God's rule). There was, however, no *single theory of the atonement* in the early centuries of the Church.

A context of Christ's substitutionary death in both an individual and systemic sense based upon restorative justice is quite different than one based upon retributive justice. Both are *objective* views which see substitution as central. However, in Flood's restorative justice model based upon the early patristic framework seen in context, our relationship with God is rightly set by God's action to transform and heal. Transformation is a real change in us, effected by God's actions. It is not a change in God effected by appeasement or retributive punishment of the innocent Christ, nor is it a mere impersonal satisfaction of "the law."

Flood interacts with the historic view of penal substitution as he calls for a correct contextual reading of the early fathers. While his general emphasis upon *restorative* justice is more appropriate than that of *retributive* justice, in the light of the present work one must ask about Paul's view. Paul's own thought does not first of all revolve around the narrative of justice, but rather around the narrative of grace. This, of course, is first seen in Paul's salutations. His thought is *subjective* and personal, not mechanistically *objective*. Grace and peace accrue from God *the Father* and the *Lord Jesus Christ*. In Paul's thought, it is *restorative grace* that effects God's peace. God's grace does not stand in conflict with God's righteousness or his rectifying activity. In fact, restorative grace *is* God's rectifying activity in Christ.

69. Flood, "Substitutionary Atonement," 143.
70. Flood, "Substitutionary Atonement," 158.

In the penal substitutionary view of the atonement, the cross becomes a "manifestation of God's wrath," "a paradigm of parental punishment" of a "patriarchal" God. In feminist criticism, this has been viewed in terms of sadomasochism and divine child abuse. Carroll and Green suggest that atonement theology is "misappropriated and misrepresented when coerced into the popular mold of the model of penal substitution," even though it is well-illustrated in popular church life in America.[71] The contemporary penal substitutionary view is often attributed to Anselm, although his view focused on the consequences of sin for humanity and the cosmos rather than upon any attempt to appease a vindictive God. Given Anselm's social order, God was portrayed in terms of a feudal lord who deserved honor and proper service. Working justice called for paying what was due in the lord-vassal relation, i.e., satisfaction of debt.

Atonement Assessment

Anselm's position offers an implicit reminder that the salvific significance of Jesus's death is always interpreted within a given sociological culture. Theological interpretation has its origin within a given cultural specificity. Within Anselm's thought, the feudal system of a cultural patronage was provided divine sanction. Anselm's model of the atonement reflects a socio-historical period relatively foreign to the modern world, and, as some might say, that of Paul's world as well. A part of the problem is that Anselm never argued that his understanding was rooted in Scripture. Even so, atonement theology has often been equated with a theory of penal substitution *attributed* to Anselm, whose thought has often been seen to be *incorrectly* derived from the apostle Paul.

Humankind, in biblical thought, belongs to and is subject to God who created them. The archetypal story of the Fall points to the problem of sin, which damaged and disrupted the divine-human relationship. The need is for the restoration of relationship, for reconciliation and regeneration. Humankind, under the corruption of Sin, is not able to right itself. God the creator on his own initiative acts to recreate and to redeem, to reconcile a wayward and burdened humanity with himself. Consequently he sent his Son out of love for his fallen creation (John 3:16). In contrast to elements of the continuing archetypal story in Genesis 1–11, God determines not to act with judgment but with the intent of redemption, reconciliation, and regeneration. Redemption, as it turned out, ultimately came with a high cost—namely, the death of his Son. The "price paid" was not a "substitutionary ransom," but a willing and personal act of redemption that sought to rescue, rectify, and restore.

71. Carroll and Green, *Scandal of the Cross*, 259–60.

Presuppositional Problems

Assumptions about what God could or could not do lurk in background of all atonement theories, such that God *could not* forgive without a sufficiently pure and valuable sacrifice (Gregory the Great) or unless his offended honor were vindicated (Anselm).

In many "historic" expressions of the atonement, positions taken and the developed theories are based upon either faulty presuppositions or the presuppositions of a given historical matrix that called them forth. They are based upon a "logical" argument rather than biblical thought, which in essence is co-opted in support. However, if the underlying presuppositions are not accepted or in fact are denied by the biblical texts, the resultant theory should be rejected.

What does the phrase "Christ died for us" mean? Finlan answers the question in the light of proffered options: it may mean he died as a martyr to save us, or, he died in our place as a penal substitute, or, he ransomed us by paying the price to buy our freedom, or, he died as a sacrificial and typological "new place of atonement," or, he took on our curse and bore away our sins according to a typological, scapegoat model.[72] It is evident that not everyone hears the same thing when "atonement" is mentioned. According to Finlan, the various metaphors utilized by Paul suggest a *transaction* by which salvation is "bought with a price" (1 Cor 6:20).[73] For Paul, one *could* speak of *Transactional* atonement. To do so, however, would be to speak from the distance of an "objective observer." Paul himself spoke from the vantage point of personal experience "in Christ." One should perhaps speak theologically in terms of a *Transformational* atonement.

The ransom/rescue and *Christus Victor* perspectives present Jesus as dying to overcome supernatural powers of sin and evil, including the devil's ownership over humanity as a result of the Fall. In some form, along with the doctrine of *theosis*, this is still the main theory of atonement within the Eastern Orthodox Church. In the West, where there is an interest, the widest held substitutionary theory is that of penal substitution. The satisfaction theory of Anselm focuses upon a debt of honor owed God, while penal substitution focuses upon the necessity of God's justice. God sent the God-man, Jesus Christ, to provide the necessary satisfaction such that "justice" and "righteousness" might be satisfied. Christ becomes the necessary sacrifice on the part of God in behalf of humanity, such that Christ takes humanity's debt upon himself in order to propitiate God's wrath and satisfy his justice—and God's "righteousness." Divine attributes become immutable.

The so-called "objective" view of the atonement focuses on the demands and satisfaction of divine justice. Forgiveness of human sin cannot take place before divine justice is satisfied. Anselm's model was informed by two aspects of the medieval life of his time—(1) the feudal system of lords and serfs and (2) the penitential system

72. Finlan, *Problems with Atonement*, 58. Finlan emphasizes scapegoat imagery.
73. Finlan, *Problems with Atonement*, 59.

of the church. Honor and satisfaction marked his description of the atonement in his medieval world of chivalry and feudalism. His society was carefully ordered by reciprocal obligations. Anselm lived "in an age consumed by the seriousness of sin and divine wrath," characterized by the recounting of sins, along with a procedural means of remission and absolution.[74] By contrast, we may live in an age where "sin" is not taken seriously and God is transcendently remote, at best. Some doctrines of "the Atonement" may well have contributed to both perspectives. The penitential system in place at the time of Anselm stood as a means of payment for sins, for which excess payment could be stored up as merit, which in turn could even be transferred to cover the debt of others.

In defense of this "objective" substitutionary viewpoint in *The Fundamentals*, Johnson maintained that the Bible is full of substitutionary atonement texts, texts that are found everywhere, being most abundant in the apostle Paul.[75] However, he only cites Rom 3:25 and 2 Cor 5:2 from Paul as support for his sweeping assertion. As he critiques other alternatives to substitutionary atonement, he suggests they tend to praise God's love and "forget His holiness and His awful wrath."[76] An inadequate view of the *state* of human sin and also of human guilt is thereby expressed, such that only repentance is needed without the need of propitiation. Johnson does not seek to set forth substitutionary atonement theory, for it is enough he says "to hold the doctrine without a theory," just as the earliest fathers of the Church did.[77]

Johnson develops eight reasons in support of substitutionary propitiation by Christ as the sin-bearer, who made "atonement" for the world.[78] Johnson sought to oppose the central alternative of his time, the "moral influence" theory, which suggested that Christ's mission was "to reveal the love of God in a way so moving as to melt the heart and induce men to forsake sin."[79] He rejects it as an insufficient theory, especially when it threatens or supplants the substitutionary atonement as the sole appointed means of salvation. Johnson acknowledges that objection to the substitutionary atonement often revolves around definitions of the words guilt, punishment, and penalty. The preaching of a Christ who bore our sins before God on the cross has

74. Baker and Green, *Scandal of the Cross*, 153.

75. Johnson, "Atonement," 3:70.

76. Johnson, "Atonement," 3:71. Cf. Morris, *Atonement,* 161–76.

77. Johnson, "Atonement," 3:72.

78. Johnson, "Atonement," 3:72–77.

79. Johnson, "Atonement," 3:65. His statement does highlight the weakness of the "moral influence" theory, which again is anthropological in its orientation. Such a view fails to take seriously the power of Sin, as Paul understood, and its effect upon humankind and the whole cosmos. It suggests that if only the human heart can be "warmed" or "moved" enough, then humans can solve their problems. There really is no need for any divine victory over the power of Sin, which Paul on the other hand would identify as the "first cause." Johnson's view reflects the matrix of his time, emerging from the optimism of human progress of the nineteenth century.

always moved the heart, although proclaiming one who dies to show he loves is only horrific.[80]

Theological Development

In due course of history, the essentials of the Anselmian tradition passed through medieval scholasticism, the Reformation, and Protestant "Orthodoxy" of the seventeenth century as the "objective" view of the Atonement. It remains present in the penal substitutionary appraisal of the Atonement. The model stresses the personal and individual aspects of atonement, but neglects the social and the communal. As Tambasco suggests, by way of critique, Christ does something *for* us, but nothing *to* us or *with* us according to this view.[81] And, it may be added, we have no soteriological responsibility. We are but passive recipients, either way. Whether Anselmian in origin or post-Anselmian in detail, such a popular viewpoint has its origin in Anselm's thought and has proven to be quite problematic in some quarters of Christianity until the present day. To the extent that "Jesus paid it all," there is no need for a more comprehensive divine indicative or a cruciform Christian imperative.[82] For Paul, God's divine action in the resurrection transformed the apparent shameful defeat inherent in a Roman cross into victory—for Jesus, and through a cruciform imperative, for us as well.

Overall, the topic of "atonement" is a topic with which the church has wrestled for twenty centuries. Debate on the nature of atonement will not end any time soon. While the category of "substitutionary atonement" is a broad one, the dominant conception of the atonement in the contemporary period in America has been that of the *penal* substitution model. The penal substitution theory suggests Jesus received full and actual punishment due humanity, suffering the unbridled wrath of God on the cross *in their stead*. Penal substitution is thus a particular kind of substitution, in which the substitution is that of Christ's punishment instead of our punishment. Christ dies "in our place." Christ's sufferings become the substitute for personal penalty, and thus preserve the divine Law, including its curse. The penalty of sin is avoided by humanity, as Christ is substituted in the place of our punishment. It is a surrogate Christology.

It is a surrogate Christological viewpoint, rationally based, that in actual practical terms essentially renders personal responsibility in discipleship largely irrelevant.

80. Johnson, "Atonement," 3:69–70.

81. Tambasco, *Atonement*, 16.

82. There is no need even for the entire ministry of Jesus, as the so-called "Apostles' Creed" suggests by its *entire omission of the ministry of Jesus* between the Virgin Birth and Jesus's suffering and passion under Pontius Pilate. All creeds are born of specific historical contexts challenged by particular needs that call forth apologetic affirmation in the given matrix.

Penal substitution developed with the Reformed tradition and presents the view that Christ by his own sacrificial choice was punished (penalized) in the place of sinners (substitution), thus satisfying the demands of God's justice so that he could justly forgive sins. It is thus a specific variation of substitutionary atonement which understands Jesus's death in the sense of punishment. It revolves around the idea that divine forgiveness must at the same time satisfy divine justice of punishment in a thoroughgoing legal and human sense. God is either not willing or not able to simply forgive sin without requiring legal satisfaction or criminal penalty for it. As a result, God himself gave the person of his Son in order to suffer death, curse, and punishment deserved by a fallen humanity as due penalty for our sins. Earlier fathers and theologians expressed strong concern for the original sin of Adam.

As Baker and Green acknowledge, most Christians in the West have encountered the doctrine of penal substitution "in Sunday school classes, heard it proclaimed by pastors and evangelists, sung it in hymns, or read it in tracts or books of basic doctrines."[83] A basic summary of penal substitution may suffice for current purposes: God must punish us for our sins, the penalty of which is death. However, God the Father sends Jesus the Son to suffer the punishment we deserve by dying on the cross. Because Jesus paid the penalty *for us* and *in our place*, God can regard us as not guilty. We believe we are sinners who deserve hell. Jesus died in our place, however, such that relationship with God is restored so we can go to heaven. Jeffery et al. express this in the following manner, "God became man in order to save humanity from God's punishment for sin, and Christ accomplished this by enduring and exhausting this curse in our place, as our substitute."[84] Usually, such a view in popular language is capsuled in a single sentence: "Jesus died for my sins, so I could go to heaven." The upshot is that God the Father, understood as an unforgiving judge, was willing to participate in some manner in the killing of his Son, in order to save at least some others.

Needless to say, one does not find this in Paul. The scenario suggested above is like that of a hurricane that must exhaust its fury, after which and only then, the sun finally shines brightly again. The exhaustion of God's curse and punishment meted out upon Christ in our place is a perspective far removed from Paul. Paul does not portray God as a wrathful, punishing avenger, nor implicitly in Paul, does Christ portray God in that manner. God did not put Jesus to death, nor did Jesus seek to divert the hurricane of God's wrath away from us. "Grace to all of you and peace from God our Father and the Lord Jesus Christ." Paul's understanding of the gospel was one of *restorative* grace, which *could* be understood in terms of "restorative justice," but most certainly not "retributive justice."[85]

---

83. Baker and Green, *Scandal of the Cross*, 167.

84. Jeffrey et al., *Pierced for Our Transgressions,* 173. Such a view reminds one of a god who is like a hurricane that must exhaust its fury before the sun can shine again, as set forth below.

85. Cf. Flood, "Substitutionary Atonement," 159.

The doctrine of penal substitution received full expression during the Reformation period and has been subject to continual criticism on biblical, logical, and moral grounds.[86] It appears to posit a fracture or division within the Godhead, pitting the Father against the Son. There seems to be no room left for divine forgiveness or pardon. How can justice be served by punishing the innocent and allowing the guilty to go free? How can the infinite suffering and permanent death of so many be balanced by the finite suffering and *temporary* death of the singular figure of Christ? It seems rather disproportionate, even increasingly so in the light of continuing history and burgeoning population figures. Was Jesus's suffering sufficient to cover the sins of all people for all time (or at *least* the "elect"), or, is Christ still suffering to cover subsequent generations? How does an automatic operation of grace of perfect satisfaction through singular punishment confer the freedom from the penalty of sin upon the many beneficiaries, who number in the billions?

It is a matter of debate as to whether early church fathers subscribed to penal substitution, although all contemporary parties in debate wish to claim the early witness of Justin Martyr (c. 100–165 CE), Eusebius (c. 275–339 CE), Athanasius (c. 300–373 CE), and Augustine (354–430 CE) for their own cause, irrespective of the contexts in which their language of atonement is to be found. Penal substitution themes are shared with other atonement theories, although penal substitution itself is a distinctively Protestant understanding of the atonement which differs from both Roman Catholic and Eastern Orthodox formulations. It is often set forth as a hallmark of evangelical faith and is most often attributed originally to John Calvin. In terms of its concrete influence in the United States, it is the Reformed theologian Charles Hodge of Princeton who popularized the doctrine.

Not all branches of Christianity accept substitutionary atonement as the central meaning of Jesus's death on the cross, either historically or currently. Eastern Orthodoxy focuses upon *theosis*. Roman Catholicism incorporates substitution into the idea of penance associated with the satisfaction view of Aquinas. While variations on the theme may occur in Protestantism, perhaps most Evangelical Protestants today assume an interpretation of penal substitution. While almost all atonement theories involve some idea of substitutionary atonement, the specific ideas of satisfaction and penal substitution drawn from the legal sphere represent later developments in the Roman Catholic Church and in Calvinism.

Key texts in Paul are often set forth in support of substitutionary atonement. These include Gal 3:10–13, 2 Cor 5:21, and Rom 3:25. These verses are often treated in a formulaic, non-contextual manner. Contextually, they address other issues. As discussed in an earlier chapter, these verses do not support atonement theory that has been claimed for them. Among other exegetical considerations, Paul would not have set forth a doctrine of the atonement in singular, isolated verses. To be sure, Jesus was

86. Cf. Brondos, *Paul on the Cross*; Finlan, *Problems With Atonement*; Baker and Green, *Scandal of the Cross*.

put to death on a cross. When one considers atonement, the historical event rather naturally calls forth sacrificial and substitutionary imagery by way of explanation. While this note may play in the background in some atonement theories, it takes on a dominant penal character with required punishment in contemporary penal atonement doctrine.

As may be seen, in the Western Church the major focus has been upon justice and legal issues of satisfaction and punishment or reparations, at least since the time of Anselm. In the Anselmian formulation of atonement, Christ's substitutionary death provides satisfaction of God's honor as an alternative to punishment. On the other hand, penal substitution requires a death payment to satisfy the moral consequences of sin. It is a matter of required justice rather than lost honor. In both, however, necessary satisfaction is accorded by a necessary substitution of some kind that covers an otherwise unnecessary debt. For example and by contrast, Eastern Orthodoxy does not incorporate substitutionary atonement into its doctrine of the cross and resurrection. The Eastern Orthodox view is that Christ died to cleanse humanity and restore the image of God *in* humankind. The power of death over humans is defeated from within, as one takes on the image of God. It is not a case that Jesus had to die to fulfill God's requirements or to meet God's needs or demands.

The doctrine of the Trinity enters into the penal substitution picture, in that God is seen to take the punishment upon himself through his Son, rather than placing it upon another or third party. If the death of Christ deals with sin and injustice (penal substitution), resurrection marks the renewal and restoration of righteousness. However, the focus is simply upon Christ's death. There is a restriction of symbol (*cross*), a misplacement of focus (*justice*), a revision of meaning (*sacrifice*), an imposture of necessity (*punishment*), and a misapplication of metaphor (*wrath*). Needless to say, little attention is given to the historical ministry of Jesus and his forgiving ways, nor is much attention given to Paul's "grace and peace."

The alternative moral influence theory has historically come into conflict with the penal substitutionary view. The two views exhibit radically different criteria of salvation and judgment. The moral influence model focuses upon the inner moral change of character in people, while the penal substitution view denies the saving value of moral change. The latter focuses upon faith in Christ's death in our behalf and *in our place,* such that trust is placed in what Christ has done for us. The result has been a strong debate and divide between liberal Protestants (moral influence) and conservative Protestants (penal substitution) since the time of the Reformation. It is argued by some that the moral influence view was held universally during the first several Christian centuries, while the penal substitution view does not emerge before Anselm and the subsequent Reformation.

Moral influence supporters argue that penal substitution represents a radical departure from historic Christian faith, while defenders of penal substitution claim an early date on the basis of the mixing of ransom/rescue and substitution in early documents such as Diogenetus, *Epistle* 9 (second century). God took upon himself the burden of our iniquities. That is to say, punishment and death were impending upon us, as "He gave his own Son as a ransom for us, . . . For what other thing was capable of covering our sins than His righteousness? . . . O sweet exchange! . . . That the wickedness of many should be hid in a single righteous One, and that the righteousness of One should justify many transgressors!" (Diognetus, *Epistle* 9.9). Moral influence advocates argue that penal substitution portrays God as either unable or unwilling to forgive wrong actions, such that full and complete punishment is required, regardless of repentance. Such a view is morally reprehensible according to many and does not thereby reflect a loving, forgiving God.

Historical atonement theory has moved well beyond Paul. Given theory may be evaluated and embraced or not on its own merits by individual interpreters. Variations on the theme continue to be proposed. It is not simply a matter of interpretation, however, but rather a *matter of imposture*, of eisegesis rather than exegesis. Paul has been pressed into the service of support of later theories that his letters simply do not support. The theories express views of God, of Christ, of the Christ event, of Christ's death, of the "mechanism" of soteriology that Paul never thought and with which he would not agree. One may again refer to examination of the discrete Pauline passages set forth earlier.

Atonement theories, including penal substitution, have been perpetrated in Paul's name and have claimed his support. In the present writer's judgment, Paul would likely criticize them and dismiss them as heterodox gospels which were not gospels at all. He would accompany his dismissal with words as harsh as he wrote to the Galatians (cf. Gal 1:8–9). Paul would revert to the Gospel of God and to the soteriology expressed therein, "Grace to you and peace from God the Father and the Lord Jesus Christ." Why? Because the powers have been overcome, Christ is now Lord, and because nothing can sever us from the love of God in Christ. The *fact* of Paul's gospel and the *experience* of that gospel stands at a great distance from the satisfaction of penal substitution. So does Paul's view of God. In Paul's view, one is to live in faithfulness to God, even if that faithfulness involves and even requires a cruciform imperative.

Theories of the atonement may divide at the point of the personal and impersonal. One must use metaphors to speak of God—Sovereign, Judge, or even Father. Some metaphors are more "personal" than others. As Grensted suggests, "No theory can stand which makes God less than personal, in the fullest sense in which man can understand the term . . . ."[87] It is significant that Paul understood both God and Christ in personal terms—God as "Father" and Christ as "Lord." The Gospel of God itself was understood in terms of personal encounter and relationship, not in terms of a judicial transactionalism. Paul, for example, *experienced* the Gospel through said personal encounter and developing cruciform relationship.

---

87. Grensted, *Doctrine of the Atonement*, 372.

However costly atonement must be, salvation is not cost-free for the believer. This is perhaps one of the greatest fallacies proclaimed in modern-gospel circles of "popular Christianity." It is inherent in the statement "Christ died for my sins so I could go to heaven" found in much common theology, in much preaching, and in much hymnody. For Paul, who suffered much as an apostle, Christians must "suffer with Christ (Rom 8:17). One is "united with him in a death like his" (Rom 6:5). One has the "mind-set of Christ" in oneself (Phil 2:5). Connection with Christ involves co-suffering and co-death (symbolic or not). Perhaps it is no surprise why Paul has lost popularity in the contemporary world of Christendom.

Salvation in Paul models a pattern of dying and being raised from the dead, following in the steps of Christ's effective death and resurrection. As the apostle to the gentile world, Paul's motif of Christ dying for others may echo the major theme of the "noble death" or "effective death" well known in Classical and Hellenistic literature and philosophy. Martyr-deaths were seen to have vicarious saving power.[88] However, if such a view influenced Paul, he did not take it over unchanged nor did he emphasize it.

While at least some early Christian theology developed along the lines of a martyr theology (cf. 4 Maccabees) and Isaiah 53, whereby death is seen to have saving, purifying value for the community, that was not the direction of Pauline development and understanding. As segments of the Christian community at large focused upon Isaiah 53 in the light of the developing martyr theology of Judaism, "they were thereby able to formulate a theology of Christ's suffering and death as vicarious atonement, i.e., as substitutionary or representative for all humanity."[89] The martyr and Servant theology of late Judaism and/or early Christianity was also developed within the context of temple sacrifice.

For Diaspora Judaism and Diaspora Christianity, animal sacrifice was not operative nor any longer central because of proximate distance from the temple in Jerusalem. Nevertheless, sacrificial theories were analogously or metaphorically applied to the lives of human beings themselves. Early Christians could understand the life and death of Christ as an atoning sacrifice. This understanding thus moved well beyond just "moral example," being truly representative and substitutionary on the one hand, yet as in Paul calling for participation on the other hand.

Paul's metaphors interpenetrate as they interpret one another. Paul does not limit himself to a single image as does much atonement theology, but rather he employs a range of metaphors. They do not take away from one another, but rather enhance one another. Paul may use social metaphors, for example, to describe the beneficial *results* of Christ's death for believers—redemption or deliverance (a payment, monetary, or Exodus metaphor), justification (a judicial metaphor), adoption (a familial, relational metaphor), and reconciliation (a diplomatic or familial metaphor). Expressed differently, the results for humans are liberation, reconciliation, rectification,

88. Finlan, *Problems with Atonement*, 52–55.

89. Tambasco, *Atonement*, 67–68.

and re-identification as children of God. All of these aspects herald regeneration and new life, both now and in the resurrection; they are transformational and not merely transactional.

Theological Reductionism

Unfortunately in a later period of Christian history, reduction of metaphors and misperception of the symbolism of blood sacrifice led to the presentation of Christ as a *penal substitute*, whereby God effected a "balancing of the scales" for a sinful humanity. The shed blood of Christ, like that of a sacrificial animal, became understood as a vicarious punishment of sin in order to satisfy God's justice, an act of appeasement or *propitiation* of God for sin. As Tambasco characterizes it, Christ in taking our human existence "could truly take the place of all humanity and, in shedding his blood, undergo the punishment we all deserve, satisfy God's justice, and thereby be a perfect once-for-all sacrifice for our sins."[90] The difficulty with such a view is that is misplaces the emphasis of the meaning of the death of the sacrificial animal in the Old Testament sacrificial system and Jesus's death in the New Testament. The focus in the Old Testament is upon life, as seen in Lev 17:11. It also suggests a legal transactionalism marked by a limited temporalism that allows the individual to leave "God's court room" in a justified mode (cf. Wright). It does not necessarily call one to a renewal of covenant relationship. There is a difference between a temporal transaction and sustained rehabilitation in covenant worship.

Theological reductionism continued into the time of Luther and Calvin in the Reformation period, certainly as it pertained to the atonement or meaning of the death of Christ. Luther repeats Augustinian teaching on universal sin and divine rescue, accepting for a time the *theosis* doctrines of the Greek fathers. Most often when Luther is summarized outside of Lutheran circles, he is mentioned in conjunction with *justification by faith* and *sola scriptura* ("scripture alone"). However, as Finlan observes, both Luther and Calvin presented a dramatic, frightening scenario of divine violence restrained by a divine mercy that had to be mediated through violence.[91] There appears to be a kind of schizophrenia reflected in their position. In a day and age when literal sacrifice was no longer practiced, the Reformers take it for granted that a sacrificial death was required to deal with human sin, although they never explain why that is so.

In his commentary on Gal 3:13, Luther suggested Christ should be seen as the greatest transgressor, blasphemer, persecutor, adulterer, and murderer as he bore the sins of all men imputed to him on the cross. One should note Luther's statement again. Christ was made guilty of the sins of the whole world and was therefore cursed by God; he became a sinner under the wrath of God. Of his own good will, Christ bore

90. Tambasco, *Atonement*, 69.
91. Finlan, *Problems with Atonement*, 75.

the punishment of the wrath of God for our person, not for his own. Christ "set Himself against sin, death, the curse of the law, the wrath and judgment of God," such that he overcame them in his own body.[92]

Paul has a focus on the "powers" and the Two Ages. In the light of the dawn of the Age to Come "in Christ," Paul likewise focuses upon life in the Age of Transformation, as he encourages Christians in Rome to present themselves as a sacrifice, as those living, as those holy, as those acceptable to God—for that is their logical worship or reasonable service (Rom 12:1). Most English translations are deficient at this point. Paul also encourages transformation or metamorphosis (μεταμορφόομαι) by the renewal of the mind (Rom 12:2).

One should note Paul's emphasis falls upon worship and service, as one lives in a transformative covenant relationship. Romans 12:1–2 represents some of Paul's most significant words that he ever penned, especially relevant as an imperative for a contemporary age. It is through a transformative cruciform imperative of worship that one finds the will of God and, in the process, discovers it to be good, acceptable (or pleasing), and perfect. Therein is atonement in its most true sense or form (*at-one-ment*), for it issues forth in an humble spirit and thankful worship, exhibited in right relationships underwritten and enabled by grace and peace.

92. Luther, *Commentary on Galatians*, 163–75. Christ becomes the active heroic martyr who overcomes even the wiles of God. Children are taught "Jesus loves me, this I know, for the Bible tells me so." And it has been said (sometimes attributed to John Killinger), "Jesus was God's answer to a bad reputation." Theologians should take note.

9

Paul and New Horizons

T HERE is a difference between Christianity and Christendom. Christianity may be
characterized as a religion of faith in what God has done in Christ and how we
are to live in the light of that. By contrast, historically speaking, Christendom becomes
the religious entity formulated and maintained by the wielding of political power by
the clergy and politicians of Church and State through the centuries. Regardless of
apparent veneers and trappings, the underlying focus is upon human power. Paul
proclaimed the one, but not the other. He was focused upon the power of God—what
God had done in Christ. In the one, the "cross" remains a symbol of divine victory
through suffering love. In the other, the "cross" unfortunately becomes a symbol of
domination. In the one, atonement is a celebration of the grace of reconciliation and
rehabilitation. In the other, it is today too often understood only in terms of an ancient
judicial transaction and divisive theology.

Modern Christendom is not a godless world, for many gods find worship there.
What is important, however, is that modern Christianity be a God-filled world. Taking
the gospel of Paul seriously can help us to avoid idolatry and to embrace the Gospel of God.

It is hazardous to speak of "assured results" within scholarship generally, much
less within Pauline scholarship, in the light of the fact that the study of Paul and his
letters has been and will be a continuing enterprise among Pauline scholars for the
foreseeable future. Advancing knowledge and contributions from other fields such
as archaeology, sociology, literary methodologies and definition, Judaic studies, early
Christianity, church history, et al., may all have a continuing impact upon the treatment and comprehension of the apostle Paul.

Contemporary applicational or contingent issues may also arise. Various groups
sought to claim Paul for their side in the early centuries of the church. Contemporary enclaves today may seek to claim Paul as their own patron saint for their own

theological or ideological cause—or, on the other hand, divorce Paul as irrelevant, idiocentric, idiosyncratic, or simply too hard to comprehend.[1]

Interpretation of Paul varies according to subjective experience. There will always be those interpreters of Paul who cannot themselves personally move beyond the strictly rational and legal sphere of theological understanding to embrace a theology based more upon the personal. And, there will always be those interpreters of Paul who embrace the grace and peace of a personal God who welcomes redeemed and reconciled persons as his children "in Christ," because God has acted to rectify his entire cosmic creation including humankind. Because *God* has chosen to rectify his creation, his rectification is not in conflict with his "righteousness" and "holiness," but instead is born of it.

And, how hard it is to scrape off theological barnacles that cling so tenaciously. How hard it is to out-grow parental beliefs and behaviors inculcated in early childhood that even subliminally impact theological growth to maturity. How hard it is to climb out of theological canyons carved by long-flowing theological waters and theological convictions wrought by rote repetition of theological dogmas. Paul faced that very problem as a trained Pharisee within the Judaism of his day. He was a persecutor of what he perceived to be the aberrant theology of a Jewish sectarian movement, later called "Christian." The vision of his call experience afforded by God (Gal 1:11–17) was so vivid and powerful that Paul was compelled to develop a new theological understanding that constituted the Gospel of God. He was called upon to repent. He was compelled to exchange an older theological perspective for a new theological understanding. The Ages had changed, and so did Paul's theology. It was the Age of Transformation.

Theological Renewal

Paul faced the very problem of theological renewal that has been faced before in Christian history and that we might face in our own day. In a struggle with Nomistic Evangelists who in his judgment proclaimed a *heteros* (ἕτερος) gospel "of a different kind," he personally proclaimed that those in Christ are not slaves but children of freedom who inherit the blessings of God the Father (Gal 4:21–31). "In/for/by/with freedom Christ has set us free; therefore, do not again become subjected to a yoke of slavery" (Gal 5:1). It was that freedom in Christ that brought fresh perspectives to Paul the Pharisee and sustained Paul the "Christ-follower" throughout his life and ministry, even through much personal suffering. And, it can sustain us above and beyond our customary theological canyons in which we have too long lived, looking only for the next bend of the river, or enjoying the limitations of our own personal encampment.

---

1. Cf Zetterholm, *Approaches to Paul*. Zetterholm's work offers an even-handed descriptive review of many perspectives on Paul, from the traditional Reformation view to what he terms a "radical new perspective." See also, McKnight and Oropeza, *Perspectives on Paul*.

All this is to say that Paul will continue to be interpreted anew within the context of different and quite varied matrices. New views may arise to challenge and older views may hang on or die hard. This has, in fact, happened in the last half century with the rise of the so-called "new perspective" of Paul and the ensuing debate it has engendered. And, on the other hand, outside of scholarship, Paul may increasingly be simply ignored, especially if there is no "Pauline cell phone app." The more complicated something becomes in our day, the less interest is expressed. The more dogmatic one becomes, the less open one becomes to new alternative vistas. Or, to use a "travel" analogy, if one has been to the tourist sites while traveling in the protective "cocoon" known as a bus, one has "seen the country" and has the digital "pictures" to prove it. Been there, done that. Nothing more to see here. And, over time, the pictures become tucked away in a "cloud-land."

Still, for those with maintained interest, there appear to be some "reassuring results" which have asserted themselves in contemporary Pauline studies. Paul's gospel was an eschatological gospel that emerged based on his understanding of an essentially Jewish story of fulfilment. Older viewpoints which place the origin of Paul's foundations in other quarters appear to be rather quaint today. One wonders how some of them even arose in the first place. While foundationally Jewish, Paul's gospel developed within the context of various matrices, which certainly colored and sometimes determined his responsive address to issues which arose over the course of his ministry.

Beker's rubric of "coherence" and "contingency" with regard to Paul's expressed theology remains as a useful model for dealing with Paul's ministry and theology. As the present author would express the rubric, Paul exhibited *consistent convictions* in his address of *contingent circumstances*. Paul proclaimed the Gospel of God within matrices that were cosmic, political, ethnic, social, and religious. Unseen cosmic powers ruled the imagination and lives of people living in the first century world and were seen to pose a constant threat. It was a world populated by spirits both favorable and unfavorable to human existence.

In many ways, the real Paul "comes to us as one unknown" (to parody Schweitzer, *The Quest of the Historical Jesus*), perhaps even as one whom we really do not want to know. To meet Paul "again for the first time" (to parody Marcus Borg, *Meeting Jesus Again for the First Time*), requires growth and alteration of our own comfortable theologies and ideologies; it requires "repentance," to go beyond the theological mind-set and lifestyle we now have. To examine "what saint Paul really said" (to borrow from N. T. Wright, *What Saint Paul Really Said*), is to scrape off some dead barnacles and to examine afresh the beauty of the original theological surface of the remarkable Pauline wood. What Paul wrote, he wrote before he was "Saint Paul" with a capital "S." Although we may not wish to admit it, we are far more at home in "Paulinism" and may not wish to welcome the stranger, Paul.

However, once one becomes more familiar with Paul, "the man in Christ," within his own world, Paul's gospel itself begins to find a reincarnation. By way of example, one may consider again the atonement or "storm center" in Pauline studies, namely, Paul's understanding of the cross of Christ. The church of the modern era has continued to wrestle with the meaning of the cross as it has focused on the meaning of atonement. On the other hand, many already have their "pictures" (even digitized)—nothing more to see here, "Jesus died for my sins so I could go to heaven," next destination, no pun intended. The atonement is a somewhat mysterious but ancient transaction. The cross is relegated to church steeples, jewelry, and gravestone markers. Nothing more to consider here.

Still, many different explanatory theories for both cross and atonement have been formulated, as has been seen. Pauline metaphors have been appropriated through time in various ways. While Pauline texts rest at the center of atonement theories based upon New Testament thought, interpretation of Paul's words have varied greatly. Regardless of the variation, as Culpepper affirms, *any view of the atonement* that suggests "the idea of an angry Father inflicting punishment upon his innocent and loving Son must be rejected as unbiblical."[2] It should also be rejected as non-Pauline. Indeed, an appropriate doctrine of atonement will reflect a worthy conception of God, as well as of human beings. God is a holy God who does not condone willful sin. God is a God of love who cares for his creation. God is a God of wrath who does not forego judgment of evil and sin. God is not schizophrenic, however, such that his love is antithetical to his wrath. As James Stewart suggested long ago, God's wrath is his love "in agony."[3]

Anthropomorphic Justification

As the church of the ancient world settled down after the time of Paul for an extended life in the world, it turned its attention toward anthropological justification. The focus was more than just anthropomorphic soteriology. Justification took the form of institutional development with consolidation of the power of the bishops. It took the form of apologetics and polemics in a theological struggle against Gnosticism and "heresy," as well as a political struggle against external persecution. As later children of the Reformation, however, we are accustomed to thinking only in terms of anthropomorphic justification in the light of cross and atonement. The present work has marked a reconsideration of the entire issue from a Pauline perspective.

In terms of modern perspectives, one may consider Ridderbos, who advances an anthropocentric view of justification, who is cited only as example by way of

---

2. Culpepper, *Interpreting the Atonement*, 152. That an "angry God who must be mollified" is absent from Paul is supported first of all by every single one of Paul's salutations, as the present work has established.

3. Stewart, *Man in Christ*, 221.

illustration.[4] Justification has both a substitutionary and corporate dimension. Statements should be formulated and read with care, if one is seeking the Pauline emphasis. One should be sensitive to external intrusion into Paul's thought. One might, for example, consider the following sentiment expressed by Ridderbos. "Christ's death and resurrection occurred for our sins and unto our justification, could take place in our behalf and in our stead for the very reason that as the Son of God he entered into our mode of existence, and in that mode of existence God not only delivered him up 'for us, 'but also made us to be 'in him.'"[5]

When *Paul* says Christ's death took place "in our behalf," he suggests a result that was "to our advantage" or "for our benefit." Paul does not say "in our stead," as Ridderbos subtly slips into his characterization. Paul speaks of atonement, but not of *substitutionary* atonement, except in the traditional sense of a sacrificial offering. Even at that, Paul emphasizes obedience more than sacrifice in the use of his metaphors. Ridderbos goes on to say that Christ's death was the demonstration of judgment of the old aeon and the old man, that justification unto life and the new creation came to light in Christ as the second Adam.[6] Paul is clear. Romans 3:26 suggests "justification" is *theo*centric. The Gospel of God is first of all about God, and for that very reason, it has relevance for humankind as creature. For *Paul*, the Gospel of God is meant to be "in Christ," in suffering as well as in victory and glory. God's victory was and would be victory for all—for *all*, who were "in Christ."

One might pursue Ridderbos's formulations a bit further, again only by way of example. Romans 5:9–10, according to Ridderbos, is best elucidated by Rom 3:25. This is effectively to interpret the "known" by the "unknown." Ἱλαστήριον is seen to be propitiation or the means of propitiation drawn from the cultus of sacrifice. Sacrificial terminology is also seen to be found in 1 Cor 5:7, 1 Cor 11:25, Rom 5:9–10, and Eph 5:2. Jesus is the one who died "for us" or "for our sins"—1 Thess 5:10; 1 Cor 15:3; 2 Cor 5:14; Rom 5:6, 8; 14:15; et al.. But are all these references sacrificial and cultic? Are they all literal rather than metaphorical? Are they all indicative rather than imperative? Do they all focus on "death" rather than life?

According to Ridderbos, Romans 3:25–26 is unmistakable in its clarity—Christ's death is propitiatory. His blood is atoning blood that covers the sins for which until now God has held back the judgment and passed over. The righteousness of God reveals itself in Christ's death as God's demanding and vindicatory righteousness. First Corinthians 5:7 does not just view the voluntary nature of Christ's death. The substitutionary character of Christ's death on the cross recurs time and again—1 Thess 5:10; Gal 1:4; 2:20; 1 Cor 15:3; 2 Cor 5:14; Rom 4:25; 5:6, 8; 8:32; 14:15. However, "for us"

---

4. The present writer offers high praise for Ridderbos's work, although he differs with Ridderbos's position. Although older, his work is recommended and commended and is used merely by way of example with regard to the general issue at hand.

5. Ridderbos, *Theology*, 169.

6. Ridderbos, *Theology*, 169.

need not mean "in our place." The death of Christ has taken place "in our favor." Yet in Gal 3:13, 2 Cor 5:21, and Rom 8:3, Ridderbos finds that the thought of substitutionary sacrifice that atones is unmistakable in these verses.[7] In this interpretation, payment for human sins has been held in a ledger-like "accounts receivable" category, but it is now time to transfer to an "accounts paid" category. This does not appear to be Paul's understanding. Paul does not express his theology by ledger accounting.

In affirming Christ's death as an atoning death of eschatological significance, Ridderbos's discussion of Christ's death as "atonement" is dominated by a discussion and defense of propitiation.[8] According to Ridderbos, the idea of God as the Author and Initiator of reconciliation is in no respect in conflict with "the idea of the propitiatory sacrifice that must cover and atone for sin before God."[9] The idea of propitiatory sacrifice is directly linked to the doctrine of justification. The revelation of the righteousness granted by God on the basis of grace also exhibits the hallmark of an "eschatological judicial verdict, . . . a manifestation of God's vindicatory and demanding righteousness in the atoning death of Christ." In the decisive, central act of propitiation, God himself provides the means of propitiation, such that Christ's death as atoning death "comprises one of the most essential definitions of God's work of redemption in the fullness of time."[10]

Really? In what sense is Christ's death "God's" work at all? God was not a co-conspirator in Christ's death in the judgment of the present writer, as has already been set forth earlier. The divine indicative begins with incarnation and resurrection, and it overcomes the worst that Sin and the powers could accomplish. Again, *Paul* does not express his theology on the basis of ledger accounting.

Word Become Flesh

Humans were created in and with freedom. Were humans mere robotic automatons or puppets, God could have effected "salvation" (if one may call it that) through mere coercion or autocratic action. God sought to appeal and attract human beings to live in loving faithfulness. However, he did not seek to compel and coerce. On the other hand, God himself did not have to be compelled or coerced to forego a "wrathful stance" toward humanity—at least not according to Paul.

To live in loving faithfulness out of freedom is to achieve full humanity. As a man *in Christ* and as an apostle *of Christ*, Paul came to know the freedom and fullness of God's grace. Paul preserves even for his gentile churches the familial address of "Αββα ὁ πατήρ" (Gal 4:6). As he writes to the Roman church/es that he has never visited, he reminds them of their identity as children of God and what that means. "You did

---

7. Ridderbos, *Theology*, 190.

8. Cf. Ridderbos, *Theology*, 192, for his comments on Rom 3:25.

9. Ridderbos, *Theology*, 190.

10. Ridderbos, *Theology*, 193.

not receive a spirit of slavery again unto fear but you received a spirit of adoption by which we cry out, Abba Father" (Rom 8:15). The Spirit of God itself bears witness with our spirits that, indeed, we are God's children—and if children, also heirs of God and fellow heirs of Christ (Rom 8:16–17).

Yet there is more that combines both indicative and imperative: we are heirs of God and fellow heirs of Christ, "if we suffer together in order that we may also be glorified together" (Rom 8:17). To recall God as "Father" reminds us of our adoption as his children. That identity is a call to live out of familial covenant relationship that is ongoing under the Lordship of Christ. Thus, he could commend an incarnate gospel of reconciliation to all his churches: "Grace to you all and peace from God our Father and the Lord Jesus Christ." In Christ the Lord, raised by God from the dead, grace and peace came that is available to all.

A true father, just as a true mother, cares for a child in a process of growth toward maturity. It is in the reciprocal context of love and care that at-one-ment finds its finest hour. It is marked by familial, covenant commitment. It is perhaps sad that in many quarters of Western Christianity that we spend more time devoting attention to judicial theology than we do with familial or adoption theology, or, with law and penalty than with rehabilitating love and adoptive graces. "Grace" is not first to be sung, but it is to be experienced. "Peace" is not the absence of theological fear, but rather the very presence of redemptive grace.

As Culpepper notes, somewhat paradoxically, the one who was by nature the Son of God in time became the Son of Man and eternally united deity to humanity in one person.[11] The Word had to become flesh. Sin had closed human beings off from God, such that salvation must come from God's side. It must address humankind as it is, as the sinful race of Adam, if redemption is to be effective. In Paul's understanding, the Gospel of God has accomplished that in Christ, as God gained incarnational victory through a sacramental cross as well as victory over a Roman cross enacted and erected by combined powers.

Atonement Compulsion

Finlan speaks of the reason that atonement is so compelling in Western Christian thought and of the underlying *psychology of atonement*, which certainly moves beyond the matrices of earlier Christian thought, Paul included. One is reminded of Stendahl's "introspective conscience of the West" emphasis. Finlan suggests that two fundamental and universal instincts about life and divinity are expressed in atonement theologies—(1) there is a debt to be paid, nothing is free; and (2) ritual establishes order, either by conservation or restoration.[12] Atonement ideas emerge from

11. Culpepper, *Interpreting the Atonement*, 133.

12. Finlan, *Problems with Atonement*, 80. Essentially, his characterization involves (1) payment and (2) order.

the sacrificial cult, in which one gives something to the god in order to get something from the god. Sacrifice marks the restoration of order (conservation of order), through a transactional reinstatement of the hierarchy of order by payment of spiritual debt through whatever currency. It should be understood, however, that any such cultic action marks a human attempt to control the divine. In a sense, it can become idolatrous.

Finlan notes that the notion of "payment" made to God to undo a penalty is materialistic. Although he has been charged with modernizing and negativism, Finlan speaks of "making sacrifices" as a necessary part of moral development. Atonement doctrines thus turn God into an offended lord or a temperamental heavenly judge[13] Finlan may thus speak of the "materialistic atonement" of a modern age. The notion that all sin carries with it a penalty has moral worth, but it represents, as he suggests, an adolescent stage of moral development. A view that emphasizes the harshness of God is largely the legacy of the harshness of parents and other authority figures. "As parents become less frightening figures, God becomes less frightening."[14] Indeed, as the present writer would affirm, if one has ever seen a woodcut portrait of Luther's parents, as in Bainton's *Here I Stand*, perhaps one can better understand Luther's problems in his portrayal of God.[15]

In a cycle governed by guilt, Finlan points to the historical result and problem of the guilt-gratitude cycle. One learns to develop manipulative strategies of bargaining, appeasement, diversion, and payment through self-punishment and pain. In the Middle Ages, these strategies took the form of penances, self-flagellations, promises of building chapels, and other attempts at negotiation with God. None of these concepts reflect the simple Gospel teaching of Jesus that disciples should *trust* God. Jesus did not describe God as one to be manipulated, but rather as a heavenly Father who delights in giving every good thing to his children (Matt 6:30–33; 7:7–11). Jesus sought to curb fear, not to encourage it. "Stop being afraid, little flock, because the Father is delighted to give the kingdom to all of you"(Luke 12:32). None of the afore-mentioned strategies of negotiation reflect the theology of Paul, either, for he commends grace and peace from God the Father.

In terms of a guilt-gratitude cycle, common in the Western religious marketplace, sacrificial soteriological and redemption doctrine perpetuates intense anxiety with regard to a portrait of a most temperamental and judgmental God. This God is characterized by rage and wrath in the interests of preserving his own sovereignty and righteousness. Reformation thought that focuses upon guilt, coupled with undeserved rescue from destruction at the expense of God's innocent Son, has a powerful psychological effect. It provides emotional appeal and an escape mechanism. One is offered escape from condemnation, but also escape from responsibility. Through appeal to the emotions of guilt and gratitude, the experience of repentance is encouraged.

13. Finlan, *Problems with Atonement*, 81.

14. Finlan, *Problems with Atonement*, 82.

15. Cf. Bainton, *Here I Stand*, 26.

Yet as some church fathers realized, repentance is a human solution to a problem that is greater than humanity's ability to address or solve. Confession and liturgy offer only temporary relief in a ritual setting, as may be seen in the weekly pronounced liturgies found in many churches today and often simply read aloud in unison. As a point that should be noted, a reminder is offered that Paul did not emphasize repentance and forgiveness. There is even a derived "Roman Road to salvation" in some Christian quarters, drawn up with resultant a-contextual misappropriation of Paul's words in Romans, to support a guilt-wrath theology.[16]

Reformation conceptions of satisfaction focused on guilt create a sense of greater *indebtedness* and *fear* that towers over any sense of gratitude, marked by perpetuation of sacrificial beliefs and emotions that replace actual sacrificial rituals. While the sacrificial cult lies long dead (pun intended), the cult of sacrificial doctrine and placation of a wrathful God remain alive and well. Whereas the ancient world understood atonement in terms of *ransom* or *rescue*, perhaps the modern world needs *relief* from the heavy weight of a transactional atonement perspective, especially those of inherent violence. Relief from violent atonement doctrine, but not atonement itself.

Atonement has become interwoven with other Christian doctrines such as incarnation, the compassion of God, and the eventual vindication of those justified, such that the loss of these beliefs and others may today be feared should one surrender any particular atonement doctrine. However, as Finlan observes, when honestly received, truth is liberating; when it is responsibly borne, freedom leads to maturity. True freedom is growth and not anarchy. It means moving beyond the doctrines of arbitrary and punishing gods. It means moving beyond "theological childhood." One comes to a more mature concept of God as a divine parent who is interested in our growth and transformation of his children "from one degree of glory to another" (2 Cor 3:18).[17] In some cases, it means exchange of doctrine long-held for another perspective which is more mature and adequate—not theology for God's sake, but for ours.

Upheaval and New Horizons

Many people do "like" Paul (or "Paul") and find support in his letters for their own foundational theology, however that may be formulated. For others, to read Paul is to engage in a "theology of irritation," for Paul may seem ever more irrelevant in a new and very different age. Others *never* read Paul, as a result of apathetic neglect. The question may be asked of each and of all, to what extent have we encountered Paul

---

16. The "Roman Road" to salvation, popular in some quarters of Christianity, is artificially constructed of the following verses taken out of context from the text of Romans and arranged in the following order—Rom 3:23, 6:23, 5:8–9, 10:9–10. Individual soteriology results from "believing in" the truth of Paul's statements. The gospel Paul proclaimed was not first of all focused on individual conversion, nor was it expressed in "post-it-note" theology.

17. Finlan, *Problems with Atonement*, 124.

and not just some version of "Paulinism"? The real Paul is not as infinitely plastic as he appears to be in the wide-ranging world of biblical scholarship or as staid and static as he appears to be in the dogmatic formulations of systematic theology, rehearsed regularly in manifold ways in ecclesiastical contexts. As the present writer has asserted more than once, the historical Paul and his thought have been strongly overlaid with theological barnacles, with the accompanying result that Paul himself has become a "theology of ideology" rather than a "man in Christ." Yet our version of "Paulinism" with which we may be so familiar and so comfortable does not either challenge nor irritate nor even assure so much as does the real Paul, whenever we may catch even a partial glimpse of him. The reason, of course, is precisely because we hold to *our version* of Paul.

We much prefer a static, mentalized, and transactionalized "Roman Road of personal salvation" to a dynamic and holistic Gospel of God which calls for a transformative identity in terms of a cruciform imperative. We would rather wear a cross or carry a crucifix, while singing "Jesus paid it all," than to be confronted with our own cross, as both Jesus and Paul asserted. It is much easier to let Jesus alone remain the crucified one of theological formulation, than to be crucified with him as Paul found his own identity to require. The real Paul, the non-theological Paul, knew that to be "in Christ" was to be crucified together with him (Gal 2:19; Rom 6:6; cf. Phil 1:20–21). After all, "Christ" remained the crucified one who died but who now lived as Lord as a result of God's resurrection and exaltation action.

The real Paul knew there was no resurrection apart from dying a cross-kind of death to self in obedience to the God who offered his Gospel of good news in Christ. While we may debate what Paul meant in Rom 3:25 in terms of our particular brand of "the atonement," and whether we should understand "propitiation" or "expiation," or whether it is "substitutionary" or "participatory" or even "penal," we may well miss Paul's own placed emphasis. Presumably, Paul knew exactly what he meant in Rom 3:25, within the matrices of his world. Be that as it may, Paul's own emphasis falls upon the actions of the God who *is* right and who rectifies the one who lives faithfully before him (Rom 3:25b–26). Both indicative and imperative is supported by a surplus of divine mystery.

Since the time of F. C. Baur, scholars have sought to define the key to Paul's thought in various ways. Paul Achtemeier suggests that the question of a coherent center is the key question for anyone who is interested in Paul's theology, the central core which may give coherence to Paul's situation-conditioned statements found in his letters. Proposals have been set forth which emphasize a doctrinal center for Paul's theology, while yet other proposals have found their locus in the traditional fate of Jesus. Justification by faith, for example, has been set forth as the time honored *doctrinal center* since the time of Luther. However, it has often been observed that this doctrinal theme tends to emerge in polemical contexts in letters like Galatians and Romans, while exhibiting a virtual absence in the majority of Paul's letters. It is not likely the theme of Romans, for example, and it even occurs in a subordinate position in Rom 1:17. Achtemeier asserts that justification by faith does not constitute the doctrinal center of Paul's theology. He suggested other concepts—such as righteousness, Christology, and ecclesiology—likewise did not represent Paul's doctrinal center. Achtemeier found the "generative center" of Paul's theology to rest in the resurrection

On the other hand, the death of Jesus on the cross does not appear to be the *traditional center* of Paul's theology as is so often assumed. To be sure, the death of Jesus is a more widely mentioned element than justification by faith within Paul's letters themselves and appears to be highly significant to Paul's understanding of Jesus Christ (cf. Gal 2:20; 3:1; 1 Cor 2:2; 2 Cor 5:14; Rom 8:32). Paul realized how difficult the cross was for his converts to accept. It was foolishness to gentiles and was a stumbling block for Jews (1 Cor 1:18, 23; cf. Gal 5:11).

Paul could attribute a rich variety of sacrificial theological meanings to the death of Jesus—a paschal lamb that enables escape from death (cf. Exod 12:7, 12–13; 1 Cor 5:7), a sacrifice which initiates a new covenant (Exod 24:5–8; 1 Cor 11:24–25; 2 Cor 3:6), and a sin offering for those already within the covenant (Lev 4–7; 1 Cor 15:3; Rom 4:28; 6:10). Paul can also employ an obedience metaphor, as Jesus's act of obedience in dying on the cross cancels the effects of Adam's disobedience (Phil 2:8; Rom 5:19). In view of Paul's inconsistency of expression, Achtemeier concluded that the crucifixion of Jesus did not constitute "the central conceptual core" of Paul's theology.[18] Still, the cross remains significant in Pauline thought, albeit it in a different sense than is commonly thought in much atonement doctrine found in Christendom today.

A Cross Imperative

Paul was a man "in Christ." That determined both his Christian and his apostolic identity. The Son of God defined both Paul's gospel and Paul's role in proclaiming it. Paul could do no other than proclaim the Gospel revealed to him in his divine call. A "call" is but the first experience of living out a "calling." Christian experience becomes a living and dynamic union with the risen Christ, such that the corporate union of all Christians together grows to become the *pleroma* of the cosmic Christ (Eph 1:23). Significantly, as Fitzmyer indicates, this means that apostolic suffering on behalf of the church found in the lives of individual Christians fills up what is lacking in the tribulations of Christ.[19] One may question whether anything was "lacking" in God's Gospel. It is perhaps better stated simply to assert that there is a continuing cross imperative that is definitional for all Christians in the face of temporal tribulations.

18. Achtemeier, "Quest for Coherence," 137. Indeed, the resurrection provides the generative center of Paul's entire ministry. Apart from the resurrection, there is no divine encounter, no revelation and call, no commission or apostleship. There is no gospel to proclaim (cf. Gal 1:1, 15–16; 1 Cor 15:12–19).

19. Fitzmyer, *Paul and His Theology*, 93; cf. Col 1:24.

Paul's cross imperative has caused some to assert that Paul felt salvation was dependent upon himself, that he completed the suffering of Jesus. In a singular sense, that was not the case. In a collective sense, all Christians were to follow Christ in a "cruciform" existence. This is not to say that *apostolic* suffering adds anything to the redemptive value of Christ's cross, but it is to point to the cross imperative that exists for all Christians, beginning with apostles. Perhaps in the end, as those "in Christ" remain faithful to a cruciform imperative, witness is given to the overall Gospel of God in terms of its profound power to redeem and recreate.[20]

One becomes a joint heir with Christ in terms of glorification, provided one suffers with him (Rom 8:17). One has the responsibility of holding fast to the gospel (1 Cor 15:2), of remaining established and steadfast in its hope (Col 1:22–23). There is a race to be run (Phil 3:12–14; 1 Cor 9:27), such that carefulness and watchfulness (Gal 5:15; 1 Cor 3:10; 8:9; 10:12) and self-scrutiny (1 Cor 11:29–30; 2 Cor 13:5) are called forth. However, in view of the imperative of the Pauline gospel, *apostasy* remains as an accompanying corollary during the time of eschatological tension for the believer.[21]

The Catalytic Cross: Remythologization?

We have adopted an under-realized eschatological view in favor of an over-emphasized anthropocentric individualism. We are left with a gospel of guilt, doubt, and anxiety too dependent upon a heavenly gospel that does not equip one for earthly living, for it is an unrealized gospel. Paul preached a gospel of a cross "in Christ," that for this world paradoxically offered a mode of coping with the adversities of life through a mode of suffering love and self-giving. Yet for Paul the cross only made sense in the light of the radiant, the generative center of the resurrection.

Cousar perceptively reminds one that Paul's emphasis on Jesus's resurrection as anticipatory of future resurrection can be modified in four different directions according to Paul's audience and literary context as reflected in his letters.[22] For Corinthian enthusiasts who exhibited a triumphalism of current heavenly existence with an excessive emphasis of spiritual gifts (such as speaking in tongues), there is the stark and shattering reminder that there is an earthly struggle with rulers, authorities, and powers. In spite of what Paul saw to be the nearness of the Telos (1 Cor 7), Paul sought to curb misplaced spiritual excess. For a second group of those who had grown weary and fatigued, who had lost vision and who had exhausted resources, Paul sought to redirect hopelessness to renewed hope (2 Cor 4:13–18).

For a third group of those who grieved and suffered the perplexity of doubt with a heart that grew faint, Paul offered strong words of hope albeit couched in apocalyptic

20. Gorman emphasizes kenosis and theosis in understanding Paul's narrative soteriology. See Gorman, *Inhabiting the Cruciform God.*

21. Cf. Dunn, *Theology of Paul*, 497.

22. Cousar, *Theology of the Cross*, 100–102.

terms (1 Thess 4:13–18).[23] For those who deny or disdain the physical nature of life, Paul maintained a unity of body and spirit, avoiding any gnostic dualism, thereby dignifying bodily activities (1 Cor 6:14–20, where the verbs and pronouns are plurals). As Cousar observes, the "this-worldliness" of Paul's gospel consists of an ethic confirmed ironically (and paradoxically) by the apocalyptic nature and presentation of Jesus's resurrection.[24] God's Gospel is one infused with and informed by an abiding hope, collective and cosmic in nature. Without hope from beyond ourselves, humankind is destined to perish.

We live at some distance from Paul and within different matrices than Paul. One reason some may find Paul less and less relevant is because of the coherent mythologization of Paul's world compared with our own. Rudolf Bultmann, of course, addressed the issue of demythologization in the mid-twentieth century. The issue seems to become more acute as time continues into a postmodern world. Bultmann identified the cross of Christ as an act of God which achieved relationship (i.e., at-one-ment), in spite of all its ambiguity as an historical fact.[25] Paul acknowledged that the cross carried with it ambiguity—it appeared to be folly, when in reality it was to be understood as a saving act (1 Cor 1:18–25). To understand the cross in terms of grace and love can only be appreciated in the context of resurrection and of the obedience of faith. It can only be celebrated in the context of communion. It summons. It is an invitation. As such, Jesus's cross can only be understood by one who is willing to live the cross. The one who is not crucified with Christ is not dead to the world nor is the world dead to that one.[26]

One does not understand the cross until one embraces the cross. It is not understood merely through the crafting of doctrines. That becomes a "substitution" in reverse. Only through acknowledgement of the cross and understanding does knowledge of the resurrection and fellowship in it come (Phil 3:8–10). As Bultmann further states, "just as a world phenomenon in all its ambiguity corresponds to God's judgment in the cross, so also to God's saving act in the resurrection there corresponds a world phenomenon—the Christian kerygma, which remains a 'stumbling block' and 'folly' until the judgment of the cross is acknowledged and accepted."[27]

Through the cross Paul is crucified to the world and the world to him (Gal 6:14). Christ is proclaimed as the Crucified (1 Cor 1:17, 23; 2:8; Gal 3:1). *For Paul*, both cross and resurrection are contemporary events of the present, not mere facts of the past, for one shares in dying-rising through baptism. One celebrates both cross and resurrection in the Eucharist. The whole life of the believer is thus a "being crucified

---

23. While apocalyptic may be summarized by many characteristics, perhaps the underlying thematic element of apocalyptic is the sustaining concept of hope.

24. Cousar, *Theology of the Cross*, 102.

25. Bultmann, *Faith and Understanding*, 1:114.

26. Bultmann, *Faith and Understanding*, 1:240.

27. Bultmann, *Faith and Understanding*, 1:241.

with Christ" (Gal 2:20), whereby one always bears the death of Christ in one's body (2 Cor 4:10). The resurrection is not isolated in the past, but marks the beginning of new life and humanity in the continuous present.

The reconciling act of God in the cross is at the same time the beginning of the "ministry of reconciliation" and the "word of righteousness/rectification." God's power for salvation is revealed in the preaching of the Word. According to Bultmann, "When Paul spreads the Word abroad, he spreads life." There, kerygma, which becomes saving event for Bultmann, centers upon the cross and resurrection.[28] For Paul, one always lives under a living Lord, the crucified yet living one who beckons.

The core of Bultmann's demythologization thus rests with the interpretation of the cross and resurrection. This also rests at the core of Paul's Gospel of God. The two elements are central to the earliest kerygma (1 Cor 15:3–4). The crucified Jesus is established as Lord of the entire cosmos through God's raising him from the dead (Rom 1:1–7). Paul's gospel sets forth the ramifications of that divine action for human living. Viewed historically in detachment, the cross becomes one fact beside others. Viewed religiously and mythologically, as Paul so understood it within the matrices of his world, it "receives the power of faith's interpretation."[29] Within the realm of theology, as Edwin Good suggests, it becomes either the cross of the "sacrificial Lamb of God" in the thought of some or the throne of *Christus Victor* who "overcomes Death and Satan and their hosts" in the thought of others.

In Good's perspective, however, sacrificial mythology "is no longer significant in our day" and the notion of triumph over Satan is "absurd" in a contemporary culture which believes in neither Satan nor his hosts.[30] Let it be said that Paul himself acknowledged that he preached a gospel that was foolishness to gentile Greeks and a stumbling block to Jews who looked for "signs." Our age has its own "mythologies" which differ from those of Paul's day; this point should not be overlooked. What would Paul say to our own day? The present writer believes that Paul would still hold to a Gospel of God that offered humankind deliverance from its own destructive bent, and from "the powers," however those might be described in a postmodern world.[31]

So the question becomes how the *intention* of mythology can still be preserved in terms of proclaiming an intelligible and effective message. In much atonement theology, the cross is an event that happened but once, by divine necessity. In Bultmann's understanding, according to Good, the importance of the cross is not that it happened once, but rather that it inaugurated a new historic situation of challenge to the hearers of the gospel that is to be found in the kerygma, sacraments, and life itself, as it

28. Bultmann, *Faith and Understanding*, 1:307.

29. Good, "Meaning of Demythologization," 33.

30. Good, "Meaning of Demythologization," 33. Whether one believes in Satan or not, there does appear to be what could be termed satanic evil in the contemporary world.

31. Cf. Scroggs, *Paul*; Wink, *Naming the Powers*; Wink, *Engaging the Powers*.

pertains to both judgment and redemption.[32] For Paul, the cross was not only that which *happened* once. It is that which *happens*. For Paul, the "cross" and "atonement" are not static entities in a systematic theology. Rather, they are dynamic realities of actually living "in Christ" that bring to the fore a dynamic of equilibrium of living with oneself, other selves, the created order, and God. Such living, born of grace, results in peace defined as *shalom* or "well-being."

In the preaching of the Resurrection Gospel (cf. Rom 1:4), the church and its kerygma became a part of the resurrection story. The church proclaimed the Jesus who died as the one who was raised and exalted by God. Faith itself is the life of resurrection, not the belief that a man named Jesus died on a Roman cross in the first century. Faith itself rests in the God of Resurrection, not in the tacit transactionalism of static theological dogmas. For Paul, the church stands on the new life of the resurrection as its primary article of its faith, or, it does not stand (cf. 1 Cor 15).

The resurrection is not amenable to "proof" as faith, nor can it be demonstrated apart from faith's testimony. Nor can it be manipulated by humans, for it is an action of God. "Crucified with Christ, risen with him"—the cross and resurrection become existential categories of the Christian life, rather than mythological conceptions. Neither represent merely past tales or facts, for both the cross and the resurrection intrude into consciousness at every turn. Each in its own way defines the responsibility of Christian living and love in action.[33]

With regard to the cross specifically, John Macquarrie raises and answers a significant question: How could an event from another time and place serve as an atonement for sins and means of salvation today? The answer is to be found in thinking of the cross as a disclosure for new existence which is a current possibility. In Bultmann's understanding, faith in the cross of Christ is to make Jesus's cross our own. "In 'dying with Christ, we also 'rise with' him. When we take up the Cross, we experience it as atonement, we become 'at one' with ourselves and with God, we enter on the new life." While Bultmann's perspective with regard to the historical aspects of the New Testament has been controversial in his theology, it follows as a necessary consequence of his existential exegesis.[34]

Bultmann's *Theology of the New Testament* exhibits a strong focus on anthropology. He asserts that Paul "was won to the Christian faith by the kerygma of the Hellenistic Church."[35] Heinz-Horst Schrey acknowledges that Bultmann's identification of theology and anthropology might result in "a mollified individualism, as world and history are reduced to the behavior of individuals to one another." The implication

---

32. Good, "Meaning of Demythologization," 33. Cf. Bultmann, "New Testament and Mythology," 37; *Theology*, 1:282–306.

33. Good, "Meaning of Demythologization," 34.

34. Macquarrie, "Philosophy and Theology in Bultmann's Thought," 135. Macquarrie understood the true nature of atonement.

35. Bultmann, *Theology*, 1:187.

raises the question as to whether Bultmann's emphasis upon anthropology absorbs the whole of theology "into some sort of ethical behaviorism," for which Schrey advances Bultmann's interpretation of the cross as an example. Schrey objects to Bultmann's existential hermeneutic in favor of an emphasis upon the cross as a "once happening event" that makes salvation possible, as emphasized in Hebrews, for example. For him, the "dread of mythologizing" obstructs the singular significance of the cross.[36]

Although many challenges may be presented to Bultmann's theology, Bultmann appears to be in support of both the Synoptic and Pauline traditions on the issue of a believer's cross in the understanding of the present writer. This is, indeed, what the present writer has termed a cruciform imperative in Paul. If one wishes to do "New Testament Theology," then the perspective of the writer of Hebrews and others should certainly be taken into account. They should be examined contextually and exegetically. However, one should not impose the perspective of Hebrews or 1 Peter upon Paul in dogmatic fashion. As indicated in the preface to the current work, one cannot legitimately criticize Paul because he does not espouse the view of Hebrews or that of 1 Peter. Neither should one read one's own views back into Paul in deliberate fashion.

Christianity today appears to be quite satisfied with its homogenized understanding of the canonical biblical literature, especially as it lives in search of identity and authority. The biblical scholar finds oneself under the pressure to write at a popular level of diminishing attention spans ("140 characters") or "power point" slides with few words. Preachers feel compelled to perceive the gospel in terms of capsuled "self-help" for individuals on the one hand, or, on the other hand, easy recognition of a "sound and a feeling" of theological tenets and platitudes, rehearsed many times over in liturgical settings of a doctrinal Christendom.[37] It is doubtful that Christians today understand the complexity of doctrines and metaphors labeled "atonement"—or, that they even want to do so. It may be a sad fact today that most Christians are not interested in thinking deeply about *any* theological doctrines and entertain only a simplistic transactional view of atonement, for example.

Then, too, it is hard to "entertain" as long as one is speaking about the cross, especially "our cross." It is much easier to live with a surrogate Christology—"*Jesus* died, so *I* could go to heaven." It is much easier to place "Jesus's cross" into some type of safe and appealing doctrinal repository (such as Easter or "the Atonement") before returning to more appealing and entertaining topics or activities for the "normal time" of the Christian year. In reality, the Christian liturgical year has more "normal time"

---

36. Schrey, "The Consequences of Bultmann's Theology," 199. Cf. *Kerygma and Myth*, where Bultmann asserts that to believe in the cross means to take up the cross of Christ as one's own—to be crucified with Christ. This is in keeping with Paul and the synoptic tradition.

37. Years ago now, the present writer heard one preacher say to another, "I don't preach on sin anymore because it does not motivate baby-boomers." In the present writer's perspective, this problem extends to other significant areas of Christian understanding. What does a minister preach in our day that motivates a present generation that finds it ever more difficult to get outside its own frame of reference?

than special rotating emphases. What if "normal time" and time between Sundays was designated as "cross time," the time to actually live out the Christian faith?

It appears that we live in a day and age characterized by biblical apathy, as well as ideological prejudices. Far too often, one is simply confronted with a culturized Christianity (to borrow from Niebuhr) or "doctrinalized Christianity" (in search of authority), either one of which seems like a "galaxy far, far away" from the matrices of Paul's world in which he lived and proclaimed his experience of the Gospel of God in Christ. Paul, as a pastor, may well have faced the issue of distance that many pastors face, namely, how to engage disinterested laypersons in things seriously theological (cf. Gal 3:1–5; 1 Cor 3:1–4). A static "religion" triumphs over a dynamic theology, a doctrinally defined "gospel" over the Gospel lived out. Rote repetition of such even lures the one who is pastor into such placid definition.[38]

While there may be a problem of "demythologization," there is also a problem of "remythologization" to be faced. Theological "atonement domains" have made it more important (when even relevant) to be "in Christendom" than to be "in Christ." However, rote recitation of ancient creeds born in galactic matrices now far, far away represent for many an element of general irrelevance in a postmodern world, perhaps aside from those who are frozen in a museum of apologetic. Ironically, perhaps, over-rehearsal of doctrinal dogmas in liturgical settings may lead to biblical apathy and little real attention given to Paul—or, more importantly even, to the Gospel itself.

The Scandal of Paul's Cross

Fast forward. What constitutes "faith" today? What constitutes "gospel"? What *is* the character, result, and goal? What apologetic or polemical view of "atonement" must one embrace to be "really Christian"? What must one do to be "really Christian"? Which "doctrine" must one recite? Which "doctrine" must one believe?

To turn the cross into a "theory," as Bultmann long ago realized, was to choose a much easier way, such that we need not concern ourselves with the harder way of realizing the meaning of the cross within our own living. "Substitutionary Atonement" itself becomes a substitute for living faithfulness.

In the present writer's understanding, among other things, the cross becomes the place, the event where all the forces of evil meet the rectifying power of God. The "powers" committed Jesus to death. One also sees the commitment of divine love to rectification, to that which is right, even if that should result in the greatest evil being perpetrated by "powers" in opposition to God. God did not put Jesus to death in order to enact some type of transactional charade that then enabled God to "forgive" and "redeem." In fact, as has been stressed, Paul does not emphasize repentance and

---

38. And, it may be that an overburdened clergy, charged with leadership of Christian churches yet guided by pragmatic concerns, are content to simply reinforce time-honored dogma without encouraging examination or depth of thought or even living.

forgiveness, as found in some other New Testament writings or as found in pietistic conversionism on a commercial scale.

Rather, God's redemptive and rectifying purpose would not be deterred even by the greatest of evils. God's power to raise the dead trumps any power to bring about death. The meaning here is not the enactment of a passion play, or, necessarily, its re-enactment. The meaning here is not that of recovery from a prior tragedy, which it was, but rather the meaning revolves around the ultimate parabolic demonstration of God's power to bring life out of death. Jesus's death, thereby, marks the opportunity of resurrection, the divine announcement in action that the Age to Come has truly dawned. And if, in this singular instance, God has brought about the resurrection of the dead, then Christ for Paul is but the firstfruit of the future general resurrection of those in Christ, in the light of the New Age which has now dawned and which is new reality.

It is in this vein that Paul emphasizes the cross in a Christian imperative. Just as Christ's death on the cross led to resurrection, so also the Christian's death in terms of a cruciform life will call for a share in the resurrection of the one who now lives as Lord. Paul works back from the reality of the resurrection to the hidden realities of the cross. Rather than defeat, it was and is the prelude to victory. Rather than only divine judgment upon human sin, it was indeed the gateway to the rectification of the entire cosmos at the Telos. God redeems in victory that which appeared as certain defeat and that which appeared to be unredeemable. The resurrection becomes a clarion call to cruciform living, rather than the signature of a divine recovery effort. The power of the cross is found in death to the "flesh" and to "the world," while the power of the resurrection heralds the reality of new life in a New Age (cf. Rom 6:3–11).

In North America, at least, a misguided theology of *both* the cross and resurrection feeds a kind of triumphalism that finds no place in Paul. As Walter Bruggemann observes, "North American dominant cultural values are massively resistant to a theology of the cross, precisely because the cross places suffering at the heart of God's character and at the heart of meaningful, faithful human life."[39] And further, "Paul's theology of the cross . . . [is] more radical, more dangerous, and more pertinent than we have been wont to think."[40] To meet the resurrected One is to meet a new Lord, who directs one to one's own crucifix life. Paul's interpretation of Jesus's death may be terribly difficult to hear, as his dominant themes sound alien and jarring for those engaged in self-indulgent consumerism.

The strangeness is difficult for those who preach and even greater for those who hear, such that neglect and apathy is becoming an ever-greater reality within the church. There is an apathy fed by disinterest and short attention spans, that is coupled with ignorance of the scriptures, fed by faulty focus of topical themes in preaching. There is a remoteness of contextual issues that makes Paul's message problematic, but

39. Brueggemann, "Editor's Foreword," viii.
40. Brueggemann, "Editor's Foreword," ix.

this is reinforced by an optimistic trust in religious illusion fed by the need for the placid security of individualism.

The church is not called to either religious illusion or to a religious imperialism to be lived out according to the standards and approval of the world of alternate powers. Cousar's warning is appropriate: "As the church learns to forsake its imperialistic struggle and to bear its cross, it must do so in the promise of the resurrection, else it will not be able to bear the cross for long."[41] There is a difference between Christianity as Paul understood "being Christian" and Christendom. The church is not designated to become a new, alternative empire, but rather the new people of God in Christ, serving Christ, one another, and the world in love—and in suffering. It is a new creation based upon God's eschatological action in Christ.

Righteousness is more an eschatological quality of rectification and reconciliation than it is a "moral" quality in search of self-justification. God's Gospel of rectification involves more than just a focus on individualistic soteriology. It is loving rectification in action for the entire cosmos, as well as for the new *people* of God constituted by the church—a people with a new identity, which, if it is Christ's church, is open to all. And "all" is a rather inclusive word.

The church has perhaps always engaged in a self-serving quest for religious security in terms of a search for a "safe haven of redemption without the risks and ambiguities of faith."[42] The church's quest for religious security has largely been satisfied in an individualistic soteriological ideology of the cross far removed from Paul, supported by annual membership that ensures immortality.

Pauline theology in the strictest sense will always be a challenge to comfortable and static religious ideology, regardless of whether a "Pauline" label has been pasted upon it or not. James Stewart objected to Harnack's portrayal of Jesus as ethical example. "The evangel of an ethical example is a devastating thing. It makes religion the most grievous of burdens. Perhaps this is the real reason why, even among professing Christians, there are so many strained faces and weary hearts and captive, unreleased spirits. . . . If Harnack's Christ [as ethical example] is all, we are left without a Redeemer."[43] In like manner, to leave Paul on the playground of the theologians is to leave aside keen insight into the very nature of the Gospel of God as it is to be actually lived out in the everyday world.

In contrast to Harnack, and according to Stewart, Paul's concept of Christ "grows lyrical," as to be "in Christ" and to have "Christ within" becomes "release and liberty," an endless song in the heart characterized by the "carrying power of love," even in the face of cruciform living.[44] Of this, Paul himself became the prime example. While Stewart's words sound rather idyllic and even moralistic in the light of Paul's

41. Cousar, *Theology of the Cross*, 108.

42. Cousar, *Theology of the Cross*, xi.

43. Stewart, *Man in Christ*, 168–69.

44. Stewart, *Man in Christ*, 169–70.

cross-imperative, Paul's own faith *in Christ* did take on a lyrical quality in spite of suffering, as may be seen in his salutations, doxologies, and benedictions, among other things.

Christian living is certainly to be moral, but not moralistic. It is to be relational, but not overly ritualistic. It is to embrace divine rectification, but not to succumb to a relishing self-righteousness. It is to embrace the core values of being in Christ incarnationally. The Christian church has the model of both Jesus and Paul before it, yet Paul has been turned into a doctrinaire theologian and Jesus into an ethical teacher or example. The "cross" of both has been turned into a piece of jewelry, wall art, or a church steeple. It has become a marker of Christendom, rather than a reality of Christian living.

The cross remains a scandal for the Christian faith, even as it was a scandal in Paul's first century world. As Walter Brueggemann suggests, it is a "dynamic phenomenon in the memory, narrative, and life of the church, . . . it is a concrete event that restlessly becomes paradigmatic in various contexts and circumstances of the life of the church. For that reason, its claim, power, and threat must repeatedly be reasserted and rearticulated."[45] A careful re-articulation that actually follows Paul's emphasis rather than a customary anthropological ideology or fashion statement will not likely be popular.

Paul's cross imperative remains a scandal for the modern "glory" gospel—a gospel that Paul would perceive to be as false as the Judaizing gospel of the Nomistic Evangelists that was plaguing the Galatians. Paul's cross imperative remains a scandal for Christian divisions and devalued spiritualities that are pressed into service through egocentric doctrinal formulations and misplaced spiritual gifts and activities—all of which Paul would see as problematic as those issues facing the Corinthian Christians, or, the churches of Galatia.

The cross remains as the catalytic center of a true Christian imperative and true Christian living, according to Paul, precisely because it emerges out of the divine imperative of the Gospel of God that culminates in life.

Too Many Pauls?

One should not misunderstand the point on the basis of idealism. A better, more comprehensive understanding and appreciation of Paul is needed. In this regard, not every "Christian" painting is a portrait of Paul. However, many purport to be, such that it is both inevitable and OK that a "Pauline gallery" of portraits exist, drawn from all periods of Christian history and that multiple portraits even characterize a given age. It is OK that new portraits be painted for a postmodern age. In fact, they may be greatly needed. But each theological portrait should be viewed for what it is and in

45. Brueggemann, "Editor's Foreword," vii.

the light of the pigments, techniques, and artistic content that characterize the artist and the given age in which he or she lived, even if of "Paul." They should bear a recognizable resemblance to the Paul reflected in our source material, namely, the New Testament. Again, every portrait *of Paul* should be exegetically responsible, historically plausible, theologically informed, hermeneutically beneficial. Not all portraits are or will be "masterpieces," nor might they pass the scrutiny of later critics. At the very least, however, each one should be recognizable that they are not just portraits, but portraits *of Paul.* There was in actuality only one Paul.

In like manner, there is only one Gospel of God, even though God's singular Gospel may be proclaimed through many different gospel portraits, including that of Paul himself. Not all portraits of the Gospel are "masterpieces"—some are fair representations, others are simply misrepresentations. However, Paul's portrait of God's Gospel can be very helpful in the scrutiny of later, alternative representations. Paul's portrait remains foundational for Christianity for many different reasons, in the judgment of the present writer, not the least of which are the standards Paul supplies for evaluating alternative gospel portraits in relation to the Gospel of God.

Paul's portrayal from the very dawn of Christianity remains valuable and irreplaceable, in spite of its many perceived ambiguities. Paul made a unique contribution to the establishment and comprehension of the Christ event and earliest Christianity. He cannot be held responsible for what later Christendom made him to be, nor for later conceptions of "gospel" developed within Christendom. When the theological barnacles are carefully removed, the Pauline portrait still shines brightly in terms of what in the end really matters. And what "matters" may still impact us.

Paul experienced a catalytic call and a catalytic Gospel. Paul proclaimed a catalytic gospel. His understanding of the Gospel was proclaimed in concrete settings of contingency. We are called upon to understand the Gospel in our contexts and to express that Gospel, though not necessarily in Paul's words. Paul experienced freedom from convention, liberation from slavery. Paul did not "write" Scripture, but he ultimately became "scripture." We need to hear Paul in a manner that sets *him* free from the "letter" of Scripture and dogmatic theology. We need to hear the words of "a man in Christ" in the earliest years of Christian identity. Perhaps we have been offered too many "Pauls" and not enough Paul.

As we separate Paul from what he has become, Paul begins to breathe again and his letters begin to speak their challenge rather than to confirm our dogma and prejudices. Paul calls us to wrestle with the challenges of our day, even as he did in his day. We are not called first of all to respect *Paul*, but rather to embrace and proclaim *the Gospel*. Or, perhaps to express that differently, Paul calls and challenges us to allow ourselves to be embraced by the Gospel and to live accordingly—creatively, dynamically, with a new orientation, in the context of love's hope as a new people of God in Christ.

If we allow the catalytic Gospel which Paul knew to take hold of us, then it is we who shall be changed and not the Gospel. It is we, as Stewart suggests, who shall become more "lyrical" in the Gospel daily. In this endeavor, Paul and his letters can still have a catalytic function for us.

Paul's own uniqueness of person and his place within Christianity will not be found anywhere else other than in his letters. He deserves the right to speak. We have the responsibility to at least listen—and maybe hear. Only then will we be in position to evaluate the many iconic Pauls which emerge, with images of thought drawn from many matrices. Only then can we propose viable alternatives, if so inclined. It may even be the example of Paul himself which grants one permission to repent—to change or alter one's own theology, in order to embrace a more adequate gospel for a new day.

Paul himself experienced a shattering, life-changing event. Theologically, Paul repented. New identity called forth his theological expression. Paul knew that it was by the grace of God that he was who he had come to be (1 Cor 15:10). Had there been no resurrection there would have been no Christian faith and no apostle Paul. Paul the Pharisee would not have moved beyond the Law or his evaluation under the Law that one who is hung on a tree is cursed by God (Gal 3:13; Deut 21:23). The resurrection was central to Paul's call (Gal 1:1, 15–16) and to the Gospel of God (Rom 1:4). That active grace of God "in Christ" challenged and changed Paul's theology which he blamelessly held prior to the Christ event (Phil 3:6).

The Gospel of God

Jesus's cross did not change Paul's Jewish theology, but the resurrection did. Jesus's cross written in history did not change Paul's theology, but the cross to which Paul was called did, as he became crucified with Christ. Jesus's resurrection changed Paul forever; it was even the resurrection that changed Paul's former understanding of Jesus's own cross. No longer an emblem of shame and defeat and even divine curse, the cross became the symbolic emblem of God's victory and God's grace. It became the symbol of living and grace, even through suffering. It became the symbol of a New Age, an Age of Transformation, inaugurated by God's resurrection of Jesus. And it was that same grace of God that Paul commended to all of those who were and who are "in Christ." One is not in Christ by oneself. As Paul himself would say, "one God and Father of us all. . . one baptism . . . one faith . . . one Lord . . . one hope . . . one Spirit . . . one body." As Paul himself would say, "Grace to *all of you* and peace from God *our* Father and the Lord Jesus Christ." Amen.

Through a very Jewish story. Through a cross. Through a Gospel. With hope of resurrection. God rectifies. God reconciles. Our indicative. An indicative for the whole of creation. Then and now. *Life* "in Christ." A gospel story. Through a cross, the Gospel of God. Our imperative. Our dynamism. Our salvation. Our equilibrium. A praise of God's glory. Through a cross, resurrection. God's indicative to us. Through a cross, God's imperative to us—gift of life from God the Father and the Lord Jesus Christ. A praise of God's glory. A fragrant offering. Grace and peace. Amen.[46]

46. See Appendix B, "Amazing Gospel."

Appendix A

Paul and the Death of Christ

A Survey of References

2 Thess 1:2 et al.

To assume Jesus is Lord is to assume resurrection following Jesus's prior death. This would be true of all Paul's salutations, which presume death and resurrection.

1 Thess 1:10

We wait for his Son from heaven, whom God raised from the dead, Jesus who delivers us from the wrath to come.

1 Thess 2:14–15

The Jews are those who killed both the Lord Jesus and the prophets. [Paul, a Jew, states historical fact as he writes to gentiles. He does not engage in anti-Semitism.]

1 Thess 4:14

We believe Jesus died and rose again.

1 Thess 5:9–10

God has not destined us for wrath, but to obtain salvation through our Lord Jesus Christ, who died for us so that whether we wake or sleep we might live with him.

Gal 1:1

God raised Jesus from the dead.

Gal 1:3–4

Our Lord Jesus Christ gave himself for our sins to deliver us from the Present Evil Age, according to the will of our God and Father.

Gal 2:19–21

Paul died to the Law that he might live to God; he was crucified with Christ and lives with Christ, who gave himself in love. If rectification came through the Law, then Christ died for no purpose.

Gal 3:1

Paul had portrayed a gospel of Christ crucified to the Galatians.

Gal 3:13

Christ redeemed us from the curse of the Law. [Gentiles are not expected to obey Jewish ritualism in Christ.]

Gal 5:11

Paul mentions the stumbling block of the cross in contrast to the gospel of circumcision proclaimed by the Nomistic Evangelists.

Gal 5:24

Paul speaks of those in Christ having "crucified the flesh together with passions and desires. This is a "cross imperative," but it implies Christ's own crucifixion.

Gal 6:12

Paul mentions that the Nomistic Evangelists seek to avoid being persecuted for the "cross of Christ."

Gal 6:14–16

Paul glories in the cross of the Lord Jesus Christ, by which he himself has been crucified unto a new creation.

Phil 1:21

For me to live (is) Christ, and to die (is) gain; i.e., Paul will experience the resurrection, having followed Christ in death.

Phil 2:8

Jesus became obedient unto death, even a cross kind of death.

Phil 3:7–11

Paul speaks of the loss of all things in view of the surpassing worth of righteousness in Christ, a sharing in his death and in the power of his resurrection.

Phil 3:18

Paul acknowledges that many conduct themselves as "enemies of the cross of Christ."

1 Cor 1:13

By his personal question to the Corinthians, Paul implies Christ's crucifixion.

1 Cor 1:17

Paul mentions the power of the cross of Christ.

1 Cor 1:18

The word of the cross is folly to those who are perishing, but for those who are being saved it is the power of God.

1 Cor 1:23–24

Christ crucified is not folly, but rather the power and wisdom of God.

1 Cor 2:2

Paul decided to know nothing except Jesus Christ and him crucified—and this is the power of God (v. 5); i.e., the power of God is demonstrated by resurrection. Faith does not rest in human wisdom, but in the power of God to raise the dead.

1 Cor 2:8

Paul, in a second class, contrary to fact, conditional sentence affirms that the rulers of the Present Age crucified the Lord of glory.

1 Cor 10:16–17

The cup of blessing is a participation in the blood of Christ; the bread, participation in his body. [Distinctive metaphors are employed.]

1 Cor 11:23–26

Bread is Christ's body for us; the cup is the new covenant in Christ's blood. Both are celebrated in remembrance of the Lord's death in the light of his resurrection and the Parousia.

1 Cor 15:3–5

Christ died for our sins according to the scriptures and was raised on the third day according to the scriptures. He made resurrection appearances.

1 Cor 15:12–22

Christ has been raised from the dead, with the result that all may be made alive in Christ.

1 Cor 15:56–58

We have victory over the Law, Sin, and Death through our Lord Jesus Christ—note again that an implicit resurrection theme is expressed.

2 Cor 1:9

God is the one who raises the dead, who will deliver.

2 Cor 4:14–15

We know that he who raised the Lord Jesus will raise us also with Jesus and bring us with others into his presence through extended grace to God's own glory.

2 Cor 5:14–15

The love of Christ controls us, Christ died for all; i.e, he died and was raised for our sakes that all might live to the one who died and was raised in their behalf.

2 Cor 5:17

If anyone is in Christ, such a one is a new creation (i.e., one has died and been raised with Christ).

2 Cor 5:19–21

In Christ God was reconciling the world to himself, not counting trespasses against humankind; for our sake he made him sin [noun] who knew no sin, so that in him we might become the righteousness of God. (On v. 21, cf. Gal 3:13—Jesus bore the fearful consequences of sin.)

2 Cor 8:9

The grace of our Lord Jesus Christ, that though he was rich, yet for your sake he became poor, so that by his poverty you might become rich. [While Paul uses a different metaphor, this verse may clarify Paul's meaning in 2 Cor 5:21.]

2 Cor 13:4

Christ was crucified in weakness, but he lives by the power of God. (V. 5—the result is that we shall live with him by the power of God.)

Rom 1:4

Jesus is designated son of God in power by his resurrection from the dead.

Rom 3:21–26

Rectification and redemption is in Christ Jesus, whom God publically set forth as an expiation by his blood, to be received by faith, that one might live out of God's rectification based upon faithfulness.

Rom 4:24–25

There is an accounting of our faith, we who believe in God who raised Jesus our Lord from the dead, he who was put to death for our trespasses and raised for our justification. He "was delivered up because of the sins we had committed, and raised up because of the justification that was to be granted to us" [Barrett]; "He died and rose again in order that we might be delivered from the guilt of our sins" [Dodd]. Our trespasses led to his death, his resurrection to our rectification.

Rom 5:6–10

Christ died for the ungodly (v. 6), as God showed his love for us (v. 8). The result is justification by his blood (v. 9), as we are reconciled through his death (v. 10) and saved through his resurrection life (v. 10). Reconciliation and rectification emerge from the reality of Jesus's death. Salvation from wrath will come as a result of his resurrection and our reconciliation with God.

Rom 6:3–11

We were buried with Christ in baptism into death; we are raised unto a newness of life. We are now dead to Sin and alive to God in Christ Jesus (v. 11). Neither Death nor Sin have dominion any longer. If we have died with Christ, we live in hope of resurrection life.

Rom 7:4

We belong to him who has been raised from the death, and have new life in the Spirit (v. 6).

Rom 8:3

Jesus is sent by God in the likeness of sinful flesh, with the result that Sin is condemned and the just requirement of the Law is satisfied. I.e., Jesus came to dwell in the same sinful flesh (being weak, not evil), but he defeated Sin in its own den. Jesus in the flesh was subject to the assaults of Sin but remained sinless. As an offering for Sin, he defeated Sin so that his sinless life and self-sacrifice for Sin was the undoing of Sin. Jesus lived under the dominion of Death in the flesh, but by his death and resurrection he became victorious over that dominion (cf. Rom 6:9). I.e., Jesus entered the sphere of Sin (personified), but it was Sin that lost the case. Sin lies dead apart from the Law (Rom 7:8). Jesus lives in full obedience to the Law, and thus conquers both Sin and Death through the power of God.

Rom 8:31–39

Reminiscent of Abraham's offering of Isaac, God gave up his own son (παραδίδωμι, "I hand over, deliver up"—cf. Rom 1:24, 26, 28) as a vicarious offering in an ultimate display of love. Cf. Rom 5:8—Jesus died (as a result of humanity's taking the life he offered), but God raised him from the dead for our intercession (v. 34). Supremely, it is the love of God in Christ Jesus our Lord which is demonstrated (v. 39)—a love from which we cannot be severed.

Rom 10:9

Confession of Jesus' Lordship, i.e., that God did indeed raise him from the dead, results in our faith, rectification, and our salvation.

Rom 14:7–9

Christ is Lord through death and resurrection.

Col 1:20

Peace by the blood of his cross. Jesus is Son (v. 13), the image of God and the first-born of all (new?) creation (v. 15), the first-born of the dead (v. 18), in whom the fullness of God dwells in reconciliation (v. 20). Cf. v. 22. The cross is related to peace, as battle is to victory. Cf. Col 2:15.

Col 2:12–15

God canceled the bond of our trespasses with all its legal demands in the cross.

Eph 1:3–10

God destined us in love to be children (lit., sons) through Jesus Christ, which includes redemption through his blood and forgiveness of trespasses through his grace (v. 7).

Eph 1:19–20

The immeasurable power of God in us was accomplished through the resurrection and exaltation of Christ.

Eph 2:1–6

God in his rich mercy and love (v. 4) made us alive with Christ (vv. 5–6), we who were dead in our trespasses and sins (v. 1, v.5). This comes by the gift of God (v. 8). Christ's death is implied in reference to resurrection to life.

Eph 2:13–17

Through his blood Christ Jesus has broken down the dividing walls of hostility by (1) abolishing in his flesh the Law and (2) creating one new person in the place of two (cf. Rom 7). Hostility between humanity and God, and between Jew and gentile is abolished. The death of Christ on the cross, followed by resurrection, has brought about reconciliation and peace.

2Tim 1:10

Jesus abolished death and brought life and immortality through the gospel.

2 Tim 2:8

Jesus Christ is risen from the dead.

2 Tim 2:11–13

A Christian hymn? If we have died with him, we shall also live with him.

Appendix B

Amazing Gospel

I T likely goes without saying that the favorite hymn of the American Christian church has been John Newton's "Amazing Grace," which he wrote in 1779. John Newton was born in London in 1725 and died in London in 1807. His mother was a devout Christian who died when Newton was but seven years of age. When he was but eleven years of age, Newton went to sea with his father, a sea captain who did not share his wife's Christian interest. He later served in the Royal Navy aboard a British man-of-war, after which he joined the crew of a slave-trading ship and became engaged in the slave trade for a number of years. He was called to the ministry in mid-life and began to preach in 1758. [1] He published more than 250 hymns and wrote his own epitaph as follows.

> John Newton, Clerk
> Once an infidel and libertine,
> A servant of slaves in Africa:
> Was by the rich mercy of our
> Lord and Savior, Jesus Christ,
> Preserved, restored, pardoned,
> And appointed to preach the Faith
> He had labored long to destroy.
> Near sixteen years at Olney in Bucks;
> And twenty-seven years in this church. [2]

The hymn "Amazing Grace" as found in the *Methodist Hymnal* includes Newton's original five verses, as well as the anonymous concluding verse ("When we've been there ten thousand years, . . ."). The familiar final verse was apparently added by a hymnic "scribe," who either felt compelled to worship or who sought to make the hymn "better" by *making concrete* the expressed satisfaction of *divine mystery* ("I shall possess within the veil, . . .") that John Newton originally penned in his concluding

---

1. See "John Newton," in Forbis, *Handbook to the Baptist Hymnal*, 417; "Amazing Grace," in Job, *United Methodist Hymnal*, 378.

2. Forbis, *Handbook to the Baptist Hymnal*, 417.

verse five. Newton's fifth and final verse has been dropped from many hymnals, in favor of the anonymous addition.

If one is familiar with the hymn, it should be noted that there is no mention of "cross," or of "blood," or of "required sacrifice," or of "atonement" in "Amazing Grace." None of those things that are customarily emphasized so much in either Christian worship, in creeds. or in Christian theology appear in Newton's hymn. This favorite hymn of the Christian Church, which is almost mystical in its appeal, has a focus that is simply and squarely upon the powerful transforming grace of God. It thus invites the heart to soar in celebration, as it sings God's praise.

At its core and at its zenith, the apostle Paul's own broad central theme of the "Gospel of God" invites one to worship the God of Israel known through incarnational expression in Jesus Christ through the presence of God's abiding Spirit. In fulfilment of God's foundational promise given to Abraham (Gen 12:3), God's Gospel of salvation is extended *to all* on the basis of his grace in Christ, being sealed by the presence of his Spirit of promise. Ephesians 1 becomes a magnificent summary of the Gospel of God, as Paul expresses both doxology (Eph 1:3–14) and prayer of thanksgiving, as he rehearses God's accomplishment in the Gospel (Eph 1:15–23). Christians are to live as a "praise of God's glory" (Eph 1:6, 12, 14). The Church is to live as the body of Christ, actualizing the fullness of the One who fulfils all things in all (Eph 1:22–23). Ephesians 1 for Paul is the equivalent of "Amazing Grace" for John Newton. As a "man in Christ," Paul the apostle invites us to leave our slave ships of human bondage and formulated theology, in order to experience a *theo*logy of freedom and praise.

And so it is that the present writer offers the following hymn of praise to God the Father, informed by Paul's theology, particularly and including Romans 8. While the present writer has written an alternative tune, "Amazing Gospel" may be sung to the familiar tune of "Amazing Grace."

"Amazing Gospel"

(To the tune of "Amazing Grace")

The Gospel of our God I see, His mercy great for thee!
His word of hope for all a-bounds, That grace of God so free!

Amazing Gospel, sweet the sound, that calls my heart from tears.
Though once enslaved, I now am free, for life beyond all fears.

From Sin and Death and Law, all three, I have indeed been freed.
For God has giv'n His grace to me, His love and joy and peace.

His Love beyond the cross I see, his Son, he reigns as Lord.
Nor height nor depth shall sever me, for I shall live in Him.

And so for all the hosts of God, lies God's own table spread.
And there the Lord himself shall be, His brothers, sisters free.

A theology to be proclaimed.
A theology to be lived.

And so, Lord, Let it be!

AMEN.

Bibliography

Achtemeier, Paul J. "Apropos the Faith of/in Christ: A Response to Hays and Dunn." In *Pauline Theology*, edited by E. Elizabeth Johnson and David M. Hay, 4:82–92. Society of Biblical Literature Symposium Series. Atlanta: Scholars, 1997.

———. "The Continuing Quest for Coherence in St. Paul: An Experiment in Thought." In *Theology and Ethics in Paul and His Interpreters: Essays in Honor of Victor Paul Furnish*, edited by Eugene H. Lovering Jr. and Jerry L. Sumney, 132–45. Nashville: Abingdon, 1996.

Aland, Kurt, et al., eds. *The Greek New Testament*. 3rd ed. (corrected). Stuttgart: Biblia-Druck, 1983.

Aland, Barbara, et al., eds. *Novum Testamentum Graece*. 27th ed. Stuttgart: Deutsche Bibelgesellschaft, 1993.

Aquinas, Thomas. *The Summa Theologica of St. Thomas Aquinas*. 2 vols. Literally translated by Fathers of the English Dominican Province, edited by Paul A. Böer Sr. Repr. Houston, TX: Veritatis Splendor, 2012.

Athanasius. "On the Incarnation of the Word." In *Nicene and Post-Nicene Fathers*, Second Series, edited by Philip Schaff and Henry Wace, 4:36–67. Repr. Peabody, MA: Hendrickson, 1999.

Augustine. *Augustin*. In *Nicene and Post-Nicene Fathers*, First Series, edited by Philip Schaff. Vols. 1–8. Repr. Peabody, MA: Hendrickson, 1999.

Aulén, Gustaf. *Christus Victor: An Historical Study of the Three Main Types of the Idea of the Atonement*. Translated by A. G. Hebert. Repr. Eugene, OR: Wipf & Stock, 2003.

Bainton, Roland. *Christendom: A Short History of Christianity and Its Impact on Western Civilization*. 2 vols. The Cloister Library. New York: Harper Torchbooks, 1964.

———. *Christianity*. The American Heritage Library. Boston: Houghton Mifflin, 1964.

———. *Here I Stand: A Life of Martin Luther*. New York: Abingdon, 1950.

Baker, Mark D., and Joel B. Green, *Recovering the Scandal of the Cross: Atonement in New Testament and Contemporary Contexts*. 2nd ed. Downers Grove, IL: IVP Academic, 2011.

Barclay, John M. "The Gift Perspective on Paul." In *Perspectives on Paul*, edited by Scot McKnight and B. J. Oropeza, 219–36. Grand Rapids: Baker Academic, 2020.

———. *Paul and the Gift*. Grand Rapids: Eerdmans, 2015.

———. "What Makes Paul Challenging." In *The New Cambridge Companion to St. Paul*, edited by Bruce W. Longenecker, 299–318. Cambridge: Cambridge University Press, 2020.

Bartsch, Hans Werner, ed. *Kerygma and Myth*. Harper Torchbooks. The Cloister Library. New York: Harper & Row, 1961.

Barry, J. "Penal Substitutionary Atonement in the Church Fathers." *EQ* 83 (2011) 195–216.

Bassler, Jouette M., ed. *Pauline Theology Volume I: Thessalonians, Philippians, Galatians and Philemon.* Minneapolis: Fortress, 1991.

Bauer, Walter. *A Greek English Lexicon of the New Testament and Other Early Christian Literature.* Translated and adapted by William F. Arndt and F. Wilbur Gingrich. 2nd ed. Revised and augmented by F. Wilbur Gingrich and Frederick W. Danker from Walter Bauer's 5th German ed. Chicago: The University of Chicago Press, 1979.

Beilby, James, and Paul R. Eddy, eds. *The Nature of the Atonement: Four Views.* Downers Grove, IL: IVP Academic, 2006.

Beker, J. Christiaan. *Paul's Apocalyptic Gospel: The Coming Triumph of God.* Philadelphia: Fortress, 1982.

———. *Paul the Apostle: The Triumph of God in Life and Thought.* Philadelphia: Fortress, 1984.

Betz, Hans Dieter. *Galatians: A Commentary on Paul's Letters to the Churches in Galatia.* Hermeneia–A Critical and Historical Commentary on the Bible. Philadelphia: Fortress, 1979.

Bonner, Gerald. "Augustine as Biblical Scholar." In *The Cambridge History of the Bible*, edited by P. R. Ackroyd and C. F. Evans, 1:541–63. London: Cambridge University Press, 1970.

Bray, Gerald L., and Thomas C. Ogden, eds. *1–2 Corinthians.* Ancient Christian Commentary on Scripture 7. Downers Grove, IL: InterVarsity, 2005.

———. *Romans.* Ancient Christian Commentary on Scripture 6. Downers Grove, IL: InterVarsity, 2005.

Brondos, David A. *Jesus' Death in New Testament Thought.* 2 vols. Mexico City: Theological Community of Mexico, 2018.

———. *The Parting of the Gods: Paul and the Redefinition of Judaism.* Mexico City: Theological Community of Mexico, 2021.

———. *Paul on the Cross: Reconstructing the Apostle's Story of Redemption.* Minneapolis: Fortress, 2006.

Bruggemann, Walter. "Editor's Forward." In *A Theology of the Cross: The Death of Jesus in the Pauline Letters*, by Charles B. Cousar, vii–ix. Minneapolis: Fortress, 1990.

Brunner, Emil. *The Word and the World.* New York: Charles Scribner's Sons, 1931.

Büchsel, Friedrich. "ἱλάσκομαι, ἱλασμός." In *TDNT* 3:316–23.

Bultmann, Rudolf. *Essays, Philosophical and Theological.* London: SCM, 1955.

———. *Faith and Understanding, Volume 1.* Edited by Robert W. Funk. Translated by Louise Pettibone Smith. New York: Harper & Row, 1969.

———. "New Testament and Mythology." In *Kerygma and Myth: A Theological Debate*, edited by H. W. Bartsch, 1–16. Translated by R. H. Fuller. London: SPCK, 1957.

———. *Theology of the New Testament.* Translated by Kendrick Grobel. 2 vols. New York: Charles Scribner's Sons, 1951, 1955.

Buttrick, George A. *The Interpreter's Dictionary of the Bible.* 4 vols. Nashville: Abingdon, 1962.

Calvin, John. *Institutes of the Christian Religion.* Translated by Henry Beveridge. 2 vols. Grand Rapids: Eerdmans, 1989.

Carroll, John T., and Joel B. Green et al. *The Death of Jesus in Early Christianity.* Peabody, MA: Hendrickson, 1995.

Cousar, Charles S. *A Theology of the Cross: The Death of Jesus in the Pauline Letters.* Overtures to Biblical Theology. Minneapolis: Fortress, 1990.

Culpepper, Robert H. *Interpreting the Atonement.* Grand Rapids: Eerdmans, 1966.

Dahl, Nils Alstrup. *Jesus the Christ: The Historical Origins of Christological Doctrine*, edited by Donald H. Juel. Minneapolis: Fotress, 1991.

Davies, Brian, and G. R. Evans, eds. *Anselm of Canterbury: The Major Works*. Oxford World's Classics. Oxford: Oxford University Press, 1998.

Donfried, Karl P., ed. *The Romans Debate*. Rev. and exp. Peabody, MA: Hendrickson, 1991.

Dunn, James D. G. "Once More, ΠΙΣΤΙΣ ΧΡΙΣΤΟΥ." In *Pauline Theology Volume IV: Looking Back, Pressing On*, edited by E. Elizabeth Johnson and David M. Hay, 61–81. Society of Biblical Literature Symposium Series. Atlanta: Scholars, 1997.

———. *Romans 1–8*. Word Biblical Commentary 38. Nashville: Thomas Nelson, 1988.

———. *The Theology of Paul the Apostle*. Grand Rapids: Eerdmans, 1998.

Edwards, Mark, and Thomas C. Ogden, eds. *Galatians, Ephesians, Philippians*. Ancient Christian Commentary on Scripture 8. Downers Grove, IL: InterVarsity, 2005.

Eisenbaum, Pamela. *Paul Was Not a Christian: The Original Message of a Misunderstood Apostle*. New York: HarperCollins, 2009.

Elliott, Neil, and Mark Reasoner, eds. *Documents and Images for the Study of Paul*. Minneapolis:

Fee, Gordon D. "Toward a Theology of 1 Corinthians." In *Pauline Theology: Volume II: 1 and 2 Corinthians*, edited by David M. Hay, 37–58. Minneapolis: Fortress, 1993.

Ferguson, Everett. *Backgrounds of Early Christianity*. 3rd ed. Grand Rapids: Eerdmans, 2003.

Finlan, Stephen. *Options on Atonement in Christian Thought*. Collegeville, MN: Liturgical, 2007.

———. *Problems with Atonement: The Origins of, and Controversy about, the Atonement Doctrine*. Collegeville, MN: Liturgical, 2005.

Finlan, Stephen, and Vladimir Kharlamov, eds. *Theōsis: Deification in Christian Theology*. Princeton Theological Monograph Series, edited by K. C. Hanson et al. Eugene, OR: Pickwick, 2006.

Flood, Derek. "Substitutionary Atonement and the Church Fathers: A Reply to the Authors of *Pierced for Our Transgressions*." *Evangelical Quarterly* 82 (2010) 142–59.

Fitzmyer, Joseph A., SJ. *Paul and His Theology: A Brief Sketch*. 2nd ed. Englewood Cliffs, New Jersey: Prentice Hall, 1989.

Forbis, Wesley L., ed. *Handbook to the Baptist Hymnal*. Nashville: Convention, 1992.

Fredriksen, Paula. "Who Was Paul?" In *The New Cambridge Companion to St. Paul*, edited by Bruce W. Longenecker, 23–47. Cambridge: Cambridge University Press, 2020.

Freedman, David Noel, ed. *The Anchor Bible Dictionary*. 6 vols. New York: Doubleday, 1992.

Furnish, Victor Paul. *Theology and Ethics in Paul*. Nashville: Abingdon, 1968.

———. *The Moral Teaching of Paul: Selected Issues*. 3rd ed. Nashville: Abingdon, 2009.

González, Justo L. *Church History: An Essential Guide*. Nashville: Abingdon, 1996.

———. *A History of Christian Thought*. 3 vols. Rev. ed. Nashville: Abingdon, 1987.

———. *The Story of Christianity*. 2 vols. Rev. and updated. New York: HarperCollins, 2010.

Good, Edwin M. "The Meaning of Demytholization." In *The Theology of Rudolf Bultmann*, edited by Charles W. Kegley, 21–40. New York: Harper & Row, 1966.

Gorday, Peter, and Thomas C. Ogden, eds. *Colossians, 1–2 Thessalonians, 1–2 Timothy, Titus, Philemon*. Ancient Christian Commentary on Scripture 9. Downers Grove, IL: InterVarsity, 2000.

Gorman, Michael J. *Cruciformity: Paul's Narrative Spirituality of the Cross*. Grand Rapids: Eerdmans, 2003.

———. *Inhabiting the Cruciform God: Kenosis, Justification, and Theosis in Paul's Narrative Theology*. Grand Rapids: Eerdmans, 2009.

Grant, Robert M., and David Tracy, *A Short History of the Interpretation of the Bible*. 2nd ed., rev. Minneapolis: Fortress, 2005.

Green, Joel B. "Death of Christ." In *Dictionary of Paul and His Letters*, edited by Gerald F. Hawthorne and Ralph P. Martin, 201–9. Downers Grove, IL: InterVarsity, 1993.

———. "Kaleidoscopic View." In *The Nature of the Atonement: Four Views,* edited by James Beilby and Paul R. Eddy, 157–85. Downers Grove, IL: IVP Academic, 2006.

Greene, G. Roger. "Amazing Gospel." Unpublished hymn, copyright 2005.

———. "God's Lamb: Divine Provision for Sin." *Perspectives in Religious Studies* 37 (2010) 147–64.

———. *The Ministry of Paul the Apostle: History and Redaction*. Lanham: Lexington Books/ Fortress Academic, 2019.

———. "The Portrayal of Jesus as Prophet in Luke-Acts." PhD diss., The Southern Baptist Theological Seminary, 1975.

Gregory of Nazianzus. "The Second Oration on Easter." In *Nicene and Post-Nicene Fathers: A Select Library of the Christian Church,* Second Series, edited by Philip Schaff and Henry Wace, 7:288–301. Repr. Peabody, MA: Hendrickson, 1999.

Gregory of Nyssa. "Great Catechism." In *Nicene and Post-Nicene Fathers: A Select Library of the Christian Church,* Second Series, edited by Philip Schaff and Henry Wace, 3:471–509. Repr. Peabody, MA: Hendrickson, 1999.

Grensted, L. W. *A Short History of the Doctrine of the Atonement*. London: Longmans, Green & Co., 1920.

Gundry-Volf, J. M. "Expiation, Propitiation, Mercy Seat." In *Dictionary of Paul and His Letters.*, edited by Gerald F. Hawthorne and Ralph P. Martin, 279–84. Downers Grove, IL: InterVarsity, 1993.

Hague, Dyson. "At-one-ment by Propitiation." In *The Fundamentals: A Testimony to the Truth*, edited by R. A. Torrey et al., 3:78–97. Los Angeles: The Bible Institute of Los Angeles, 1917.

Hanson, R. P. C. "Biblical Exegesis in the Early Church." In *The Cambridge History of the Bible*, edited by P. R. Ackroyd and C. F. Evans, 1:412–53. London: Cambridge University Press, 1970.

Hay, David M., ed. *Pauline Theology, Volume II: 1 and 2 Corinthians*. Society of Biblical Literature Symposium Series. Minneapolis: Fortress, 1993.

———. "Pauline Theology After Paul." In *Pauline Theology Volume IV: Looking Back, Pressing On*, edited by E. Elizabeth Johnson and David M. Hay, 181–95. Atlanta: Scholars, 1997.

Hay, David M., and E. Elizabeth Johnson, eds. *Pauline Theology, Volume III: Romans*. Society of Biblical Literature Symposium Series. Minneapolis: Fortress, 2002.

Hawthorne, Gerald F., and Ralph P. Martin, eds. *Dictionary of Paul and His Letters*. Downers Grove, IL: InterVarsity, 1993.

Hays, Richard B. *Echoes of Scripture in the Letters of Paul*. New Haven, CT: Yale University Press, 1989.

———. *The Faith of Jesus Christ: The Narrative Substructure of Galatians 3:1—4:11*. 2nd ed. Grand Rapids: Eerdmans, 2002.

———. *The Moral Vision of the New Testament: Community, Cross, New Creation: A Contemporary Introduction to New Testament Ethics*. San Francisco: HarperSanFrancisco, 1996.

———. "ΠΙΣΤΙΣ and Pauline Christology." In *Pauline Theology Volume IV: Looking Back, Pressing On*, edited by E. Elizabeth Johnson and David M. Hay, 35–60. Society of Biblical Literature Symposium Series. Atlanta: Scholars, 1997.

Heim, S. Mark. *Saved from Sacrifice: A Theology of the Cross*. Grand Rapids: Eerdmans, 2006.

Hengel, Martin. *The Atonement: The Origins of the Doctrine in the New Testament*. Philadelphia: Fortress, 1981.

Hill, Charles E., and Frank A. James III, eds. *The Glory of the Atonement: Biblical, Historical,& Practical Perspectives*. Downers Grove, IL: InterVarsity Academic, 2004.

Hodge, Charles. *Systematic Theology*. 3 vols. Repr. Peabody, MA: Hendrickson, 2016.

Holmes, Michael W., ed. *The Apostolic Fathers: Greek Texts and English Translations*. Grand Rapids: Baker, 1999.

Howard, George. "Faith, Faith of Christ." In ABD 2:758–760.

Humphreys, Fisher. *The Death of Christ*. Nashville: Broadman, 1978.

Ignatius. *Ignatius*. In *Ante-Nicene Fathers*, edited by Alexander Roberts and James Donaldson, 1:45–132. Repr. Peabody, MA: Hendrickson, 1999.

Irenaeus. *Irenaeus*. In *Ante-Nicene Fathers*, edited by Alexander Roberts and James Donaldson, 1:309–602. Repr. Peabody, MA: Hendrickson, 1999.

Jeffery, Steve, et al. *Pierced for Our Transgressions: Rediscovering the Glory of Penal Substitution*. Wheaton, IL: Crossway, 2007.

Job, Rueben P., chair.*The United Methodist Hymnal: A Book of United Methodist Worship*. Nashville: United Methodist, 2001.

Johnson, E. Elizabeth, and David M. Hay, eds. *Pauline Theology, Volume IV: Looking Back, Pressing On*. Society of Biblical Literature Symposium Series, edited by Gail R. O'Day. Atlanta: Scholars, 1997.

Johnson, Franklin. "The Atonement." In *The Fundamentals: A Testimony to the Truth*, edited by R. A. Torrey et al., 3:64–77. 4 vols. The Bible Institute of Los Angeles, 1917.

Josephus. *Josephus*. Translated by H. G. Thackeray et al. Loeb Classical Library. 9 vols. Cambridge, MA: Harvard University Press, 1926–1963.

Kähler, M. *The So-Called Historical Jesus and the Historic Biblical Christ*. Repr. Philadelphia: Fortress, 1956.

Käsemann, Ernst. *Perspectives on Paul*. Translated by Margaret Kohl. Philadelphia: Fortress, 1969.

Kelly, J. N. D. *Early Christian Docrines*. Rev. ed. New York: HarperOne, 1978.

Kittel, Gerhard, and Gerhard Friedrich, eds. *Theological Dictionary of the New Testament*. 10 vols. Translated and edited by Geoffrey W. Bromiley. Grand Rapids: Eerdmans, 1964–1976.

Knox, John. *Chapters in a Life of Paul*. Rev. ed. Macon, GA: Mercer University Press, 1987.

Ladd, George Eldon. *A Theology of the New Testament*. Rev. ed. Grand Rapids: Eerdmans, 1993.

Liddell, Henry George, and Robert Scott. *A Greek-English Lexicon: With a Supplement 1968*. Revised by Henry Stuart Jones and Roderick McKenzie. New York: Oxford University Press, 1994.

Longenecker, Bruce W., ed. *The New Cambridge Companion to St. Paul*. Cambridge: Cambridge University Press, 2020.

Louw, Johannes P., and Eugene A. Nida. *Greek-English Lexicon of the New Testament Based on Semantic Domains*. 2 vols. 2nd ed. New York: United Bible Societies, 1988, 1989.

Lührmann, Dieter. "Faith, New Testament." In *ABD* 2:749–758.

Luther, Martin. *Commentary on Galatians*. Translated by Erasmus Middleton, edited by John Prince Fallowes. Repr. Grand Rapids: Kregel, 1979.

McGrath, A. E. *Christian Theology: An Introduction*. 5th ed. West Sussex: Wiley-Blackwell, 2011.

———. "Theology of the Cross." In *Dictionary of Paul and His Letters*, edited by Gerald F. Hawthorne and Ralph P. Martin, 192–97. Downers Grove, IL: InterVarsity, 1993.

McKnight, Scot, and B. J. Oropeza, eds. *Perspectives on Paul: Five Views*. Grand Rapids: Baker Academic, 2020.

Macquarrie, John. "Philosophy and Theology in Bultmann's Thought." In *The Theology of Rudolf Bultmann*, edited by Charles W. Kegley, 127–43. New York: Harper & Row, 1966.

Malina, Bruce J. *The New Testament World: Insights from Cultural Anthropology*. 3rd ed., rev. and exp. Louisville: Westminster John Knox, 2001.

Manschreck, Clyde L. *Melanchthon: The Quiet Reformer*. Repr. Eugene, OR: Wipf & Stock, 2008.

Martin, Ralph P. *Reconciliation: A Study of Paul's Theology*. Grand Rapids: Zondervan Academie, 1989.

Marty, Martin E. *A Short History of Christianity*. 2nd ed., rev. and exp. Philadelphia: Fortresss, 1987.

Martyr, Justin. *Justin Martyr*. In *Ante-Nicene Fathers: The Writings of the Fathers Down to A.D. 325*, edited by Alexander Roberts and James Donaldson, 1:159–306. Revised and arranged by A. Cleveland Coxe. Peabody, MA: Hendrickson, 1999.

May, Herbert G., and Bruce M. Metzger. *The New Oxford Annotated Bible with the Apocrypha*. Revised Standard Version. New York: Oxford University Press, 1977.

Mertens, Herman-Emiel. *Not the Cross, But the Crucified: An Essay in Soteriology*. Lovain Theological & Pastoral Monographs. Louvain: Peters, 1992.

Metzger, Bruce M. *A Textual Commentary on the Greek New Testament*. London: United Bible Societies, 1971.

Mish, Frederick C., ed. *Merriam-Webster's Collegiate Dictionary*. 11th ed. Springfield, MA: Merriam-Webster, 2014.

Mitton, C. L. "Atonement." In *IDB* 1:309–13.

Moo, Douglas J. *Theology of Paul and His Letters: The Gift of the New Realm in Christ*. Biblical Theology of the New Testament Series, edited by Andreas J. Kostenberger. Grand Rapids: Zondervan Academic, 2021.

Moore, George Foot. *Judaism in the First Centuries of the Christian Era: The Age of the Tannaim*. 3 vols. Repr. Peabody, MA: Hendrickson, 1997.

Morgenthaler, Robert. *Statistik des neutestamentlichen Wortschatzes*. Zurich: Gotthelf-Verlag, 1958.

Morris, Leon. *The Atonement: Its Meaning and Significance*. Downers Grove, IL: InterVarsity, 1983.

———. *The Cross in the New Testament*. Grand Rapids: Eerdmans, 1968.

Moulton, W. F., et al. *A Concordance to the Greek New Testament*. 5th ed. Edinburgh: T. & T. Clark, 1978.

Neill, Stephen, and Tom Wright. *The Interpretation of the New Testament 1861–1986*. Oxford: Oxford University Press, 1988.

Ogden, Thomas C., gen. ed. *Ancient Christian Commentary on Scripture*. Downers Grove, IL: InterVarsity, 2001–.

Origen. *Origen*. In *Ante-Nicene Fathers*, edited by Alexander Roberts and James Donaldson, revised by A. Cleveland Coxe, 4:223–669. Repr. Peabody, MA: Hendrickson, 1999.

Osborne, G. R. "Hermeneutics/Interpreting Paul." In *Dictionary of Paul and His Letters*, edited by Gerald F. Hawthorne and Ralph P. Martin, 388–97. Downers Grove, IL: InterVarsity, 1993.

Packer, J. I. "What Did the Cross Achieve: The Logic of Penal Substitution." The Tyndale Biblical Theology Lecture, 1973, delivered at Tyndale House, Cambridge, July 17, 1973. https://www.the-highway.com/cross_Packer.html.

Plevnik, Joseph, SJ. *What Are They Saying About Paul?* New York: Paulist, 1986.

Richardson, Alan. *Introduction to the Theology of the New Testament*. New York: Harper & Row, 1958.

Ridderbos, Herman. *Paul: An Outline of His Theology*. Translated by John Richard DeWitt. Grand Rapids: Eerdmans, 1975.

———. *Paul and Jesus: Origin and General Character of Paul's Preaching of Christ*. Translated by David H. Freeman. Philadelphia: Presbyterian and Reformed Publishing, 1958.

Roberts, Alexander, and James Donaldson, eds. *Ante-Nicene Fathers: The Writings of the Fathers Down to A.D. 325*. 10 vols. Revised and arranged by A. Cleveland Coxe. Repr. Peabody, MA: Hendrickson, 1999.

Robertson, A. T. *A Grammar of the Greek New Testament in the Light of Historical Research*. Nashville: Broadman, 1934.

Sanders, E. P. *Paul, the Law, and the Jewish People*. Minneapolis: Fortress, 1983.

———. *Paul and Palestinian Judaism: A Comparison of Patterns of Religion*. Philadelphia: Fortress, 1977.

———. *Paul: Past Master*. Oxford: Oxford University Press, 1991.

Schaff, Philip, ed. *Nicene and Post-Nicene Fathers: A Select Library of the Christian Church*. First Series. 14 vols. Repr. Peabody, MA: Hendrickson, 1999.

Schaff, Philip, and Henry Wace, eds. *Nicene and Post-Nicene Fathers: A Select Library of the Christian Church*. Second Series. 14 vols. Repr. Peabody, MA: Hendrickson, 1999.

Scheck, Thomas P., trans. *Origen: Commentary on the Epistle to the Romans Books 1–5*. Washington, DC: Catholic University of America Press, 2001.

Schrey, Heinz-Horst. "The Consequences of Bultmann's Theology for Ethics." In *The Theology of Rudolf Bultmann*, edited by Charles W. Kegley, 183–200. New York: Harper & Row, 1966.

Scroggs, Robin. *Paul for a New Day*. Philadelphia: Fortress, 1977.

Shelley, Bruce L. *Church History in Plain Language*. Updated 3rd ed. Nashville: Thomas Nelson, 2008.

Stendahl, Krister. *Paul Among Jews and Gentiles and Other Essays*. Philadelphia: Fortress, 1976.

Stewart, James S. *A Man in Christ: The Vital Elements of St. Paul's Religion*. Grand Rapids: Baker, 1975.

Stupperich, Robert. *Melanchthon: The Enigma of the Reformation*. Cambridge: James Clarke, 1965.

Tambasco, A. J. *A Theology of Atonement and Paul's Vision of Christianity*. Zacchaeus Studies. Collegeville, MN: Liturgical, 1991.

Tannehill, Robert C. *Dying and Rising with Christ: A Study in Pauline Theology*. Berlin: Alfred Töpelmann, 1967.

Taylor, Vincent. *The Atonement in New Testament Teaching*. 3rd ed. London: Epworth, 1958.

———. *The Cross of Christ: Eight Public Lectures*. London: Macmillan, 1957.

Tertullian. "The Five Books Against Marcion." In *The Ante-Nicene Fathers*, edited by Alexander Roberts and James Donaldson, 3:271–475. Repr. Peabody, MA: Hendrickson, 1999.

———. "The Prescription Against Heretics." In *The Ante-Nicene Fathers*, edited by Alexander Roberts and James Donaldson, 3:243–65. Repr. Peabody, MA: Hendrickson, 1999.

———. "On the Resurrection of the Flesh." In *The Ante-Nicene Fathers*, edited by Alexander Roberts and James Donaldson, 3:243–65. Repr. Peabody, MA: Hendrickson, 1999.

Thielman, F. "Law." In *Dictionary of Paul and His Letters*, edited by Gerald F. Hawthorne and Ralph P. Martin, 529–42. Downers Grove, IL: InterVarsity, 1993.

Tidball, Derek et al., eds. *The Atonement Debate: Papers from the London Symposium on the Theology of Atonement*. Grand Rapids: Zondervan, 2008.

Turrettin, Francis. *The Atonement of Christ*. Translated by James R. Willson. Repr. Eugene, OR: Wipf & Stock, 1999.

Vermes, Geza. *The Complete Dead Sea Scrolls in English*. Rev. ed. London: Penguin, 2011.

Wiles, M. F. *The Divine Apostle: The Interpretation of St. Paul's Epistles in the Early Church*. Cambridge: Cambridge University Press, 1967.

Williams, David J. *Paul's Metaphors: Their Context and Character*. Peabody, MA: Hendrickson, 1999.

Williams, J. Barry. "Penal Substitutionary Atonement in the Church Fathers." EQ 83 (2011) 195–216.

Wink, Walter. *Naming the Powers; Engaging the Powers: Discernment and Resistance in a World of Domination*. Minneapolis: Fortress, 1992.

———. *Naming the Powers: The Language of Power in the New Testament*. Philadelphia: Fortress, 1984.

Wright, N. T. *Jesus and the Victory of God*. Christian Origins and the Question of God 2. Minneapolis: Fortress, 1996.

———. "The Letter to the Romans." In *The New Interpreter's Bible*, edited by Leander E. Keck et al., 10:393–770. Nashville: Abingdon, 2002.

———. *Paul and His Recent Interpreters: Some Contemporary Debates*. Minneapolis: Fortress, 2015.

———. *What Saint Paul Really Said: Was Paul of Tarsus the Real Founder of Christianity?* Grand Rapids: Eerdmans, 1997.

Zetterholm, Magnus. *Approaches to Paul: A Student's Guide to Recent Scholarship*. Minneapolis: Fortress, 2009.

About the Author

G. Roger Greene is professor of Christian Studies at Mississippi College in Clinton, Mississippi, where he has taught since 1979. He previously served as an associate professor of religion at Palm Beach Atlantic College. He has taught courses in New Testament Greek, the Gospels, Acts, and the letters of Paul. In addition, he has taught courses pertaining to the intertestamental period, text and canon, the New Testament world, and distinctive ideas of biblical thought. He has participated in archaeological work in Israel and has led travel groups to the lands of the Bible, including Israel, Jordan, Greece, and Turkey. He is an ordained Baptist minister and a graduate of The Southern Baptist Theological Seminary, with an undergraduate degree from Louisiana Tech University. He currently serves as the senior professor in the Department of Christian Studies at Mississippi College, where he continues to teach a full range of courses in the field of Greek and New Testament studies.

Subject Index

lived in the flesh and died at the hands of sinful humankind, 12

living in Paul, 22, 82

made a substitute and a surety, 232

"made sin" for our sake, 164

as the Mediator who made us sons of God, 231

in no temple other than the body of Christians, 102

not injured by death, 204

not offering appeasement to God, 166

not undergoing punishment for sin, 23

as now Lord, 80

offered himself as a necessary sacrifice, 215

offering infinite satisfaction, 220

one's incorporation into, 77

overcame the curse of the Law, 162

Paul not calling "God," 42

Paul's concept of "growing lyrical," 281

placating the wrath of God, 231

as a place where mercy might be received, 168

as propitiation, 165

saving us from the tyranny of Law, 153

sent by God in terms of incarnation, 162

shouldered payment required by justice, 215

submitted to the consequences of sin, 145

succumbed to a forbidden and defiling death, 162

suffered death out of love for humankind, 145

taking humanity's debt upon himself, 253

"Christ crucified," Paul preaching, 19, 121

Christ dying for others, as a motif of Paul, 180–81

Christ event, 79, 92, 134, 136, 187

"Christ hymn," on significance of Jesus's death, 103

"Christ-bearer," as also a "cross-bearer," 101

Christendom, 263, 281, 283

"Christ-follower," Paul as, 264

Christian actions, stimulating, 75

Christian community, as God's beachhead, 69

Christian ethics, connection with the christological meaning of the cross, 111

Christian existence, Paul's understanding of, 94

Christian faith, requiring the resurrection, 26

Christian history and thought, study of, 134n8

Christian life/living

confirmed by the presence of the Spirit, 124

cross and, 64, 67, 107–9, 119

founded upon conformity to Christ's death and the imitation of Christ, 104

living, 79, 106

as moral, but not moralistic, 282

polarity of in the New Age, 92–95

wrestling with the vicissitudes of life, 91

Christian tradition, Paul building upon "earlier," 128–29

Christianity

American, literalized metaphorical language, 148

animal sacrifice as not operative, 260

Chalcedonian, 216

compared to Christendom, 120, 263, 281

the cross as a symbol of, 1, 22, 46

culturized, 279

current understanding of canonical biblical literature, 278

early, 23, 42

Eastern, 214

as God-filled world, 263

Latin, 214

Paul's portrayal of, 283

Paul's vision of, 179, 188

as a "salvation by grace," 89

as soteriology, 137

Christians

committed to crucifixion, if need be, 108

cross imperative for all, 273–74

"died" in Christ, 75

Paul admonishing to "become imitators of God as beloved children," 72–73

Paul writing to, 67n3, 116

suffering with Christ, 260

understanding the cross event, 191

Christocentric living, of Paul, 95

"christocentric" theology and ethics, of Paul, 72

christological aspects of Pauline theology, 80

Christology

of Christ as the second or last Adam, 45

easier to live with a surrogate, 278

of Paul, 42, 72, 122–23, 191n57

Christ's death. *See* death of Christ Jesus

Christus Victor: An Historical Study of the Three Main Types of the Idea of the Atonement (Aulén), 195, 244

Christus Victor model

declining after the sixth century, 197

as a dominant view prior to the time of Anselm, 137

as the earliest theory of atonement, 195

on Jesus overcoming powers of sin and evil, 253

portraying conflict, struggle, and victory, 196

rooted in the Incarnation, 138

roots of, 244

logical precision, not doing justice to Paul's metaphorical language, 62
"logical service," of believers, 73
Logos concept, Irenaeus employed, 199
Lombard, Peter, 217
longing after God, no focus in Paul on, 147
"Lord of Glory," presuming both resurrection and exaltation, 26
Lord's Supper, 16, 180, 189, 190. *See also* Eucharist
love
    as an action of the will of God, 141
    as characteristic of one who is mature in Christ, 114
    creative and redemptive power of, 70
    as the dominant quality of God for Grotius, 235
    faith working through, 89–90
    as fulfilling of the Law, 115–16
    gift of God's, 87
    as greater than righteousness, 141
    language of as devotion expressed in sacrifice, 90
    as the means by which one lives, 87–88
    motif as key to Paul's thinking, 109
    overcoming the evil of the Present Evil Age, 115
    power of revealed and made real, 81
love of Christ, 163, 291
love of God
    Augustine pointing to, 208
    delivering from all condemnation and powers, 153
    God's wrath as identical with, 247
    Jesus's death as a demonstration of for Abelard, 222
    Luther filled with a sense of, 229, 231
    as the motive power of atonement, 217
    Paul's teaching on, 140–41
    proclaimed by Paul, 149
    redeeming Christ, 185
love of neighbor, 115, 127
Luke, Paul writing much earlier than, 15n34
Luther, Martin, 229–30
    assuaged his guilt under "a theology of the cross," 52
    on Christ bearing the sins of all men, 261
    emphasis upon the "Law" and the "Wrath of God," 245
    Käsemann defending the insights of, 24
    looming after the time of the Reformation, 119
    marked a revival of the classic theme, 245
    parents of, 270

personal pilgrimage of salvation and discipleship, 23
placed stress upon the victory of Christ, 234
rejected belief in man's free will to do right, 238
on the supremacy of the loving grace of God, 238
on universal sin and divine rescue, 261
Lutheranism, Käsemann and, 28, 31
lyrical quality, of Paul's faith in Christ, 282

Macquarrie, John, 277, 277n34
man "in Christ"
    hearing the words of, 283
    Paul as, 44, 266
Manichaeans, Augustine's argument against, 211
Mark, shaping his "gospel," 123
martyr, image of, 23
martyr theology, as not the direction of Paul, 260
martyr-deaths, having vicarious saving power, 181
martyrdom, in the face of persecutions, 108n28
Mass, emphasis upon, 244
masters, treating slaves justly and fairly, 114
"materialistic atonement," of a modern age, 270
matrices
    alternative, 183–84
    historical, 191
McGrath, A. E.
    on "atonement theory," 2n6
    on the cross, 27, 32–33
    on the death of Christ, 15
    on Käsemann, 24, 28
    on misunderstanding of an already "realized resurrection," 25
    on the paradigm of the suffering of the believer, 108
    on passing through "the shadow of the cross," 126
    on Paul's distinctive emphasis, 28
    on the theology of the cross, 49
medieval doctrine of merits, protest against, 237
Meeting Jesus Again for the First Time (Borg), 265
Melanchthon, Philip, 229, 230, 239
members, caring for one another, 114
mercy of God, 6, 236
mercy seat, 128, 168
Mertens, Herman-Emiel, 51
"message of the cross," Christian gospel as, 51

Scripture Index

Old Testament

Genesis

Exodus

Leviticus

Numbers

Deuteronomy

Joshua

1 Samuel

2 Samuel

Deuterocanonical Books

Pseudepigrapha (Old Testament)

Dead Sea Scrolls

1 Corinthians

2 Corinthians

Ephesians

Augustine of Hippo
48, 133, 137, 208–14, 216, 217, 229, 238, 257

Confessions

10.43.69   209

Enchiridion on Faith, Hope and Love
    213

108   213

Exposition on the Psalms

51.6   209n57

Against Faustus   211

14.3   208, 211n65
14.3–7   213
14.4   208, 211, 212n67
14.4, 6   212n69
14.6   208, 211, 212, 212n69
14.7   211n66

On Nature and Grace

26.29   209n57

Sermon

130.2   245n52

Sermon 263, On the Ascension
    208n54

On the Trinity

4.13.17   208
13.11.15   208
13.13.17   209n55

13.14.18   209n55
13.16.21   209

Clement of Alexandria   225

Clement of Rome   204, 225

Council of Nicea   205n38

Council of Trent   227, 228

Cyril of Jerusalem   208

Didache

16:5   144n30

Eusebius of Caesarea   200–202, 257

Ecclesiastical History   201

The Proof of the Gospel (Demonstraito Evangelica)   201

10.1   201
10.8   201

Gregory of Nazianzus   206–7

Second Oration on Easter

7:431   207nn48–49

Gregory of Nyssa
196, 200, 206, 207, 208, 245

Great Catechism

22	200n18, 206
24	206

Sermones

130.2	206
134.6	206
263.1	206

Gregory the Great
216, 253

Hippolytus of Rome
225

Ignatius of Antioch
138, 139, 197–98, 202, 225

Epistle to the Magnesians

5	139n19

Epistle to the Romans

6	198
7	198

Epistle to the Smyrnaeans

1	197

Epistle to the Trallians

8	198
9	197

Irenaeus of Smyrna
48, 137, 193, 196, 198–200, 206, 215, 225, 244

Against Heresies

1.1	199
3.18.7	199
3.19.6	200
5.1.1	199
5.21.1	199
Preface, Book 5	199

Justin Martyr
198, 257

Dialogue with Trypho
198

40.4	144n30
95	198
111.2	144n30

Second Apology

13	198

Nicene Creed
205n38

Origen of Alexandria
48, 137, 182, 196, 199, 200, 204, 217, 225

Against Celsus

1.68	200
8.17	200

Commentary on Matthew

16.8	245

Printed in the USA
CPSIA information can be obtained
at www.ICGtesting.com
LVHW071025161123
764127LV00024B/362

9 781666 745863